Conscience, Consensus, & Crossroads in Law

Semiotics and the Human Sciences

Roberta Kevelson
General Editor

Vol. 8

PETER LANG
New York • Washington, D.C./Baltimore • San Francisco
Bern • Frankfurt am Main • Berlin • Vienna • Paris

Conscience, Consensus, & Crossroads in Law

Eighth Round Table on Law and Semiotics

Edited by
Roberta Kevelson

PETER LANG
New York • Washington, D.C./Baltimore • San Francisco
Bern • Frankfurt am Main • Berlin • Vienna • Paris

Library of Congress Cataloging-in-Publication Data

Round Table on Law and Semiotics (8th : 1993 : Penn State in Reading)
Conscience, consensus, & crossroads in law : 8th Round Table on Law and Semiotics / edited by Roberta Kevelson.
p. cm. — (Semiotics and the human sciences, vol. 8)
Includes bibliographical references and index.
1. Semiotics (Law)—Congresses. 2. Social conflict—Congresses. 3. Law—Philosophy—Congresses. I. Kevelson, Roberta. II. Title. III. Title: Conscience, consensus, and crossroads in law. IV. Series.
K213.R68 340'.1—dc20 94-38633
ISBN 0-8204-2511-7 (hardcover) CIP
ISSN 1054-8386

Die Deutsche Bibliothek-CIP-Einheitsaufnahme

Conscience, consensus, & crossroads in law / 8th Round Table on Law and Semiotics. Ed. by Roberta Kevelson. - New York; Washington, D.C./Baltimore; San Francisco; Bern; Frankfurt am Main; Berlin; Vienna; Paris: Lang.
(Semiotics and the human sciences; Vol. 8)
ISBN 0-8204-2511-7
NE: Kevelson, Roberta [Hrsg.]; Round Table on Law and Semiotics <8, 1994, Reading, Pa. >; GT

The paper in this book meets the guidelines for permanence and durability of the Committee on Production Guidelines for Book Longevity of the Council on Library Resources.

Printed in the United States of America.

Acknowledgements

Once again, The Center for Semiotic Research in Law, Government and Economics at Penn State expresses its appreciation to its friends and renews its commitment to sponsorship of its annual, international Round Tables on Law and Semiotics.

The Eighth Round Table on Law and Semiotics was held April 27, 28, 29, 30, 1994 at Penn State, at Reading, Pennsylvania. As is customary this colloquium was a global event: transnational, cross-cultural, interdisciplinary. Although the Center is primarily concerned with a Peircean approach to semiotics, it continues to be inclusive, welcoming all voices and perspectives. In good humor, yet with utmost seriousness the participants continue to develop these meetings as exemplars of pluralism and open exchange.

We thank, for their ongoing support, the several offices of Penn State which contribute to the success of these meetings: the Berks Campus, the C.E.S., the Philosophy Department, the College of the Liberal Arts, the Office of Research and Graduate Research. We again give special thanks to Cindy Palecek for preparing the manuscript for publication.

In particular, we thank The Xerox Foundation whose support over many years has made possible the convening of these Round Tables and its publications which serve a growing 'community of inquirers' as evolving, open-ended reference tools.

This year a shadow falls over this event: our good friend and colleague, Gordon E. Whitney, died just a few months before this Eighth Round Table, in December, 1993. Gordon brought to us the richness of a lifetime of service, of scholarship and especially of caring, sensitive relationships with other people. He explored with us, he listened, and he shared in open trust his ideas and values. Gordon said much to remember; but especially he leaves us his grasp of Peirce's notion of Chance and Community in the following:

> 'The force behind the cosmos is a mind, one vaguely like that of a man. Matter is law abiding, but lacks the ability to take new habits as do living beings, yet as law keeping and in submission to the continuity of the cosmic order, it shows itself to be the product of a creative mind,' Note 7, 'Peirce's Reasoning Love as an Aesthetic Ideal,' in *Law and Aesthetics*, ed. R. Kevelson, 1992:377-400.

Table of Contents

Chapter One

On Passages and Possibilities: Introduction

Roberta Kevelson*

I

The alliterative titles of the Round Table volumes sometimes succeed in conveying the notion of a search for 'primitives' by participants of the annual, international colloquia on problems and issues — discovered and invented — in legal semiotics. Alliteration is that device which is mnemonic in function, but is also a strategy designed to suggest a return to origins, to the so-called 'primitive.'

This assumption, that the idea of the 'primitive' is somehow equatable with a more simple stage of human development and the development of the social institutions, has been long consigned to a multipeaked range of ideational eruptions regarded as the cumulative mountains of errors which testify to human inquiry and reflexion. We cross these ranges of mistakes at our peril; we find passages if we're lucky and somehow learn to depend upon one another in the art of getting footholds. So we have come to discover that 'the primitive' is not simple, but is a term for complexities in evolutionary processes not apparent prior to inventions of new instruments and methods of observation. Semiotics is such a means; it is that theory of signs which was produced via the method of pragmatism. Or so Peirce tells us.

The several topics of this year's meeting, linked alliteratively, indicate fresh starts, moments of choice and hence of indecision, of points of transition, of places here and now in a world where almost every legal culture is in crisis and whole codes of human conduct are at stake. For law is the ground on which the ethics of human behavior get played out. Law is the crux of what Locke has termed the 'Conduct of the Understanding,' and is that which Peirce reinterprets when he assigns to Ethics the mediating role in the Normative Sciences which are, as a triad of Logic, Ethics, Esthetics, the fulcrum upon which his entire philosophy spins. Ethics, which seeks to explain the principles upon which human conduct — good interaction — is based, is fueled by the structures of thought which constitute a comprehensive logic on the one arm, and a referent theory of Esthetics, a 'science of value,' on the other arm. Under Ethics are 'layers' or levels of semiotic function analogous to that which, as a model, is often used by scholars of human evolution to show stages in the development of people, from early to now. The idea of 'early' is often equated with simplicity; but we have begun to understand in this century that early is but another mode of complexity, and the primitive has dimensions we have yet to discover.

By the same token, the bottom layer Peirce graphed under the heading, Ethics, is that most close to actual social interaction, such as we live, in everyday life. The conflicts of everyday life are both incurred and resolved by a kind of cryptography, that is to say, by a consensual manner of agreeing with selected systems or codes of value derived from various sources: art, religion, custom, quirks and chaotic reconfigurations of usual patterns. Mediating between this closest-to-actuality of everyday life and Ethics is Law as system, order, culture.

Tentatively we may say that the dominant sign-function of everyday life is Iconic, as the closest approximation of the observable or visualizable and hence *sensible* dialogic, interactive human behavior. Law represents this Iconicity *as* a dually-functioning Index or double-edged blade, oppositionally constructed as is the institution of all types of Law, whether adversarial or inquisitorial. The principles which operate in legal systems and legal orders are representations of ethical codes or norms; at this level values become symbolized and conventionalized.

In a 'closed society' it is assumed that transitions from Esthetics to Ethics, and from the Ethical Code to the Law, ie. to actual social life and return, is circular. It has been wrongly assumed that the same *matter* of conscience lives in all members of a social group, who share consensually, tacitly, as a kind of homogeneous human nature, in 'rules for right action.' Perhaps in utopian societies — some notions of Utopia — such homogeneity is ideal. But utopian ideals have become suspect, especially in recent years. Studies of complex systems of various kinds show over and over again that development, growth, self-determination and the freedom to break/stretch boundaries is, one may adduce, more desirable than utopian representations of homeostasis. Even current studies of crystals show that the increases of crystal formations are not necessarily reduplication or cloning, but rather tend to asymmetry in some manner; they become, after their fashion, more complex even at this presumably elemental level of the primitive.

What has become far more interesting in our time are possibilities for change that occur as junctures, as crossroads at levels of iconicity in human interaction, as indexicality of conflicts in and of the law, and as symbolicness at that level where norms crystallize and thus come to represent values *as* conventions.

Peirce's emphasis on the openness of the universe, and the chance for chance, anticipates presuppositions of modern investigators of complex systems. While some insist that chaos is 'framed' within deterministic systems, others argue that the notion of genuine novelty and change is not possible within the boundaries, however plastic and flexible, of strict determinism. Neither is it the case that only *some* times are opportunities for choice or change; rather *all* times are, in this actual world, opportunities for decisions or choice — at the level of intentional action — of more general change in response to context, circumstance and readiness to move from a norm and to break with habit. If Logic reenforces the general rule, the predictable, and if the dominant realm of Values represents the meaning of the Permanent and the Continuing, it is at the place of this middle where Law lives that the *meaning* of Experience lives: the meaning of Experience is signified by tension, interaction, change.

II

Morris Cohen, a great admirer of Peirce and a much-loved proponent of legal pragmatism, was keenly aware of unresolved inconsistencies of 'self-rule,' or democratic 'majority rule' which derives as idea in large measure from Locke. Cohen, deeply committed to the ideal of open, democratic, dynamic society also knew the tightrope one walks between habitualized consensual values, and continuous change which comes dangerously close to no rule. Cohen says that all crises on the level of actual exchange, as well as indecisions in institutional mouthpieces which represent such crises in law, economics and government, must come to expedient agreement. Leaders do not have the luxury of waiting until a thoroughly-investigated seminary kind of inquiry decides, on the basis of logic and formal reason, which way to go. Unfortunately right reason does not move as quickly as exigencies in human affairs require. So decisions must be made, and made with somewhat better justification than by tossing coins, reading runes, deciphering tortoise shells, holding fingers to the wind, or by dueling in the public arena. All of these ways of settling opinion still prevail today, in all societies, in modern industrialized as well as in emergent states: the primitive persists everywhere, as we know. But, Cohen says, despite the intense interest of all parties involved in disputes of law and polity and the temptation to rely on variations of mere chance or 'might makes right,' the best interests, short- and long-term, is to seek satisfaction through some rules of order, of law. 'Otherwise we fall into a state of perpetual war or anarchy,' (Cohen, 1931, *Reason and Nature*, at pages 24-25).

Locke's notion of 'majority-rule' has come to be seen as a working myth. The idea of 'consent' to which it is related in Locke's thought is not only increasingly viewed as a much overrated concept, but as a malignant one as well, since it presumes a cohesive bond, a social agreement to values, which obtains between those who do affirm such symbolized norms and those who are born into such a climate of value without having chosen them. The members of a society — formerly regarded as numerical as well as ideational 'majority' — who use such rules of conduct as points of reference in their own everyday interpersonal behavior — are today confronted at every stretch of the common road by those who reject values imposed upon them, and thus claim that they did not consent and do not share in a consensus of value. In genuine deference to the reasonable assertion by those who do not include themselves among the group of consenting governed many legal systems of many modern democratic societies have attempted to accommodate the law to serve everyone. The result, in individual legal societies — *jural societies* in Francis Lieber's terms — as well as in the larger global society of international states and crossnational legal systems — is an instability ready and open for 'chaos' in a technical sense, for anarchy in a legal-political sense, and for incomprehensibility and Babel in an everyday and merely interhuman sense.

William Kendall argues convincingly that Locke's position on majority-rule, equivalent with the representation of sovereign will, is a mistaken interpretation by the mainstream of Lockean scholars. In the same spirit as Cohen, Kendall maintains that the Locke we want to take more clear cognizance of is that Locke as 'prince of individualists,' to whom the notion of individual is a relate, or relative term, in a whole organization which consists of connections *between* individuals. The target or object for this relationship of individuals is always some absolutist, authoritarian power. Thus it is against this State that the community of individuals revolt. The overturn and change of Status Quo is the significant act of individuals-in-community. Kendall suggests that the American Revolution serves for Locke as prototype of change against habitualized, formalized and merely conventionalized referential authority, (William Kendall, 1959, *John Locke and the Doctrine of Majority-Rule*, Urbana, 64-67).

Acccording to Locke's view, as understood by Kendall, it is not the Individual against Majority-Rule which is the leading principle of consent; but rather it is the relationship of individuals against absolute authority or fixed principle which characterizes a free society. Kendall says that Locke 'puts' individuals into a hypothetical 'state of Nature' because he wants to create a place — *a locus standi* — or context which represents the ground of experience of people interacting in the world: a community of individuals does not spring from thin air but is seen to grow, to evolve, out of some presupposed 'primitive' level of interaction, (Kendall, *op cit*, at page 66).

The community of individuals who convene for the Round Tables on Law and Semiotics create such a relationship or community *in some respects* (as Robert Boyle speaks of the *ad hocness* of relations based on mutuality and reciprocity). The main 'respect' or commonality which is the cohesive force of this conference is Semiotics, or Legal Semiotics in particular, as an instrument for observing, probing, discussing crossroads in law as opportunities for reconfiguring human values, for reassessing the lay of the land for law from the perspective of global rather than chauvinistic national interests.

One of the first problems to be recognized in the emergence of Semiotics as a new way of seeing and saying *vis-a-vis* the pragmatic opportunities of crises in human conduct at all levels — iconic, indexical, symbolic (as mentioned above) — was the problem of translation and paraphrase. We have yet to work out appropriate equivalences of the idea of Property, for example, which is integral with a Lockean concept of individuals-in-community against authoritative instantiated and conventionalized sovereignty. Throughout the modern world this term means various kinds of value: sometimes it is used as a representation of an individual's achievements or attributes, ie., what one 'has' as equivalent with what one 'is' in interaction with others. Sometimes the word Property does not carry these connotations, but stands for negotiable counters or assets or wealth in a more generalizable sense, yet restricted to material things. 'New' Property expands to include artifacts and other tokens of cultural values. Property is also understood in a new sense of phenomenality: thus *Intellectual* Property extends the meaning of the term — evolves it — to indicate ideational phenomena of such kind as might be marked with the inventor/creator's special 'brand' and be registered or copyrighted even as cattle is imprinted with the ranch's sign. Property is a boundary and hence a sign of complex relations as in Hohfeld's sense.

Government largess or entitlements are viewed as property, with constraints (see Kevelson 1990). Further, securities which people pay for become, when managed by government administrators, interpreted as entitlements and thus, by extension, as public property. Distortions and ingenuities that represent changes in 'conscience, consensus and crossroads in law,' on both international and intranational levels are topics examined by participants of this conference from the general perspective of a loosely defined notion of legal semiotics.

Indeed, in every respect the community of individuals who come together for these colloquia do represent, in my opinion, a Lockean community of individuals who resist the absolute authority of even an authoritative definition of Legal Semiotics. This idea called Legal Semiotics also evolves, is annually revolutionized, as it grows and becomes in response to those who interact with it, who cultivate its meaning.

The subtopics of the Round Table of 1994 are: *Evolution of Legal Semiotics: Attempts at Synthesis*; *On Crafting Authority: Institutional Iconoclasm; Law and Literature*; *Comparative Law and Legal Cultures*; *Ideological Conflicts: Competing Norms and Values*; *Insiders and Outsiders: Rackets and Subtexts*; *Law, Language and Logic*. Participants represent almost every continent in the world, several special areas within legal studies and jurisprudence, and a range of academic disciplines that includes Philosophy, History, Sociology, Administration of Justice, Linguistics, Communications. I introduce our contributors in alphabetical order since this is the best way I know to resist fitting people into procrustean grids by country, by discipline, by even the very topic chosen as a 'locus' for inquiry. In this way the flexibility of this semiotic mode of inquiry is emphasized in much the same manner that alliteration represents the ground levels of our human affairs: the Primitive. The Primitive (as idea) evolves.

In each of the following papers is a juxtaposition that each inquirer uses in a special, selective way to signify experiential contexts out of which our ideas grow, bear, and seed themselves. These volumes have, for almost a decade, been a source of cross-reference — of cross-pollenization and self-seeding.

This volume then is a mediator between those who have already come to serve this growing community and those who will emerge. Next year the Round Table on Law and Semiotics will focus on Conflicting Ideologies in

Law. But in its basic function as a Methodological Tool — a function of Peircean Pure Rhetoric — this volume is both cataphoric and anaphoric: it is at the crux of problems on the very problem of 'crossroads in law' and of moot questions of conscience and of consensus.

III

The editor as maker of montage takes on, in addition to red-lettering comma errors, a compositional task. In its best sense the composition is a reassemblage of materials/texts taken out of their original context and placed in new juxtaposition or contingent relations with new textual neighbors. It has been my pleasure, as well as matter of principle in editing these volumes, to preserve the separate and distinct voices of all contributors; this requires sustaining profound respect for the style of expression each one prefers. I rewrite as little as possible, and only when some word or phrase is inadvertently omitted, or interferes with the sense of the text. Despite the fact that there is a pervasive and sometimes heavy-handed apparent sense of obligation on the part of many editors today to take charge, to rewrite, to standardize, and to manage, I have little sympathy with the managerial mind or the bureaucratic turf it feeds upon.

Nevertheless, just as any response in any mode of communicative activity involves some creation of new meaning, and just as any paraphrasing or translation also involves the growth of meaning from original into transliterated new text, it is unavoidable that some reordering takes place in collecting individual papers into a new whole. The meaning of the papers as they were initially presented in the special subtopical sessions mentioned above takes on a new, thin layer of significance when regrouped in this volume. Further, the seeming neutrality of presenting papers in alphabetical order takes on the tint of my own manner of *mentioning*. But this is a minimal and forgivable liberty of editorship. I suggest in the following only a provisional grouping, and leave it to the reader to make her connections between authors as suits her purposes, realizing that we have here a community, in some respects. These respects may vary as we read and reread and as fresh connections between themes and subthemes become observable.

The largest grouping of papers, unplanned but unmistakable, is that dealing with one or another aspect of comparative legal cultures. In this group I include Ralph Lindgren's focused paper on the paradox of permanence and change, and on the significance of enduring pattern in his 'Seals, Oaths and the Primacy of Ritual.'

From a very different approach, but in close relation with Lindgren's work is Leon Sheleff's 'Customary Law as Common Law.' Sheleff compares and contrasts tacit as well as explicit assumptions of both common law and civil law systems. He argues that the customary modes of interactional behavior provides a ground for Common Law as it does not in Civil Law. The protolegal customary normative interaction of a society is distinguished from customary law as oral, or unwritten law. Clearly, the primitive is not the simple, but that which is closest to actual lived experience, Sheleff suggests.

B.D.D. Radipati's paper, 'Legal Semiotics and Normative Imposition in an African Context: The Case of the San/Bushmen,' argues that there are often several levels of law, or lawlike behavior, coexisting in a single society. The example given is the triadic situation that exists for the San/Bushmen in several areas of Africa. The oldest inhabitants of these regions, it is claimed, do not have any concept of law as generally defined; but there is a legal order of native tribes imposed upon this oldest and a-legal society; superimposed over these two layers, coeval with them, are several interpretations of European-derived law. The paper is especially intriguing since it does not hold that the means of settling disputes among the San/Bushmen according to the most ancient customs is in any way prototypical of a legal culture. It is not a mode of law, Radapati, argues, but an alternative to law.

In yet a very different approach from the other papers in this collection is the correspondence between Robin Paul Malloy and Sharon Hom on their interpretations of the marketplace in China. This correspondence, presented as a dialogic exchange, is entitled 'Impressions of a Market Economy in China: Letters of Exchange.' Some of the questions raised have to do with the possibility of transplanting a concept, such as 'market economy', from 'native soil' to another cultural ground, and what modifications this concept undergoes in response to a new environment.

The problem of conflicts between legal cultures was also examined from a distinctly other perspective by Pierre Legrand. He walks us through some twisting, fascinating byways that legal codes take, in transposition from one legal culture to another. Legrand's locus is Quebec and problems connected with the 'newly-enacted Quebec civil code.' Legrand's paper, focused on this problem of a legal code, is an adventure in the peregrinations of a legal concept, through time and space and cultures, in 'Civil Codes and the Case of Quebec: Semiotic Musings around an *accent aigu.*'

Since the umbrella of comparative legal cultures is a generous one, I also include under it Stephen Hicks' paper on topologies of legal cultures, entitled 'Comparative Law and Legal Cultures.' Hicks seeks to establish family resemblances between kinds of legal cultures in order to be able to constitute more general and more comprehensive legal types. The tendency to ever greater generalization, always in tension with the particular thing-in-itself, is part of that semiotic process whereby a *token*, or 'property' of a *type* may, in another context and for another purpose, become a 'general' or Type of itself. So Peirce has argued. From another point of view Hicks seems to share this Peircean assumption.

Helen Endre-Stacy's paper, 'Land Usage as Privileged Discourse in Anglo-Australian Law' deals with the '*Mabo* decision' of the Australian High Court, which as recently as 1992, finally ended the use of '*terra nullius*' in Australian law. The end of application of this concept revealed an intricate aspect of the law which represented a complex pattern of dealing with the dispossession of Aboriginal peoples' claims to lands. Endre-Stacy shows that the effect of the *Mabo* decision was disruptive of an ongoing method of dealing with aboriginal claims, and that the disruptive effects of Mabo has had far-reaching consequences on Australian law.

Another view of legal cultures in transition is Jan Bekker's 'Poets' Reaction to Apartheid Laws.' Here Bekker sharply contrasts the rich and powerful poetry of black Africans with the 'oppressive and humiliating' conditions from which this poetry emerged. The writing of poetry, according to Bekker, is a means of opposing, even transforming on some personal, communal level, the injustices of apartheid legislation. This poetry seems to have become a perceptible current from the beginning of the 1960's, and today can be called an evolving custom of dissent. Bekker has selected several pieces of legislation, and shows some of the poetry written in response to apartheid legislation. The changes in the laws have not brought about secure or even tolerable community. Vestiges of apartheid are still everywhere. But out of the old order new symbols become visible. They sing, says Bekker, in the many voices of the Poets.

The second 'largest' topic in this reworked montage has to do with aspects of criminal justice. The following four authors are concerned with punishment, with sentencing, with prisons, and with the need to establish a theoretical framework for this aspect of the law.

In Donna West's paper, 'The Mentally Retarded Defendant as Interpretant: Semiosis of Admission,' it is argued that the mentally retarded should be separated from others who break the law since they lack, in many instances, ability to understand the law or to connect one kind of infraction with another which is related to it. She argues that respect for the law and lawful behavior requires the ability to act in accordance. Those who break the law, but are *unable* to avoid doing so, should not be subject to the same penalties as those able to choose.

Bruce Arrigo's 'Reflections on the Future of Criminal Justice: Issues for Theory, Method and Practice,' is a close evaluation of leading theories on aspects of criminal justice. In fact it is a report on the 'state of the art' of this special concern of Legal Semiotics.

An imaginative, ironic and even scathing condemnation of the worst of present tactics of criminal justice is presented in Robert Ginsberg's 'A Utopian Proposal for the Improvement of our Prisons.' Ginsberg's paper is irony reflecting on itself, since it parodies the notion of prisons as country-club retreats of lawbreakers, as they are imagined by law-and-order types. He proposes that the 'poshness' of prisons be improved. But he says, as well, and with tongue in other cheek, that the whole idea of punishment may be as foolhardy as the notion of a prison utopia.

In tandem with criminal justice topics are notions of crime and illicit behavior. These subtopics are dealt with in inquiries both profoundly serious and fun: William Pencak writes in 'From Racket to Natural Law: The Permutation of Smuggling into Free Trade,' of the shady sides of our founding forebears in early North American colonies. From the perspective of the legal-historical semiotician Pencak shows a tradition of illicit acts made legal, for purposes of mercantile profit and wellbeing. The point is made, theoretically and anectdotally, that this notion of individuals-in-community did not drift down from some ethereal and rarified strata, but had their starts, if not in the mud, in common pay-dirt of less than ideal human deals and compacts. Legislature, Pencak shows, is indeed an interpretant of values. But values are themselves inventions of wants, needs and often greedy wishes.

Bill Scott examines deceit and fraudulent acts in the special area of Intellectual Property. His paper, 'The Literary Fraud: An Intractable Problem for Law and Semiotics' examines problems that concern 'meaningful representations' that are phoney, ie., that are meaningful misrepresentations. Here, too, the 'commercial value' which motivates the making of, 'literary fakes and forgeries' cannot be discounted, since genuine esthetics forces govern the making of ethical norms, and hence of laws that protect deliberate deceits.

In a similar vein another paper on manipulations of truths by law is Chris Braun's 'Signs of Value: The Laws of Accounting Theory.' Braun shows how tax laws are capable of generating multiple truths: the law creates not only Persons which are not people, but it creates property that has no referent in the actual world. This method of making something out of nothing is a kind of representation, or mirror-image *illogic*. Yet Braun argues convincingly that the 'accounting sign system' has the means by which universally-accepted, or consensually agreed upon referents may evolve (or produce) 'multiple truth signs.' If the initial premise is permitted to hold, an entire ensuing structure may count as a truth-representation. And if the initial premise is not required to be absolutely true, but is pragmatically *workably* true, (in a Peircean sense) it may produce indefinitely since it is counterfactual only with respect to another 'fictive' assumption and not to a 'real' or actual world.

From quite another perspective Kevin Jackson looks at the problem of resolving disputes among 'truths' created by the law. 'Corporations and Conflicting Norms: Modal Frameworks for Vague Transnational Precepts' examines problems in modal logic. Peirce regarded his shaping of a logic of possibility as perhaps his greatest accomplishment. Jackson, while not concerned here with Peirce's work on modal logic, nevertheless presents an important study on the use of modal logic to examine *vagueness* in underlying structures of laws involving such vague notions as *Negligence*, and other notions of damage by omission.

The next group of papers discusses the *method* of semiotics, namely, the Method of Pragmatism. The approaches are as varied as the individuals writing on this topic. But for this time, in this respect, they constitute a community of interest.

On this keynote I introduce Denis Brion's paper, 'Making a Difference and Making all the Difference: Community and the Dilemma of Difference.' Brion argues that we create our differences, and that they are not 'given' to us as impersonal or neutral data. From this point of view, a pragmatic point of view, he takes a critical look at the recent work of Minow on American law, on its privileged paradigms, and on her suggested ways of changing all that (1990). Brion's critique of Minow is largely his opposition to her contention that hardened value attitudes have an absolutist or near-deterministic influence on how the law behaves, especially with respect to minority populations. Brion contrasts this consensual basis that Minow presumes with the idea of a more viable, free-wheeling, choice-making community. He takes up the problem of the meaning of the idea of Community, and in doing so clearly shows that ideas, even of consensus and community, are not given once and for all times: they continually evolve and change. Individuals as related members of community are themselves growing and evolving. The problem of permanence and change in Community is a problem of paradoxical thinking, Brion concludes. It is an indispensable mode of those who want values which both endure and at the same time represent possibilities for change.

Virginia Black comes at this paradox from yet another door. She argues in 'The Illicit Reduction of Ontology to Epistemology in the Legal Enterprise' that the tension is between History and Nature. Historical forces represent change. Natural existence represents the fixed and the lasting. Her opposition to what she sees as a 'focus on semiotic neopragmatic possibility' is in agreement here with Corrington (1993) since there is, she says, the tendency to lose sight of the virtually permanent, the pro-visionally eternal.

'Pragmatism and the Limits of Rationality,' by Jay Knaack, which seems appropriate to introduce at this point, argues that we need to develop the capacity not only for paradox, but also for listening to several discourses in concert: the political, the legal, and the economic. Knaack's thesis is not, in Montesquieu's manner, focused on the 'separation of powers,' but rather on the chorus which consists of individual voices unified. Knaack's emphasis is on the importance of revisiting the concept of Political Pluralism and reinterpreting it in a fresh manner, not unlike Locke's concept of Individuals and Majority Rule discussed above.

Alfred Neeley, in 'Evolution and 19th Century Legal Pragmatism: Darwin and Holmes,' brings us into an event of the kind that revolutionizes an entire pattern of thought, with infinite reverberations. The meeting of ideas of Darwin, Holmes and Peirce is momentous: it shifted emphasis on states of things to processes of transition itself. Neeley looks critically at each of these principals, and how they resisted the influence of the other and yet, nevertheless, appropriated even from that which each opposed. The study is a penetrating inquiry into the community of law which, in analysis, is not one voice but many. Law, as a complex discourse, is itself an ongoing evolutionary process which takes its course from its intellectual environment. It transforms both itself and its environment thereby.

The reciprocity between discourses is especially marked in the ideas that derive from the chemistry (and alchemical vestiges) of Robert Boyle and his colleague friend, John Locke. Roberta Kevelson's paper, 'Boyle's Lock'n'Key: Consent and Contract' shows that the relation of individuals in community, illustrated by Boyle's famous metaphor of the lock and key, is adapted by Locke in his 'Consent' theory. Later it is interpreted by Peirce, and becomes as it evolves a leading metaphor of political pluralism, of legal pragmatism, and of a general notion of community.

Our introduction concludes with the papers of Bruce Rockwood and Willem Witteveen. Both of these papers explore aspects of relations between law and literature. Rockwood extrapolates from the situation of Salman Rushdie in 'Speech as a Universal Right: International Law and the Case of Salman Rushdie.' He shows that not only does the general notion of an 'international legal order' consist of an organization or 'system of sovereign states,' but consists also of value systems that cut across national boundaries and exert authority and constraints upon individual freedoms, of such as Salmon Rushdie, from which there is no sanctuary. The problem he probes is at the cutting edge of concepts of self-determination, of human rights, of international law. This problem challenges the sovereignty of states since it questions whether a world community can intervene in affairs of sovereign states to demand cessation of violations of human rights. Further, it challenges ideologies and theologies which are not state-bound, and questions the extent to which intervention is possible or desirable on behalf of individuals.

Witteveen's paper, 'Seeing Rhetoric as Law as Literature,' shows the force of the work of art — of literature as an aesthetic value-bearer — in bringing into a unified text a means of evoking emotions or powers of bringing about objectives, which is the function of rhetoric as pragmatic prime mover. Witteveen turns to Kafka's parables which illustrate a mode of paradoxical thinking that well may serve the dual aims of both Logic and Rhetoric in law: The open hand and the closed fist coexist in inclusive rather than exclusive relationship in literature and in such a manner as to persuade the *actual* legal actor — the lawyer and the judge — that such is *possible* in the *practice of law*. Thus the law may come to represent the paradoxical logic of a Kafka, and thereby may bring back to everyday life the resolving of disputes in human affairs, new values or value-symbols which liberate relations of people in community and thus stretch boundaries of ideas hardened into inflexible forms.

Not least, there is one *Index* which points up the various concepts that interact in this collection. Only a subject index is ever provided. This is offered as a kind of implied editorial commentary, since it selects and 'measures' the significance of a multitude of ideas of which this montage is composed. It is a choice from among at least a million 'topics.'

Recall an early study in the development of modern semiotics by Boris Uspensky: *A Poetics of Composition* (University of California Press, 1973). Here Uspensky says that 'Intrusion of art into life changes the borders of the artistic space without destroying them . . . Efforts to violate the borders of the artistic space . . . seem to be motivated by an understandable desire to bring together, as closely as possible, the represented world and the real world, in order to achieve the greatest degree of verisimilitude — of realism — in the representation,' (at pages 138-139).

**Roberta Kevelson is Distinguished Professor of Philosophy at Penn State.*

Chapter Two

Reflections on the Future of Criminal Justice: Issues for Theory, Method and Practice

Bruce A. Arrigo*

I
Introduction

This essay was originally conceived of as a well-documented and theoretically-animated analysis, exploring the peripheral core of law and criminology. The ideological impetus for the initial work included the very technical and often cumbersome language of French post-structural theory (e.g., Lacan, Foucault, Irigaray, Baudrillard, Derrida), some neo-Marxian insights developed by Frankfurt School critics (e.g., Habermas, Adorno, Balkin, Benveniste), and the emerging wisdom of several heterodox intellectual trends (e.g., chaology, quantum physics/mechanics, catastrophe theory). Having completed a draft of this first paper and following a sufficient period of time in which to digest its relevance, a related and more foundational question now presents itself; namely, what is the future of criminal justice? Put another way, what projections can be made about the theory, method, and practice of justice-related enterprises in light of postmodernity and its deracinating agenda? Accordingly, this essay speculates upon the future of the discipline.

Before we proceed, a clarification on the article's purpose is warranted. The issue under consideration relates less to rigorous and meticulous analysis and more to experimental and heuristic exploration. In other words, the aim of this essay is to provisionally consider how criminal justice, as a free-standing academic discipline, must embrace the challenges of postmodernity if it is to endure, indeed thrive. Inevitably this means that in the pages which follow certain controversies within the field will require some elucidation. However, this elucidation will itself be less deductively or inductively proven and more reflexively and intuitively described. Thus, the reader is asked to experience, to appreciate, the more *human* and *mythic* dimension of that which is presented rather than to systematically and positivistically critique its erudition. As the British philosopher-physicist Lancelot Whyte cautioned over three decades ago when assessing the growth and direction of aviation research: 'there are today many problems more important than high-speed flight. Beneath them all lies one supreme need: the cultivation of the *imagination*' (as cited in Bevan and Kessel, 1994: 506; emphasis added). Thus, the call in this article is for each reader to travel beneath the waters of his/her soul and touch that force which breathes meaning into an 'alternative vision of what is and what might be' (Henry and Milovanovic, 1991: 308).

II
On Postmodernity and Theory-Building in Criminal Justice

There is a dearth of ideological scholarship designed to advance the specific field of criminal justice. Much of the literature which passes as theory in the academy borrows significantly from the related social science disciplines of sociology, psychology, economics, history, anthropology, philosophy, and political science, etc. The behavioral sciences, too, have helped shape the conceptual identity of this unique area of study. Here contributions from epidemiology, biology, psychiatry, and forensic medicine have played crucial roles in defining our understanding of crime and justice. Indeed, evidence for this eclectic construction of and hybrid regard for the theoretical underpinnings of criminal justice is perhaps most apparent in introductory and theory textbooks respectively (see, Inciardi, 1993; Senna and Siegel, 1990; Abadinsky and Winfree, 1992; Vold and Bernard, 1986).

Despite the paucity of discipline-specific ideological research, it remains clear that criminal justice is a vastly popular and fascinating domain of inquiry (Surette, 1991; Barak, 1994). Droves of students register for CRJ courses often with excitement and anticipation. Large segments of the viewing public are mesmerized by TV shows, films, docu-dramas, and the like bringing violence, brutality, and bloodshed into their living rooms. Many politicians, educators, activists, entertainers, moralists, and athletes feel compelled to redress perceived injustices, represent the interests of violated or marginalized constituencies, or agitate for structural and institutional reform. As these endeavors suggest, the criminal justice system, for better or worse, assumes an important and privilege position in society.

After all, it is this apparatus which is called into question and it is this apparatus which is mobilized in response.

Given the overwhelming popularity of criminal justice, one might assume that the discipline would stand on less tenuous footing. However, when we couple the field's mass appeal with its lack of discipline-specific theoretical grounding, a vexing problematic *is* apparent. In short, no one really knows what law and order, punishment and control, victimization and violence mean — at least not according to criminal justice per se. Theoretical speculation abounds but this speculation is itself the product of *outsiders* (sociologists, historians, psychiatrists, biologists) making sense of, imposing order upon, a field of inquiry which is something more or something other than what the reductionism of others claim it to be.

Here, then, we can begin to identify a link between postmodernism and theory-building in criminal justice. The language of these other scholars, given their discipline's unique orientation, is necessarily based upon a specialized grammar. The coordinates of these other grammars are defined by that particular discipline. Thus, we can speak of *linguistic coordinate systems* (Milovanovic, 1986: 285-96) where meaning is communicated from within a specialized discourse (e.g., the language of psychiatry differs from that of history, or the language of anthropology differs from that of political science). The encoding of criminal justice, though, particularly in the context of theory construction, is subject to these competitive grammars with their own system of signs (i.e., unique languages and signifier-signified anchorings). As a result, criminal justice thought represents the ideological interests of many but its own, distinctive voice remains uncultivated or, worse still, silenced.

The suggestion that an articulation of what criminal justice thought uniquely signifies remains fundamentally unknown because the field lacks a distinctive language is no small claim. If the proposition is accurate, than the implications for method and practice are profound. How knowledge is constituted in the academy and how business is conducted in the field may be vastly different from what we presently take to be legitimate truth claims or appropriate work habits. By analogy, recent developments in postmodern feminist literature, particularly those works concerned with questions of crime, law, justice, and community, have endeavored to make sense of differences (i.e., gender, race, and class) communicated within the discourse of conventional crimino-legal theory-building (e.g., Smart, 1989; MacKinnon, 1989; Cornell, 1991;1993; Young, 1990; Arrigo, 1992;

1993a). Collectively, these studies contribute to our awareness, regarding the powerful role language plays in representing 'phallogocentric interests' (Lahey, 1985: 538; see also, Smart, 1989) or malestream thought. Thus, by extension, embedded in such notions as law, crime, victimization, and control, is a singularly encoded understanding of reality where individual identity is always and already a reduction enveloped in masculine meanings. Postmodern feminists remind us that the invitation, the challenge, is to develop a language system(s) (an *écriture féminine*) liberated from the misogynous trappings of (prevailing) phallocentric language and culture (Arrigo, 1992: 21-24; see also Arrigo, 1994a).

Returning to theory construction in criminal justice a similar argument can be made. Postmodern feminists identify and then deconstruct the discursive coordinates by which law and criminology are constituted. They accomplish this by pointing out how the values embedded in conventional (malestream) language foster the invalidation of women and feminine ways of knowing. However, the imposition of *outsider logics* defining crime and justice also communicate values. These values are an expression of meaning compatible with the specialized coordinates of those (academic) groups engaged in justice-related semiotic production. Further, in the competitive rush to explain the macro/micro causes of crime, delinquency, and/or deviance there is a tendency by social and behavioral scientists, knowingly or not, to 'shave off' parts of the criminal justice discipline as if it were a sub-specialty within their own academic realm. Thus, for example, sociology generates the growth of *criminology*; psychiatric medicine fosters advances in *psychopathology*; economics spawns the evolution of *criminalistics*. Lost in the process is the possibility for establishing alternative (perhaps more liberating) ways of communicating the dynamic nature of crime and justice by invoking the uncultivated argot of criminal justice.

Making room for the unencumbered voice, the grammar, of criminal justice thought is sorely missing in theory construction pursuits assessing crime and justice. Given this absence, one is not to assume that the plea is for the elimination of intellectual enterprises advancing our understanding of crime and justice informed by other linguistic codes. Our appeal relates more to envisioning what crime and justice might otherwise signify if a discourse-specific grammar were cultivated. Thus, we are distressed by the perceived lack of fundamental inclusion for what we take to be a glaring oversight in theory-building. The question concerning the future of criminal justice in light of postmoderinity can be further amplified by exploring methodological practices in the academy. Here the pivotal issue hinges on the orthodox manner in which truth claims are made. It is to this matter that we now turn.

III
On Postmodernity and Research Methods in Criminal Justice

Thus far, the scarcity of criminal justice thought per se has been linked to theory competition in both the social and behavioral sciences. Intended or not, the semiotic cleansing of outsider logics is, in large measure, responsible for the impoverished theory of a free-standing discipline. The legacy of postmodernity signals the importance of validating or re-claiming the coordinates which define excluded voices. The grammar of criminal justice, whatever it may be, remains silenced and warrants articulation. Another concern which must be addressed, if the discipline is to endure on its own terms, is the question of methodology. Here methodology refers to the conditions under which we come to know, legitimate, and esteem what we claim to be truth.

A shared and reified theme developed by social and behavioral scientists investigating issues and controversies in crime and justice involves an understanding of social problems, events in the life world and individual actors in the social order. Traditional researchers maintain that the world is essentially retrievable, reducible, knowable and, therefore, predictable (Arrigo, 1994b; Milovanovic, 1994). This linear and positivistic regard for the totality of human existence has been staunchly challenged and rejected by several postmodern ideologues (Barthes, 1988; Foucault, 1972; Lyotard, 1984; Dews, 1987; Sarup, 1989). Moreover, the center piece of criticism for a growing cadre of crimino-legal commentators persuaded by the postmodern perspective entails the dismantling or debunking of all over-arching principles of reason, logic, order, and meaning contained in the *natural scientific* approach to sense-making (Arrigo, 1995a; 1993b; Milovanovic, 1992; Gelsthorpe and Morris, 1990; Cornell, 1991; 1993).

The privileged method of analysis by researchers who profess to be engaged in criminal justice scholarship emphasizes empirically rigorous, objectively verifiable inquiry. What is troubling about this approach is the extent to which the method *reduces* violence, harm, and suffering wielded upon victims to dispassionate, elemental, ordinary realities. Behavior that is reasonable, interaction that is explainable, desires that are predictable, discourse that is intelligible, awarenesses that are conventional, symbolize the argot of empirical knowledge (Arrigo, 1993a: 135-140; 1994a; 1994b 1994c). Moreover, the natural scientific method, as the privileged investigatory model in crime and justice studies, fails to consider the embedded assumptions (values) implicit in its understanding of the human condition and the human spirit. As one virulent commentator admonishing the positivist approach asserts:

> Modern science . . . has separated subject and object, mind and body, self and other, human and animal, man and woman and earth. All objects in the modern world, even the human subject and human body, are treated as lifeless, as cadavers (Malhorta Bentz, 1993: 122).

Unlike 'scientific' knowledge which is esteemed in conventional methodological studies exploring controversies in crime and justice, postmodern analysis seeks the discovery of 'narrative' knowledge (Sarup, 1989: 120-121; see also, Arrigo, 1992: 24-27; 1993a: 33-37 on *imaginative discourse*; Lacan, 1985: 143-47 on *mythic knowledge*; Cornell, 1991: 168-196 on the *imagination and utopian possibility*). Truth, justice, reason, progress and other similar abstractions are based on myths, symbols, metaphors, representing the historicity of a given culture as an incomplete and unfolding life story. Postmodern thought seeks the discovery, articulation, and affirmation of repressed voices (excluded stories), and the linguistic coordinates which constitute their logos. In this regard, then, knowledge is provisional and relational; that is, logic is local not global (Dews, 1987), meaning is contingent not certain (Surup, 1989), understanding is fragmented not complete (Lyotard, 1984), truth is a departure not an arrival (Barthes, 1988).

If the discipline of criminal justice is to break free from the dictatorial hold of the competitive discourses which claim to advance the field albeit in their name, then a replacement model of scientific inquiry is needed. The postmodern sciences appear to offer a forward-looking agenda, simultaneously affirming the stories of heretofore linguistically marginalized citizens and groups, while more authentically, more completely, advancing our understanding of those narratives accounting for crime and justice. In this regard, then, *language as method* tells us something more or something other about the social order, individual actors, and the interconnectedness of both.

The discussion on theory-building signalled how criminal justice is deprived of its unique grammar. The review of research methodology identified the predominant investigatory approach, informing studies claiming advances in criminal justice. Further, this section identified a replacement model for making claims about how we come to know. However, it remains to be seen how these insights relate, if at all, to the future operation of justice-related endeavors. It is to this matter that we know turn.

IV
On Postmodernity and Practice in Criminal Justice

Questions concerning the future of criminal justice practices must be linked to an understanding of social change in the workplace. The knowledge claims of orthodox empirical studies provide for social transformation but this very change is itself rooted in institutional responses to the undifferentiated complexities in the environment. But here the system's outcome-responses reduce the human and structural complexities *on the institution's terms*, yielding a functional (linear and predictable) result in social planning. Change in the context of criminal justice typically results in a tension-reduction dynamic in which the operative discourse and the prevailing method endure. Thus, the essential core of what passes for reform is nothing more than the reaffirmation of system-supporting declarations with their corresponding and limiting truth claims.

The postmodern perspective on social change is mindful of the nonlinear components of the social order. Nietszche (1980) and his notion of transpraxis offers guidance here (see also, Deleuze, 1983; Henry and Milovanovic, 1991: 305-309). Unlike Hegel's (1807/1977) reaction-negation dynamics regarding the master-slave relationship, Nietzsche points to a more active change phenomenon which includes deconstructionism and reconstructionism (see also, Bernstein, 1975: 31 on class control and *de-contextualizing and re-contextualizing* processes). Following Hegel, when one reacts to perceived hierarchical power relations and seeks to repudiate them, the act of negating creates new forms of domination (i.e., the reproductions of relations to productions) which also wield their marginalizing effects on human subjects. Conversely, with Nietzschean transpraxis, critical attention is directed toward the reconstitutive effects, inherent in any attempt to neutralize or challenge that which is negated.

Several insights developed by Lacan (1975; 1977; 1985; 1991) further suggest the possibility of fostering genuine social change. His treatise on the *de-centered and desiring subject* as well as his analyses on the *discourses of the hysteric and analyst* explore the intra-psychic and intersubjective semiotic processes by which repressed voices can find unencumbered expression and legitimation. Elsewhere I have examined his psychoanalytics as they relate to overlapping issues in law, criminology and psychology (Arrigo, 1995b; 1994c; 1994d; 1994e). What both Lacan and Nietzsche offer is a version of historical change in which the imposed parameters of conventional speech and knowledge are transcended. In other words, irony, unpredictability, indeterminacy, contradiction, serendipity, and flux supplant the more linear and homeostatic dynamics of traditional language patterns and thought processes. Social planning, then, requires a *double negation* or *negative dialectics* (Adorno, 1973). Criminal justice practitioners must break free from the restrictive linguistic categories of traditional reason and rationality advanced by the privileged scientific method constituted by outsider and competitive grammars. Moreover, the subject in discourse, the criminal justice professional, must become a divided self, embodying that difference which constitutes his/her logos (see Pecheux, 1982 on *dis-identification* and Cixous, 1990 on *lé dépensé*).

In justice-related pursuits some movement in this direction of change can be traced to the peacemaking agenda (e.g., Pepinski and Quinney, 1991; Pepinski, 1993; 1989; 1986). Accordingly, postmodernists recognize the harm, suffering, and pain caused by acts of violence and 'seek to examine [what legal and criminological pursuits] might reduce [them] through transforming the totality of relations of which [the harm, suffering, and pain] [are] a part' (Henry and Milovanovic, 1991: 309). Therefore, social change and social justice require a responsible and active debunking (deconstruction) by crimino-legal practitioners, addressing the politically constructed, ideologically articulated, and media-driven dimensions of social problems (Barak, 1988: 585). The task here is not to construct 'new and different' versions of truth, justice, law, crime, etc., in ways that typify systematic reconstitutions. This exercise would foster nothing more than the reaction-negation problematic implicit in Hegelian thought. Rather, the peacemaking agenda envisioned here considers the *duality* (or mutuality) implicit in our understanding of victimization, control, punishment, law, and order, and endeavors to change our *linguistic* (and therefore social) relationship to such phenomena in ways that foster a replacement (more liberating) experience of human subjects and the life world.

V
Conclusions

This essay has been a very modest attempt to speculate upon the future of criminal justice in light of postmodernism. The discipline is at a crossroads and is in desperate need of its own discourse-specific theory. In order to adequately confront the challenges of crime and justice in the future, an alternative method more synchronized with the *far-from-equilibrium* conditions of the human condition and the social order is essential. In addition, a vision of change which moves beyond the limitations of linear and institutional responses must be developed. Throughout this more mythic and human enterprise the call is for each of us (scholar, practitioner, student, and victim) to experience a more authentic — perhaps more liberating — existence. Thus, the future of criminal justice is an invitation to make us all a bit more moral (honest) by reminding us of our relationship to others and our communities. That other disciplines (e.g., feminist theory) have, in part, been persuaded and guided by the postmodern perspective gives us pause for hope. Criminal justice must now do the same if it is to be appropriately poised for the future.

**Bruce A. Arrigo is Assistant Professor in Administrative Justice at Rowan College of New Jersey.*

REFERENCES

Abadinsky, H. and Winfree, T. L. Jr., 1992, 2d ed., Chicago: Nelson-Hall.

Adorno, T., 1973, *Negative Dialectics*, New York: Continuum.

Arrigo, B., 1995a, forthcoming, *The Contours of Psychiatric Justice: A Postmodern Critique of Mental Illness, Criminal Insanity and the Law*, New York: Garland.

_____, 1995b, forthcoming, 'Desire in the Psychiatric Courtroom: On Lacan and the Dialectics of Linguistic Oppression,' *Current Perspectives in Social Theory*.

_____, 1994a, 'Rethinking the Language of Law and Justice: Postmodern Feminist Jurisprudence,' in eds. D. Caudill and S. Gold, *Radical Philosophy of Law*, New Jersey: Humanities Press.

_____, 1994b, 'The Peripheral Core of Law and Criminology: On Postmodern Social Theory and Conceptual Integration,' (working file).

_____, 1994c, 'Legal Discourse and the Disordered Criminal Defendant: Contributions from Psychoanalytic Semiotics and Chaos Theory,' *Legal Studies Forum* 18(1): .

_____, 1994d, 'The Insanity Defense: A Study in Psychoanalytic Semiotics and Chaos Theory,' in ed. R. Kevelson, *The Eyes of Justice*, New York: P. Lang, 57-83.

_____, 1994e, forthcoming, 'Towards a Theory of Punishment in the Psychiatric Courtroom: On Language, Law and Lacan,' *Journal of Research in Crime and Delinquency*.

_____, 1993a, 'An Experientially-Informed Feminist Jurisprudence: Rape and the Move Toward Praxis,' *Humanity and Society* 17(1): 28-47.

_____, 1993b, *Madness, Language and the Law*, New York: Harrow and Heston.

_____, 1992, 'Deconstructing Jurisprudence: An Experiential Feminist Critique,' *Journal of Human Justice* 4(1): 13-30.

Barak, G., 1994, *Media, Process and the Social Construction of Crime: Studies in Newsmaking Criminology*, New York: Garland.

Barthes, R., 1988, *The Semiotic Challenge,* New York: Hill and Wang.

Bernstein, B., 1975, *Class, Codes and Control*, London: Routledge and Kegan Paul.

Bevan, W. and Kessel, F., 1994, 'Plain Truths and Home Cooking: Thoughts on the Making and Remaking of Psychology,' *American Psychologist* 49(6): 505-9.

Cixous, H., 1990, *Reading With Clarice Lispector*, Minneapolis, Minn.: University of Minnesota Press.

Cornell, D., 1993, *Transformations: Recollective Imagination and Sexual Difference*, New York: Routledge.

_____, 1991, *Beyond Accommodation: Ethical Feminism, Deconstruction and the Law*, New York: Routledge.

Deleuze, G., 1983, *Nietzsche and Philosophy*, New York: Columbia University Press.

Dews, P., 1987, *Logics of Disintegration: Post-structuralist Thought and the Claims of Critical Theory*, London and New York: Verso.

Foucault, M., 1972, *The Archeology of Knowledge*, New York: Pantheon.

Gelsthorpe, L. and Morris, A., 1990, eds., *Feminist Perspectives in Criminology*, Milton Keynes: Open University Press.

Hegel, F. W., 1807/1977, *Hegel's Phenomenology of Spirit*, trans. A.V. Miller, Oxford: Oxford University Press.

Henry, S. and Milovanovic, D., 1991, 'Constitutive Criminology: The Maturation of Critical Theory,' *Criminology* 29(2): 293-315.

Inciardi, J., 1993, 4th Ed., *Criminal Justice*, Fort Worth: Harcourt Brace Jovanovich.

Lacan, J., 1991, *L'envers de la Psychanalyse*, Paris, France: Editions du Seuil.

_____, 1985, *Feminine Sexuality,* New York: Norton.

_____, 1977, *Ecrits: A Selection*, trans. A Sheridan, New York: Norton.

_____, 1975, *Encore*, Paris, France: Edition du Seuil.

Lahey, K., 1985, 'Until Women Themselves Have Told All That They Have to Tell . . .,' *Osgoode Hall Law Journal*, 23: 519-541.

Lyotard, J-F, 1984, *The Postmodern Condition: A Report on Knowledge*, Minneapolis, Minn.: University of Minnesota Press.

MacKinnon, C., 1989, *Towards a Feminist Theory of the State*, Cambridge, Mass: Harvard University Press.

Malhorta Bentz, V., 1993, 'Review of James M. Ostrow's Social Sensitivity,' *Humanity and Society*, 17(1): 121-123.

Milovanovic, D., 1994, 'Dueling Paradigms: Modernist V. Postmodernist Thought,' paper presented at the Annual Meeting of the Western Association of Sociology and Anthropology, Saskatoon, Saskatchewan, Canada (March 3-5).

_____, 1992, *Postmodern Law and Disorder: Psychoanalytic Semiotics and Juridic Exegesis*, Liverpool: Deborah Charles.

_____, 1986, Juridico-Linguistic Communicative Markets: Toward a Semiotic Analysis, *Contemporary Crises*, 10, 281-304.

Nietzsche, F., 1980, *On the Advantage and Disadvantage of History for Life*, Cambridge, Mass.: Hackett Publishing Company.

Pecheux, M., 1982, *Language, Semantics and Ideology*, New York: St. Martin's Press.

Pepinski, H. and Quinney, R., 1991, eds., *Peacemaking in Criminology*, Bloomington: Indiana University Press.

Pepinski, H., 1993, 'What is Crime? What is Peace?: A Commentary,' *Journal of Criminal Justice Education* 4(2): 391-394.

_____, 1989, 'Peacemaking in Criminology,' *The Critical Criminologist* 1 (Summer): 6-10.

_____, 1986, 'This can't be peace: A Pessimist Looks at Punishment,' in eds. W. B. Groves and Graeme Newman, *Punishment and Privilege*, New York: Harrow and Heston.

Sarup, M., 1989, *Post-Structuralism and Postmodernism*, Athens, Georgia: University of Georgia Press.

Senna, J.J. and Siegel, L.J., 1990, 5th ed., *Introduction to Criminal Justice*, St Paul: West Publishing.

Smart, C., 1989, *Feminism and the Power of the Law*, London and New York: Routledge.

Surette, R., 1992, *Media, Crime and Criminal Justice: Images and Realities*, Belmont, California: Brooks/Cole.

Vold, G.B. and Bernard, T. J., 1986, *Theoretical Criminology*, 3ed., New York, Oxford: Oxford University Press.

Young, I., 1990, *Justice and the Politics of Difference*, Princeton: Princeton University Press.

Chapter Three

Poets' Reaction to Apartheid Laws

Jan Bekker*

I

This paper compares and contrasts concepts created by apartheid laws with the language in which African poets expressed themselves about the effects of these laws. The point of departure is that the laws created symbols that were interpreted differently by the two main population groups, the whites and the blacks.

Some of the conditions arising from these symbols were outright unfair, oppressive and humiliating. Other similar conditions may obtain after the demise of apartheid. The laws were virtually churned out in reams. Apart from acts of Parliament there were thousands of proclamations, government notices and other directives that regulated the lives of Africans from the cradle to the grave.[1] The following extract from S. Sepamla's poem 'To Whom it May Concern'[2] is, for instance, a fair reflection of official policy at the time:

> Please note
> The remains of RN 417187
> Will be laid to rest in peace
> On a plot
> Set aside for Methodist Xhosas[3]
> A measure also adopted
> At the express request of the Bantu.

There was no shortage of poetry either. From the early 1960's Africans in South Africa produced a significant number of poems in English.[4]

In view of the large number of poems and the variety and volume of laws, it was impossible to cover all the poems and the whole range of apartheid legislation. I have, for instance, decided not to deal with poetry emanating from security legislation, nor with poetry referring to the land acts. But the poems chosen do cover the most outstanding black/white legal, social and economic relations.

City Johannesburg by M. W. Serote[5]

This way I salute you:
My hand pulses to my back trousers pocket
Or into my inner jacket pocket
For my pass, my life,
Jo'burg City.
My hand like a starved snake rears my pockets
For my thin, ever lean wallet,
While my stomach groans a friendly smile to hunger,
Jo'burg City.
My stomach also devours coppers and papers
Don't you know?
Jo'burg City, I salute you;
When I run out, or roar in a bus to you,
I leave behind me, my love,
My comic houses and people, my dongas and my
ever whirling dust,
My death
That's so related to me as a wink to the eye.
Jo'burg City
I travel on your black and white and robotted roads
Through your thick iron breath that you inhale
At six in the morning and exhale from five noon.
Jo'burg City
That is the time when I come to you,
When your neon flowers flaunt from your electrical wind,
That is the time when I leave you,
When your neon flowers flaunt their way through the
falling darkness
On your cement trees.
And as I go back, to my love,
My dongas, my dust, my people, my death,
Where death lurks in the dark like a blade in the flesh,
I can feel your roots, anchoring your might, my feebleness
In my flesh, in my mind, in my blood,
And everything about you says it,
That, that is all you need of me.
Jo'burg City, Johannesburg,
Listen when I tell you,
There is no fun, nothing, in it,
When you leave the women and men with such
frozen expressions,

Expressions that have tears like furrows of soil erosion,
Jo'burg City, you are dry like death,
Jo'burg City, Johannesburg, Jo'burg City.
Johannesburg is the epitome of South Africa's economic achievements.

It is the country's financial capital — the local counterpart of London, New York, Zurich, Tokyo. But it is also, except in size, a huge replica of each and every town and city in South Africa: it consists of a 'white' city and way beyond a 'black' city. The two were legally defined, distinct entities. The two together — the joint area — was defined as an urban area, that is an area under the jurisdiction of an urban (white) local authority. But part of it was defined as a location or Native village.[6] A location was in turn an area where a (white) urban local authority provided accommodation, whereas in a Native village blacks could erect their own houses on sites leased from the local authority.[7]

This poem portrays a black man's experience of these two components of what may be termed the larger Johannesburg. He enters Jo'burg city at dawn and leaves for the other city at dusk. Jo'burg city offers little comfort. There he has to have his pass book and be continuously on the alert of muggers. His experience in the other city is even more cheerless. In fact, his description of the black city is probably the most poignant to be found in prose or poetry, and I quote:

And as I go back, to my love,
My dongas, my dust, my people,
my death,
Where death lurks in the dark
like a blade in the flesh.

Jo'burg and its black counterpart were creatures of statute. Corollary legislation made the legal distinction for the people concerned even more painful. In terms of section 31 of the Blacks (Urban Areas) Consolidation Act,[8] curfew regulations could be proclaimed declaring that no black male or female shall be in a (white) public place or a specified (white) area within certain specified hours after dark without a written permit signed by his/her employer. In practice the curfew hours were between 9 or 10 pm and 6 am, and a siren sounded or a bell rung to announce the hours.

The poet therefore had to leave Jo'burg city when (its) 'neon flowers flaunt(ed) their way through the falling darkness.' The converse also applied, but not in such crude form. Non-residents (mostly whites) had to have visitors' permits to enter locations.[9]

The laws referred to have been repealed and substituted by racially neutral legislation and further integration of local authority affairs are in the pipeline. However, the picture sketched by Serote is still basically the same. Jo'burg city is still there and Soweto also, and a large number of blacks commute to and fro. The number of blacks living on the periphery of the central business district has, however, increased considerably and by day the central business district is crowded with blacks.

In Johannesburg one still has to keep one's hand on one's rear pocket to protect one's wallet, and in Soweto death still lurks in the dark more than ever.

The two components symbolising apartheid have therefore not disappeared. And they are not likely to merge — at least not in the foreseeable future.

The Master of the House by O. M. Mtshali[10]

Master, I am a stranger to you,
but will you hear my confession?

I am a faceless man
who lives in the backyard
of your house.

I share your table
so heavily heaped with
bread, meat and fruit
it huffs like a horse
drawing a coal cart.

As the rich man's to Lazarus,
the crumbs are swept to my lap
by my Lizzie:
'Sweetie! eat and be satisfied now,
To-morrow we shall be gone.'

So nightly I run the gauntlet,
wrestle with your mastiff, Caesar,
for the bone pregnant with meat
and wash it down with Pussy's milk.

I am the nocturnal animal
that steals through the fenced lair
to meet my mate,
and flees at the break of dawn
before the hunter and the hounds
run me to ground.

This poem depicts the uncomfortable socio-legal relationship between blacks and whites. It is laden with symbols of the unequal black/white relationship.

The Master in the title illustrates the assumption of authority by the white owner of the House. The poet on the other hand is an anonymous entity, a faceless man, an inferior being. The House symbolises the fact that the whole country was the white man's domain. The Master's table, heavily heaped with bread, meat and fruit, is moreover symbolic of the Master's affluence, whereas the poet must vie with the dog for leftovers.

The dog, Caesar, occupies a central position in this scene. It symbolises the state apparatus, the police and the officials. One had to dodge the dog to gain entry to the backyard of the house, and risked being hunted, if detected. The poet's interaction with the dog suggests dehumanisation and inferiority.

There is a painful contrast between the Master's life and the poet's cohabitation with his wife — by stealth.

Servants' rooms in the backyards of white-owned houses are still a common phenomenon — so also the turret-like constructions on top of apartment buildings. In the heyday of apartheid the occupation of these rooms was regulated by section 9 of the Blacks (Urban Areas) Consolidation Act. The gist of that section for present purposes was that all blacks were obliged to reside in a location, black village or black hostel with certain exceptions of which the following one is relevant:

> '(A)ny black employed in *bona fide* domestic service and occupying accommodation approved by the urban local authority, which is provided by his employer on the premises on which he is so employed. . . .'

In South African laws the masculine gender includes the feminine, but here the masculine 'he' is rather ironic, because male domestic servants are few, compared with women. There are in fact some 800,000 black females in domestic employment in South Africa.[11]

Be that as it may, blacks not covered by the exceptions committed an offence by residing outside a location, black village or black hostel.

In practice many husbands and boy friends shared these rooms with their wives and girl friends. But it was illegal and both employer and the illegal 'resident' could be prosecuted, if the 'resident' was found on the premises.

These guests led a precarious life. Regular nocturnal raids were made on premises irrespective of whether there was a report made or a suspicion that there were illegal occupants. The nightly re-unification of couples, however, remained part of the South African scene. The law worked on the assumption that the couples could be kept asunder; being merely human brought them together from after nightfall to the break of dawn.

The law has been repealed, but the scene sketched by the poet still prevails. There are still hundreds of thousands of little square rooms with minimum facilities in the backyards of white Masters in the turret-like constructions on top of apartment buildings. The male occupants are still by and large faceless strangers. But relations are not quite as harsh as they used to be. The Masters would nowadays freely allow, even encourage, the erstwhile illegal visitors, especially to encourage a maid to stay in service and to make her happy. Some Masters nowadays even erect prefabricated wooden, zinc or asbestos structures, in which black men are allowed to live in exchange for keeping the Master's garden. An amicable relationship would sometimes develop between the Master and occupant and Caesar would no longer constitute a threat. But the Master is still the Master and the House and the room in the backyard still symbolise the dichotomy between black and white. Ironically some blacks that moved into 'white' areas use the same rooms to accommodate their own domestic servants.

Maybe, even today a black poet may ask:

Who am I?
That question you will never know
Because you do not wish to know
Many names have you called me
But you cannot confuse me
One thing that I know
You will never know me.[12]

The Start of a Removal by S. Sepamla[13]

On a Monday morning

when some people were hailing taxis
others rushing to buses and trains

when teachers and school-children
were packing their books
peeping out of windows to see so-and-so
their time-keeper
was leaving for the factory or office-job

when the local businessman
eyes large and sleepy
like he was an owl
sat at the till
waiting for the early customer
to make his insomnia worthwhile

when the housewives started bending
their overused frames
raising dust on the pavement
in front of their yards
with home-made grassbrooms

when a midwife wearily flung
instructions at an old lady
whose daughter had just
given birth to her third child
by her third 'boyfriend'

the first five families
woke up
to the drone of bull-dozers
and the impatience of heavy-duty trucks

The removal had started!

II

A removal has a peculiar meaning in South Africa. It referred to the removal of people of colour from areas proclaimed as group areas for the white population group, from so-called 'black spots,' that is areas which were predominantly occupied by blacks, but falling outside a homeland, and from informal (squatter) settlements. It has been reported that more than three and a half million people, of whom a few were whites, were removed in the process of rearranging South Africa's human geography.[14]

Removals could be effected by different laws, but I shall discuss this poem in the light of the Prevention of Illegal Squatting Act,[15] because, despite the official abolition of apartheid, removals under that Act are still possible.

The difference between the title of the poem and the heading of the section in the Act is significant. The title of the poem is a bland statement. But for most readers it has on account of the notoriety of removals an emotional content. The heading of the relevant section of the Act reads: 'Orders for ejectment and transfer of trespassers and for demolition of structures.' It reflects an attitude, an assumption of authority. Such assumption of authority over a section of the population characterises a closed society, in this case the apartheid society.

Referring as it does to orders for ejectment, transfer of trespassers and demolition of structures, it conveys the message that the provisions are aimed at criminals. The Act is in fact categorised as part of South African criminal law. The lawgiver found it easy to create this picture of criminality, because exclusive and absolute rights to property are held in high regard. The poet on the other hand also had an easy task to create sympathy, because obviously the squatters were homeless and so-called squatter's camps were their only homes. The Act, by the way, is racially neutral. It speaks of 'persons.' In South Africa, however, a squatter in South Africa means an African (black) who settles on land without right or title.[16]

The Act categorizes the people to be removed as persons, individual human beings. They are nevertheless a faceless group, the objects of a removal exercise. The poet sees them in a more compassionate light: people on their way to work, teachers, school-children, a local businessman, an early customer, housewives, a midwife, an elderly mother, a wayward daughter, even a newborn babe. These people constitute a community, although individually going about the business of living.

'Monday morning' reflects a state in the affairs of the people involved. It is traditionally a beginning, a revival of activity after a break. It also suggests in this poem a blue Monday, a Monday on which anything might go wrong. In the implementation of laws authorising removals, Mondays had a specific official significance. For fear of violent protests and unfavourable press coverage, removals had to have an element of surprise and were never carried out over weekends, but often on Mondays and invariably early morning when people were weakest to resist.

Lastly, the law does not refer to bull-dozers and heavy-duty trucks, but says that a court convicting a squatter shall — '. . . make an order for the summary ejectment of such person from the land or building concerned,' '. . . issue such further orders, give such instructions and confer such authority as may be reasonably necessary —

(i) to give effect to the . . . order of ejectment;

(iii) to ensure the demolition and removal [of the structures concerned].'[17]

In the implementation of these judicial powers bull-dozers and heavy-duty trucks have become the ominous images of removals. The officials concerned had a fleet of trucks that were deployed all over the country wherever needed. Bull-dozers were obviously not that movable and were locally hired as the occasion demanded.

These heavy-duty trucks and bull-dozers in operation were immortalised in cinema, short story, novel, drama and poetry. They have come to stand for more than ordinary law enforcement. They reflect brute force, legal nevertheless, to create demographic white areas.

The Squatters Act has since been amended to make it possible for squatter areas to be upgraded. However, the provisions for removal remain intact. But, more importantly, the terminology for dealing with squatters has undergone relexification. The same things are called by different names. Squatter camps are called informal settlements; 'emergency camps' are no longer in vogue.

Even the judges have become unfrozen. Whereas formerly squatters were illegal and that was the end of it, they now go out of their way to find that under certain circumstances squatters may acquire rights[18] and may even order shacks illegally demolished to be re-erected.[19] What a sea-change — the remover acting illegally!

Counter 14 by M. Dikobe[20]

Around Albert Street
Are faces pale, haggard and desperate
Lips cracked with cavities
Scrambling over job-seeking

In a yard
Twenty feet high
Bounded from sightseeing
  many more
Seated, shifting, yawning

Not even a bazaar
Would have so many customers
Queuing
Their fate
On a white face

'Escort'
72 hours grace
Out of the urban area
To starve, rob, steal
In own homeland.

The significance of this poem is its stark description of the application of the pass laws. Counter 14 was one of the counters in the pass office at 80 Albert Street in Johannesburg where black people were ordered to leave the urban area. Such orders, officially endorsed in reference books, revolved around the application of the notorious section 10 of the Blacks (Urban Areas) Consolidation Act, which provided that 'No Native [later Bantu, then Black] shall remain for more than seventy-two hours in an urban area, unless . . .' (there were certain exceptions and conditions).

A 'Native' for this purpose meant a member of an aboriginal race or tribe of Africa.[21] The apartheid legislation assumed that there were discrete and unassimilable population groups. The dominant (white) group furthermore fabricated by legal definition an urban area and assumed powers to keep 'Natives,' as defined, out of that area, by creating the concept that their mere presence in an urban area was unlawful. The courts placed a judicial stamp of approval upon this legal fabrication. In *R v Mdingani*[22] it was held that *all* Natives falling within the purview of section 10 were unlawfully within the urban area and that once they had thereafter resided for more than seventy-two hours therein, their residence had become unlawful.

As a result some 18 million people (blacks) were prosecuted and fined or imprisoned for contravening pass laws in one form or another.[23]

The poet paints the human face of these unlawful Natives. In Albert Street their unlawfulness was stamped in an identity document, called a reference book. And so the book came to symbolise the oppressiveness of the pass laws. Resentment was sometimes expressed by a burning of books. But the pale, haggard and desperate faces of the bearers of the books speak of their plight. Being seated, shifting and yearning reflect their helplessness.

In actual fact Albert Street was as depressing as intimated by the poet. Hundreds of blacks milled around, then somehow found their way into the yard, bounded from sight-seeing by an enclosure and eventually in a queue, slowly shuffling up to counters where white clerks conducted brief enquiries into each one's presence in Johannesburg. Some got permission to stay, many were endorsed out of the area in terms of official guidelines complementing the law. The law and regulations were by no means as clear as might have appeared at first blush and could give rise to misapplications.[24]

However, there was very little judicial intervention in the application of the laws. Few cases went on appeal or review and in cases that did go on appeal the courts regarded themselves as bound by the rule that they applied law as they found it. More specifically, in regard to the wording of the Act the courts adopted the following principle of interpretation:

Where the language of a statute is unambiguous and its meaning is clear, the Court may only depart from such meaning if it 'would lead to absurdity so glaring that it could never have been contemplated by the legislature or where it would lead to a result contrary to the intention of Parliament as shown by the content or by such other consideration as the Court is justified in taking into account.'[25] The courts nevertheless sometimes added to or subtracted from the meaning of certain words and phrases. The meaning of the word 'remains' often required further elaboration, because its so-called ordinary meaning did not cover the variety of eventualities under which persons were found in the urban areas. For instance, it was held that an accused's stay in an urban area must have been voluntary. A period during which he was detained by the police could not be taken into account when the 72-hour period was calculated.[26]

The abolition of influx control in 1986 prompted another poet, Karen Press, to write a poem with the title 'April 23rd, 1986,'[27] adding the explanation: 'On this day the Minister of Constitutional Development and Planning announced the abolition of influx control, and the Minister of

Justice tabled new security legislation in parliament.' The poet was obviously sceptical.

The scepticism of this poet is understandable. The abolition of influx control did not bring about any real change, except that it enabled many more Africans to converge upon the towns and cities.

In the meantime Africans have acquired real political power, and the country has a new constitution and a bill of rights. The necessity to distinguish between groups and areas has therefore fallen away. But most of the people who turned up at Albert Street were workseekers. They don't go to pass offices any more — they go to labour bureaux. They cannot be endorsed out of the area, but most of them are shown away, because there is no work for them.[28] The labour bureaux have thus become the symbols of their plight.

Ballad to the Coffee Cart by C. Themba[29]

A little tin shack on wheels,
Jars a Jo'burg pavement,
Like a busy ant the roadwife peels
Potatoes, stirs porridge, blind to enslavement.

It is the blackman's Coffee Cart,
Simpler, cheaper, nourisher,
And, oddly, so near to the heart
Of this Metropolis' chestnut worker.

Coffee is the least of its wares;
Sour milk, Mahewu, dumpling and meat —
Staples all — but I love most the democratic airs
Of the easy-smiling women who come to eat.

If only the guys with the burning meat,
And the slick restaurants where stomachs smart,
Did not agitate against that dinner on the street,
You'd meet me during lunch at the Coffee Cart.

This poem is symbolic of the restrictive economic activities of Blacks in metropolitan areas. Coffee carts are commonly found in cities, especially in and around industrial areas and in the less well-to-do shopping areas on the fringes of central business districts. They were exclusively patronised by Africans doing menial work, such as cleaners, janitors and messengers.

The poet refers to the owner of the coffee cart as 'roadwife.' She symbolises thousands of African women traders engaged in a marginal day-to-day existence, selling small quantities of commodities on pavements, at taxi ranks, at entrances to railway stations — in fact everywhere. Their economic activity is crucial to the circulation of goods and money, but on the long term they are not likely to improve upon their precarious existence. Their trade is not a stepping stone to big business. As a group they are likely to be kept out of more lucrative trading activities by established businesses and traders (mostly men) who have access to capital.

The coffee cart simply served cheap food. Although 'coffee [was] the least of its wares' it acquired the name 'coffee' cart, probably by reason of the fact that the early customers had coffee and something to eat and the workers had coffee breaks during the day.

The poet concisely describes the cart in only six words: 'A little tin shack on wheels.' In legal parlance it was a 'movable structure' or 'stationary vehicle.'[30] But compare the more detailed description by a magistrate after an inspection *in loco*:

> It is a movable wooden structure, the front being mounted on several bricks. The structure has a gabled roof, is 6 feet high, 4 feet broad at the front and 3½ feet on the side. At the front there is an opening and a serving shelf with a roof over it. The roof is made of wood is hinged and is held by a support, when the support is removed the roof swings down and closes the opening. On one side there is an entrance door about 5 feet high and 3 feet broad which can be locked by means of a padlock. There is a wooden floor, and two shelves are fitted on the side opposite the door. Inside there were a few loose paraffin tins, a box, a candle, 4 plates and other oddments.'[30, 31]

The poet's use of 'wheels' and the magistrate's use of the word 'movable' to describe an essential character of the cart, symbolise the fiction that blacks were birds of passage. After office hours they were forbidden in that area; the proprietor had in any event only a passing right to trade in the so-called white area.

In strict law it was supposed to be even more mobile, because the trader was meant to carry on his/her business elsewhere than at a fixed place and to travel with his/her goods from place to place with a vehicle propelled by him or herself.[32]

'Inside,' according to the magistrate, 'there were a few loose paraffin tins, a box, a candle, 4 plates and other oddments.' In contrast, according to the poet, the [white] guys went to 'slick restaurants.'

So far the mobility. Another feature of the coffee cart that comes out in the poem and the legal/official version is the simplicity of its wares. The poet says it consists of potatoes, porridge, sour milk, Mahewu, dumpling and meat — a simple fare. Justice Kuper in *R v Tshingila* confirmed that the trader 'supplied tea, coffee, vetkoek, and bread in slices, the cakes were cold. . . .'

The menu is not only a sign of the poverty of the 'chestnut workers' (the poet's words) or the 'natives employed in the area' (the judge's words), but also points to features of African culture: the sour milk, Mahewu, dumpling and meat — favourite African food and 'simpler, cheaper, nourisher than' the white man's 'burning meat.' Yet again it emphasises the difference between the haves and the have-nots.

The coffee cart setting is moreover a typical African one. It is a familiar South African scene: 'the blackman's Coffee Cart' where 'easy-smiling women . . . come to eat.'

The poem ends on a cheerless note. The poet in effect says that the Coffee Cart community was broken up by reason of the fact that the guys in the slick restaurants agitated 'against the dinner on the street.' It was indeed possible to have a coffee cart removed, because, as intimated by the poet in the first verse, it jarred a Jo'burg pavement. That would be in contravention of road traffic bylaws. However, it would seem that the poet was aware of the judgment in *R v Tshingila* where it was held that a coffee cart proprietor must have a restaurant licence, which would place it in the same category, albeit not quality, of the 'slick restaurants' frequented by the [white] guys. In *casu* 'the roadwife' was charged for trading without a hawker's licence, and the judgement was that she should have had a restaurant licence. She was, ironically, therefore acquitted on the charge of trading without a hawker's licence.

Be that as it may, life was made difficult for hawkers and pedlars and 'roadwives' generally for many years. They were continuously prosecuted for trading without licences, obstructing traffic and selling foodstuff under unhygienic conditions.

Many of these restrictive laws have been repealed or ameliorated, but the socio-economic scene of the coffee cart has not changed. There are literally thousands of African traders jarring pavements to eke out a living.

They do keep themselves alive and are euphemistically referred to as constituting the informal sector of the economy. The prospects of rising above the level of roadwives are, however, gloomy. There is still a sharp contrast between them and the guys (this time round black and white) frequenting slick restaurants. The gap is unlikely to grow narrower in the foreseeable future.

III
Conclusion

The human scene in South Africa is rapidly changing and no one can predict the future. I have, however, cautiously shown how the past might project itself into the future. Squatters, for instance, will be with us for a long time to come and we may very well witness more removals.

In a more general sense, too, the anguish and powerlessness expressed in the poems are timeless. Bureaucrats are bureaucrats wherever and whenever. Some of the poems remind one of *The Trial* by Kafka. They express a helplessness that is not confined to time and place.

The new constitution has created a host of new symbols hitherto unknown in this country, although even the National Party has for some time been introducing a new range of terms, e.g. negotiation, minority rights, free enterprise, devolution of power, the right to own property, deregulation, privatisation and so on and even transformed some of the concepts into law, e.g. by repealing the Land Acts and the Group Areas Act.

However, the new constitution reels off a whole array of new concepts. Some are ideals, such as a 'need to create a new order.' Others are substantive law, for instance, an Act of Parliament must be made for the payment of special pensions to 'persons who have made sacrifices . . . in the establishment of a democratic constitutional order.' The reality, as with the ideology of apartheid, may turn out to be different.

The new symbols are in some respects more universal than the old ones and probably more functional. They will at least serve as bridging symbols. Others, such as affirmative action may cause new tensions. One could go on endlessly about the new symbols. I confine myself to a few constantly recurring in a barrage of affirmative action literature: empowerment, equal opportunities, disadvantaged communities, access to resources, appropriate support, space and opportunities, and black trainees.[31] These concepts are obviously racially biased. The terminology is aimed at justifying black advancement despite constituent disabilities, such as a lack of learning, a lack of capital resources, a lack of entrepreneurial skills and so on. The terminology will inevitably be adjusted, depending upon the success or failure of affirmative action. Poets will no doubt in due course respond — either gleefully or sadly.

**Jan Bekker is Professor of Law at Vista University.*

ENDNOTES

1. The large number of subordinate laws, proclamations and government notices, was due to the fact that the State President (formerly the Governor-General) was given wide legislative powers in respect of blacks 'to meet rapidly the ever changing needs of a primitive people, emerging from barbarism. It provided a means of meeting emergencies . . . and of legislating for the peculiar needs of the Natives in their own areas. . . .' H. Rogers, *1949, Native Administration in the Union of South Africa*, 30. Second edition by Linington, P.A.

2. M.V. Mzamane, 1984, ed., *Selected Poems*, 19.

3. Separate areas were allocated in graveyards for different ethnic groups, but I could not get confirmation that a distinction was made between various religious denominations.

4. Several reasons have been advanced for this spate of English language poetry by African poets. One is that 'poetry has been used by the African poets . . . to 'nationalise' the English language: that is, to transform the English language — one of the official languages — into a language expressing the emergent culture and aspirations of the majority of South Africans.' J. Cronin, 'The law that says/Constricts the breath-line. . . . South African English Language Poetry Written by Africans in the 1970's, 1985, *The English Academy Review 3*, 26.

5. M.W. Serote, 1982, *Selected Poems*, 22.

6. G. Davis, 1959, *et al, Urban Native Law*, 95.

7. *Ibid.*

8. Act 25 of 1945.

9. Municipal regulations provided for that — See Davis *et al, op cit* 188-189.

10. O.M. Mtshali, 1971, *Sounds of a Cowhide Drum*, 55.

11. According to the South African Central Statistical Service there were 805 340 black female domestic workers in 1991.

12. G.S. Mama, 1974, in ed. D. Bunyan, *25/25 Twenty Five Years of English South African Poetry*, 1989:5.

13. T. Couzens, and E. Patel, 1982, *The Return of the Amazi Bird — Black South Africans Poetry 1891-1981*, 232-233.

14. *Land in South Africa* P.C10, a publication compiled by the Human Awareness Programme, 1989.

15. Act 52 of 1951.

16. D.R. Beeton, and H. Dorner, 1975, *A Dictionary of English Usage in Southern Africa*.

17. Section 3(1) of Act 52 of 1951.

18. In *George Municipality v Vena and another* 1989 2 *SA* 263 (A) the Court held that if prior permission was granted for the erection of a structure, and the structure is destroyed by fire, the provisions of the Squatters Act cannot without more ado be invoked to demolish the re-erected structure.

19. *Fredericks and another v Stellenbosch Divisional Council*, 1977 3 *SA* 113 C.

20. Couzens and Patel *op cit* 298.

21. The term is defined in section 1 of the Act.

22. 1956 4 SA 39, C.

23. Between 1916 and 1981 the figure was 17,12 million. Influx control was abolished five years later in 1986. *Report of the Committee for Constitutional Affairs of the President's Council on An Urbanisation Strategy for the Republic of South Africa*, PC 3/1985, 147.

24. In *Oos-Randse Administrasieraad v Rikhoto*, 1983 *SA* 595, A, at 610 the judge remarked that the complexity of the act and regulations made them very difficult to interpret.

25. Per C.J. Innes, in *R v Venter*, 1907 *TS* 910 at 915.

26. *R v Molele*, 1960, 1 PH K61, 0.

27. A. Coetzee, and H. Willemse, 1989, *Iqabane Labantu (Poetry in Emergency)*, 126.

28. In 1991, according to the South African Statistical Service, there were 94, 978 unemployed whites, 229, 252 coloureds, 48, 146 Asians and 1, 746, 273 blacks.

29. Couzens and Patel *op cit* 166.

30. See Davis *et al, op cit* 167.

31. 1956 4 *SA* 632 (T) at 633.

32. Davis, *et al*, *op cit* 167.

Chapter Four

The Illicit Reduction of Ontology to Epistemology in the Legal Enterprise

Virginia Black*

If you place the nature of truth in one sort of character and its test in something quite different, you are pretty certain, sooner or later, to find the two falling apart.

Brand Blanshard, *The Nature of Thought*

I
Setting the Terms of the Problem

In a tribute essay to John Smith, the Yale University process philosopher, Robert Corrington in 'Beyond Experience: Pragmatism and Nature's God,'[1] describes a split in the philosophical and literary tradition between nature and history. History is the endlessly changeable, the Heraclitan flux. Nature is fixed.

Critical of contemporary neopragmatism in its emphasis on variance, procedures, and operations — how something is known — Corrington writes:

> [In neopragmatism] the human process is but one of innumerable others and . . . whatever distinct features it has are features derived from an unlimited domain that has neither origin nor goal . . . .the neopragmatic focus on semiotic possibility and historical/contextual pluralism assumes that the self has more hermeneutic maneuvering room than it actually has. At the same time, *it makes human history (and temporality) the genus of which nature is a mere species*. (my itals) As we shall see, the correlation between nature and history is the exact opposite of this. . . .'

What Corrington seems to mean by this nature/history subordination is that the relative, the transient, the in-flux is made, wrongly, the foundation of the permanent, whereas it should rightly be the other way around. Corrington has exposed a startling contention. Can anyone seriously hold, except trivially, that the natural order that exists, that is real and has discernible properties, relations and conditions, is in thralldom to how we communicate about it — that *how* man knows depends not at all on what it *is* that he knows? The thesis Corrington criticizes is inside-out as well: it violates a ground rule of explanation, namely, that the more puzzling takes clarity from the less puzzling.

What seems like a substantive insight, namely, that *knowing* the identity of object X is the same as declaring, 'That is X,' and hence requires a human mind and human language is, in my judgment, a mere analyticity, confounded by the rhetoric of emphasis. No one doubts that we do not have an ant's eye view of reality. We have a human's eye view of reality. Given this platitude, it is a mere logical truth, but a truth apparently bearing an appealing psychological impact, that the physical objects we perceive define their identity through a human preconception without which they would not *be* the objects that they are.[2] This acknowledged and done with, certain prominent human-mind-and-language independent objects like planets and antelopes still require to be distinguished from how occasions and perspectives shape our discussions and theories about them.

The story goes that Galileo was demonstrating through the magnifying lens of his telescope that the planet Saturn had moons. This was not an 'interpretation.' Religious authorities, however, refused to accept the reality because saturnian moons did not coincide with terrestrial pre-eminence and special creation. 'It is only a spot on the lens,' they declared. Now we have to ask: Which party interpreted? It was the party that refused the testimony of their senses.

If anything exists and has shape and size and mass independent of man, who no doubt *measures* these properties, it is material entities in the sky. Language is a lens whose spots can distort entities in the sky. But if anyone today confuses these distortions with the stuff they distort, rational and empirical remedies are available, not for their denial but for their correction in the direction of a never fully-perfected truth.

The operative or performative question, 'How do you know?' validly catalyzes an epistemological frame of enquiry, sets it in motion into testifying on behalf of the truth or falsehood of some actual statement. But just as the prefix, 'It is true (or false) [that p . . .],' been shown to be rhetorical and empty of content, so also 'I know that p. . . .' has been shown to be a rhetorical use of 'I know.'[3] These locutions contribute nothing of substance to what p describes. 'I know that . . .' only adds emphasis to p; the sentential prefix is redundant. While this does not at all make meaningless the desire to know, it suggests that efforts to wash a muddy ontology with the allegedly clearer waters of an epistemological bath may be subject to this hidden redundancy. One has to look and see.

In the distance I see a cow. That is what I see. The cow is real. It exists. But exactly what makes it possible for me to see the cow (identify the object *as* a cow) is a question with long drawn-out answers to which even only the sciences of psychology and biology are not sufficient to comprehend. One needs, as well, cognitive and *gestalt* psychology, and certainly conceptual support from the philosophies of knowledge. But since only subject matters can be epistemologically assessed — how do we know them and what vindicates our belief in them? — it makes no sense to distinguish the latter without a science of 'the furniture of the world.' Like particulars and universals (general terms), sense and denotation are distinct categories of understanding.[4] Sometimes these activities even refer to the same thing.[5]

This useful contingency does not, however, *ipso facto* turn ostending into interpreting. Both activities can make mistakes. But the remedy is no more further to reinterpret the language than further to take another look. That the term 'cow' is by convention, making it convenient to give an instant label to what this second look reveals is, as we indicated, the result only of an analytic truth regarding our human — what else! — perspective on reality.

The perverse contention that Corrington exposes suggests that the complex and obscure can be used to explain what is simple and less obscure. Yet to understand anything, it is commonly agreed that we need a measure, a limit we can fix on to explain what is difficult. Certainly we need, at least, the more obvious, the already known, to account for our perplexities about the extraordinary.

The conditions of the natural order — its mind-independent objects, states and events, even its cycles and regularities, being relatively stable and already explained — are the limits and fixities through which the unknown, the complex, or the dependent and constructed features of the world are normally approached. *How* we know these objects, states, and so on, is itself an inquiry suffused with problematics. In any case, there must be *something* to know before the epistemological question meaningfully arises as to how this something is known. History looks at nature to take its bearing, not the other way around. An ontological perspective is presupposed.

Epistemology's great endeavor is having contributed to a method of enquiry that has served science and so many other disciplines triumphantly. This does not imply, though, that its language and methods of enquiry so manipulate its subject matters that they cannot be said to have an existence and nature independent of the tools of knowing.

Changing the terms a little in order to examine certain legal phenomena, but following by analogy Corrington's concern that 'first things' have been subjected to relativities that are given logical primacy of place, it has become the mode in certain circles to talk as if nature and its denoted objects are always and irrefutably subject to the conventional vagaries of linguistic interpretation, which latter is itself subject to time and place, person, popularity, and power.[6] It is, after all, through language (through signs and symbols, models, icons, and graphics) that we understand most of what we do understand; certainly language precises and nuances for us the cognitive units, abstractions, and theoretical terms we require for sophisticated communication. Using Corrington's analogy, just as nature, mistakenly he thinks, has been subordinated to history, to the ever-changeable — as a species is subordinated to its genus — so by these thinkers ontology, that is, what exists and its characteristics, is seen as a species of the genus epistemology wherein linguistic interpretation is sovereign — and always running scared of usurpation! What is real and what these real things are like, no longer are logically anterior considerations. Indeed, even the claim to know them without the medium of signs is held to be naive and pretentious. Identity, what things are, moves always through symbolic mediation, through signification controlled by the language conventions, agreements, mind-sets, and cultural histories of diverse peoples, through 'universes of discourse' and the later Wittgenstein's 'forms of life.' The identity and features of objects in the world, even those ostensively noticed, are subject to human, often idiosyncratic, constructions for which there are no discoverable criteria adequate or fully agreed to for distinguishing their true representation from their false; the situation-relativity of language absorbs the entire lot. From such a view, it follows that meta-language absorbs the object language; and meta-meta language absorbs the meta-language, *ad infinitum*.

On this view, the content, referents, and substance of our vision and speech, and especially its material subjects — the ontological realm we are inclined to believe in as a reference point for trying out our grasp of more remote, sophisticated, and occipital realities — succumb to conceptualizations that emerge from widely varying, selected, or unconscious perspectives. Values, purposes, contexts, decisions, biases, arguments, qualifications, communal norms, powers and authorities — and finally, even if innocently, indeterminacies of translation and renderings — know no beginning-or end-point. Denotation and ostensive reference, a real grasp of an object, is a phantom if an object is held to be an entity independent of semiotic manipulation.

I disagree with this reduction of ontology to epistemology, of what we know to how we know it. And I want to illustrate my disagreement drawing upon an area of enquiry that seems paradoxic at first glance. This area of enquiry is certain aspects of law. It is paradoxic because law and social life deal not centrally with the material objects whose oneness we find easy to locate and name and sometimes easy to communicate without the blessings of vocabulary, but with the 'esoterica' of social life. It is paradoxic because our social life, of which law is a pervasive institution, is notably constituted by 'choice-inclusive' ideas[7] and thus by higher-order concepts quite buried in speech habits. Journalists, ideologues, and political authorities also use media semiotics to persuade and compel their way. These linguistic stratagems enter mainstream vocabularies of natural language, feed back on themselves and associated ideas, and glide forward into the natural language like a tadpole into a frog. The result is a discourse whose connection with hard being is amorphous and light-miles away from the data it presumably accounts for.

It is paradoxic, too, that the antinomy, ontology vs. epistemology, matters less with certain legal phenomena, since social and legal phenomena are largely constructed by our beliefs and actions, are complexly influenced by the beliefs of others that are communicated through language (reflexivity and feedback in social phenomena), and often demand justification — and also since contestable concepts rampant in the social sciences are notoriously ripe for interpretation.

Nevertheless, the illustrative arena through which the ontological/epistemological antinomy is questioned is drawn here from law and from things relevant to law.

II
Law

Thesis. Taking certain legal and judicial phenomena as examples, I want to show that in certain crucial instances, it *does not matter* which viewpoint we take, which we hold primary and which secondary, which logically anterior, which dependent and derivative. Law as a system and its procedural and administrative auxiliaries contain elements for knowing that we have arrived at just solutions to social problems (epistemology). But these elements are laminated upon the reality that law governs (ontology). Hence *how* we know what is just (legally right, morally true, etc.) is, by and large, *what* we come to know is just. Legal ontology and legal epistemology are, at crucial junctures, woven of one continuous thread whose segments are indistinct, blurring one into the other until the question, Which is which? is meaningless.

In consideration of particular problems, however, as in the application of the law to a given case, ontological or epistemological enquiries may be differentiated, one taking precedence if its sequence as first or second bears some practical import. For instances, in trying to discover what something is (a washed-out footprint or an eroded depression in the mud?), a provisional separation of the two domains of enquiry may be useful: 'What is this and how do you know?' may be appropriately answered by separate approaches. Epistemology 'comes first' if, for example, an alleged fact needs to be re-thought; if doubts about witness and testimony are articulated; or if the query, 'How do you know?' is a strategic one in some litigatory instance. Adversarial legal systems quite naturally emphasize these cognizable subjects; quite naturally they intensify the search for method, for 'how-to' criteria and procedures, for authoritative meaning strictures that cohere with already accepted truths, or for adequacy and relevance of proof.

But besides the interests of the litigant and his defender in demanding proofs, the morality of law — justice — has always demanded the causal and logical vindication through reasons that we ascribe to the epistemological endeavor, since reasons validate our belief in statements that are made. Justice is degraded by prejudice, unreason, naked authority, and dogmatism that abjure 'showing how and why.' Accordingly, the epistemological disposition during law trial — questioning the grounds for claims made, emphasizing 'let's be sure' — takes on, for a time, a luminous urgency.

Does ontology ever dominate, or does it ever entirely eclipse the desire to know *why* something is so? Is there any form of knowledge that demands no 'justified true belief'? Revealed theology comes first to mind. So far as I know, queries for reasons in this sensitive domain are by and large quiescent. As to whether the claims of revealed theology are knowledge, its expositors and advocates must answer the question with terms drawn from the discipline, many of whose meanings are interior.

Some years ago it was modish in college poetry classes to ridicule translation. Tampering with symbolic meaning and imagery — interpretation, historical exegesis, biographical, contextual analyses — was out of fashion. Re-thinking a poem's own language, a critical task previously thought essential to locating an idiom that would make its meaning clear, was denounced by the new canons of poetic appreciation.

Within this hands-off school of thought, the word 'ontology' was bandied about: the poem was said to have its own ontology, its own existence and being. This approach, in my judgment, is basically a right one, with the proviso that sometimes facts about the poet and her times may bring to light a larger perspective of what she is trying to convey. Focus on anything other than the poem inclines to subordinate its dignity in its own right. The poem is not *about* something else that is more important, as if the poem were secondary, a vehicle for another more real reality. The poem is itself a real object, a unique, symbolic 'particular.' Because its meanings are internal, the way to understand a poem is to reject its translation into a more familiar idiom. Understanding a poem is simply to read it, to expose oneself to it, again and again if necessary, directly acquainting oneself with it, like standing in front of a painting or like meeting a person on the street, until its individuality, its 'face,' becomes familiar and remembered. A poem is self-referring.

Some poets contend they cannot tell anyone what their poem means because this invites alternative symbolization, imagery, metaphors, etc., that they did not choose. It invites mistakes, ridicule, diminishment. Instead, they welcome readers into an act, not of proliferating versions of an original, like the studio art of copying — but of creation, into an idiosyncratic gestalt of self-reflexive artistry. This is not a surrender to subjectivity, because there is no objective meaning that is the correct one to which to compare the poem. The poem's language *is* the objective meaning of itself, and so also is our understanding of it. The poem's being and how we know what it means are a single, indistinguishable reality.

These poets' modest disclaimers about the meanings of their poems are a sincere and proper response to the fact that a real item, like a statue, has been brought into the world, where before there was nothing. Unlike a painting or statue, a poem uses linguistic signs and so the tendency is to think its meaning lies hidden but for the translation that discloses its referent. But this confuses poems with ordinary descriptive sentences whose meanings sometimes denote objects that are other than themselves. With poetry, there can be no meta-performance about meaning.

If poems, using language, denote themselves, why can objects not denote themselves? The case for objects is even clearer, for they use no language at all.

Back to Law. In theory, as I hope to show, the ontological and epistemological projects often merge; they are conceptually indistinguishable, one meaningless without the other, and sometimes they mutually reduce to an equivalence.

But not always. In the application of law to concrete cases, a gap occurs in that a specific judicial outcome (let's call this the *ontology of decisional justice*) does not exhaustively represent the evidence proffered for the decision (let's call this the *epistemology of procedural justice*). *How* the decision was reached, *how* the court or the judge knows where justice lies, is not logically equivalent to the rules and facts offered as its foundation, similarly as an operational definition in science is only a partial identification of all that a general natural law conveys.

How Do You Know This? The question is ambiguous in any context. Depending upon what one understands is wanted in the situation, it admits of a plurality of answers. These answers may overlap or be quite independent, may be direct or quite indirect.

1. *Observation statements may satisfy the query*, (a legal witness may aver that she saw so-and-so). 2. . . . *or presentation of a physical object* (material evidence, such as a weapon, a clot of blood, a body). 3. *Facts already known may be relevant* (the defendant belongs to Carpenters' Union 285; the victim was on the second floor when he was struck). 4. *Inferences may be appropriate* (the plants are wet so someone has been in this room recently; the tires are still hot so someone has just parked this car). 5. *Testimony may be called for* ('I never made a contract with Mr. Horn'). 6. *Necessary conditions may be sought* (If thus-and-so was the case, then it had to be that . . . also prevailed). 7. *Documents or records may be subpoenaed.*

What we note about the above types of evidentiary materials in support of the epistemological question — How do we justify saying that we know this? — is that all of them are facts, or are presumed to be; and close scrutiny would reveal, I think, that all have either logical or causal connections to the *desideratum*. Statements in evidence of facts are facts themselves; and in matters of law, it is facts that confirm or disconfirm the critical, How do we know this? questions. 'Facts, judicially noticed, are equivalent to evidence.'[8] [The same pattern occurs in the sciences where hypotheses and laws *entail* their confirming evidence.]

Through the lens of a microscope, two biologists differ, let us say, on whether what they see is a virus or bacterium. 'Why do you think this is a virus?' asks one of the other. 'Because it has few features of a bacterium,' replies the other. Evidence is presented in the form of a negative contrast. The negative contrast makes reference to the nature (properties) of an organism. The epistemological quest is satisfied by the ontological status of the datum.

Confirming a statement as true, normally settled by evidence, is subsidiarily a question about the relevance of the evidence itself. This could not be true if the world and not our varied constructions of it did not contain the final and most trustworthy answers as to what evidence is related to what. To turn this logic around makes evidence masters instead of servants. It makes truth and falsehood subservient to someone's personal sense that his inquiry has been comfortably closed.

From what we have said above, human laws, judicial proceedings, and the like furnish apt examples for our thesis: Namely, no impenetrable boundary exists between the ontological and the epistemological project for many legal phenomena. They comprise a unity of effort and outcome.

Because factual materials used in law are meant to eliminate appearances, deceptions, distortions, falsehoods, causal relevance and accuracy (empirical truth) furnish to curial phenomena their ontological dimension: What is real (really to be believed) as opposed to what is only an appearance? What is true as opposed to what is deceptive? Here sense and reference — the epistemology and the ontology — come out to be the same. The problem is answered in both ways simultaneously. The 'logic' of the answer is one.

Where circumstantial evidence must be weighed for its contribution as admissible evidence, and where the adversarial stance conceals, if it can do so, the relevant realities that cloud its cause, the logical identity of both perspectives — that of identifying the object of enquiry and that of confirming the object of enquiry — cannot be overestimated.

The same is true when what are called for are not natural conditions, that is, facts learned through the senses, but rules, procedures, reasons, precedents, arguments, standards. These paraphernalia are legal realities.

They are, for any given system, legal facts — what we have come appropriately to call 'institutional' legal facts. Accordingly, the epistemological ambiguities resident in, 'How do you know this?' may, instead of facts, be resolved by citing the relevant rules and the like (' . . . because in the S case just like this one, such-and-such was the precedent, or so-and-so was the holding'). And these existing rules and procedures (the institutionally ontological realities of the legal system) stand also, similarly as the sensory facts cited above, as confirming materials leading toward a just resolution.

The legal justice which, above, we called *decisional* (in contrast to procedural) represents the moral authority of the law as it closes a case. But it cannot be said that a summing up of all the evidence on both sides, even when the ambiguities of factual evidence and legal procedures are resolved, yields like an arithmetical formula the just outcome. If we idealize this evidence to a limit by assuming that *everything* relevant has been accounted for, then again, ideally, we might think the decision should equal the assembly of vindicating materials. We might think the just decision should be an incorporated statement of all the evidence both factual and procedural, sensory and rule-bound.[9] But this is not so. There is no epistemological-ontological equation marking a neat summing up, even of legal materials idealized to a relevant totality. Neither discipline exhausts the sources and functions of the other. After the evidence is assessed that faces both toward the physical and social reality pertinent to law and toward the institutional reality of rules, a gap remains. A logical gap is left for judgment, for someone to evaluate, on the terms as he understands them, the legally relevant data.[10] An arithmetic machine can derive an evidentiary equipollence if all that is wanted is numbers. But in law, such an equipollence is unconvincing and dysfunctional: Discretion, value-pondering, and equity would be eliminated from the justice of the law. Without these, law would scarcely be a human project.

When, therefore, it is time for an ultimate legal judgment, epistemology and ontology depart their tight alliance. Ontology sets out the case with its events, materials, and rules, just as nature sets out its elements and continua for the human mind with its symbolic capacities to understand. But the evaluative reflections that follow — How do I know which resolution is the just one? How shall I judge this case fairly? — begins its rumination on a kind of existential path in that some reasons are missing and may never be known. Indeed, the innuendoes of subtle human relationships are not open to reasons. The legal map is put aside. Responsibility, autonomy, and the challenge of the judgment resume the journey.

Meaning. At this decisive decisional juncture, the question of legal meaning, something we have not said much about, reaches its core. If the ontological dimension of nature includes only what exists and its features, then meaning questions would seem to be left by and large to the epistemological dimension; criteria and procedures of knowing rest heavily on what is meant — what sense is given to things. Meaning, in any case, seems to be today the semiotician's foundational nutrition. Perhaps it is this division of labor that once submerged meaning questions under the 'warranted assertability' thesis whereby evidence is held to be identical with the meaning of what it is that is evidenced or known (tested, confirmed, verified, etc.)

Nevertheless, within the legal domain, the meaning question does not rest only on theory of knowledge. It straddles both camps. It is singularly neither a species of epistemology nor a species of ontology.

No doubt interpretation of legal concepts is a meaning enterprise that hangs heavily on language. Be they general rules, precedents, laws of evidence, or abstractions like equity, harm, due process, burden of proof, property, contract, *mens rea*, negligence — these concepts' meanings emerge in part from 'operational definitions,' that is, from decisions about them and their actual uses in past cases, tidied up through a kind of theoretical completion that generalizes their meanings and makes them available for future cases.

But the confrontation of legal facts in the form of sensory evidence is a meaning enterprise of quite a different sort, because for a first-order empirical description *p* to be known *as true* is to know what *p* refers to, stands for, identifies, represents. Not language or sense, but reference stands as its ground. For a skeptic (which is the appropriate stance for an attorney weighing the evidence of his opponent), the burden of proof is always to turn back to the reality the referent is meant to signify, to check it out at its baseline, to demonstrate, as we said, that the alleged reality is not a mere appearance; and to draw upon this ineluctable veracity: namely, that unless reference is in itself a function that stops enquiry in the direction it is going, even linguistic interpretation can have no range of meaning. And vice versa. The referring function of an idea that is not contextually limited in its interpretation can never be satisfied. If it cannot, then the useful distinction between sense and reference, and between appearance and reality, disappears. What we have here is something comparable to C.S. Peirce's synechism, a term denoting real continua in the natural order. '. . . the external referents of true laws [Peirce means law of nature] are real continua [my itals.] which, since they involve unactualized possibilities, contain real generality.'[11]

Elsewhere I have shown that along with the grave misfortune of never authorizing trust in a language-unclothed reality, the distinction between particulars and universals, or general terms, so relevant to clear thinking and to philosophical discourse, vanishes from sight.[12] Even abstract ideas that imply, say, dyadic or triadic interpersonal relationships — a commonly confronted situation in curial phenomena — are without sense unless they can take their core bearing from referents, like persons whom we directly know. Autonomy, responsibility, right, dignity — the reasons-for-being for the morality of law — take their meaning from our capacity to individuate and to recognize *sans parlance* sentient beings. A baby knows its mother without the blessings of vocabulary. But speech is seldom first learned in the absence of the pre-existing objects of a primal order never fully submissive to the secondary order of language and sense.

Use and Mention. The object — meta-language distinction directs attention to the important differences between referring directly to a state of affairs and only mentioning that we or someone else has talked about this state of affairs. In law cases, the distinction is crucial. Suppose that whenever Mrs. Smith said that Mr. Johnson reported something to her: '. . . and he told me that . . . ,' we believed she said or believed this herself? The evidentiary confusion would be incommensurable, justice, a play of words.

Referential or denotational integrity by which is meant that things exist pretty much as we perceive them (respecting the critic's warnings against taking things naively to be only as they appear) safeguards against the mistake of discoursing as if all language were only about language (all 'uses' really were 'mentions'), a result of the neglect to allow ostending to be a legitimate and often foundational knowledge operative.

The compulsion of signification leaves us only with meta-languages, one atop another, remote from the subject matter and calling for yet another layer of interpretation that can go wrong. Again, under this bizarre demand, the complex and obscure is made to explain the simple and less obscure; the less puzzling taking clarity from the more puzzling, invoking the impractical to resolve, in the case of law, the eminently practical.

Couple such a philosophy with the 'infinitely interpretable' thesis, and the legal postulates that controversial issues must be joined and that cases finally must be decided would be contradicted and undermined.

III
Justification and Values

No subject seems more laden with problems of knowing than what we call 'values.' The subject of values constitutes a complete philosophy. Their meaning, criteria for validity or truth, justification, and how we know what they are or ought to be — seem perennially in question by debunkers of one sort or another who want to show that somehow values are not 'real.' The justification of values, what they mean, how we know them, whether they are true, is an apparently interminably fascinating preoccupation for epistemological argument.

Nevertheless, despite thousands of books laden with complex and heady justifications for the reality or unreality of human values — good, bad, and neutral — the positive law when dealing with a legal case *takes whatever values appear in its proceedings as given.* Their ontological status is taken as primitive, sound, and unentangled, not further reducible or given over to complex questions of, 'How do you know?' Doubts regarding their existence, definitions, or properties in the minds and beliefs of the protagonists, the actors and agents in a courtroom drama, do not arise. The existence and nature of stated or inferred values (interests, purposes, intentions, etc.) do not transliterate into questions about their meaning or vindication. Theoretical imponderables, in such a setting, are irrelevant, idle.

As an ongoing case at law ensues, the values of the involved personnel are not justified *in situ.* As contemplated by jury or judge, they are not subject to argument, knowledge criteria, examination, checks, criticism, 'warranted assertibility,' rejection. They are not tested for their validity or existence. Spoken or implied values in trials do not suffer the humiliation of, 'How do you know you think this is good? Are you sure you did right? Were your purposes the same as you now describe them?' 'Mrs. Hunt. . .!' with exasperation, 'why is it exactly that you object to Mr. Murphy's dog upsetting your garbage can every day and spilling its rotten contents onto your lawn? Come now — justify that disgust you have — confirm that it really is a disgusting spectacle, or we shall not be able to do anything for you here.'

Courts are not the place to validate the reality, magnitude and attributes, the approvability or disapprovability, sources, functions, or higher-order purposes of values referred to in the utterances of a testator, witness, plaintiff, or defendant. These values may be community norms, conventional and mundane or even reformed and enlightened. Or they may appear in quite other forms, say, in the form of *mens rea* or as some mindless desire of the moment, warranting no justification whatsoever — and given none.

Despite thorny philosophical problems about the ontological status of values and value discourse, the stated values uttered and made explicit in ordinary curial settings where trials at law are going on, have, for the purposes of resolution and justice, to be taken as real: they motivate actions. Their first-hand reports simply *are* the beliefs which constitute partial definitions of the actions that are being juridically considered, and as such, are conceptually indifferent to further representations and meta-representations about what they mean or through what evidentiary or justificatory mechanisms they may be known and validated. These latter considerations are absent.

We have not been talking here about the general values that legal systems have grown up with and that every judicial philosophy would justify almost without a second thought. Right and justice and desert are deeply indigenous to the law's judicial interior, to its reason-for-being. These are values that have already been developed, time-tested, and accepted; their presence or absence furnishes law and jurisprudence with their heroic, interlocutory dramas and disasters.

All social subjects, theoretical, systematic, practical, are value-drenched; scarcely an ounce of data emerges from the source-points of these sciences — which are human beliefs and actions in their individual, associative, and corporate forms — without values in the form of purposes, interests, intentions, wants and desires, obligations, rights, and of course rules and standards — being assumed or enunciated.

What we might call judicial values like presumption of innocence, clear preponderance of evidence, beyond reasonable doubt, and the like, reside, first, in well-tested practices that over time and on the whole have proved their worth in assisting the deliverance of justice. And secondly, procedural values like these serve to thwart serious violations of personal dignity. Courts and their processes, offices, and presumptions are a kind of idealized problem-solving institution. We should not wonder, then, that right ends and means, proper and good relationships, official obligations and responsibilities, promises and other kinds of expectations that manifest judicial bearing should have been justified and legitimated over the centuries.

Also, it is expected that certain courts should publicly justify their judgments, and so certain values are made explicit and take a paramount place within these realms of discourse. Supreme Court opinions in the United States reflect this obligation to enunciate the values and facts on which justices' opinions and decisions rest. Since justification arguments always convey values, such as the reference to the dignity of man in Justice Thurgood Marshall's minority opinion against allowing the several states to determine whether or not to install the death penalty[13] — the sheer existence of such judicial decisions implies the ontological status, the givenness, of the value(s) therein denoted.

To summarize: value language in ongoing cases at law has ontological status when the language is identical with the (unquestioned) belief in the value. As with the example of poetry, proffered value language demonstrating value beliefs, when sincere, is the reality that moves its agent to take the action he has taken; and it is this action that is under judicial review.

To borrow an analogy, the 'protocol' statement described in philosophies of science is the last-ditch location for intractable evidence linked causally and through entailment in confirmation of an empirical claim. The protocol statement refers directly to some non-mediated sensory quality whose authenticity as an existing state or condition must be assumed as a rock-bottom sensory truth or else all other empirical evidence of whatever kind or level of abstraction reducing to this truth comes to nothing. As C.S. Peirce put it, ' . . . our knowledge has a definite starting point in propositions which give direct reports of phenomenal observation and . . . whatever is asserted in those judgments of perception must be accepted as given.'[14]

Similarly, the value claims in legal proceedings issuing from the mouths of protagonists are protocol: unless they are taken as declared, the evidence of higher order-abstractions or of irreducible social and legal constructions built upon them are a house of cards.

I have tried to show that the legal enterprise contains both practical and theoretical regions of enquiry where questions of knowledge do not at all intrude upon, damage, or eliminate questions about what kinds of things exist or what their natures are that we can depend on without epistemological/interpretative interception. These ontological questions are valid in their place and may even take precedence. But often, too, the two areas of enquiry share a common goal or blend into a single problematic, to which our response has also to be one piece.

Adventures with language and what language can do, do not bury ontology under epistemology or subsume, in Corrington's words, nature under history. On the contrary, the imaginative underworld of meaning that excites our human needs to play attests to our yearning to uncover the sometimes shadowy crevices of a concealed reality.

**Virginia Black is Professor of Philosophy at Pace University.*

ENDNOTES

1. *American J. of Theology & Philosophy*, V. 14, n. 2, May 1993, 148-9.

2. The analytic nature of this point and others relevant to the dismissal of ontology are discussed more fully in Virginia Black, 1993, 'Putting Power in its Place, A Criticism of Legal Deconstruction,' *ARSP BEIHEFT, Concept and Conceptions of Practical Reason*, eds. Alexy and Dreier, Stuttgart: Franz Steiner Verlag.

3. Roderick M. Chisholm, 1966, *Theory of Knowledge*, Englewood Cliffs, New Jersey: Prentice-Hall, Inc., 106. Also pertinent is Chisholm's reference to J.L. Austin, 'What, then, of Austin's remark 'To suppose 'I know' is a descriptive phrase, is only one example of the descriptive fallacy. . . .' 17.

4. Virginia Black, *op. cit.* See also Virginia Black, 'A Way Out of the Realist Indeterminacy Morass,' *U.C. Davis Law Review*, Vol. 26, no.3, Spring 1993.

5. Gottlob Frege, 1952, 'On Sense and Reference,' trans. Max Black, *Translations from the Philosophical Writings of Gottlob Frege*, Oxford.

6. See Mark C. Taylor, *Descartes, Nietzsche and the Search for the Unsayable, N.Y. Times*, Feb. 1, 1987, sec. 7 (Book Review), at 3. We can add Foucault, Adorno, Unger, de Man, and Fish, all deconstructionists in their way. Also implicated in the flight to the unqualifiedly relative are the American neopragmatists Quine and Rorty. Their view is not to be confused with C.S. Peirce's 'pragmatic realism.'

7. This is a phrase I find eminently descriptive of many social concepts. It was likely coined by John Lachs for his Fourth Annual Patrick Romanell Lecture, 'Human Natures' presented at the Eastern Division meeting of the APA, 1989, and appearing in *Proceedings and Addresses of the APA*, Vol. 63, no. 7.

8. *Black's Law Dictionary*, 1968, Revised Fourth Ed. (*Zickefoose v. Thompson*, 347 Mo. 579, 148 S.W. 2d 784, 792). St. Paul: West Publishing Co., 657.

9. cf. Hilary Putman's 'idealized warranted assertability,' a qualified position Putnam reached after abandoning the philosophical positivist's narrow verification theory of meaning. See the entry, 'Putnam, Hilary,' by Thomas Tymoczko, 1992, *A Companion to Epistemology*, eds. Dancy and Sosa, Oxford: Blackwell Publishers.

10. C.S. Peirce's use of the term 'abduction' to describe the 'leap' toward a hypothesis to explain facts which neither deduction nor induction fully accounts for, may be appropriately analogized here. The law, as given, is authoritative and certain; but because the facts may not be complete, the conclusion is only probable. Since probabilities cannot characterize legal decisions, 'probability' in law is reflected as a factor to be weighed so as to reach a reasonable (non-deductive) judgment.

11. Murray G. Murphey, 1967, 'Peirce, Charles Sanders,' *The Encyclopedia of Philosophy*, Vol. Six, New York: The Macmillan Company & The Free Press, 76.

12. Virginia Black, works cited.

13. *Gregg v. Georgia*, 1972.

14. Murphey, work cited.

Chapter Five

Signs of Value: The Laws of Accounting Theory

Christopher K. Braun*

I
Introduction

Generally speaking, a law or set of laws can be broadly defined by reference to some set of standards, beliefs, or norms, whether they be created by society at large, a sub-group within that society such as a professional association, or internally produced by the individual actor, which determine the appropriateness or inappropriateness of a given course of action, event, conclusion, or outcome. These laws can range from the simple rules of casual social interaction to the determination of net income by a certified public accountant ('CPA').

Accounting theory, and its manifestation into the laws of financial statement construction promulgated by the Financial Accounting Standards Board ('FASB'), is really, from a semiotic viewpoint, a complex system of signs whose purpose is, in part, to provide meaning to the object term 'net income.' All businesses have a 'net income' and it is a common belief that the true 'net income' of a firm can be determined in the abstract and reported on a financial statement under the heading (i.e. sign) 'Net Income After Tax.' Yet, as will be shown in this paper, the abstract true 'net income' can actually be reported in almost unlimited numerical amounts on the income statement due to the functional equivalency of the signs CPAs use in the process. Importantly, these differing amounts assigned as 'net income' are equally taken as the true 'net income.' This phenomenon is what I term the creation of multi-equivalent signs from one object which are, in turn, interpreted uniformly to be true in that they are *all* in accord with a single object which, in this case, is true net income.

The importance of this sign system to our lives cannot be underestimated. Every day, billions of dollars of financial transactions sweep the globe. These investments are centered around the determination of the economic viability of the underlying entity. This determination is made possible by the preparation of financial statements by CPAs who provide a uniform telescope through which investors view economic events. As such, CPAs determine the 'truth' about historical operations and thereby significantly influence investment decisions. Therefore, investment decision making is nothing more than the simple interpretation of signs.

This paper shall accomplish three things. First, in order to appreciate the sign system of accounting, it will be necessary to understand what is meant by the term 'generally accepted accounting principle' and how this term is the overriding object, in the Peircean sense of the term, of the accounting sign system. Second, I will provide a detailed example of how the object of generally accepted accounting principle can be manifested in the form of four functionally equivalent, or universal, signs when inventory values are being reported on an income statement in the computation of net income. Third, and finally, I will discuss the concept of the universally functionally equivalent sign system called accounting by graphically representing it.

II
Generally Accepted Accounting Principles: The Creation of a Sign System's Basic Elements

The primary body responsible for the articulation of acceptable accounting procedures and the treatment of various issues is the FASB. The FASB was created in 1973 and consists of seven members who have a detailed knowledge of accounting, financial, and economic issues. Three of the seven members are CPAs and the other four come from government, business, or academia. The primary responsibility of the FASB is to identify emerging issues in the accounting field which require new or unique treatments. In doing this, the FASB, in response to an emerging issue, will appoint a task force, conduct research, hold public hearings, and eventually vote on whether or not to adopt a new rule regarding a certain accounting issue. These new rules come in the form of officially governing Statements of Financial Accounting Standards which subsequently form the bedrock of generally accepted accounting principle, or 'GAAP.' These official Statements become binding on all CPAs in their preparation of financial statements and require that CPAs from all over the country treat similar issues in a similar way. The adherence to the Statements furthers uniformity among the financial statements of various firms which, in turn, allows potential investors to rely on the legitimacy of the financial information they may read, for instance, in a prospectus at the time of their investment decision.

Other bodies also exert an influence on the formulation of GAAP. These bodies include the Securities and Exchange Commission which is the government agency with final authority over the form and format of the financial statements of publicly held firms. Further, the American Institute of Certified Public Accountants is the nation-wide professional organization of CPAs. By exerting a voice on the FASB, by developing Statements of Position and Practice Bulletins, and by requiring continuing professional education of its members, the AICPA plays a key role in the GAAP setting process.

Arguably, the most fundamental and important project the FASB undertook was the drafting of six Statements of Financial Accounting Concepts ('FACs') which provide the overall theoretical framework for the purposes and uses of GAAP in the preparation of financial statements. In particular, Statement of Financial Accounting Concept #2, entitled 'The Qualitative Characteristics of Accounting Information,' discusses the requirements that all accounting representations in the form of financial statements must meet in order to be considered GAAP. It is in FAC #2 that the sign system of accounting information was built and it is against this FAC that the legitimacy or illegitimacy of any financial statement is measured. Further, it is from this FAC that one can trace the groundwork for the creation of multi-equivalent or universal signs in the accounting sign system. Indeed, the FASB itself laid the groundwork for repeated future reference to FAC #2 when it stated the following:

> Statements in the series are intended to set forth objectives and fundamentals that will be the basis for development of (GAAP). The objectives identify the goals and purposes of financial reporting. The fundamentals are the underlying concepts of financial accounting — concepts that guide the selection of transactions, events, and circumstances to be accounted for, their recognition and measurement, and the means of summarizing and communicating them to interested parties. Concepts of that type are fundamental in the sense that other concepts flow from them and repeated reference to them will be necessary in establishing, interpreting, and applying accounting and reporting standards.[1]

In the Peircean sense, the concepts of selection, recognition, measurement, and communication are the accounting fundamental principles through which the objects (i.e. net incomes) of the sign system are interpreted. The financial statements, which seek to convey the above selection, recognition, measurement, and communication of transactions, are the signs of the sign system of accounting. The potential users (i.e. shareholders, creditors, managers, etc.) of the statements, in whose mind an interpretation of the above signs are to be made, will become the interpretants of the accounting sign system. For Peirce, truth existed in the accord, or the identity, of a interpretant and its object. An ideal interpretant, in the mind of the observer of the sign, is the equivalent sign of the sign observed. In this triad of object-sign-interpretant, one can deduce the presence of the perfect opportunity for communication of the form of the object (i.e. financial information) through the sign to its interpretant.

What the FASB sought to do in FAC #2 was to lay out the governing criteria for the selection, recognition, measurement, and communication of any identifiable event of accounting information and, in essence, set forth the criteria that a bit of accounting information must meet in order to be considered an object for anything. If an accounting bit of information fails to meet these criteria, it is not selected, recognized, measured, or communicated. It may exist in fact, but it is not recognized as producing any sign of its existence and GAAP shuts off any potential interpretation of it. Consequently, no sign triad exists for that bit of information. This is of course an interesting difference between the accounting sign system and the traditional Peircean sign system. In the traditional Peircean sign system, virtually anything can be an object and set off the sign triad. In the accounting sign system, only certain qualitatively correct bits of accounting information are granted this privilege.

As noted, the characteristics discussed in FAC #2 set forth the baseline propositions of the definitional parameters which prospective objects must meet in order to function in the accounting sign system. The following characteristics must be present in order for a piece of accounting information to be recognized as an object in the accounting sign system:

1. understandability;
2. benefits exceeding costs;
3. materiality;
4. comparability; and
5. decisional usefulness:
   5(a) relevance (i.e. predictive value, feedback value, and timeliness);
   5(b) reliability (i.e. verifiability, neutrality, and representational faithfulness).

The first of these characteristics, understandability, is the characteristic which allows a user to perceive the significance of what is being presented.[2] Naturally, financial statements and the information they contain should be orderly, clearly presented, and presented pursuant to some uniform format principle which allows all users to make informed decisions. What must be made clear here is that we are not assuming that anyone could use and/or understand well organized accounting data. The presumed user, against which we judge the understandability of what is presented, is presumed to be a person of at least some business expertise who possesses the time necessary to study the information in order to understand it. Interestingly, the FASB has thereby admitted that the accounting sign system requires, to a certain extent, a user who has prior knowledge of and exposure to accounting sign concepts. In other words, prior accounting sign interpretation is assumed and individuals without prior experience in accounting sign interpretation are not considered in the determination of the creation of the accounting sign manifestations themselves.

Comparability, materiality, and cost/benefit are important links in the chain of accounting theory. Financial statements of differing corporations would be said to be comparable if they possessed 'the quality or state of having certain characteristics in common.'[3] To be sure, we do not mean virtual identity but a sufficient amount of common characteristics, arrived at through a quantitative assessment, which leads to a subjective assessment of the existence of comparability. In the words of the FASB:

> Greater comparability . . . is not to be attained by making unlike things look alike any more than by making like things look different . . . . (we) must not disguise real differences nor create false differences.' [4]

The concept of materiality serves as a screen for the user of financial information and prevents that user from being overwhelmed by information that is of no consequence. This 'big picture' notion requires CPAs to screen out the minutiae and deliver statements which include all relevant and reliable information which is material enough (i.e. important enough in the context of the entity) that it is worth reporting. The question asked is: 'Is this item large enough for users of the information to be influenced by it?'[5] Materiality is a subjective test in that an item is considered material if 'it is probable that the judgment of a reasonable person relying upon the report would have been changed or influenced by the inclusion or correction of an item.'[6]

While materiality operates to the benefit of the user, cost/benefit, to a degree, operates to allow the CPA the discretion not to track items if the cost of doing so would exceed the benefits of the information gained. Naturally, costs come in the form of expenses incurred on person hours to keep track of the information and of the time allocated by the users in disseminating the information after it is reported. Of course, benefits are much harder to quantify and lie strictly in the realm of personal subjective assessment. Nevertheless, if it is felt that the costs (either quantified or unquantified) exceed the benefits of doing something it will not be done. An obvious example of this would be a CPA for General Motors refusing to locate $100,000 of missing inventory in a total inventory count of 10 billion. Not only is the amount immaterial in comparison to the total count, failing to locate the missing inventory will not impair the comparability of GM's financial statement with Ford's, and finally, it might very well cost a large sum of money and require an enormous effort on the part of the CPA to actually find the missing inventory. While the above is an obvious example, it represents to a degree the factors to be taken into account in assessing the cost/benefit rule.

For the FASB, the most overriding accounting principle is that financial information which is presented be of the kind which allows a useful decision to be made.[7] The FASB is not requiring that the decision need be the correct one in the view of hindsight. It is merely requiring that the decision that was made be a reasonably plausible one given what the user knew at the time he or she knew it after informing themselves of the factors presented in the financial statement. Decisional usefulness exists if the inferences that were drawn from the accounting signs that were presented were reasonable in light of what was potentially knowable within the sign system at the time the decision was made.

In particular, decisional usefulness can be defined in terms of the information's relevance and reliability. All accounting data must be relevant in that it must have predictive value, possess feedback value, and be presented upon a timely basis. Overall, it must be possible for the information to make a difference in any decision which could be made.[8] Timeliness is simply the time frame in which information reaches the user. If it is out-of-date upon reaching the user it could be the most understandably useful information in the world but it will not provide the user any benefit. Therefore, financial statements are presented within a reasonable time frame after the end of a period which, for most large

American corporations, is three to four months after the close of a fiscal or calendar year. It is generally accepted that the financial statements of large corporations are still useful three to four months after the end of the period in that it is believed that at that point they still possess the ability to influence a decision.[9] Predictive value is not meant to infer that CPAs make crystal ball projections as to the future earnings of an entity. Predictive value, as that term is used, refers to a process of judgment that takes place within each individual user of the information and the impact of the information upon any future expectations that individual person may create about the reporting entity's future performance.[10] Information has predictive value if it forms, confirms, or changes an individual's expectations about the future of the entity.[11] Feedback value is the opposite of predictive value. Rather than focusing on the future, feedback value confirms or corroborates the user's past decisions about the entity. For instance, one quarter ago a shareholder bought IBM after she read the latest quarterly statements. This is an example of relevant information being provided to an individual who uses the information to form an expectation about the entity. In particular, that IBM's performance will be better in the future and that the price of the stock will rise. The quarterly statement has provided predictive value to the user. Three months later, the same shareholder decides to sell IBM stock on the basis of the next quarterly financial statement. Her decision is based upon the feedback value of the latest financial *vis-a-vis* her earlier decision. Her earlier decision has been confirmed as having been a decision which lead to her losing money as the price of IBM stock dropped sharply after the release of the latest quarterly information.

The concepts of predictive value and feedback value provide a link between past, present, and future financial statements. The statements, which are the signs in the accounting sign system, are therefore affected by past, present, and future interpretations of the meaning of their objects. These sign-statements will be interpreted in the context of prior interpretations of prior sign-statements of the same reporting entity. Indeed, companies purposely prepare comparative balance sheets which present a rolling review of the latest three years of balance sheets. As Peirce argued, interpretation is a process akin to thinking in a logical fashion and this thinking will bring about other signs of an object. These other signs, or interpretant signs, are themselves again interpreted into new signs in an infinite series which leads to the creation of new ideas about the financial health of the reporting entity. Therefore, Peirce's notion of the endless viaduct of idea potentiality can, in the accounting sign system, be seen as the gradual interpretation and reinterpretation of quarterly sign-statements by current and potential investors. Thus, downward movements of stock prices, as the result of a sell-off, are the products of the creation of a sell interpretant in the mind of some investors after they analyze the newest quarterly financial information. Conversely, the upward movement of stock prices, which results from shares being purchased, is the result of the creation of a buy interpretant in the minds of some investors. The cyclical movement of stocks shown on stock charts (which would plot the 52 week ending price for a share) are graphical representations of the endless viaduct of idea potentiality as it is seen from the mind of the investing public. Peirce's notions, which seem abstract and difficult to grasp, can be physically embodied in the price clearing mechanisms of an economic system as those mechanisms are reflected in what a willing buyer and a willing seller are agreed is a fair price. The workings of a sign system can thus be visually identified in the context of an economic, financial, and accounting analysis of a reporting entity.

Accounting data must be reliable in that it is verifiable, neutral, and representationally faithful. Representational faithfulness refers to the degree of sameness between a bit of accounting information which is reported and 'the phenomenon it purports to represent.'[12] Simply put, if a balance sheet lists one thousand units in ending inventory it is presumed that the units in fact exist and are in fact in ending inventory. If they are indeed in ending inventory, the balance sheet assertion of existence is representationally faithful. This concept is also a direct reference to the functioning of signs. Perfect signs perfectly signify their objects and the interpretant created in the mind is the exact equivalent sign of the sign being signified. It can be said, in a real sense, that signs are representationally faithful to their objects and Peirce termed the most representationally faithful signs and their interpretants as 'rational interpretants.' This is opposed to the creation of a dynamic interpretant which is not quite the same sign as the object signified. The possibility of dynamic interpretants breeches the question of verifiability. Verifiability is the 'ability through consensus among measurers to ensure that information represents what it purports to represent or that the chosen method of measurement has been used without error or bias.'[13] To continue the above example, the presence of one thousand units in ending inventory would be verifiable if another inventory count with a different set of persons, using the same methods such as visual inspection and count, would arrive at the existence of one thousand units in ending inventory at the end of the period. This is simply the replication test. Can another person using the same method arrive at and therefore confirm the same assertion? If they can, the information deduced from the measurement is verifiable. Within the context of a sign system, the FASB has placed a high degree of emphasis on the creation of rational interpretants in the mind of the financial statement user and, to extend this logic, would like to insure that all other financial statement users 'verify,' or replicate, this rational interpretant upon their own reading of the financial statements.

Neutrality refers to the supposed lack of political agendas in the standard setting process and the information that is presented as a result of it. More precisely, neutral information does not consider the effect 'that the new rule may have on a particular interest.'[14] By this it is meant that CPAs do not attempt to 'color' what is reported to further a particular interest such as the interests of management. Instead, CPAs 'let the chips fall where they may' and are loyal to the verifiable and representationally faithful events, not the potential consequences of reporting those events.

III
GAAP Inventory Practice: An Established Sign System's Truth

It can be said with little doubt that for most manufacturing firms inventory is the single most important variable which determines the ultimate success or failure of the entity. For these firms, inventory represents the single largest investment of current funds and may very well be the single largest class, in dollar terms, on their balance sheets. Therefore, tracking inventory and purchases and related sales is of critical import to all manufacturing firms and the cost of goods sold, which consists of material, labor, and factory overhead which was incurred in the production process, can be the single largest item of expense on many manufacturing firms income statements. Accordingly, the cost of goods sold ('COGS') has a primary impact on the determination of the net income of the firm.

After reviewing the basic five elements of the accounting sign system's standards of recognition of an object of accounting data, one would expect that there would exist uniformity in the measurement of items such as depreciation and inventory for purposes of the income statement. Surprisingly, there are four methods for valuing your inventory as part of your COGS. There are also four methods of computing depreciation. Therefore, four identical firms with identical sales and identical units of ending inventory and equipment can report four different COGS values and four different depreciation values and therefore 16 different net incomes from the same facts. As will be seen, each of these 16 differing values is generally accepted and taken as an accurate depiction of the 'truth' of the events and are consequently taken as being signs which are in accord with their objects with the consequence that each interpretant produced is also said to be in accord with its object which is true net income. An example will illustrate this unusual signification present in the sign structure of accounting data by illustrating the four differing inventory methods.

ABC Beer Wholesaler, Inc. starts its new calendar year with 500 kegs of beer in inventory which it purchased for $1 a keg for a total cost of $500. ABC purchased the following kegs at the following prices and times during the year:
March 1: 200 kegs at $2 p/kg for a total cost of $400;
April 1: 300 kegs at $3 p/kg for a total cost of $900;
June 15: 250 kegs at $2.00 p/kg for a total cost of $500;
November 12: 600 kegs at $4.00 p/kg for a total cost of $2400.
Total kegs available for sale: 1850
Total cost of kegs available for sale: $4700
Ending inventory 12/31/XX: 200 kegs
Sales revenue p/kg: $10
G & A and other operating expenses: $0
Total sales revenue: $16,500 ($10 times 1650 kegs sold)
ABC has a choice of four inventory methods which are:
1. Specific identification which would place in the cost of goods sold account the costs actually associated as being identified with the actual kegs of beer sold;
2. Average cost identification which would place in the cost of goods sold account the average cost of each keg purchased without regard to which kegs were in fact sold;
3. Last-in-first-out identification ('LIFO') which would place in the cost of goods sold account the latest purchases first and would work upwards from the bottom of the purchases list without regard to which kegs were in fact sold; and

4. First-in-first-out identification ('FIFO') which would place in the cost of goods sold account the earliest purchases first and would work downwards from the top of the purchases list without regard to which kegs were in fact sold.

It should be remembered at this point that each of the above four methods are GAAP and are used routinely in today's business world. The computation of COGS, and therefore net income, under each of the four methods would be as follows:

1. Specific Identification: The CPA ascertains that of the 1650 kegs sold 400 came from beginning inventory (cost of $400); 150 from the March 1 purchase (cost of $300); 250 from the April 1 purchase (cost of $750); 250 kegs from the June 15 purchase (cost of $500); and 600 kegs from the November 12 purchase (cost $2400). Total COGS: $4350; **Net Income: $12,150;**

2. Average cost: Total inventory cost of $4700 divided by 1850 kegs equals an average cost per keg of $2.54 times 1650 kegs sold equals COGS of $4192. **Net Income: $12,308;**

3. LIFO cost: To account for 1650 units we would start at the bottom of the purchases list and work upwards until we find 1650 units. This would produce the following schedule:
    11/12 600 kegs at $4: cost of $2400;
    06/15 250 kegs at $2: cost of $500;
    04/01 300 kegs at $3: cost of $900;
    03/01 200 kegs at $2: cost of $400;
    01/01 300 kegs at $1: cost of $300. Total COGS: $4500
    Net Income: $12,000;

4. FIFO cost: To account for 1650 units we would start at the top of the purchases list and work downwards until we find 1650 units. This would produce the following schedule:
    01/01 500 kegs at $1: cost of $500;
    03/01 200 kegs at $2: cost of $400;
    04/01 300 kegs at $3: cost of $900
    06/15 250 kegs at $2: cost of $500

11/12 400 kegs at $4: cost of $1600. Total COGS: $3900
Net Income: $12,600

In periods of rising prices, LIFO will produce the lowest net income as it assigns the highest cost goods to COGS thereby decreasing net income. Conversely, since FIFO assigns the cheaper earlier goods to COGS it will produce the highest net income.

IV
Multiple or Universal Truth?: Visualizing the Accounting Sign System as Both

Any sign system will utilize Peirce's object-sign-interpretant triad. However, it will be seen from the following diagram that the accounting sign system employs a dramatically different triad.

```
                      spec. id. sign-----     HOUSE
                        av. cost sign-----      of
                         LIFO sign-------      the
                /        FIFO sign-------      GAAP  \
              /                                        \
           /                                            \
        /                                                \
object::::::::::::sign:::::::::::GAAPprism:::::::::interpretant
   +              +                +                    +
   +              +                +                    +
   +              +                +                    +
REAL OR        multi-        colors multi-        mult equiv signs
TRUE NET       equiv         equiv signs          seen as same;
INCOME         signs         uniform by           all in accord
                             est. parameters      w/object; all are
                             of recognition       true
```

It is generally understood by the lay public that, as an abstract proposition, the real or true net income of any firm can be tabulated with accuracy and reported. However, from the above inventory illustration, this has been shown to be false. Since each of the four inventory methods are GAAP, each can be said to represent the real net income of the firm. Indeed, four identical firms using four different inventory methods will arrive at four different net incomes. Who is right? Which sign (i.e. income statement) is most in accord with its object? The answer is that all four signs are in accord with the *same* object. They do not have individual objects as in the traditional Peircean model. There is one object of net income and that is an object which meets the five qualitative characteristics of accounting information discussed earlier. Since, by definition, each of the four inventory methods also meets independently each of the five qualitative characteristics they all are signs which refer back to an *identical* object. This is an important distinction to remember. I am not suggesting that there are multiple objects of net income. There is only one object true net income (i.e. one that meets the five qualitative characteristics) and each sign of net income, which outwardly signifies a different truth about the net income of the firm, refers back to it.

Arguably, however, it would be remiss to overlook the obvious: even if each of the four signs refer back to the same object there are still four signs and in the abstract there exists four possibilities for differing interpretants to be created. What prevents each sign from throwing off an individualized signification to the mind of each and every different observer? The answer is that the interpretation and the creation of the interpretant goes through a lens of accounting theory before signs undergo signification. As a consequence, each of the four signs of net income are filtered into one sign which is then interpreted as being in accord with its object and is therefore true. What results is the classic Peircean model of one object, one sign, and one interpretant. Four signified multiple truths have become one interpreted universal truth.

The lens of accounting theory which forces a uniform interpretation is buttressed by the FASB's enormous power to promulgate the requirements of inventory accounting and therefore force all CPAs to choose from one of the available methods. Simply put, since all CPAs must follow GAAP as promulgated by the FASB and all financial statements of publicly held corporations must be prepared in accordance with GAAP, the ability of the FASB to artificially create a filtering lens through which all financial statement signs must pass through is quite real indeed. At this point, one might ask a question. What prevents the individual observer from unofficially creating a uniform measure of their own for inventory accounting and thereby employing it to make investment or credit decisions? The answer is that nothing does; however, this option is really not viable. One would presumably pick one of the four methods, or a close variant thereof, as an individualized yardstick. A banker who extends credit might require, on an internal basis, that all credit applications report inventory on a FIFO basis. This is fine as far as it goes. The banker has established absolute uniformity; however, she has not moved the inquiry any closer to the real truth of the matter in the sense that she knows for a fact just what exactly is in ending inventory and what its real value is. Indeed, ascertaining the real truth may be impossible for many firms whose inventory is fungible and/or stored together. For instance, an oil storage depot mixes the oil it purchases at different times and different prices into a huge uniform tank mix.

Unfortunately, any method of inventory valuation utilized will have its advantages and disadvantages.[15] For instance, LIFO reports a very good COGS number and therefore presents well the financial health of the firm in terms of its ability to replace its inventory on a current cost basis and sell it at a profit. This occurs since the COGS number consists primarily of the latest purchases which presumably are the closest approximation of the current market price of the inventory the firm must purchase to be viable. Conversely, FIFO reports an artificially deflated COGS number and, from a current replacement cost perspective, overstates income and a firm's ability to go on. However, FIFO does report on the balance sheet a very reliable, in terms of its approximation to current fair market value, ending inventory number as under the FIFO method the most expensive goods, which were purchased last, are still considered in inventory. Therefore, such ratios as working capital, which is current assets (including inventory) minus current liabilities, are good measures of the liquidity of the firm under FIFO. Conversely, LIFO reports a grossly distorted ending inventory number as the units shown on the balance sheet as being in ending inventory could literally be, for book purposes, the ones we bought our first year in operation fifteen years ago. Consequently, the working capital ratio can be misstated badly under LIFO. LIFO is excellent for tax purposes since it reports the lowest net income and therefore the lowest taxes are paid. However, you would also report a low net income to your shareholders and creditors which could affect the capital position of the firm. Likewise, FIFO reports a high net income to the shareholders and creditors but also a high net income to the IRS so more taxes are paid! Indeed, unfortunately, it is against the law to use LIFO for tax and FIFO for book!!

The above discussion proves that any inventory method has the flaws of its virtues in terms of accounting theory. Therefore, ultimately, it is up to the subjective CPA, in consultation with management, to 'pick a poison' and adopt a method of inventory which under all the circumstances works best for them in the particular instance. However, in allowing this flexibility to 'pick your own truth poison' the FASB has created a sign system whereby all versions of the truth will be treated equally in the sense that each is seen as being in accord with one object true net income. The FASB has admitted that its sign system is somewhat confusing in that the real truth will be somewhat muddled by the adoption of differing methods of accounting for it. About this consequence, the FASB stated the following:

> No model, (*i.e.. sign system*) however sophisticated, can be expected to reflect all the functions and relationships that are found within a complex organization. To do so, the model would have to be virtually a reproduction of the original. In real life, it is necessary to accept a much smaller degree of correspondence between the model and the original than that. One can be satisfied if none of the important relationships are lost. . . . perfect reliability of accounting information is equally unattainable. [16] (emphasis added.)

In other words, since perfect accord between an income statement and real net income is impossible, accountants have endeavored to create a system that operates on an implicit assumption that the financials presented are in perfect accord with the unreportable and/or unquantifiable reality known as real net income. After all, if everyone verbalizes the same account and everyone really believes it to be the truth and people act on it as if it were the truth can not it be argued that it is in fact the truth? Isn't it the truth as much as the real truth which no one is recognizing, in the accounting sense of the term, because it is either immaterial, too costly, not relevant, not understandable, or unachieveable?

V
Conclusion

The accounting sign system is a system in which one universally accepted interpretant of a single object is created from multiple true signs. This is possible due to the authority of the FASB to limit the number of accounting objects that are recognized as being valid and through its authority to control the creation of signs which signify these objects. Ultimately, through this process, interpretants are controlled through a lens which is provided to all potential users of the information. The accounting sign system is one in which reporting the abstractly pure true event is made subservient to a belief that uniformity of interpretation of what is reported, as long as what is reported is still relevant and reliable, is the paramount goal.

**Christopher K. Braun is Assistant Professor of Accounting and Taxation at Millersville University.*

ENDNOTES

1. *Statements of Financial Accounting Concepts of the Financial Accounting Standards Board*, hereinafter *Statements*, Irwin Publishing, 1990:26-82.

2. *Id.* at 34.

3. *Id.* at 65.

4. *Id.* at 67.

5. *Id.* at 68.

6. *Id.* at 70-71.

7. *Id.* at 42.

8. *Id.* at 48.

9. *Id.* at 51.

10. *Id.* at 48-50.

11. *Id.*

12. *Id.* at 52.

13. *Id.* at 34.

14. *Id.* at 62.

15. However, all of the above methods meet the GAAP requirement that, from a periodicity perspective, expenses and revenues are matched pursuant to some uniform system which is consistently applied. It is this consistent allocation of decreases in owner's equity (ie. expenses) to particular periods of revenue recognition that lends comparability and uniformity to financial statements. Again, we see here that the accounting sign system, and its manifestation of the matching principle, is not necessarily concerned with what is being reported. After all, the four firms noted matched different expenses with the same revenues. Rather, the

matching principle requires that some allocation and connection between expenses and revenues take place over a period of time on a consistent basis. It is this consistency which ultimately leads to a uniformity of interpretation of the same object in spite of the four differing significations of that object being presented.

16. *Statements*, *supra* note 1 at 56.

Chapter Six

Making Differences and Making all the Difference: Community and the Dilemma of Difference

Denis J. Brion*

I
Introduction

Not long ago, an article appeared in the *Washington Post* in which an anthropologist recounted a stroll that he had taken in the area around Key Bridge in Georgetown with three Aluku Maroons — people of African descent from French Guiana.[1] His companions astonished him by pointing out numerous plants growing in the odd and unlikely places that such flora find in the urban environment, plants that he knew only as weeds and that they knew as valuable herbs and medicinal plants.

> Some plants could cure illnesses when properly prepared and prescribed by a Maroon herbal healer. Others could induce trancelike states or usher in spirit possession when handled by a knowledgeable practitioner. Still others could be used to address ailments Americans would consider psychiatric. . . . Where most of us would have seen the unwanted presence of weeds — mere targets for passing dogs — the Maroons had found an affirmation of the richness of plants and their curative properties.

This small tale illustrates, of course, the notion that the world that we experience and the differences that we see are not given to us but instead rest strongly on choices that we make.

What I want to do is take a recent scholarly work that explores difference and the problems of oppression that arise from the fact of difference. This exploration is of interest because it proceeds from this notion of the constructed nature of difference. Despite my agreement with its thesis that differences are constructed and not natural, I propose to offer a critique of its propositions and conclusions.

The work in question is Martha Minow's 1990 book, *Making All the Difference: Inclusion, Exclusion, and American Law.* In this book Minow urges what I will refer to as a relational paradigm as the preferred alternative to the transactional, rights-based paradigm of social relations that the law now both ratifies and fosters. This is a significant work, not least because it pulls together several strands of thought that have had considerable recent currency in legal discourse — the dialogic process,[2] the 'different voice' of the feminine,[3] and the 'communitarian turn.'[4]

The lens through which I will offer my critique is one of the illustrative examples on which Minow builds her analysis — the dispute that arose in Cleburne, Texas over the proposed location of a group home for the mentally retarded in a residential neighborhood. The Cleburne City Council had denied a regulatory permit for the group home in reaction to strong opposition to the facility from neighboring residents. After a protracted course of litigation over the denial of the permit, the United States Supreme Court invalidated the permit denial.

Clearly, of course, in terms of the liberal values that dominate our public discourse, the outcome to this dispute is unassailable. The exclusionary attitudes of the neighbors toward fellow humans in need of sympathy and support were socially pernicious. And the action of the feckless City Council in bowing to these attitudes of course could not have been allowed to stand.

My purpose is to offer something of a dissent from this seemingly unassailable outcome to the group home dispute. This dissent will begin with the given circumstances of the human condition. First is the postmodern moment in which we find ourselves. Second is the necessarily conventional and incomplete World which we experience. And third is the semiotic nature of human existence — the process by which we make the World that we experience is the process of making differences. I propose to argue that Minow's relational paradigm and the way that it resolves legal disputes over powerless and oppression involve a troubling incompleteness.

In developing this critique, I will first offer a more detailed description of the Cleburne group home dispute and the relational 'take' on it. I will then engage in a deeper consideration of the relational paradigm and its consequences. Finally, I will offer a reconsideration of the Cleburne dispute, not simply as a critique of the relational approach to the dispute, but instead as a means of developing a particular way of using the relational approach in addressing endemic problems of difference and power.

II
Cleburne and Difference

A. *The Cleburne Dispute*

Cleburne, Texas is a city of 19,000 population some thirty miles southwest of the Dallas-Fort Worth area. In 1980, Cleburne Living Center, Inc. [CLC], an operator of group homes for the disabled, applied for a special use permit for the use of a house in a residential area for a group home for thirteen mentally retarded men and women. The local zoning regulations required that CLC obtain the written approval of 'the property owners within two hundred feet' of the proposed group home in order to be granted the special use permit. When many of the neighbors instead protested, the Cleburne City Council denied the permit application.

CLC then challenged the permit denial in Federal District Court, on the grounds that the Council's action discriminated against the mentally retarded in violation of their right to the equal protection of the laws. Ultimately, in 1985, five years after the dispute had arisen, the Supreme Court invalidated the action of the Cleburne City Council in denying the special use permit.[5]

As has become the norm in constitutional litigation, several opinions accompanied the Court's decision.[6] The majority opinion was based on the City Council's concern over 'the negative attitude of the majority of property owners located within 200 feet of the . . . facility, as well as with the fears of elderly residents of the neighborhood.'[7] Because of this 'irrational prejudice,'[8] the Council's action was not 'rationally related to a legitimate governmental purpose.'[9]

In a concurring opinion, Justice John Paul Stevens picked up on, and emphasized, the concerns expressed in the majority opinion — 'this permit was required because of the irrational fears of neighboring property owners, rather than for the protection of the mentally retarded persons who would reside in . . . [the] home.'[10] Stevens went on, 'I cannot believe that a rational member of this disadvantaged class could ever approve of the discriminatory application of the city's ordinance.'[11]

B. *The Relational Approach*

Let us now turn to Martha Minow's treatment of this dispute under her relational approach to the law. Minow begins where I would begin, with our thoroughly conventional World. The world that we experience is a human construct — 'Given our limited ability to hold the complexity of the world in our minds, we summarize and simplify through language.'[12] Each of us is strongly embedded in our world because it comes into being through social interaction. It is a world made up of categories and distinctions that 'shut off any understanding of our connections with one another as human beings,'[13] a world that deploys power in a hierarchical structure. Thus, 'difference' counts heavily in the experience of power. Because we are [necessarily] so strongly embedded in our world, we easily forget that it is a social construct. Thus we assume — erroneously — that differences are immutable properties of persons and things rather than a consequence of choices that we have made — and can unmake.

Minow then describes the dilemma of difference through the situation of a hearing-impaired schoolchild, a young girl called 'Amy.'[14] How does a school respond to her needs? Does it include her in a classroom of non-hearing impaired children, thereby treating her the same as her classmates and thereby becoming insensitive to her difference and stigmatizing her on that basis? Or does it provide a separate program for her, thereby treating her differently and thereby stigmatizing her on that basis?

According to Minow, several implicit assumptions underlie the differences that we perceive and act on.[15] First, we assume that differences are intrinsic, rather than viewing them as expressions of comparisons between people on the basis of particular traits. We typically adopt an unstated point of reference when assessing others — the point of reference being the norm by which we determine who is different and who is normal. We treat the person doing the seeing or judging as without a perspective, rather than as inevitably seeing and judging from a particular situated perspective. We assume that the perspectives of those being judged are either irrelevant or are already taken into account through the perspective of the person who is doing the judging. And, finally, we assume that the existing social and economic arrangements that provide the context for these perceived differences are natural and neutral.

From this, Minow lays out her principal thesis — 'the difference dilemma is a symptom of a particular way of looking at the world.'[16] As I shall later argue, this thesis does not necessarily follow from the starting assumptions that Minow sets forth. Because of this, her approach to the relational paradigm misunderstands the nature of difference and the possibilities that the relational approach offers.

According to Minow, there are in concept several approaches to solving the dilemma of difference. The first is what she terms the *abnormal-persons approach.*[17] This approach divides society into two classes of persons, the normal and the abnormal. And important legal consequences follow from being assigned to one class or the other. The problem with this approach is that it replicates the feudal notion of hierarchical fixed-status relations.

The second is what she terms the *rights-analysis approach.*[18] Under this approach, legal rights apply to every individual. The historical denial of rights to certain groups cannot be defended. The problem with this approach is that it maintains the unstated norm, based on one group of people, and therefore attributes differences to those who diverge from that norm.

Third, and her preferred approach, is what she terms the *social-relations approach.*[19] This approach proceeds from the idea that there is a basic connectedness between people. People live and talk in relationships and never exist outside of them. The advantage of this approach is that attributions of difference are sustained only if they do not express or confirm the distribution of power in ways that harm the less powerful and benefit the more powerful.

Minow demonstrates how the social-relations approach would apply to the two circumstances of difference which we have considered. Under this approach, the task of judgment should not be the application of general principles to a problem. Instead, the task of judgment should be a process of taking the perspective of another: 'those who would judge should reflect on their own relationships to the one they would judge, not just the actions and motives of that other person.'[20]

Take Amy, the hearing-impaired schoolchild.[21] The relational solution, instead of treating the unimpaired students as the norm and the problem as being located in Amy, would instead treat Amy's problem as embedded in the relationships among all the students. Thus, the solution to this problem is to instruct all the students in the use of sign language, and then conduct the class in both spoken language and sign language simultaneously.

Similarly, the ultimate outcome of the Cleburne, Texas group home dispute was correct in terms of the relational approach.[22] The abnormal-persons approach makes differential treatment seem natural, unavoidable, and problematic. The rights-analysis approach presumes that most social arrangements are natural and inevitable, although it does invite proof that a given assignment of difference reflects prejudice and error. Under the social-relations approach, however, differential treatment becomes a problem of social choice and meaning. Thus, it is a problem for which all onlookers are responsible.

III
The Matter of Community

Despite my agreement with much of what Minow offers by way of both propositions and prescriptions, I am not fully comfortable either with the 'relational' outcome to the *Cleburne* dispute, or, more especially, with the deep implications of the approach to reaching that outcome. In particular, as we will see, the focus of my critique will be on her assertion, 'the difference dilemma is a symptom of a particular way of looking at the world.' In order to explain more fully the nature of my discomfort, let me turn to another local community as it, too, experiences intrusion from outsiders.

A. *The Nature of Community*

In August 1989, resident youths in the Italian-American Bensonhurst section of Brooklyn killed a young black man who had come there on what turned out to have been an altogether innocent errand.[23] In the intensive media attention that followed, we witnessed black protest marches through Bensonhurst with Bensonhurst residents lining the march route chanting, 'Go home,' while they held up signs which read, 'We're not racist.'[24] To anyone who observed this,[25] the assertion — 'We are not racist' — simply is not convincing.

What can we learn, however, by giving these Bensonhurst residents the benefit of the doubt? Assume that they mean what they say, and that what they say is objectively true as well, and not the product of self-delusion. Assume also, however, that, like anyone else trying to express deep and complex feelings, they have a problem of articulation. Indeed, to anyone who has seen the newspaper photographs or television news segments depicting the vehemence in the faces of the Bensonhurst residents who were onlookers at the black protest marches through their community, their very vehemence suggests the problem of inarticulation — expressing with emotion the ineffable, and expressing with emotion their frustration at it being ineffable:

> 'I think it's a shame. I'm out here yelling and screaming at these people, but not because they're black,' resident Tom Citera, a construction worker, said before the march. 'It's because they come into our neighborhood.'[26]

Surely there is a paradox in this. In order to explore this paradox, let us shift our focus once again, to look at this paradox from another perspective. And let us begin with someone who is unusually articulate.

Eva Hoffman's 1989 book, *Lost in Translation: A Life in a New Language*, is a memoir about her emigration at the age of thirteen from Poland to Canada and then to the United States. The memoir literally is about language — it is about how feelings that can be articulated in one language cannot be articulated in another. At one point, she found herself asking herself:

> Should you marry him? the question comes in English.
> Yes.
> Should you marry him? the question echoes in Polish.
> No.[27]

Her memoir is about how she sees her journey to becoming an American as the process of losing one language and assuming another, and how language is the manifestation of the world, a world that is the particular creation of a particular culture:[28]

> My sister has returned to her Polish name—Alina. It takes a while for me to switch back to it; Alina, in English, is a different word than it is in Polish: it has the stamp of the unusual, its syllables don't fall as easily on an English speaker's tongue. In order to transport a single word without distortion, one would have to transport the entire language around it.[29]

Repeatedly, Eva Hoffman's memoir recounts conversations that she had during her time of transition, in particular, conversations that quickly turned into argument between people occupying two radically different psychic worlds who were utterly failing to understand each other. She recalls her freshman year college roommate:

> Even a relatively intelligible person, like Lizzy, poses problems of translation . . . . The human mean is located in a different place here, and qualities like adventurousness, or cleverness, or shyness are measured along a different scale and mapped within a different diagram. You can't transport human beings whole from one culture to another any more than you can transliterate a text. Nevertheless, Lizzy and I set out to understand each other with a will — and we run into misunderstandings with the rude surprise of rams butting into each other in the middle of a narrow bridge.[30]

In a recent essay,[31] the philosopher Ted Cohen addressed the problem of metaphors and jokes that misfire:

> Suppose you make a metaphor and I don't comprehend it. Or again, suppose you tell a joke and I don't laugh. In both cases something has not come across: something has not gotten from you to me. What does this show? It shows that we are different, certainly, at least with regard to this metaphor and this joke, at least on this occasion. . . .
>
> My favorite way of thinking of these things—both offering metaphors and telling jokes—is in terms of a context of community. They are, typically, devices or occasions for establishing modes of intimacy, ways of sharing which render a group of people more than a collection of individual, different people.[32]

In describing the successful use of metaphors and jokes, Cohen asserts that, 'These successes, on my view, occasion communities of intimacy.'[33] Here, we see both creation and celebration. We surely use these devices — jokes and metaphors — for 'establishing modes of intimacy.' Surely also we use them to recognize and enjoy modes of intimacy that are already in being.

We seek and cherish modes of intimacy because we are social creatures. More correctly, and by way of agreeing with Martha Minow, we are socially created, the ongoing product of groups that, for each of us, are located somewhere along a spectrum that reaches from the larger society to an intimate community. As Eva Hoffman puts it:

> Human beings don't only search for meanings, they are themselves units of meaning; but we can mean something only within the fabric of a larger signification.[34]

Because we are socially created, we function fully only in a social milieu, and that functioning works best within the community that has formed us or that is still shaping us. And, because we are socially created, we cannot avoid deep paradox in trying to do justice in a political society that accords strong protection to a mythical autonomous individual.

I want to pursue this line of thought by looking into a more particular question — What is 'community?' We can capture a crucial aspect of community by defining it as a common, particular world manifested through, and largely created by, a common, particular language. For two people to be members of a community means not having to struggle in conversation — at a profane level, 'getting' each other's jokes; at a sublime level, participating in each other's metaphors. To the extent that we have community, to that extent we function well in our social role, that is, we function well as humans. Ultimately, as Eva Hoffman tells us, 'the only reality is a shared reality, situated within a common ground.'[35]

Outsiders who intrude into a particular community, by definition, do not share its language, its common ground. Yet, because we are social creatures, we cannot simply ignore a stranger who enters onto the 'turf' of our community. That is, the very presence of a stranger in that social space is a disruption of the community; again, Eva Hoffman:

> But for all our sophisticated deftness at cross-cultural encounters, fundamental difference, when it's staring at you across the table from within the close-up face of a fellow human being, always contains an element of violation.[36]

As trenchant observers of the dynamics of successful urban communities understand,[37] the intrusion of difference manifested by the presence of a stranger demands that we do something about it — we must either push the stranger away, or do nothing, thereby risking having her presence disrupt or destroy our community, or take her in. But to take her in involves both learning her language — her jokes and her metaphors — and teaching her our language. That is, because our world is our language, for a stranger to become part of our world entails a dialectic process between her language and ours, leading to a new synthesis.

Of necessity, this involves considerable costs, both procedural and substantive. First is the transaction cost — Eva Hoffman demonstrates, through the charged and acerbic conversations that she recounts, that this mutual process of learning is difficult and therefore psychically expensive. Second is the substantive cost — this mutual process of learning will necessarily change our language, which cannot change unless our values also change. To accommodate that stranger will also, in whole or in part, cost us our values. This substantive cost is even more expensive psychically.

And both social science and neurological science are beginning to reveal the nature and extent of these costs. Anthropologists suggest that 'prejudice is hereditary.'[38] That is, mind is a collection of specific mental functions that have become soft-wired in the brain, the result of selection and evolution. Xenophobia and bigotry may have 'evolved as a mechanism to provoke our ancestors into immediate defensive action under threatening circumstances.' Thus, the rule of thumb — 'trust the familiar, fear the strange; prejudice may be an evolutionary artifact initially designed to protect 'us' from 'them'.'

Neuroscientists[39] are beginning to understand how this evolutionary artifact comes about. The mind can be described as a process that arises from a massively complex structure of 'reentrant maps' which develop through a process of 'neural Darwinism.' These maps are made up of particular physical patterns that an individual's experience forms in the neural paths of the neo-cortex. These patterns are malleable. We are not locked in to such traits as fear of the unfamiliar; but changing them comes at the real cost of real physical effort.

Thus, if we choose not to incur these costs because we find them to be too formidable, then, if we are to maintain our community intact, to ignore the stranger is not an option. Instead, we must push the stranger away.

We now have a way of understanding the full dimensions of the psychic harm that a group home thrust into a residential area brings. A measure of communality no doubt exists in even the most atomized neighborhood. To the extent that communality does exist, it is a jolting wrench to be required by law to take in a substantial element of outsiders into that neighborhood. It is jolting because the option of rejecting the strangers is foreclosed.

If the fact of communality is to be maintained, the current members themselves must change. Comfortable values must, at least in part, be given up, at considerable substantive and procedural psychic cost. Not incurring this cost, moreover, then entails that each member of the community will incur the cost of losing communality itself; the community member either must move away and seek a new community, or remain, in quite-literally-diminished circumstances.

Eva Hoffman's memoir, at its most fundamental level, is about these costs of changing one's world, a memoir, as it happens, written from the other side of our group home conundrum. She is the stranger thrust into the pre-existing community. And she was thrust because she had foreclosed the option of returning to Poland. Indeed, it may be that she was willing to incur the costs on her side of the transaction only because she had foreclosed the exit option.[40]

We now have a way of understanding the apparent paradox of the assertion, 'We are not racists.' It has nothing do to with the relative merits of the values possessed by, or the relative value as human beings of, the community members and the strangers. Before the clash of stranger and community reaches the level of the relative merits of values, resistance necessarily arises, first, from the presence of difference, and, second, from the anticipation of the formidable substantive and procedural costs of accommodating difference.

If we are to take the assertion 'We are not racists' as true, then its deep meaning is rooted in the understanding that outsiders, any outsiders, threaten the substance of our values and the fact of our communality. As the deep emotion in the faces of the Bensonhurst onlookers demonstrates, outsiders threaten us at our deepest level. We seek to reject them in order to avoid a threateningly high psychic cost.

If this account rings true, we have brought into sharper focus two distinct facets of discrimination. The exemplar of malign discrimination is the oppressive majority exploiting an insular minority through its assumed hierarchy of values that brands the minority as inferior. The exemplar of neutral discrimination is the community drawing a boundary in the face of difference in order to protect its values, not in order to oppress the outsiders and not because the outsiders' values are inferior. And, to deny a community the power to engage in neutral discrimination is to impose on that community a considerable cost. Indeed, it threatens the very existence of that community — the quintessential function of a community, after all, is boundary drawing, to establish a bulwark between those who participate in its values and those who do not.

B. *The Dilemma of Community*

Having explored the nature of community, we can now consider two contrasting notions — the value of community, and community values. These notions together capture the fundamental problem that, in our political culture, the nature of communities is complex and conflicting. They are, simultaneously, institutions that serve both benign and malign ends.

Take first the benign aspects. Despite the primacy in our political culture of the notion of the autonomous, rights-endowed individual, the community is perhaps the most important and efficacious milieu available to the individual for achieving self-definition. Moreover, despite the individual's endowment of abstract political rights, for most people the practical realization of those rights depends on communality — the particular community is also a highly efficacious institution both for the empowerment of the individual and for the protection of the individual from the power of others. Communities, then, are altogether valuable.

Indeed, Minow implicitly recognizes this. She fully understands that we are socially created. More importantly, her relational approach exactly captures the World-making paradigm of the egalitarian community. It is in the egalitarian community where difference does not amount to the oppression that Minow seeks to eradicate.

This, however, leads us to the malign aspects of community. The deep problem with the relational approach and the egalitarian communities which embody it is the incessant tendency toward fissure which plagues such communities.[41] Exactly because the well-functioning egalitarian community dissolves the power consequences of difference, it holds no hierarchy of values or organizational principles on which to establish group cohesion. Thus, as the individual values of its members evolve and play out, subgroups will form around particular value sets, which then inevitably leads to schism.

The egalitarian community has available only two solutions to this inevitable problem of fissure. Either it must establish and impose an overarching set of values, thereby transforming itself into a hierarchical community. Or it must allow the fissure process to play out. The first solution, by definition, leads to a community that, because it is now organized hierarchically, exhibits a considerable degree of internal oppression, much like the 'River City' of the musical, *The Music Man*. The second solution leads to two or more new egalitarian communities. Because, however, they are egalitarian, they therefore have no internal mechanisms to maintain cohesion. Each can thus maintain its cohesion only by drawing its boundaries strongly, by branding the values of the other splinter groups as alien and malign.[42] That is, it must oppress the outsiders.

Thus, each solution ultimately leads to difference and oppression. The crucial point is that the relational approach tends to establish egalitarian communities. And all egalitarian communities will ultimately create differences and act on them.

IV
Critique

A considerable problem with Minow's analysis is that she carries it out at a substantially abstract level. Her real-world examples for applying the relational approach are few, and, as we have seen with the two that we have explored, they present relatively easy cases. Surely adopting both the oral and the sign language in Amy's classroom is a commendable approach to her differentness. And surely the neighbors of the Cleburne, Texas group home ought not be allowed to block so useful a way of meeting the needs of the group home residents in a non-oppressive way.

We are now in a position, however, to take a more critical look at these seemingly benign proposals for dissolving difference and oppression. Two problems are evident — one is the problem of cost; the second is the larger problem of efficacy.

In Amy's classroom, the cost of introducing her classmates to sign language seems to be more than acceptable when compared to the resulting benefits. Amy now joins the new mainstream — her difference is dissolved. And her classmates can now be enriched by becoming fluent in a second language.

The matter of cost, however, is more salient in the Cleburne neighborhood. We have seen that merely to take the group home residents into this neighborhood will entail substantial procedural costs. Moreover, the substantive costs of this change will be heightened by the fact that, the more that the group home residents become part of the community — the more, that is, that the group home is successful on its own terms — the more that the functional level of human interaction within that community will be attenuated.[43]

In the Cleburne example, as we have seen, the overall benefits that the group home will generate surely will outweigh the consequent process and substantive costs that the neighbors will bear. Thus, the fact of these costs would not justify abandoning the establishment of the group home. These costs, however, cannot simply be ignored.

The neighbors to the group home may hold majoritarian values. They assuredly, however, are not part of the power elite. Thus, they find themselves in the position of having the larger society thrust on them the costs of advancing important social values.

Minow's analysis, by ignoring these costs, is incomplete. The fact of these costs — *in this case* — ought not bear on the decision whether to establish the group home. The fact of these costs, however, ought to require that the neighbors be compensated.

The larger problem is the matter of Martha Minow's deep assumptions. She starts out from the proposition that the differences that we see are an artificial construct, and that problems of oppression can be solved by dissolving the [constructed] differences on which they are based. She then, however, concludes that her relational approach will allow us to escape entirely the process of making differences. Her key proposition is that 'the difference dilemma is a symptom of a particular way of looking at the world.'[44]

Her approach assumes that problems of difference would dissolve 'if only we could interrelate . . . .' Yet, we interrelate through language. And language can only create particular worlds. And the creation of a new particular world will lead ultimately only to more difference. It may dissolve a current set of differences. It will not, however, eliminate the *making of differences*.

That is, the difference dilemma is not 'a symptom of a particular way of looking at the world.' Instead, it is a necessary consequence of having a world. Thus, it is ironic that Minow, in seeking to dissolve difference and oppression, is seeking to do justice. We need justice, however, when we find ourselves in the circumstances of justice — when, that is, there is a scarcity of the resources required to satisfy fully the needs and wants of all of society's members, and there is no unanimity within society over how scarce resources ought to be divided among these individuals.[45] The circumstances of justice are quintessentially the circumstances of difference. Minow's project amounts to an attempt to dissolve the circumstances of justice. As such, it seems to reduce to an exercise in utopianism.

V
Conclusions

Because the aims of Martha Minow's project are so desirable, I would prefer not to end on such a pessimistic note. There is, however, opportunity here only to sketch out an approach to the problems of difference. The starting point is Ronald Garet's taxonomy of modes of human existence — Individuality, Sociality, and Communality.[46] This taxonomy captures the idea that elements of each mode are present in the existence of each of us, but that the existence of each of us is dominated by one or another of these modes.

If a necessary condition for a healthy culture is the presence of a balanced mix of each of these modes, then our current culture is impoverished. Individuality is an overwhelmingly strong value our in public discourse, although the strongly hierarchical organization of productive activities precludes all but a relative few from existing in a dominantly individualistic mode. This very circumstance, in fact, has generated an increasingly noticed phenomenon, the coalescing of individuals into communities of interest. The result has been a cacophony of special interest advocacy in public discourse and an accelerating fragmentation of the social dimension.[47]

It is in the mode of Sociality where our cultural impoverishment is the most intensive. Our opportunities to exist in public spaces are confined to hierarchically-organized milieus of entertainment and commerce — the well-functioning agora, or town square, has been reduced to the lonely pseudo-dialogue of the call-in show. Our other milieus of public discourse, the state and federal legislative bodies, are almost totally given over to a process of log-rolling among the minions of special interests. As a consequence, our 'culture's descent into small, mutually opaque segments — liberalism's carefully demarcated ghettos — bars some kind of common expression of belief.'[48]

And it is the mode of Sociality that provides the most promising opportunity to attenuate the play of difference and oppression. The argument of this essay is that the inescapable attribute of the human condition is the creation of difference as a necessary consequence of the necessary human task of creating the psychic circumstances that add up to the world in which each of us exists. The conclusion of this essay is that Martha Minow's prescription for avoiding difference and oppression — that we 'relate more' — is nothing other than this inescapable process of world making. If we are to attenuate the play of difference, we must do so by revitalizing the dimension of Sociality.

**Denis J. Brion is Professor of Law at Washington & Lee University.* *The author acknowledges with thanks the financial support of the Frances Lewis Law Center in the preparation of this essay.*

ENDNOTES

1. Shelby M. Givens, 'The Walk that Wasn't Pedestrian,' *The Washington Post*, July 12, 1992, at C8.

2. E.g., Bruce A. Ackerman, 1980, *Social Justice in the Liberal State.*

3. E.g., Carol Gilligan, 1982, *In a Different Voice: Psychological Theory and Women's Development.*

4. See, e.g., Michael J. Sandel, 1982, *Liberalism and the Limits of Justice.*

5. City of Cleburne v. Cleburne Living Center, Inc., 473 U.S. 432, 1985.

6. This discussion will not consider Justice Thurgood Marshall's opinion, in which he concurred in part and dissented in part.

7. 473 U.S. at 448.

8. *Id*. at 450.

9. *Id*. at 446.

10. *Id*. at 455.

11. *Id*.

12. Martha Minow, 1990, *Making All the Difference: Inclusion, Exclusion, and American Law* 95, [hereinafter cited as 'Minow'].

13. *Id*. at 7.

14. *Id*. at 19.

15. *Id*. at 50-52.

16. *Id*. at 79.

17. *Id*. at 105-106.

18. *Id*. at 106-107.

19. *Id*. at 110-112.

20. *Id*. at 221.

21. *Id*. at 83-84.

22. *Id*. at 119.

23. This discussion is derived from Denis J. Brion, 1991, *Essential Industry and the NIMBY Phenomenon*, 184-189.

24. E.g., Andrew Sullivan, 'The Two Faces of Bensonhurst,' *The New Republic*, July 2, 1990, at 13, 16; Newsday, Jan. 10, 1990, at 8; *id.*, Sept. 15, 1989, at 81, letter to the editor; *id.*, Sept. 10, 1989, at 19; *The New York Times*, Sept. 5, 1989, at A19, col. 2.

25. E.g., *Newsday*, Sept. 15, 1989, at 81, letter to the editor.

26. *Newsday*, Sept. 10, 1989, at 19.

27. Eva Hoffman, 1989, *Lost in Translation: A Life in a New Language*, 199, hereinafter cited as 'Hoffman.'

28. See also Stuart Chase, *1956, Foreword* to John B. Carroll, ed., *Language, Thought, and Reality: Selected Writings of Benjamin Lee Whorf*, vi:

    > Whorf as I read him makes two cardinal hypotheses: *First*, that all higher levels of thinking are dependent on language. *Second*, that the structure of the language one habitually uses influences the manner in which one understands his environment. The picture of the universe shifts from tongue to tongue.

29. Hoffman, note 27 *supra*, at 272.

30. *Id.* at 175.

31. Ted Cohen, 'Figurative Incompetence (A Thesis),' *Raritan*, Fall 1990, 30, philosopher, University of Chicago.

32. *Id.*

33. *Id.* at 33.

34. Hoffman, note 27 *supra*, at 279.

35. *Id.* at 195.

36. *Id.* at 209-210.

37. See Jane Jacobs, 1961, *The Death and Life of Great American Cities*, 29-54; Oscar Newman, 1973, *Defensible Space: Crime Prevention Through Urban Design*, 22-117.

38. Helen Fisher, 'Is Prejudice Hereditary?,' *New York Times Book Review*, March 24, 1994, at 15, reviewing Robin Fox, 1994, *The Challenge of Anthropology: Old Encounters and New Excursions*.

39. E.g., Gerald M. Edelman, 1992, *Bright Air, Brilliant Fire: On the Matter of the Mind*.

40. See Hoffman, note 27 *supra*, at 209.

41. Mary Douglas & Aaron Wildavsky, 1982, *Risk and Culture: An Essay on the Selection of Technical and Environmental Dangers*.

42. For an exploration of these oppressive consequences, see Denis J. Brion, 1991, 'Modern Witchcraft: The Semiotic Power of Community Cosmology,' ed. Roberta Kevelson, *Action and Agency*, 65.

43. The nature of this attenuation may be understood through the phenomenon of 'cabin fever' to which parents who are homebound in caring for young children succumb — having to function for extended periods of time at the lower level of interpersonal relations of which young children are capable exacts a high psychic toll on the adult.

44. Minow, note 12 *supra*, at 79.

45. For a discussion of the circumstances of justice, see John Rawls, 1971, *A Theory of Justice*, 126-28.

46. Ronald Garet, 1983, 'Communality and Existence: The Rights of Groups,' 56 *S. Cal. L. Rev.* 1001.

47. E.g., James Davison Hunter, 1991, *Culture Wars: The Struggle to Define America*; Arthur M. Schlesinger, Jr., 1992, *The Disuniting of America: Reflections on a Multicultural Society*.

48. Andrew Sullivan, 'The Theatre,' *Washington Diarist* column, *The New Republic*, April 11, 1994, at 46.

Chapter Seven

A Utopian Proposal for the Improvement of our Prisons

Robert Ginsberg*

I

This proposal is not a utopian study but an exercise in utopian thinking. It addresses a concrete problem faced by current society. Imprisonment as the standard way of punishing criminals is a distinctively modern institution, an innovation upon executing, torturing, or deporting criminals.[1] Hence, proposals for prisons always incline to be utopian in thinking as they offer model institutions fit for a just society. And what we call prison reform is perennially utopian as critics recognize that radical changes are needed in prison practices if the noble values of society are to be realized. If we are to resolve the problem of prisons we must be willing to expand our thinking to its fullest, following the argument where it leads. If it should lead to the reconstruction of society, well then, shouldn't we accept those consequences? Realistically, we may have to be utopian.

Recent prison riots in America have made us acutely aware of the inadequate and overcrowded condition of our prisons, and this recognition has occurred at just that time in the life of American society when — as civil riots show — we have most need of our prisons to lock up dangerous criminals. I anticipate that your reply to another suggestion for penal reform is, *Our society has enough problems on its hands in serving good, law-abiding, taxpaying, hardworking citizens, like ourselves, so that to spend time or money on those who are the evident enemies of society would be, to use a mild word, unfair.* But this time, dear reader, we must do *something* about our prisons since we face a dire shortage of places to securely detain the hordes of criminals who are setting upon our citizens in the streets, in their homes and shops, and in the halls of government. To insure domestic peace and promote law and order, we require a first-class prison system.

The proposal advocated here is intended purely and solely for society's general good, not as a comforting or coddling of despicable criminals. While our present prison system requires a thorough reorganization to bring it up to modern-day standards, which means enormous expenditure of funds, all this effort and expense is worth the gain in security and prosperity that will follow.

Some readers may say that all we need is more cells, or more cots in existing cells, since the problem simply is to put our criminals *somewhere.* Overcrowding seems always to have plagued prisons. But that is not the core of the problem. Indeed, to just add cells or to fill the old ones beyond their capacity will act in the wrong way, increasing rather than alleviating the prison problem. The heart of the prison problem is that while we have always had some places to put criminals, we have not yet learned how to make them learn their lesson. Imprisonment, alas, hardens the criminal. Once out, the criminal is more dangerous to society than before entering. Prison is the graduate school of crime.

Others have an easy and inexpensive solution to this backfiring of the system: *Throw away the key. Make sure the criminal never gets out to prey on good people like us again.* Unfortunately, due to our lenient judges, those Supreme Court reversals, lack of evidence, denied confessions, improper arrests, unwarranted searches, appeals, pardons, parole, and so many other loopholes and escape hatches, we shall have to live with people who have been to jail, unless we decide that for the safety of society all crimes must be punished by mandatory life imprisonment not subject to appeal. This is the only alternative, short of universal capital punishment, to letting people who have served time get out to possibly disserve society.

In the long run such harsh categorical punishment may be the best answer, though you must consider that we might all be vulnerable to this unvarying treatment, for no person may have yet lived who did not break some law. Consult thy conscience, reader, as I have consulted mine.

While my proposal is utopian, it is not extreme or unrealistic. I anchor it at a down-to-earth level where you can clearly envision improvements: the physical facilities. Truly, we need more prisons and more cells. But standards must be set as well as quantity increased. Utopian vision of prison design is a marked feature of theories of prison reform. Jeremy Bentham envisioned a 'panopticon,' a wheel of cells observable from a control center, as an implementation of solitary confinement. John Haviland designed a ray system of cells springing from a center for much the same purpose. In Pennsylvania two celebrated state prisons were constructed along these two designs: the Western Penitentiary in Pittsburgh (1818), as a panopticon, and the Eastern Penitentiary in Philadelphia (1829), as a ray system.[2] A criminal could decide in which half of the state to operate, given a preference for one or another of these designs.

Punishment requires design. We should first set down the minimum space and facilities for each prisoner. This is the unit of prison design: the cell. Each inmate, let us say, must have one and half rooms. The basic room, following the Scandinavian University Student Housing Module (SUSHMOD), has no less floor space than a chamber 3.6576 by 4.572 meters. In the principal room goes the standard furniture allowance, to wit: one double bed, one table with reading lamp, one desk chair, one easy chair, one floor lamp, one bookcase (4 shelves), a radio, tv, phonograph, telephone, fax, answering machine, video cassette, compact disc player, wordprocessor, modem, laser printer, clock, two paintings, a small refrigerator, a microwave oven. The adjoining half room is the Hygienic Center (H.C.), containing a flush toilet, one washbasin (hot and cold water), one medicine cabinet and mirror, one shower-bath-bidet.

You might protest that these minimum provisions are luxurious. True, some of these furnishings you might find at a reputable motel chain. We wish to impress upon our criminals a level of decency so that they can mend their ways. This decency requires privacy and a sense of self-respect. Ex-convicts must respect the privacy of others. Our prisoners will learn the value of having a room of one's own with the basic facilities for civilized life. Hence, they will be less likely to disrupt the domestic tranquillity of others when they get out.

When you place people in a dungeon, force them to lie about in dank darkness all day and night, and crowd their breathing space with other bodies, you intensify their resentment against the good people in ordinary dwellings on the outside. For the indignities the prisoners suffer, which they attribute so unfairly to our meanness, they then want to make us suffer. Incidents of brutalization of prisoners by one another, including multiple homosexual rape, which we inadvertently insist our criminals be exposed to, will be greatly diminished by the new housing arrangements.

The prisoners will eat together the standard four meals of the day and night, though not all at once, nor in the accustomed refectories which have the appearance and aroma of mammoth garages. The dining halls will be numerous, small (seating about 40 each in a hexagonal pattern), and varied in decor. No persons will take all their meals in the same room each day. Our purpose is to humanize the eating function in prisons instead of requiring it to be the carnal necessity of trapped beasts.

Prisoners will have an interest in eating in pleasant quarters, which will help them to see others who are present as persons. This is an incentive to being well-behaved. While the mealtimes are not entirely social hours, conversation will be encouraged, soft music will be played, table service will be polite and leisurely, and the diners may take their seat wherever they wish. When the prisoners get out, we want them to sit properly in a restaurant and respect the good people who are eating there.[3]

The prison meals will be four-fifths synthetic, made of chemicals, minerals, and plant extracts such as high protein soybean substance. The food will be the most healthful imaginable and attractively presented so that the prisoners will find it appetizing and refreshing.

The prison meals will be served in shifts. Breakfast on the first shift begins at 5 Hours, lunch at 10H, dinner at 16H, and nightmeal at 23H (the prison clock will be divided into 24 hours, which is twice as useful as the American civilian system). The other shifts will vary such that the Nutrition Department will be continually in operation, preparing and serving food around the clock.

This is but one example of the maximized daynight utilization of the prison facilities. The library, art museum, cinématèque, sauna, gymnasium, scientific laboratories, tea house, and chapel will also never close.

The athletic facilities at our prisons must be considerably expanded, for their present state is regrettably insufficient. We are aiming at a healthy prisoner in body and mind who will be able to bear up well under the stress of outside life. Athletics teaches coordination of body and will, cooperation in team play, competition that is strenuous but nonviolent. In sports a person may earn the praise and esteem of others while learning to appreciate the effort of accomplishment of others. Everyone has talents and limitations. You don't have be a champion to play. You don't have to win to be appreciated. You don't have to injure anyone to be noticed. So athletics teaches our prisoners what we want them to remember: all persons are to be respected for who they are, namely, human beings.

At the core of the athletic field will be the Olympic-size swimming pool, and girdling it the great running track. Swimming and running are the golden sports. Courts for tennis, handball, volleyball, and basketball will be numerous indoors and out, though every effort will be made to conduct activities outdoors, even amid snowflakes. We want to build a criminal-citizen able to flourish under the wide variety of natural conditions in our great country.

The acreage necessary for the outdoors sports admittedly is huge, for we will provide for golf, tobogganing, baseball, skiing, cross-country running, mountain climbing, and possibly, with a change of playing habits, hockey, football, and soccer. No sports involving weapons will be permitted, as you will be pleased to hear. Boxing, the art of manly brain-damaging, will also be prohibited.

The prisons will house a fully staffed hospital, offering the finest in physical care, and an expert staff in psychiatry and social work will also be available. The medical-counseling staff will work in teams that deal with the whole person as patient instead of as a body attached to an ailment. Emotional needs, social background, aspirations, and intelligence shall be taken into account in helping ailing or troubled persons. The medical and counseling files will be confidential; no one else in or outside or prison may ever see them. The prisoners learn that society offers help to individuals. They can benefit from that help no matter how insignificant or defective they might feel.

Each prison will have its university. Vocational and remedial work in basic skills will be available, as they now generally are, but the new emphasis will be on providing college-level work for every prisoner. *Life-Long Learning (LLL) for All* will be our slogan. The liberal arts core program will require full audio-oral training in Spanish or another international language (never to be called 'foreign' language), since language offers a valuable dimension for human expression and conception. Courses in world literature will also be required, for imaginative literature is the most accessible source of insight into all human experience. The most popular course, Prison Lit, will assist the students to reflect on their experience as well as that of others. Readings include Dickens, *Little Dorrit;* Dostoyevsky, *The House of the Dead;* e. e. cummings, *The Enormous Room;* Oscar Wilde, 'The Ballad of Reading Gaol'; George Jackson, *Soledad Brother;* Brendan Behan, *Borstal Boy;* Arthur Koestler, *Darkness at Noon;* and Jerome Lawrence and Robert E. Lee, *The Night Thoreau Spent in Jail.* A course in Semiotics will be required for all advanced students to expand their imagination and their social vision to the limits. Look at the wonderful things that can be done under the heading of Semiotics! Philosophy will be available only upon petition, since it is usually taught as too dry and abstract a subject to have any bearing on human insight.

Just as in the civilian world people go to college primarily to get a good job and earn more money, these attractions will be touted in the prison world. This will also raise the educational level — and thereby the economic level — of the whole society. Education will be looked upon seriously as the key to advancement and success, whereas crime, particularly violence, fraud, and political corruption, is now regarded in that light. In celebrated cases, inmates have made outstanding contributions to scholarship, especially in the legal and sociological fields. Broader implementation of such benefits to society will be the business of the Prison University Division of Graduate Education (PUDGE). Unemployed scholars throughout America will have a chance for a satisfying teaching career behind bars.

An extensive arts program will offer the full range of expressive and creative techniques, emphasizing those which involve bodily coordination and collaboration. Criminal personalities need harmless outlets for their destructive energies. This they can find in creation or performance that is socially acceptable and requires effort and practice. We would like as many hardened criminals dancing in classical ballet as we can get. Artistic experience will also attune the savage breast of the criminal to the civilized pleasures of the arts generally accessible in society. Ex-convicts will frequent art museums and concert halls instead of their usual dens of iniquity.

The prisoners will enrich the cultural life of the community. They will be providing stable jobs for artistic personnel, critics, designers, teachers, librarians, and deans. The prisons will have the physical settings and they will stimulate that audience interest much needed by civilian artistic activities, such as repertory theaters, operatic companies, and local art galleries, many of which are obliged to close down due to lack of public interest and public funding.

The public will be drawn to the prisons as spectators at its sporting events, patrons of its arts, auditors of its lectures and courses. This will make prisoners feel that people are interested in their life and their possible contribution to life. They will also become used to the presence of the outside world in the prison so that they will not regard these as antithetical worlds. Prisoners should not think of themselves as outsiders who must prey on society. Presently, prisons are shunned by the public with distaste and fear. Consequently, the inmates feel the taintedness of their location and status. They think that they are evil and therefore must continue to be so. While *we* know that they are evil, we want to get them to think that though they have been evildoers they needn't be evil persons. That's the trick.

The prison is to be the meeting place and showcase for cultural and social programs in the community, and it will enter into friendly competition with prisons of other communities in sports, arts, and education. This encourages efforts at excellence in all the activities the criminals pursue, and it leads to pride in their accomplishments. Without pride people cannot have self-respect, without self-respect they cannot be expected to respect others, and without respect for others they are likely to injure others. A reason frequently cited these days for murder is the feeling that the victim was 'dis-ing' the poor murderer, disrespecting the humanity of that person, who then was obliged to assert respectability and human worth by killing the misinformed accuser.

Pride in one's legitimate accomplishments as a person even in prison must replace rancor and resentment that prisons now aim to induce in the heart of their inmates. These emotions turn in on themselves, eating away the soul and longing for a chance to pour out on others as revenge. Each community will also take pride in the success of its prison, just as it does in the triumphs of its hometown team or the size of its skyscrapers. Each city will be able to say: 'See, this is how well we have treated the problem of crime in the streets; we have created an outstanding prison that redeems our criminals as valuable citizens in order that we may be safe.'

The principle of reform should be clear enough for you to apply to many other areas of prison life: the criminal is to be treated as a person and in such a way as to fulfill all potentialities as responsible human being. It is not because the prisoner might be worthy of such treatment that we are to treat that person that way; we do so only because we want the prisoner to avoid interfering again in the fulfillment of *our* potentialities as human beings. No question can be raised that we deserve to have fulfillment protected and enhanced. Please bear in mind throughout this prisontation that its sole motivation is to benefit law-abiding peaceful citizens like us good folk, not to benefit confounded criminals.

I will point out just one other major requirement of our reformative principle: sex. Sex is a major part of human fulfillment. We also lock people up for nasty crimes of sexual assault. Once they are locked up in our prisons, we see to it that they are sexually assaulted. The consequence of our getting even with criminals in this manner is that when they are released they are inclined to get back at us through sexual assault or other indignities. Sex is viciously abused in this cycle instead of being a source of mutual joy.

Therefore, our prison reforms include provision for a full and healthy sex life for the inmates. They may be visited for social and sexual purposes each daynight by their spouse or appointed partner. Conjugal visits have been a traditional feature in Mexican and Scandinavian penology. We shall place no restriction on the acts engaged in, all of which will be done in privacy, nor on the sex of the partners, though they must be consenting adults (*i. e.,* over the age of 16). The prison library will house the community's erotica collection, donated by judges, civic clubs, presidential commissions, postal inspectors, as well as enterprising publishers, for a healthy awareness of human sexual experience diminishes the fear that people have of their strange desires — and their fear of strangers.

Other kinds of love and affection, in addition to the sexual, will be given ample opportunity for expression. Prisoners may be visited by their family. Even more important for the family, the prisoners may visit them. What an appropriate way to support family values, which mean so much to Americans. Young single prisoners may be permitted to attend social functions on the outside and make the acquaintance of other young people. Elderly inmates too will have their social clubs outside the walls as well as inside. In this way, everyone will have some tie of a personal and affectionate kind with the civilian world, and each will feel cared for by someone. The greatest aid to stability of personality, according to soap operas, is love. So the best way to fight crime is with love. Let the true prison be a place of love! Yet we have been exposing our criminals to hatred, only to reap its bitter fruits.

A special problem arises in treatment of perpetrators of heinous crimes. Those guilty of causing irreparable human injury, as in killing, maiming, and raping, and those guilty of gross abuse of public office, whether they be judges, police officers, mayors, congress members, generals, or presidents, would be sentenced to many years in the Double-Attention Towers from which they would have a full view of the playing fields and other prison activities, and where they would receive extra attentions and kindnesses, though never permitted to leave their glassed-in suites or to touch another human being. These will be the only prisoners whose right of suicide would not be recognized. This proposal turns Bentham's panopticon inside out, making the worst criminals the center of attention, rather than isolating them from awareness of others. Yet the result is a terrible isolation in the very presence of others. Kindness might kill their hostility. After several years, this kind of criminal might be allowed into the ordinary cells and then eventually be paroled. But anyone who has committed the supreme offense twice shall never be released from the Attention Towers.

Capital punishment is currently advocated — and widely practiced — in America as treatment for radically evil crimes, but since premeditated killing of people is the supreme evil, the ideal prison must refrain from it. Human life is the supreme human value, therefore the prison must enhance it. By pointing to the Double-Attention Towers we shall show people that even though they kill others they cannot escape being regarded as human. No one must escape being regarded as human, even those you might wish to kill. That's the message. Those in the towers will learn their lesson through kindness, though it may mean a life of unspeakable agony of remorse.

The biggest objection you may raise to this proposal for reform is cost. *Where is the money to come from for the land, the buildings, the salaries, the treatment, when we cannot find funds for comparable improvements in the community at large?* I grant that the expenditure must be huge, but so are the savings and the profit. We forget to calculate the latter pair, for all we see is the outlay of additional money as it it were being thrown into a bottomless pit, some Black Hole of Calcutta, that we think of as our prisons. *Putting money into prisons is wasting it,* you may argue. *Put criminals in there instead. Put money into projects for social betterment that need it.* Yet looked at in larger terms, the prison system is an investment which can repay us for what we put into it and give us a long-term dividend.

Let us suppose that the cost of opening and maintaining such a prison in a large American city is one billion dollars. I will list five ways in which that investment is repaid.

1. The project will create the greatest building boom in history. This will slash the lists of the unemployed by giving thousands of people stable, well-paying jobs. Moreover, since all the prison planning and building must be done in accordance with new humane rules, including interracial and sexually mixed construction crews, fixed prices on all building costs during construction, and profit-sharing between contractors and workers, the

industry will be reformed. The rules will be carried over into the private sector. This means a healthier economy, good jobs, and improvement of living conditions. Such invigoration and rectification of the economy might alone be worth the billion dollars.

2. The prisons will house a work force. Each prisoner will be responsible for a minimum of five hours of work each daynight (or 35 hours per week). They may do more if they wish, but to require any person in the modern world to work than 35 hours a week is an indignity. For the most part, this work will be factory skills, manufacturing necessities for society, such as chemical foods, medicines, clothes, communication and transportation equipment. In addition, specialized skills will be developed in the electronic fields for information processing, problem-solving, and other sophisticated services. The great oversight in our present prisons is that the labor to which we direct our prisoners is rock-breaking, laundering, or license plate-stamping, while they could be doing more highly skilled jobs productive of greater social value. Our prisoners will also work in professional, clerical, and intellectual posts, doing research, teaching in our public schools, serving on city councils, etc.

Many factories will be located adjacent to the prison, especially those that produce items needed by the prison. By the way, all of the clothes manufactured or worn in the prison will be of a standard inexpensive and hardy cloth. The garments can be colored variously by the owner with natural dyes, and minor ornaments may be added to express individuality, but no money should be wasted on expensive finery. The prison factories will also be producing for the general public. Because of their standardization, mass production, and cheap labor, the prices will be low, the quality acceptable, and the products readily available. Hence great savings to the public. Some of the prison factories may manufacture things more needed on the outside than the inside.

Finally, prisoners may be escorted on sightseeing vans to specialized factories of their choice operating elsewhere in the city. However, only necessary or socially useful items will be made by the prison work force, even if most of the other manufactured products in the future, are, as today, worthless junk.

Utopian literature, as for example Edward Bellamy's *Looking Backward* (1888), often proposes a reorganization of society's industrial system. The present proposal applies such reorganization to the small society of the prison. That in turn has salutary consequences for the society as a whole.

This is not an argument for replacing the good old American capitalist system; on the contrary, that system will likely be improved by our steps to organize the economic life of prisons.

Because our prison runs on a 24-hour daynight, the work force will be active 'round the clock in five slightly overlapping shifts (the equivalent of three shifts nowadays). This will increase production and improve the quality of products. Since the prisoners will be running the factories day and night, other citizens will be permitted to join them. The entire output of the economy will multiply overnight. Unemployment will be impossible for anyone who wants to work and who possesses rudimentary skills.

3. Our prison earns money from sale of tickets to its athletic events, theatrical productions, concerts, lectures, and guided tours, and it sells art objects, publications, and souvenirs. Fees are collected for public use of the medical facilities, which would become the principal public clinic, charging fixed modest rates. The prison will be the community's permanent center of entertainment, enlightenment, hygiene, and culture, offering excellent yet inexpensive services and products. Whenever people have free time for wholesome amusement or agreeable learning they will ask one another, 'What's on tonight at the prison?' While all fees will be kept below civilian scales, such that the billion dollar investment could not be earned back through them, yet sales at the prison help sustain its operation.

4. The prison project increases earnings from its investment, but it will also save us from wasted expenditures. It costs an American metropolis a billion dollars a year in money and property lost to crime and in crime-fighting or crime-prevention expenses. Following inauguration of our new system, this disruption of the economy, not to mention the accompanying personal suffering, will be cut by ninety percent. Almost all the crimes committed will be by first offenders, who after a stay at the prison would not return to crime. Though we can never expect to eliminate all crime, for everyone is prone to make a mistake once in life, and some are willing to make repeated mistakes, we will prevent youthful offenders from becoming hardened criminals. At present we make sure that anyone sent to prison learns a criminal trade there.

The life of the criminal, under these reforms, will lose its attractions. Young persons will not rob or injure someone in order to become fugitives from society's punishment. They will know that society will repay them kindness and help. Nor do they have to commit a crime in order to receive such prison treatment. I am happy to report that anyone who wishes may request a sojourn in the new prison without having violated any law. Since the lawbreakers know that they will end up in prison sooner or later, they might as well go directly to jail, passing up crime. (People who commit crimes solely for the purpose of getting into prison will be punished by not being admitted.) Out-prison services would be available to those who may need them but who are reluctant to commit crimes and would find moving into prison inconvenient.

We have made a life of crime a second-rate heroism for those we did not allow to compete for first-class social respect. The criminal became the big-shot, someone who counts, a force to reckon with, an underdog hounded but feared by society. In the minds of criminals and in the eyes of their associates, criminals had made something of themselves. Crime is the status ladder for the subculture of the unprivileged at the bottom of society's normal ladders of success.[4] Utopian thinkers would do well to first address the problem of subcultures or countercultures as they design the larger culture.

With the industrial boom created by the new prison, and with the new sense of social fair play, 'deprived citizens' will no longer exist. All will have a fair share to make a decent life and a decent living in a legal manner and to be respected for their efforts.

Furthermore, as the number and seriousness of crimes diminish, we will have less need for police officers, police stations, police riots, burglar alarms, electronic surveillance systems, and anti-personnel weapons carried by us good law-abiding citizens. The climate of fear will be dispelled by the sunshine of trust. The more respect and friendliness that people show to others the less likely will they become the victims of crime. Goodness is disarming.

No one will stand to lose anything monetarily by any crimes committed against them, for the community will act as insurer of all citizens against criminal acts, since the community in a sense would be at fault in not preventing the loss from having occurred. Under the present absurd system, the community only takes care of the criminal, attending to that person's needs for several years or even lifetime, while it does nothing for the victim who may have lost life-savings — or even life.

The community could afford the reparations since it will be the mandatory insurer of all. At present insurance companies make a huge profit by conducting such a business for those lucky enough to be able to pay and to be allowed to pay. Social insurance will be for mutual protection. The community will also have at its disposal a portion (called a 'tax') of the earnings of the criminals themselves, which will finance this operation and other humanitarian funds. Nowadays we make the victim work to regain the losses, while the criminal responsible for them sits idly in jail, the capability to help others left dormant.

In sum, while the initial sum needed for prison reform is titanic, equal to the cost of a month or so of modern warfare, it supplies a permanent increase in profit-making and a valuable saving of otherwise wasted funds. This is sufficient justification for its immediate adoption by an American public enlightened to its own interests.

The usual philosophical theorizing on law and society begins with what is good, only arriving at crime, if at all, as an incidental consequence. But we began our social theorizing with an inherent malfunction of society: crime. Then treating crime in terms of the crucial problem of the prison system, we can see what social implications follow for general theory. This is a prisoncentric vision of society. Thus, instead of constructing an ideal society which may have prisoners, we have constructed an ideal prison which may reshape society.

Throughout this proposal for prison reform I have stressed advantage to society as the pre-eminent concern. Our labors to remedy this sore spot in our modern lives will carry with them societal advantages in so many areas that a renovation of our life together may be accomplished. Some of the consequences of prison reform have been sketched: the level of cultural activity will be raised, the production of basic products will be increased at lower cost, more economic opportunities will abound with less economic — and social — injustice, crime insurance will protect everyone as will community-supported health and accident insurance. The 24-hour daynight, permanent operation of factories, and the five-shift work force, all established by the prison, will lead to rapid changes in society; it will be a much more active and exciting yet cooperative and peaceful life. Housing will be built in accordance with prison standards and food will be manufactured and served on its standards as well. It will become, in a word, *a prison society,* in which the model for institutions and interactions is built on respect for people. This is preferable to *an unpoliced society* or *a police state,* both of which are based on disdain for people.

You might think that the greatest danger in this proposal is that it could become too successful, for after the prisons are built and operate they would so benevolently affect people that scarce a handful of criminals will be left in them. But people will always be willing to go to our prison even if they have done nothing wrong, since it will be such a fine place to live. The prisons will remain full, though the criminal population in them gradually will be replaced by the upwardly mobile civilian. And as people move in, their degrading houses, and polluted places of work, and piteous grim playgrounds will be torn down and replaced by new prison architecture. We will have learned that stone walls do not a prison make.

Thus, by the year 2000, all the institutions and public activities of every community in America will come under the prison values. The whole country will have become a vast open prison for the benefit of all. A cooperative existence of people in society will have replaced the conflict and violence that now are the daily stuff of our lives. Human beings will have expiated the crime of their inhumanity and discovered the fruits of peace. Vengeance and neglect will have withered away as crimes of society. The word 'prisoner' will gradually have been replaced by 'guest,' meaning guest on the planet Earth, a title shared by all those inside and outside prison. And the very term 'prison' by then will have extended from the buildings and grounds to the whole social structure of respect in the life of persons. Standing for 'prized life together,' it will mean to Americans what others once meant by *polis, civitas, communitas, commonwealth, pueblo.*

So, good reader, as you look about us at this world of violence and suffering in which we find ourselves as if fellow-prisoners, can you think of any crime greater than not beginning these reforms, utopian though they be?

**Robert Ginsberg is Professor of Philosophy at The Pennsylvania State University.*

ENDNOTES

1. For a brief history see Marshall B. Clinard, 1949, 'Prison Systems,' eds. Vernon C. Branham and Samuel B. Kutash, *Encyclopedia of Criminology*, New York: Philosophical Library, 369-386, and Paul W. Tappan, 1960, *Crime, Justice, and Correction*, New York: McGraw-Hill, ch. 20, 'The History of Imprisonment,' 585-621.

2. For illustrations see *ibid.*, 632-633, and Max Grünhut, 1948, *Penal Reform: A Comparative Study*, Oxford: Clarendon Press, 47.

3. Several of the provisions for the social conduct of prisoners that are proposed here have been put in practice in special institutions, notably the California Institution for Men at Chino. See Kenyon J. Scudder, 1954, 'The Open Institution,' ed. Thorsten Sellin, 'Prisons in Transformation,' special number of *Annals of the American Academy of Political and Social Science,* vol. 293, reprinted Westport, Connecticut: Greenwood Press, 1972:79-87.

4. Cf. Marvin E. Wolfgang and Franco Ferracuti, 1967, *The Subculture of Violence*, London: Tavistock.

Chapter Eight

Semiotics, Legal Theory and the Study of Comparative Law

Stephen C. Hicks*

I

At the First Congress of Comparative Law in Paris in 1900, there was a fight for its soul. Saleilles' agenda was practical while Lambert's was intellectual. To Saleilles, the potential of comparative law lay in a legislative common law, *'un droit ideal relatif.'* To Lambert, its usefulness was to discover the natural laws of legal development through *'la vie juridique.'*[1]

The dynamic confrontation between comparative study for the narrow jurisprudential purpose of developing an international, transnational or common law, in a scientific or at least instrumental sense, and comparative study for the jurisprudential purpose of describing and accounting for the relationship between law and society, whether from an evolutionary or existential perspective, has enabled comparative law to defy labelling and categorization. This has been its latent strength.

The point is that today these are not seen as alternatives but parts of a consistent whole. Today the fact that it may incorporate as widely divergent studies as that of a particular branch of law of a particular foreign system or the relationship between families of legal systems does not prove that comparative law is only a method, but that it unites all the reflective disciplines of legal theory, such as jurisprudence, legal anthropology, legal history, the sociology of law and political science, in a study of the very relationship between rules of law in all their different manifestations and the very conception of law.

The persistent debate about the origins of what we take to be comparative law is bound up with this problem of its purpose and scope and thus with the relationship between perspective and subject matter.[2] But it is more complicated than the contrast between theory and practice. For example, comparative law can be said to have begun with the study of primitive law. Pollock said that as such it made no difference whether one talked of comparative or historical jurisprudence, for the expectation was to discover universal principles of the development of law, such as Maine's famous dictum that 'the movement of the progressive societies has hitherto been a movement from status to contract.'[3] Yet in Pollock's own words the significance of comparative jurisprudence was as 'a handmaid to the theory of legislation.'[4] It was this which served to distinguish the modern practice from all other applications of the comparative method from Plato to Montesquieu.

Although at first it expressed a distinctly idealistic and metaphysical historical perspective, as is evidenced by Comte, Maine, Spencer and Kohler, it was conceived as a new branch of legal science, the subject matter of which was the idea of universal principles of positive law, a practical end. This ambiguous interplay of the universal and the empirical was a result of the application to law of the distinct influences of the comparative method and the idea of evolutionary progress.[5] The comparative method was hailed as an intellectual advance as great as the revival of Greek and Latin learning. It was expected that the comparative study of law would, on analogy with philology and biology, reduce its data to generalized propositions arrangeable according to the essential characteristics of concepts and categories, as if like species they were objectively real and independent of both function and social context.[6] Indeed as early as 1854 a major study of the commercial laws of the world had concluded with a proposal for the unification of commercial law to be achieved by international conferences.[7] Thus, although by the time of the 1900 Paris Congress of Comparative Law the idea of the possible unification of European private law had taken hold, it never quite eclipsed the underlying sense of comparative or historical jurisprudence, because unification was progress and evolution. It has taken two world wars and their qualified successes in international political cooperation to undermine the faith in progress that historical change implied.

Today it is for the relationships among legal systems that we use legal history and not for the grand unfolding of the idea of law. Similarly, the formal analysis of rules of law has been replaced today by the cataloguing and systematizing of laws and solutions as a taxonomic preliminary to a possible universal law. But the realization of the unification of law is left to the piecemeal development of transnational law and the idea of general principles of law recognized by civilized nations because this taxonomy serves to show not the reality of legal concepts but their dependence on the society and culture.[8] In fact it is the underlying and original sense of comparative law as comparative jurisprudence that has come to the fore again. The subject matter of comparative law is as likely to be society, culture or tradition as rules of law.

However, the different conceptions of comparative law that have evolved since the early nineteenth century remain to form the framework of the field of study today. There is, therefore, a tension between science and history as the legitimate cornerstones of comparative law, between its practical and its theoretical value, and likewise allegedly between a superficial and generalizing tendency and an unscientific analysis of incomparable details. It remains true that comparative law is at the experimental and innovative stage and has perhaps suffered from the ambitions of its originators.[9] But it is also true that whether the intent is descriptive, identificatory, explanatory or reformative, there is a relationship between its scope or its subject matter and the perspective adopted on law a whole. Frankerberger identifies four theoretical orientations: the applied, the conceptual, the ethnologic and the functional; each of which results in a different theory of comparative law, method of comparison, governmental type, academic school and political persuasion.[10]

Moreover, this is itself a jurisprudential matter. Thus the two extremes of the scope of comparative law are easy enough to identify. Either it should include 'as much as is possible . . . of all peoples and all times' or it should be limited to the law as seen 'from within and in itself rather than in relation to other human standards of conduct.'[11] Obviously when looked at this way comparative law can, with justification, lend itself to the study of other methods and techniques of law, to the study of different sources and structures of law, of one area of law in different systems, of one system as a social whole or even of the overall relationships between legal systems; but this is because the very nature of law itself is taken to encompass not just rules, principles and concepts but systems of social order.

But it is with regard to comparative law's deeper value that there is most confusion. This confusion reflects a failure to grasp the perspective of comparative law as about the correlation of law and society and apply it to the field of study of law as including its forms, values and processes of development. Thus the ideal of a unified law must proceed upon an awareness of the nature of the legal experience of social order. It is this that comparative law can realistically achieve. It is properly, therefore, jurisprudential for the organization of the materials of comparative study to that end must lead to some jurisprudential conception of law as the experience of order rather than universal or common rules of law. But more importantly, it means that the essence of jurisprudence is actually comparative jurisprudence, as Austin himself realised long ago, though for different reasons, for the desire to know law and see it in its human sense as a manifestation of order is the realisation of comparative legal systems.

Certainly this is a wide claim. Others have claimed a similar importance for comparative law too, however. For example Hall has suggested that anthropology, political science and the sociology of law may form a single legal discipline because legal norms are of primary significance to social action.[12]

It has been said that the utility of comparative law is architechtonic so that no emperico-inductivist knowledge is possible without its general types.[13] Northrop classified law and legal systems into three types: status, contractual and mediational.[14] In such a way Lawson claimed comparative law could verify results obtained by theoretical analysis.[15] In effect jurisprudence and comparative law form the two essential moments of legal knowledge: content and form.[16] But of the two it is jurisprudence that cannot exist without comparative law.[17]

A hundred years ago, Jhering said 'comparative jurisprudence is the method of the future theory of law.'[18] The essence of comparative law is jurisprudence, for it is the fundamental question of the nature of law as the social experience of order that renders coherent its study, whether directed to the unification of law or mere functional comparison.[19] It has its own jurisprudence, for the changing meaning of comparative law over the years is a reflection of alternative perspectives and subject matters thought appropriate to it. But conversely the essence of jurisprudence is comparative law, for its fundamental question, the nature of law, is a question about the meaningfulness of the human experience of order in society. This is a historical, sociological, anthropological and philosophical problem and it is comparative law which makes each of these disciplines see their subject whole.[20]

Moreover, comparative law offers a total overview that none of the other disciplines of law does, for it has within it the dynamic interplay of the search for common and general principles of law and the processes and causes of legal development, both of which are grounded in the basic conception of the experience of law.

II

The idea of law involves more than the substance and procedure of law, its rules, techniques and styles; it involves the relationship of the whole to itself, as an internally consistent form of rational expression of ideals of order or justice. Therefore, it also involves an external perspective of how the whole of law, as defined internally, relates to the whole of society. This is both internal and external, but it is more than doctrine and function. The interrelatedness of both can only be interpreted from the point of view of the life of a participant in the society rather than that of a practitioner or an observer. With an adequate concept of legal experience, the given structural features and the open phenomenological variables of any legal system may be described, whether at the level of rules, categories, systems or families of law. What semiotics brings to this is such a way for interpreting experience through cultural codes that sustain the shared mentality recognized as law.[21]

A complete study of comparative law, therefore, would include a consideration of the interplay between law, society and politics and some overview of the theories and possibilities of social change and evolution. It would obviously cover western, philosophical, religious and simple legal systems, for each connotes a different way of making meaningful the experience of living in an ordered whole. It would analyse the forms and functions of their rules, the social forces and values at work and their theories, the self-concepts of the legal system. If legal systems as a whole are signs themselves of how social interactions are made meaningful, then insight is as likely to be found in the classical law of ancient Greece, Rome, or India as their modern progeny.[22] Therefore, ancient, classical and medieval legal systems have something to say as part of the whole complex of law and order about the nature of legal experience.

On the one hand such an overview combines the analytic, sociological, anthropological, historical and philosophical perspectives with their appropriate normative, factual, interpretive fields of study, whereas on the other hand it is more than a grand overview for it focusses on the very idea of order in society.[23] It is a semiotic endeavor because the experience of order in society may be the one universal attribute of human being and because it leads us to consider the role of law in social organization as a way of our being human. Perspective and field of study, therefore, come together not so much in the combination of all possible approaches but that these approaches lead to the same question, that is, how societies make meaningful the experience of order through law. Thus, the perspective is that of the search for the meaningfullness of experience and the field of study is that of the experience of order.[24]

III

To interpret this experience of law as a semiotic of social order necessitates a conceptual framework.[25] Such a framework must avoid the obvious pitfalls of applying to the whole of legal experience the characteristics of a particular system. Likewise it must not presume an essence to law. Thus the polar opposites of consent/coercion, authority/power, or autonomy/ dependence cannot account for their tension, their balance and their mutual interaction when looked at as parts of the relationship of law to society from the point of view of the person in law. Similarly the classification of historical circumstance as a dynamic of status/contract, rational/irrational or formal/substantive reduces the overall complex of society as an accommodation of self, others and whole into a partial and misleading pattern of characteristics rather than essence. In the latter, all we see is the law's self concept contrasted with its coherence over time. In the former, all we see is the law in its external relationship to the whole analysed as if transcendental to history. These two approaches of the historically contingent and analytically formal can only be brought together if we think of how law affects our experience in society, that is, how it appears to us, how it is maintained and how it realizes itself.

From a semiotic point of view, the conceptual framework of law for the study of comparative legal systems must include the *aspects* of law's *appearance* in social order in relation to religion, politics and ethics, the *qualities* of law's *maintenance*, whether original, reflective or actual, and lastly the *realities* of law's *facts*, its processes, substance and ideals.[26] Comparing law cannot take place with regard to only the rules or the reasoning of a legal system, nor its justification or self image, whether historical or philosophical, for this still assumes a sense to law; the jurist's conception is experienced as already given; the theoretical conception is given in the experience of the observer. Semiotics offers access to this function of law as one of the ways we make sense of the experience of being in society.

The *aspects* of law show how law presents itself as a part of the overall social order. Ethics is constituted by the experience of self with others; in ethics we would do unto others as they unto us. Politics, on the other hand, is constituted by the relationship of others to the whole. The self's actual needs are represented in the political realm as generalized group interests. Moreover, the person is represented by the process as a citizen, an abstraction which necessitates that the personal self be subsumed into a public self which acts towards the whole in a civil or civic fashion on behalf of others. Religion is constituted by the whole in relation to the unknowable. Lastly, law is constituted by the relationship between self and social whole. Thus, it is law's responsibility to universalize particulars and its claim depends on whether its universality can be particularized to the self.

Given then that we can see the *aspect* that law presents relative to the whole of social order, the next level of comparison focusses on the *qualities* of law itself. These qualities will obviously vary according to whether the type of order is religico-ethical, politico-legal and the role of law in the order. What is needed is some way of describing how law's role is legitimated and justified, that is, how law maintains itself in the experience of the participants in the social order, but without reducing the process to one of consent, coercion or coherence. Thus law may be justified according to the basic plan or vision of the social order, that is, its 'original' quality. It may be justified according to its accommodation of interests, desires and needs, that is, its 'reflective' quality. Lastly, it may be justified by reference to its relevance for the conditions and circumstances of the particular time and place, that is, its 'actual' quality.

IV

Again, none of these is alone likely to be an essential characteristic of a legal system, although we can go far in that direction, rather what is significant is the balance and proportionality among them. Basically, the question is whether the fundamental principles or values of the law as part of the whole social order legitimate it; or whether the content of the rules rather than the system legitimates it; or whether the results of its application are the source of its legitimacy. A basic difference can be drawn at once. The emphasis in a religico-ethical social order upon the role of law throughout the continuum of experience between self-whole-others means that the actual quality of law in terms of its fit with the particular situation is the basic justification of law.[27] In the context of politico-legal social order, there is an obvious tension between the justification of law by its conformity with social practices and by its reference to basic principles such as equal respect.

Lastly, in comparing legal systems we look to the *realities* of the law in terms of its content and substance, its process and also its ideals. There we will find the differences of the sources of law, public and private law, judicial review, inquisitorial or adversarial or mediational truth finding and so on among varieties of legal systems. But if what is to be compared includes not just the forms and functions of law, but its forces and processes of development and also their historical and philosophical implications then some means of orienting one's approach to the whole social order is necessary. Thus the significance of codification, a structure of administrative courts or reliance on religious leaders for counsel is seen in the context of how the law is justified and how the law reveals itself in the entire social order. The overall comparison of legal systems, therefore, by way of their aspects, qualities and realities cuts across the usual civil law, common law and religious law typologies for it enables differences within these families to be accounted for in terms of its overall framework.

These are the units whereby comparative law makes sense of its actual world, considered as signs in a text or discourse about the theory of law as experienced in different cultures. The key element to this experience of law is the manner in which norms are constituted as both perceived signs and expressed signs of order. Such an analysis of law itself, however, as opposed to the study of law comparatively, while more basic, will have to wait until some sense of the performative or signalling function of the individual through his or her example in experiencing order is forthcoming. But as regards legal theory and the study of comparative law, this semiotic framework of aspects, qualities and realities offers a tool for unravelling the way law represents order, order is experienced and law gets constituted normatively in experience.

**Stephen C. Hicks is Professor of Law at the Suffolk University Law School.*

ENDNOTES

1. H.C. Gutteridge, 1949, *Comparative Law* 5, Cambridge; J. Hall, 1963, *Comparative Law and Social Theory* 17, Louisiana. See also, Kamba, 1974, 'Comparative Law: A Theoretical Framework,' 23 *I.C.L.Q.* 485 at 488, trans. Weir. North Holland, 1977, K. Zweigert and H. Kotz, vol. I *An Introduction to Comparative Law* 1-2 .

2. Thus, for example, one classification has been 'vertical' and 'horizontal' approaches. The former might be historical legal systems and the latter might be contemporary. Mayda, 1970, 'Some Critical Reflections on Contemporary Comparative Law,' 39 *Rev. Jur. Puerto Rico* 431 at 453. Or, the horizontal approach may be described as a survey, whereas the vertical approach necessitates a thorough immersion in a branch of law of a particular country, Kozolchyk, 1962, 'Comparative Legal Study — Another Approach,' 14 *J.L. Ed.* 2367 at 370. The approach is meaningless without reference to its field of study. The different uses of such terms as 'vertical' and 'horizontal' only serves to warn of the danger of taking different emphases as matters of mere opinion. There is more implicit in the relationship of perspective to field of study than taste.

3. F. Pollock, 1922/1969, 'The History of Comparative Jurisprudence' in *Essays in the Law* 2, Archon. H.S. Maine, *Ancient Law* 100, 1861, Dent 1917. See also, J. Hall, *Comparative Law and Social Theory*, 16.

4. F. Pollock, *Essays in the Law, 2.*

5. For example, F. Pollock, *Essays in the Law*, 1, refers to J. Austin's, 1863/1954, 'On the Uses of The Study of Jurisprudence' in The *Province of Jurisprudence Determined*, 365, Noonday. However, comparative jurisprudence was not concerned with the utility of legal principles and was therefore only descriptive and analytic, according to Austin. Pollock also refers to Darwin, *ibid.* at 25.

6. J. Hall, *Comparative Law and Social Theory*, 3-4, 125, quoting N.D. Whitney, *1875, An Outline of Linguistic Science*, 131, quoting E.A. Freeman, 1873, *Comparative Politics*. See also, F. Pollock, *Essays in the Law*, 22 fn. 1, quoting Amari, 1857.

7. Zweigert and H. Kotz, I *An Introduction to Comparative Law*, 49, referring to Levi's 'Commercial Law of the World; or the Mercantile Law of the United Kingdom compared with the Codes and Laws of the (58) following Mercantile Countries, and the Institutes of Justinian,' 1854.

8. Kozolchyk, 1976, 'Trends in Comparative Legal Research, 24 *A.J.C.L.* 100 at 109. K. Zweigert and H. Kotz, I *An Introduction to Comparative Law* at 54. M.B. Hooker, 1975, *Legal Pluralism, An Introduction to Colonial and Neo-Colonial Laws*, 14, Oxford.

9. Tallon, 1969, 'Comparative Law: Expanding Horizons,' 10 *J. Soc. P.T.L.* 265.

10. Frankenberger, 1985, 'Critical Comparisons: Rethinking Comparative Law,' 26 *Harv. J.I.L.* 411 at 428.

11. The first quote is by Del Vecchio and the second quote is by Sereni. See Wagner, 1962, 'Research in Comparative Law: Some Theoretical Considerations,' in *Essays in Jurisprudence in Honor of Roscoe Pound* 511 at 517, 531, Bobbs-Merrill.

12. J. Hall, *Comparative Law and Social Theory*, 111-112, 117, 121.

13. Tur, 1977, 'The Dialectic of General Jurisprudence and Comparative Law,' 22 *Jur. Rev.* 238 at 245, 248.

14. Northrop, 1960, 'Comparative Philosophy of Comparative Law,' 45 *Cornell L.Q.* 617 at 621.

15. F.H. Lawson, 1977, II *Selected Essays*, 59, North Holland.

16. Tur, *supra* note 13 at 249.

17. Kamba, *supra* note 1 at 494.

18. Quoted in Mayda, *supra* note 2 at 438.

19. J. Hall, *supra* note 1 at 7, 11, 'What is Comparative Law, is not a question in the field of comparative law. It is, instead, a jurisprudential problem.' *Ibid.*

20. Kuhn, 1939, 'The Function of the Comparative Method in Legal History and Philosophy,' 13 *Tulane L. Rev.* 350 at 361.

21. John Deely, 1990, *Basics of Semiotics,* 81, Indiana.

22. R. Kevelson, 1982, 'Comparative Legal Cultures and Semiotics: An Introduction,' 1 *Am. J. Semiotics* 63 at 75.

23. Deely, *supra* note 21 at 61 on the 'umwelt.'

24. Richard Lanigan, 1972, *Speaking and Semiology* 84, Mouton.

25. Cf. Kamba, *supra* note 1 at 485.

26. See my 'A Model of Society for the Comparative Study of Law,' 12 *Rechtstheorie* 215, 1989.

27. Rosen, 1980, 'Equity and Discretion in a Modern Islamic Legal System,' 15 *Law and Society Rev.* 217. Weber referred to this as 'Kadijustiz,' implying its basis to be individual expediency. Rosen's article shows the definite regularities that are implicit in a one by one ad hoc determination. It is my position that these regularities are different from the value of the rules' content reflecting social values or interests and from the system as a whole expressing certain fundamental values.

Chapter Nine

Impressions of a Market Economy in China: Letters of Exchange

Sharon Hom*
and
Robin Paul Malloy*

China seeks to develop a market economy but what is a market economy? How do we recognize such a phenomenon and how does a country *plan* for such a thing especially when planning is itself a contradiction within the market metaphor? Looking at events and elements of Chinese culture the authors of these related essay/letters to each other seek to explore these issues. Sharon, with a Chinese background and years of experience and contact with China, uses her lens of critical theory to explore the boundaries of culture, markets and person in the 'new China.' Robin, with his background in western market theory, uses his law and economics viewfinder to perceive his first time encounter with China. He attempts to interpret his observations against a backdrop of western economic constructions. From different personal backgrounds the two contributors reflect upon each other through the window of discourse, signs and meaning.

ONE
First Impression of My Own

Dear Sharon:

In the summer of 1993, and thanks to you and the CLEEC program, I am making my first trip to China; my first trip to Asia in fact. I've never studied about Asia or China and know little about this part of the world beyond the general minimal knowledge possessed by most 'educated' Americans. I, however, have an open mind, no biased historical readings to overcome, I am ready for anything and everything. A less generous view of my own preparation, however, might be that I am drastically uninformed and unaware of my own cultural presumptions, but after all I am an American and that means I can and should be proud of my boldness.

You've asked me to participate in a three and one-half week program teaching Chinese law professors about American law. My specific topic is to be law and economics and the relationship between law and a market economy. This is a great opportunity for me to learn what the Chinese are up to and to begin spreading my own approach to the subject matter in the world's largest potential market. If just ten percent of the Chinese population would buy one of my law and economics books I could retire on royalties. Oh, for the dreams of an academic entrepreneur.

Anyway Sharon, after twenty six hours in transit I arrived in Shanghai, host city for our program. The very first images of Shanghai were going to make a lasting impression on me so despite it being almost midnight local time and in spite of my lack of sleep I was alert as could be when I stepped off my plane. The very first image that greeted me was impressive, even if not altogether expected. It was in the form of a huge wall poster. Yes, there it was, bigger than life standing proud to greet my arrival at the terminal gate . . . the man that all of China worshipped . . . not Mao, but the Marlboro Man. His western ruggedness, his staunchly independent manner, his blue jeans, his Stetson hat, his leather vest, saddle in hand, surrounded by wide open spaces . . . all proclaimed that the market economy stood proudly and boldly in the footprints of earlier peoples' heroes.

But Sharon, was this metaphor or metonymy? Was the new China the embodiment of America's staunchly independent free-spirited cowboy? Had it become a society ready to reconstruct your deconstructed images of Asian male dominance with a newly constructed deconstructed Western male image? Or — maybe it was just a wall poster, just an advertisement, but what was it selling . . . an American cigarette?

The Marlboro Man entangled my mind even as my taxi driver whisked me down a highway lined with back-to-back billboards advertising everything from electronics to high fashion furs, and luxury condos on waterfront property to pictures of mom taking an entire minivan full of children to the ballpark. I thought to myself, 'who in China has the money to buy these capitalist commodities and why does mom need a minivan in a country with a one child per family policy?' This, apparently, was the New China, the market driven China, the see us as *you* are China.

It was late and I was exhausted when I finally arrived at my hotel, the journey to it having been filled with much confusion concerning my actual destination for the night since there were two Rainbow Hotels within four blocks of each other. As luck would have it, mine was the less luxurious Rainbow. Nevertheless, it had a bed with a pillow and I soon found myself fast asleep.

Sincerely yours,
Robin

P.S. I eagerly await your arrival in the next few days.

ONE
Imaginary Chinas

Dear Robin:

In this space of time and space discontinuities, I finally get around to responding to your first letter. The morning sunlight is filtering through the bamboo blinds as I face the computer screen, acutely aware of concrete materiality, feeling the lures of diaspora. I was so struck by the coherence and self-reflexivity of your 'I' coming into first contact with 'China.' China as distinct, foreign, yet suspiciously reflecting back a mirrored Western rugged male individualism. The Marlboro Man with Chinese characteristics? Or simply the Marlboro Man as triumphant signifier of global capitalistic commodification? China as a potential market of a billion consumers of law and economics texts. But, Robin, your humanistic economics, your comparative perspectival approaches is so foreign (and threatening) to a discursive regime that speaks in totalizing ways about 'perfecting the legal system,' 'correct' analysis of the country's situation, the need for 'scientific' solutions, and of course, always in quantifiable terms (remember the recurring slogans of enumerated evils in mobilization campaigns, the world of 10,000 things?).

Listen to the way official Chinese-speak refers to legal reform goals and achievements: since the reform policies of 1978, 80 new laws (*falu*) enacted, and 58 laws and decisions (*jueding*) amended and supplemented, 550 administrative regulations promulgated by the States Council, and by

1990, judicial personnel, including judges and clerks, totalled 171,609, and the number of lawyers increased from 3,000 in 1980 to 38,708. There you have it, reform by numbers. Your call for examining the ideological bias in both legal and economic theories undermines these assumptions of the desirability and possibility of objectivity, predictability, and ordered rationality. No wonder Posner has been widely translated and understood in Chinese. I don't want to be contributing to academic entrepreneurship, but I do think your work translated (the problems of translation aside for the moment) will be enormously valuable in undermining the hegemony of current Western infiltrations. So, I find myself in dialogue with a law and economics professor!

When I look back on both the trajectory of my China scholarship and my self-descriptions, I notice a shifting from the pacing of a perpetual outsider along the borders of two cultures, yearning for belonging, to hyphenated categorizations (a Chinese-American-woman), to contextualization of be-ing within multiple categories (Chinese-American by culture, American by nationality, Hong Kong Chinese by birth) to a more recent comfort with and embracing of border crossings as a paradigm for interpreting and understanding my own experience. Throughout all of these travels, China has always been imaginary in some way.

I was born in Hong Kong, immigrated when I was five to the United States, and had never set foot on the mainland until I arrived there in 1986, to begin my Fulbright residency. And yet, when our plane landed, as our Chinese hosts drove us through a misty Beijing night, I heard it. The click of a huge missing piece of me falling into place. I almost cried in that space of relief, of inexplicable homecoming. Of course, now years later, it's less clear what that 'it' was. As the Zen saying goes, we find on the mountain top only what we bring up there. Or there is no 'there,' only the illusions that separate us from ourselves and others through false constructions. What I remember was not the image of billboards, though they were certainly already dotting the old Airport Road. What I remember arriving and on each departure is the line of trees, the way they stood, silent sentinels, in the city's struggle against deforestation, the sands and windstorms from the North. There was a time when the storms left sand drifts piled against buildings and in small mountains on the roads.

Rey Chow says in her usual provocative fashion, 'To turn the world upside down, to stake out the right to imagine each other: these are the tasks we are still faced with.' But how are we to engage these tasks without creating ourselves in the imperial mirror? How to imagine each other in non-reductionistic, non-essentializing ways that empower (there is no word for this in Chinese) and honor the other and ourselves in our full unimagined potentialities? How to escape the delusions engendered by the five second sound-bite presentation of China that has plagued the whole history of U.S.-Sino (mis)understandings? How can we transcend the constructions of the American dream avidly followed by mainland Chinese in the immensely popular Chinese soap 'A Beijing Person in New York?' Can we talk about markets in the Chinese context without becoming destabilized by a critical and necessary examination of the untranslatability of basic terms? Was it ever really possible for you to have arrived in China, either open and unbiased or uninformed? What was in your checked baggage? Or your carry-ons for that matter?

Talk to you soon. Let's have breakfast together.

Sharon

TWO
I Am a Market Sign

Dear Sharon:

Well it's my first morning in Shanghai. I rise early at the sound of the guest house staff doing morning exercise drills and marches. The Guest house that you have arranged for is a commercial undertaking of the Army. I guess even the military has to try and turn a profit — or maybe it's just that official pro-market policy requires everyone to participate. In any event, I find that making one's way in China is much like that of the U.S. at least to the extent that money is needed to negotiate the many exchanges of our daily existence.

My first real market adventure, therefore, began with an exchange of U.S. dollars for the local Chinese currency. It was here that I began to appreciate the convoluted approaches to markets favored by the Chinese. 'Change Money!' 'Change Money!' Money changers, official and Blackmarket, were eager to deal in U.S. dollars. There seemed to be no need for English, just name a currency and talk through a calculator. In hotel lobbies, the Blackmarket and street corners, by people age 12 to age 50 or more; U.S. dollars at 9.5; Deutch Marks at 18; Francs, Lire . . . all understood by numbers — numbers on the screen of a handheld calculator. When I didn't respond to the given quotation I was invited to take a calculator and punch in a counter-offer — it's the numbers that talk — the money that's prized — the holder that's marked. By manner, by looks, by style and grace, it's your person that marks you in currency terms. For money and value and profit, too, are related to everything that makes me, me and not them or you.

In simple terms, it seemed that my social existence was being marked by a dividing line of currency walls: A currency wall that marked the distinction between local and foreign.

As you know, and I learned, locals use Chinese currency, RMB, and foreigners are required to use special Foreign Exchange Certificates, FEC. The FEC is the official and legal currency required to be purchased and used by non-locals. The government sets the exchange rate for the FEC. The exchange rate when I arrived in China was about 5.7 FEC to the US dollar. At the same time 'black market' money changers on the street were paying up to 10.4 RMB to the US dollar. The RMB rate was very close to market value for the exchange of US dollars. Thus, the official rate provides great profit to the government. Both FEC and RMB are officially and artificially treated as having the same *face* value even though one FEC is actually worth about 1.7 RMB. Legally, a foreigner is required to pay in FEC for any goods or services even if marked for sale on the street in terms of RMB. Outside of hotels and other businesses that dealt exclusively in FEC, catering to foreigners, there was seldom any way of proving how many foreign customers exchanged with local businesses. As a consequence, revenue at the end of the day could be accounted for by local business people in face value using RMB instead of FEC. Thus, a taxi driver or small business person that was paid 20 FEC for instance could do their own exchange by putting in 20 RMB for the 20 FEC and walk out with the profit at the close of business. Likewise, at tourist locations such as The Temple of The Jade Buddha, ticket takers were openly pocketing FEC and replacing it in the cashbox with face value RMB even though actual values were very different. It seemed, therefore, that the government and everyone else in the society had a profitable stake in the currency markets. And, it took a few losses before I discovered I was being asked to pay in FEC and given change in RMB. No wonder my sellers always worked with a smile.

After a while I began to think that the wall between currencies was symptomatic of a Chinese inability to understand markets. (Free markets, that is.) The policy behind the FEC, it seems, is one of officially sanctioned exploitation. Every foreigner carries the mark or identifier that says 'I am exploitable in *being* foreign I must deal in FEC.' Thus, who you are governs the terms of your exchange and speaks out to merchants inviting them to exploit you for profit.

In China it appears that every man, woman and child that is not a local is a commodity, is FEC, is US dollars, is exploitable because the official government policy declares these people as outsiders. They are welcome to spend money but are never truly invited in. One of my hosts indirectly spoke of this in references he made to the Japanese. He said that the Chinese hate the Japanese but they very much welcome their tourist dollars and their investment. He added that China needed outside investors in order to get rich, therefore being friendly to the Japanese was good business. I believe he meant that the Japanese were commodities, carriers of FEC, therefore they were tolerable and useful for getting rich.

This desire to get rich quick seemed to turn even the most simple business transaction into an opportunity to milk foreign dollars. Everywhere I went I met foreigners having the same negative reaction to the Chinese currency rip-off and its many transactional variations. We all agreed this was far more problematic than anything experienced in our travels to other countries. My explanation for this is that unlike other countries I had visited, China has an official policy that 'marked' outsider. Their otherness was marked not only by their looks but by the currency that those looks represented.

Sharon, are Americans nothing more than dollars: walking symbols of capitalist wealth and excess marked by their success to be both admired and despised?

Well, it's been a very long day and I'm exhausted.

Take care,
Robin

PS. Today I met one of our program hosts from the East China Institute of Politics and Law. He informed me that they have 30 American Indian law students studying at their school this summer. On further inquiry it turned out they were American law students on a summer program from Indiana University.

TWO
Crossing Currency Walls

Dear Robin:

What marks me in China is not the currency I use, but the shoes and clothes I wear. When I was living in China and had acquired a certain no-make-up dusty-riding-your-bike style, there were a number of times that I was stopped, quite roughly in some cases, as I was entering a store or a nightclub, meant only for foreigners, or the American Embassy even. So my experience was as an outsider, or outsider treated as in insider and flipping back and forth. My literal and symbolic 'passport' was the image of the American eagle on the front of my blue passport. This passport provided the access past lines of waiting Chinese dreaming of escape, into the Fourth of July barbecues at the American Embassy, and allowed me all the privileges and immunities of a citizen of one of China's largest trading partners. These multiple (and one might say contested) 'readings' of who and what I was/am suggests not that the PLA guards at the American Embassy were engaged in Post-modernist textual interpretative strategies but rather exposes the East/West, insider/outsider dualities as false oppositional categories. What country coming into modernity has escaped the imprints of the imperialist and colonialist enterprise? Or enterprises? Is it possible today in an increasingly interdependent global market and the globalization of a commodified culture to continue to speak in the language of nation states?

I think that what is happening in China is not that the 'outsider' is marked for exploitation, or as sites for getting rich. There is something much more damaging in the realm of the spirit that will ultimately, already is, threatening the possible democratic and just futures for Chinese citizens. There is a current Chinese expression that China now has three 'lacks' (*sange wu: we daode, wuwenming, wu lianxin*): no ethics, no civilization, no conscience. I read as imbedded in the expression a deep critique of the increasing 'what's in it for me' get rich quick schemes of both officials abusing power for personal gain, of individual citizens, teachers abandoning teaching, of the continuing sexual commodification of women and exploitation of children's labor, and the environmental mortgaging of the future for present profits. A culturally over-determined reading? Perhaps, but my conversations with Chinese colleagues into the night, hearing their pain and despair at the costs and consequences of current market exploitation and that the lines of exploitation are not foreign/Chinese, but perhaps more politically accurately drawn as elite/mass/democratic/authoritarian tensions playing out in the discursive and policy making arenas.

I remember an incident when we were living in China. Jamie was five, I think, and had just lost one of his first baby teeth. Jamie who had been cared for in the States by a Chinese-speaking baby-sitter from Taiwan, Jamie who was attending Chinese primary school in Beijing, Jamie who was forgetting his English, and viewed himself as a *Beijingren* (Beijing person), mistaken by the hotel *fuyuan* as a 'local child' because of his perfect Beijing accent. As we discussed where to put his tooth for the tooth fairy, he wanted me to leave a note for her. He said tell her 'Please leave U.S. dollars.' And she did to his delight and amazement.

Then and still, I now wonder at how my child could so deeply and immediately have absorbed the valuation of different currencies. But then again, it is at that tooth-losing age that children begin to learn the language for demanding one's way in a world not of their making, and then ultimately the languages that shape their capacity to envision alternative worlds. There is a Chinese radio program that I listened to once about a doting Chinese mother and her demanding one child. In one episode, she is coming home from work and is piling a month's wages of chocolates and other goodies on the bed for her little tyrant. The husband complains about her extravagance. She says, it's too late for us. We have to give all the good things for little *baobei* (little treasure). 'Yech' was my immediate reaction. Visions of hyperactive children. In another episode, she is at the store with little *baobei*. He wants a toy, that she tells him is too expensive. He lies on the floor and makes a scene until she agrees to buy it. On top of this she buys him some more chocolate. As she asks for some, he refuses and says, didn't you say that all the good things are for me?

I have never understood the purpose of the program. Was it to instruct what not to do with children? Or what to do? After all, the mother laughs and lovingly takes her little *baobei* by the hand and they go home. There were no markers signifying disapproval of this kind of rearing these last little emperors (*xiaohuangdi*). Yet, in the sociological literature, in the press, and in conversations, people seem genuinely concerned that this generation of one-child-policy children will not know or ever have the experience of sharing, of participating in a collective society. Complaints that the student demonstrators during 1989 were students who couldn't make their beds or had parents (mothers mostly) who go to their college dorms to

wash their laundry. But the solution the following fall on the part of the leaders was to send the students from the most active universities (like Beida) to army training camps prior to the beginning of the term to 'learn discipline' and of course how to make their beds. Is military discipline the only response possible? Will such discipline really produce autonomous citizens capable of participating in a democratic deliberative process? I guess these were not the questions nor the goals. How to shift the questions?
Your friend,
Sharon

P.S. On my last trip to China, the dual currency system had been abolished, as part of China's get into GATT strategy, I think. The prices had been all marked up to reflect what would have been the dual currency difference in paying in renminbi versus waiwai. In the hotel shops, people assumed that I was from Hong Kong. Perhaps it was my Cantonese accent. Then again, it was probably my shoes.

THREE
X Marks the Spot

Dear Sharon:

On my second full day in Shanghai I set out for the 'free market section' of the city. Although the streets were full of tabletop vendors hawking their wares, the impression of a free and open market was quickly shattered after a translator told me to stand back and observe the dickering over goods and prices taking place along the street. While foreigners engaged in heated debates over prices and proceeded from one seller's table to the next, I could observe messengers moving up and down the street in advance of the prospective bidders. I was informed that price information and inventory were being arranged between sellers so that a floor price could be set on similar items between vendors. Once again the images of the free market were stronger than the practice.

Leaving the free market area with my bargained-for memorabilia of Mao, I met up with my wife and daughter for lunch. After lunch we managed to flag down a taxi for a journey across town. Our driver greeted us with smiles and said 'you English, you American.' We confirmed that we were Americans and asked if he could speak English. He said 'You American, America Rich!!' We tried to further the conversation but it became clear that he had learned only a few facts in English which he could repeat but could not really understand much else. He went on with a monologue saying 'Beijing like Washington, Clinton like Deng Xiaoping.' We smiled and said yes. Then he made his hand look like a gun and pointed at his chest and 'pulled' the trigger saying 'Garfield, bang.' Next he took his imaginary gun and pointed at his head and said 'Lincoln, bang . . . Kennedy, bang.' Pointing back at his chest he said 'Reagan, bang no dead.' He said this twice so my wife are both sure of what he said. Then he made some uncertain gestures and waved his imaginary gun around saying or asking 'Clinton.' He said something more about 'you American' but rather than listening I became concerned about this guy's stability. After all, for someone that apparently had memorized only a few facts and words in English I thought his repertoire was very strange.

At about the time that our cab driver was reciting his knowledge of American history a small motorcycle pulled up next to our cab. It had a license plate that began with the letter 'X.' I took the opportunity to change the subject matter and to point out to my wife and daughter that I had learned that the 'X' on the plate indicated it was a privately owned vehicle as opposed to being owned by the government, the party, a work unit, or a joint venture. Our cab driver immediately became very excited and animated. He started saying 'X' and drew and 'X' on his windshield with his finger. We nervously wondered what would come next. 'X,X,X,' he said and pointed to himself. 'Me X, me king, me king here!' Indeed as it turned out he had an 'X' on his license plate which indicated that he owned his own cab. We had been in a free enterprise zone even if it was limited to the interior space of his car. To this cab-driver/owner, 'X' meant empowerment through private property in the market-place. To him it meant entering a doorway currently open to only five percent of Chinese vehicle operators. I learned, however, that it takes both cash and connections to get approval for the 'X' plate in Shanghai. Maybe 'X,' therefore, is not so much a market symbol as it is an emerging new status symbol. Fundamentally, personal relationships are needed to engage in the enterprize, to obtain the 'X' mark. 'X' therefore, may merely mark passage into an inner space of official power. It may indicate one's status within the walls of personal exchange. As long as 'X' is unavailable to those without personal status and relationships it remains a problematic sign for those of us concerned with the development of a free market economy. On the other hand, the emergence of 'X' may mark an important opening in the walls of Chinese commerce and politics. It may be a doorway that weakens the foundations of state control if enough people get to experience the possibilities of independent decision making and the opportunity to come to grips with the risk and reward of private business.

Well Sharon, I know you will arrive tomorrow and our program will start the following day. I will try to reflect on my observations and put them into a final letter that will await you when you arrive.
Sincerely,
Robin

THREE
Cabbies as 'Native Informants' and Lost Dictionary Dreams

Dear Robin:

I love cabbies. In Hong Kong, in China, I have found my conversations with cabbies ranging on everything from the local prostitution business, to legal reform ('there is no law in China' view predominated), to the historical development of the particular city, to women's rights and equality, to current Chinese films, to social reform. Of course, there are questions about the golden cities of America. Once it comes out that I am a lowly academic, here to teach as opposed to cut a business deal, the reaction is usually one of respect. After all, I could be making millions, right? Of course, I have had my share of borderline psycho drivers, one that seemed absolutely intent on killing both of us as he sped in and out of traffic, intent on taking some bicycle riders with us it seemed. He avoided my desperate efforts to make eye contact in the rear view mirror. But on the whole, cabbies have been some of my best teachers, guides, and translators of the China passing us by.

What is that 'X'? It marks the private ownership of the vehicle, and the status symbol of one who has either the *guanxi* and/or the money to pass into some 'inner space of official power' as you note. I am struggling with understanding whether and how notions of 'public,' 'private' play out in the Chinese context. So your observations regarding the shift to a possible site, a doorway for weakening the foundations of state control are interesting.

But what does private mean in the context current privatization (*siyouhua*) drive? State enterprises are being transferred into not only individual (private?) hands, but also into the hands of local governments. The diversification of economic actors in this privatization process has arguably resulted in economic power being diversified, but it has also provided the opportunity for individuals in state power to ensure the transfer into their own or relatives' hands. So the 'X' might also mark the further plundering of 'public' resources by 'public' officials, the appropriation of resources that are desperately needed for collective development.

A story comes to mind invoked by the limited vocabulary available to you as audience and the cabby acting out his bizarre English repertoire. I arrived once at Beijing airport to find myself amidst a sea of Uygur in long robes. There were piles of belongings everywhere, tied with rope, bundled into large net bags, and, visible in many of them, copies of the Koran. I had the odd sensation that I had perhaps landed in the wrong country or city. Then, of course, I remember that China has more than 56 ethnic peoples, of which the Han (of which I am a member) is the large majority. I catch the eye of a weathered nut brown face and the old man smiles warmly at me, wrinkles on his forehead and at the corners of his mouth. I say something to him in Chinese (*putonghua*), but it turns out that he doesn't speak it except for one word. He points to himself, his arm encompassing the crowd of Uygurs, *shamo* (desert) he says. I repeat *shamo*. He smiles and a whole expanse of sand stretching to a distant horizon opens before us.

I once had a powerful dream about finding some ancient Chinese dictionaries, one of those BIG dreams I think. I was in a dark wood bookstore and I crawled under a counter, a kind of crypt-like space with shelves lining the walls. I discovered three sets of blue silk-bound volumes on folding panels of rice paper, nestled in oval bamboo baskets. I asked the man at the register how much they were and he replied $89.90. I say, that's not too bad, and almost buy them with my credit card, but I think it's too expensive and plan to return another day. When I awoke and for a long time afterwards, I have regretted not purchasing them, because try as I may, I couldn't find my way back to that dream store again. It's only been recently as I have been working on my Chinese-English Lexicon project of women and the law that the dream has revealed a different significance. I didn't/couldn't buy the dictionaries not because they were too expensive, but because ultimately they were not purchasable. The price has all the lucky numbers of longevity and fortune, but like the murmur of numerous

disembodied voices that comes to me at that split second before waking, the vision and the tactile memory of holding them, gesture toward discoveries beyond market exchanges. I couldn't buy them. I had to help write them.
Have a good rest and good dreams,
Sharon

FOUR
Tentative Reflections

Dear Sharon:

After a few days of wandering in and around Shanghai awaiting your arrival I began to notice more subtle things than the billboards, neon lights, and currency exchanges that told me a market economy of some sort was evolving in China. Perhaps these things were more subtle because they were so obvious and so pervasive but what I noticed was that everywhere I went there were walls. The housing structures were surrounded by walls, the factories were enclosed by walls, the countryside was burdened with endless miles of walled-in spaces. It seemed that no building, no space, no structure, no pasture could be complete without a wall. Sure, even I knew the Chinese were famous for their Great Wall but what was this obsession with walls telling me about this 'new, open and market driven China?' This question haunted me.

It occurred to me after a while that there were many walls in China. There were literal walls and there were metaphorical and invisible walls. There were walls everywhere, so many in fact that I now think it impossible that the Chinese will ever be able to build a true market economy nor even one approximating the best efforts and aspirations of the West. The walls betray their fear of markets, their distrust of the uncontrolled or potentially uncontrollable. Whether directly imposed or personally constructed they are signs of controlled and limited choice. When linked to geographic space and place they embrace a precapitalist and premarket situated mindset.

Walls, it seems, create order and balance. Walls define space and organize it. Walls create position and status because they establish a place for everything. There are fixed points of reference both within and outside the walls. Walls also have limited access doors and within walls are often found more walls, more doors, and more and more defined spaces. Walls serve a dual function; they enclose and keep in and they barricade and keep out. Walls systematize and rationalize the wide open spaces of unbound nature, of uncontrollable freedom. In China the Marlboro Man is confined to the corral.

A wall mentality is a feudal or tribal mentality. It is a way of thinking that relates to place and space. The world and one's position in it are defined by geographic location. There are insiders and outsiders and each has a specific relative relationship to a defined space. Such a manner of thinking dominated the Western world in the pre-contract era. Feudal and tribal societies constructed social order and identity out of a reference to geographicl space and one's relationship to defined areas of property. Property was status in that your relationship to it defined your membership in a particular tribe or community and 'marked' your position with respect to others. From the point of view of law and economics, property relationships were personal, status oriented and generally anti-market. It was the development of contract that changed this relationship or at least contract became an outward symbol of a fundamental shift in social organization. Contract embodied what legal economists would see as a shift to the impersonal and away from status. Contact focused on voluntary or freely chosen exchanges. It empowered individuals. Together with the rise of capitalism during the Industrial Revolution and thereafter, contract has facilitated a major departure from land or place and space as a point of reference for many issues. Capital is fluid. Capital traverses the globe in an instant by mere electronic impulse. Controlling capital and manipulating it through contract provides status and power independent of physical place.

For a market economy to work there must be open space for creativity and experimentation. People and resources must be flexible and readily movable. Merit and innovation must rise above status and personal relationships. Walls are barriers to markets. In markets, walls symbolize cartels, monopolies, and destructively pervasive government planning.

Until the Chinese come to appreciate the absence of walls, the uncertainly of choice, the potential uncontrollability of wide open space, they will not be ready for the development of a truly free market economy.

Sincerely yours,

Robin

FOUR
Walls, Mirrors and Rock-and-Roll

Dear Robin:

A propo of your story about the misunderstanding about the American Indian law students who turned out to be American students from Indiana University, I thought of Jamake Highwater's explorations of the broader ramifications of such cultural misunderstanding. Jamake Highwater quotes the poet Rene Char; 'For those who are walled up everything is a wall . . . even an open door.' Highwater adds, 'The vistas of all the great windows of walled-up cultures are simply mirrors. We see the world in terms of ourselves.' Perhaps it is cosmic irony that Deng Xiaoping, and the aging patriarchs, the military survivors of the Long March, living in cloistered privilege behind the guarded walled compounds of Zhongnanhai, proclaim an 'open door policy,' moving forward in their bifurcated vision of economic and political reform, avoiding the ghost and spirits across in Tiananmen Square, still echoing, gesturing towards inevitable futures beyond their control.

Grounded in his dual cultural orientation as a traditional Blackfeet Indian and as a Western trained scholar, Highwater makes a passionate argument for the visionary apprehension of 'the other,' the essential heterogeneity of being, and art as the transcending bridge out of solitary confinement. He refers to art in the Indian cultural context as inclusive of everything, the totality without a name. I think of art as one way out of the discursive prisons of official Chinese-speak. Official-speak shifts the terrain of permissible terms, language constructions, and labels, yet always maintaining control over the terrain. Everyone must speak in the approved codes, at least in public forums. And everyone reads the unspoken messages. Is cynicism our destiny?

Rain pours down the gilded gold tiles of the Tianlun tennis court roof. Thunder and a white snake of lightning shocks the gray sky. Bicyclists pass in yellow plastic ponchos, those who still have a long way to go, they peddle against the wind and the rain under a rumbling heaven. I sit settled into an armchair, looking out at the traffic on Wanfujing. A foreigner, dry, inside a five star hotel. I think of the 'animal market,' the dusty line of stalls, a young sleazy guy is pulling small puppies out of a ripped black plastic bag. They are tan, wet with their own urine, unable to walk. An old man peddles by and tries to sell me two rabbits huddled in a straw basket tied to the side of his bicycle.

> *'Xiaobaitu' he says pointing to the black and gray rabbits. A young man squats on the ground surrounded by baby chipmunks in tiny wire cages. A shiny black bird tries to fly out of his too small cage. Again and again it hits the bars of the cage, only to keep trying. (Beijing, June 21, 1992)*

The Marlboro Man, the minivan in a country of one-child families, and advertising billboards proclaiming the dream of luxury furs and condos is at hand. Although MTV, SONY, and AT&T have also arrived in China, no, I don't think this is 'the' new China. Rather, there are many Chinas being negotiated, shattered, envisioned behind these images. In the halls of power in secret (*neibu*) Party meetings, in the Fifth generation films that deploy western international aesthetics codes in national projects of retrieval and cultural critiques, in the appropriation of rock-and-roll by Chinese bands on tours like 'The New Long March' and names like 'The Great Wall,' or the all-women band, Cobra, in the contested sites of what are legitimate NGO acitivites as China prepares for the 1995 World Conference on Women, in the efforts of Chinese in Diaspora struggling with national allegiances and polyvocal subjectivity and experience, and in the cells of Chinese political dissidents, their 13, 15, 20 year sentences witness to the inevitability of a more democratic, open China. We can honor these negotiations by acknowledging their complexity, and conflictedness. And we can resolve to take political responsibility for our complicity for the walls, the mirrors, and the limited and limiting envisioning of choices: — Beyond the open (was it ever?) frontier or a society of commodified exchanges.

Looking forward to continuing our conversation,
Sharon

P.S. I can't help noticing Kate Moss, that girl-child languidly invoking transgressive images of anorexia and sexy children, plastered across the sides of passing buses or huge billboards near train stations in New York, modeling Calvin Klein jeans or underwear with naked vulnerability. I wonder how Chinese visitors read this ad and what this says about 'us.'

**Sharon Hom is Professor of Law at CUNY Law School, Queens College. Robin Paul Malloy is Professor of Law and Economics at Syracuse University.*

Chapter Ten

Corporations and Conflicting Norms: Modal Frameworks for Vague Transnational Precepts

Kevin T. Jackson*

I

An essential task of transnational corporate codes is to set out legal and ethical standards in the form of general precepts, expressed as rights and corresponding obligations for multinational corporations to respect wherever they do business.[1] The precepts cover such areas as human rights, employment, consumer safety, bribery, and environmental protection. However, such precepts are typically vague. Terminology used to formulate transnational precepts must be of the type that can be applied to a variety of legal, ethical, and cultural environments. The precise manner in which the precepts are to be applied and interpreted in such disparate settings cannot be explicitly listed in the texts of the corporate codes themselves.

Consequently, transnational codes are constructed against background conceptions of possibility which influence the way in which managers, executives, jurists, and other individuals apply precepts to facts by interpreting concrete meanings for legal and ethical predicates which denote indeterminate, 'fuzzy' boundaries. Standards for multinational corporations are broadly stated and are thus amenable to differing interpretations, depending on such factors as ideological orientation, level of economic development, and the national legal environment of the host country. Examples of general standards for MNCs in the global marketplace subject to widely varient understandings include obligations to: provide 'just and favorable working conditions,' disclose 'likely environmental harm,' avoid 'improper payments' to public officials, and respect employee 'privacy.'

The referents of many such precepts are not exhausted by extant *concreta* in the actual world. Many precepts have a modal dimension involving possible beings — counterparts of real flesh-and-blood people — who inhabit logical space called 'possible worlds.' On the other hand, precepts set forth what is socially obligatory, and so they express matters of *necessity*.

The abstract concepts of possibility and necessity are sytematically treated in the field of modal logic. This branch of logic is a helpful vehicle for conveying metaphysical baggage into which legal and ethical terms are packed. This paper seeks to explore how some concepts from modal logic — possible worlds, a tolerance principle, and a degree-of-truth framework — apply to problems in interpreting vague legal and ethical precepts from transnational corporate guidelines in connection with business activities in widely disparate economic and cultural milieux, such as those of Japan and the U.S., and in developed versus developing countries.

Law students subjected to the traditional Socratic classroom exercises in 'hypotheticals' consider cases with respect to: (i) their rules and principles, and (ii) possible applications of these rules and principles to factual settings. Suppose some case supports a rule saying that five days is a 'reasonable time' for a promissor to perform under a contract. The professor queries whether the rule would have applied had it been, say, seven days instead of five. What about eight, nine, or ten days? For each of such proposed changed facts the student faces a hard decision. If she continues along in the chain of slightly altered fact situations affirming that the rule still applies, eventually an absurd result is reached: the facts have changed too much for the rule to still plausibly apply. 'No way. Six months just isn't 'reasonable,' period.' However, if the student protests at any single stage that, at that precise point, the rule would no longer apply, she is hard pressed to show why the slight change between the facts at that stage and the immediately preceding stage is significant enough to take the facts outside of the scope of the rule's application. The alteration is, *ex hypothesi*, extremely slight and any demonstration of a relevant distinction made by the student comes with a peculiar sense of uncertainty and arbitrariness, which seem out-of-place, given the assumption that legal judgments are not supposed to be capricious. Vague terms make vague rules. But the existence of vague rules in a system of law suggests that legal rights are not always grounded in determinate, pre-existing standards, but are instead subject to unavoidably arbitrary judgments of those who apply rules in undecidable cases.

The hypotheticals game illustrates a major difficulty in international law and ethics in connection with norm conflicts between home and host countries. A given practice of a multinational corporation in a host country may be viewed as impermissible from the perspective of a home country. The payment of sub-minimum wages to workers in a host country is a good example of this. If we imagine a successive series of possible worlds — corresponding to alternative possible levels of economic development of host countries — with lower and lower levels of economic development iterated through the series, a practice which at first may be interpreted as impermissible comes to seem increasingly permissible, within limits. This kind of counterfactual transformation among possible worlds can be seen in connection with the notion of an 'ethical algorithm' recently proposed as a methodology for resolving conflict of norm situations that confront multinational corporations.

The conflict situation arises when the MNC follows a practice that is legal/moral in the host country, yet illegal/immoral in the home country. The MNC might face minimum wage laws when doing business in the U.S., yet also operate in a host country with no minimum wage standards. The ethical algorithm distinguishes Type 1 conflicts from Type 2 conflicts. In a Type 1 conflict, the lower level of economic development of the host country plays a role in the host's view that the practice is legally/morally permissible. For Type 2 conflicts, however, the moral reasons underlying the host's view that the practice is permissible are independent of the host's level of economic development. Instead, the moral reasons are grounded in religious or cultural values of the host country, for instance, those which condone nepotism, or low-level bribery, in some countries. If the conflict is Type 1, a 'rational empathy' test is used by the multinational manager.[2] Under this test, the practice is impermissible if members of the home country would not, under conditions of economic development relevantly similar to those of the host country, regard the practice as permissible. If, on the other hand, the conflict is Type 2, the practice is impermissible if either of the following are true: (1) it is possible to conduct business successfully in the host country without undertaking the practice; (2) the practice is a direct violation of a fundamental international human right.[3]

But the kind of questions that the 'rational empathy' test poses are not resolvable by reference to empirical facts *simplicitur* but rather implicate counterfactual methodologies imbued with a controversial, interpretive element. There are no assurances that one can arrive at a true and unbiased understanding of what the home country inhabitant's standards would be, assuming their level of economic development was reduced to one commensurate with that of the host country. Instead, there are likely to be a range of alternative possible conceptions of what business practices members of the home country might consider acceptable under the hypothetical assumption that they are living under economic conditions similar to those obtaining in the host country.[4]

What is important to note here is that the 'rational empathy' part of the ethical algorithm is distinctly modal. It requires that the interpreter imagine counterparts in other possible worlds. These are possible worlds because members of the home country do not actually inhabit the world represented by the lowered economic conditions of the host country. Imagine ways in which actual legal worlds might have been different. MacPherson might have owned a Ford, not a Buick.[5] Chaplinski[6] might have uttered those opprobrious epithets with alternative words. Suppose that in *Riggs v. Palmer*[7] the testator had been killed by the beneficiary in response to an explicit request for euthanasia. Would the ruling, and subsequent common law cases based on it, have changed? Considering alternative possible states of affairs on the basis of slightly changed fact situations constitutes the *modus operandi* for the law school game of hypotheticals.

Modal logic is a useful tool in accounting for changes that things undergo. This genre of logic provides a way of analyzing what we mean when we claim, for example, that something must have certain (essential) properties in order to still be the same thing, even though other of its (accidental) properties have changed.

II

Two key concepts of modal logic are possibility and necessity. The sense of possibility that is most significant for modal logic is the broadly logical sense. In the broad sense of possibility, a statement such as 'it is possible that P' means 'there are alternative ways that things could have happened, regardless of how unlikely they might be, such that P would have obtained.' This sense of possibility may be contrasted with another sense, according to which 'it is possible that P' means 'for all I know, P is the case.' This second sense of possibility is the epistemic sense. Because a necessary set of circumstances denotes circumstances for which it is not possible for them not to obtain, the notions of necessity and possibility turn out to be interdefinable. In other words, the statement 'it is necessary that P' means the same as 'it is not possible that not P.' This relation of interdefinability is represented as follows:

$$[]P = \underline{df} - \Diamond - P$$

In this expression, the symbol [] represents 'it is necessary that' and the symbol '◇' represents 'it is possible that.'

The interdefinability of possibility and necessity works in reverse as well. A possible set of circumstances is one for which it is not necessary that it does not occur. This is expressed as follows:

$$P = \underline{df} -[]- P$$

Another central concept in modal logic is that of possible worlds. A possible world denotes an entire set of alternative circumstances. It is a complete state of affairs that might have occurred. Symbolically, possible worlds are represented by lower case letters: **u**, **v**, **w**. Since states of affairs in possible worlds are sometimes considered with respect to the actual world (the way things actually are) it's useful to have a way of singling out one possible world as the actual one. This is done by affixing an asterisk to a lower case letter. So, the actual world is represented as **w***.

The idea of accessibility is used to stipulate which states of affairs from one world may obtain in another distinct possible world. If a set of circumstances in one world is possible in another world, the second world is *accessible* from the first. The relation may be written this way:

Acc(w*,u)

This expresses the stipulation that a possible world, **u**, is accessible from the actual world, **w***. Similarly, for the opposite stipulation — that **u** not be accessible from **w***, we may write:

Not-Acc(w*,u)

The final modal concept to be introduced is that of a counterpart. A counterpart may be thought of as a thing existing at one world which resembles another thing existing at another world. Using the terminology of possible worlds, the counterpart relation may be expressed in the following way:

> For any **x** in a world **u**, if **x** has a counterpart in some other world **v**, then for all **y** in **v**, **y** is **x**'s counterpart at **v** if no object is more similar to **x** as it is in **u** than is **y** as it is in **v**.

The counterpart relation is a three-place one. In symbols representing individuals **a** and **b** and some world **w**, the relation of counterparthood is written:

Cbaw

This symbolizes the statement '**b** is **a**'s counterpart at **w**.'

In deontic logic, the concepts of possibility and necessity are translated into normative concepts of permission and obligation, respectively. There are two primary axioms contained in the deontic system known as system D.[8] The first axiom is the principle of consistency:

(P1) OP ---> -O-P

The second axiom is the principle of conjunction:

(P2) OP & OQ <---> O(P & Q)

In this notational scheme the obligation operator **O** is used instead of the necessity operator [] to express the analogous concept of deontic, or normative, necessity.

In addition, system D contains two rules. The first rule relates to the rule of necessitation of modal logic (if a formula A is an axiom of a theorem of a system M, then the formula [] A is a thesis of M as well). This rule is formulated as:

(R1) P ---> OP

The second rule, known as the consequence principle, is formulated as:

(R2) (P ---> Q) ---> (OP ---> OQ)

System D shows why it is necessary to resolve the vagueness problem in legal rules. Under sponsorship of an argument of impeccable logical form, a vague term in a rule makes it possible that a contradiction results from some state of affairs being judged both **x** and **not x** within the meaning of the rule. Consequently, it is possible that both **OP** and **O-P** might obtain in some circumstances. This contradictory legal state of affairs may be represented as:

(1) OP & O-P

Under (P2) and (1), however, it would then follow that:

(2) O(P & -P)

Formula (2) provides in effect that some individual would be subject to a legal obligation that is self-contradictory and therefore, not possible. The danger of vagueness in rules, then, lies in the possibility of a violation, by (2), of the principle that genuine legal obligations cannot be based on logically impossible or inconsistent states of affairs. (For Kant: 'ought implies can.')

A standard account of vagueness emphasizes the semantic impossibility of applying a vague term in some instances.[9] According to this view, there are cases in which it is not possible to say whether something is, say, 'short' or 'not short.' (Imagine a dispute concerning a contract of sale for 1,000 'short' widgets which, upon inspection, buyer insists are 'not short.') The difficulty remains even when the relevant reference-class has been identified, and the object is the type of thing that is properly referred to as being either 'short' or 'not short' (as opposed to a mathematical set), and the heights of other objects that might be relevant to a comparison are known.

The problem of vagueness in such circumstances becomes a problem of meaning. Something about the meaning of a vague term precludes getting a definite answer as to whether the term applies to a state of affairs or not. All would-be answers seem totally out of place.[10]

It is sometimes suggested that words themselves are not the culprits of vagueness. Under this view, it is thought that words only serve to reveal the difficulty associated with vagueness because certain relative properties denoted by words are not completely specified. According to this argument, it seems awkward, thought it is not a contradiction, to say that an individual is both 'short' and 'not short,' provided that intended meaning is, for example, that 'x is a 'short' American, but a tall ('not short') Japanese.' This sort of example illustrates that the predicate 'short' has to be considered in relation to a properly delimited reference-class in order to generate propositions with truth value. However, it should be noted that giving due regard for this type of relativity still does not get rid of all vagueness. Relative to the class of Japanese persons, it is still not possible to say definitively of certain individuals that they are 'short' or 'not short.' Despite paying correct attention to the relativity of the particular reference-class to the other possible reference-classes, the trouble stems from the vagueness of the term 'short' itself. This opposes the claim that the vagueness of words is wholly a matter of ignoring certain relativity relations.

As a variant of the argument based on vagueness-as-insufficient-relativization, it might be said that the meaning of 'short' is not only relative to some given class, but also to a given standard of height. This standard itself would have to be specifiable with some precision. According to this argument, the meaning of a statment of the form 'x is 'short'' would be 'x is 'short (H)'' where H denotes an exact standard of height. The value of H would be given as, e.g., 'less than the average height of the relevant class.' A difficulty with this argument is shown with the following example. Clearly, it would be agreed that an American whose height is four feet is 'short.' But accepting a precise standard of height (e.g., five feet, six inches) in order to ground all judgments incompatible with this decision would be mistaken. The kind of precision offered as a solution is inconsistent with what the meaning of vague words is normally taken to be.

The vagueness of terms compels us to accept a *de minimis* (tolerance) principle. In connection with 'short,' the principle may be expressed as follows:

> (TP) Relative to any properly identified reference-class of appropriate objects, there is an increment of height i, such that if one object of the class is 'short' and is of height H and another actual or possible object is of a height equal to or less than H + i, then the second object is also 'short.'

It can be seen that (TP) presupposes that for any appropriate class of objects there is some increment of height that does not make a difference with respect to an object's being 'short' or 'not short.'

Accepting (TP), however, leads to some special difficulties. The resulting Sorites paradox (S) may be represented by this two-part scheme:

PART I:

(S1) A_1 is 'short' (relative to an appropriate reference-class of objects C).

(S2) A_1 is of height H.

(S3) A_2 is of height H + i or less.

(S4) For any pair of objects A_j and A_k (from C) if A_j is of height H and is 'short,' then for some height I if A_k is of a height equal to or less than H + i, then A_k is 'short.'

(S5) Therefore, A_2 is 'short.'

PART II:

After demonstrating that A_2 is 'short,' A_2 is then used in another application of PART I. Successive applications of PART I in this fashion eventually leads to the result that some object which is clearly 'not short' is nevertheless shown to be 'short.'

The general structure of this argument may be given as follows:

(SA) A_1 is 'short.'

A_1 is 'short' ---> A_2 is 'short.'

.

.

.

A_{n-1} is 'short' ---> A_n is 'short.'

A_n is 'short.'

Another difficulty connected with (S) results from applying a series of arguments starting from opposite points of the height range. This application eventually leads to the contradiction that some objects are both 'short' and 'not short.'[11]

In order to see how (TP) and (S) pertain to instances of rule-based vagueness, we will need to consider two features which typify vagueness in adjudication. These features are definitional transference and rule-fact application tolerance.

I indicated in a previous work that vague operative legal terms of art contained in rules typically are defined by formulas which themselves function as rules in a legal system.[12] Because a legal definition establishes an identity between the designation of the definiendum and the definiens, the vagueness of a term of art is in effect transferred to a formula, which may be in the form of directives to a jury or a set of standards for a judge. At some point in the decision process of a case, the formula must be applied to facts.[13]

This shifting of vagueness by a definition — a sort of semantical passing-the-buck — is discussed by ethicist C.L. Stevenson in his theory of persuasive definitions. In Stevenson's view, defining a 'just' person as 'impartial' and not 'unduly influenced by personal preferences' functions 'as a schema, helping to delimit the boundaries of the meanings of 'justice' by relating them to those of 'impartial' and 'undue.' No issue is likely to arise about the range of senses that these boundaries mark off, for people's attitudes are sufficiently similar to let them find, somewhere within it, a meaning they are willing to associate with the laudatory term.'[14] Even though the definition fixes the meaning of the term, 'an evaluative issue will reappear . . . when the definiens is applied to concrete cases.'[15]

There are two varieties of legal terms of art involved in the definitional transference of vagueness. The first type is defined by clusters of important criteria cashed out in ordinary language. For instance, legal definitions of 'obscene' incorporate standards like prurient interest, patent offensiveness, literary, artistic, political, and scientific value, and so on. The second kind of term is defined by a *modal* formula. Examples of terms of the latter sort are 'negligence' and the 'reasonable person' from tort law.

III

Looked at in the framework of modal logic, negligence is defined by attributes that a defendant's *counterpart* has in a *possible world*. The standard of negligence is given in terms of what a reasonable person *would have* foreseen when faced with the circumstances the defendant confronts in the actual world at which the allegedly tortious conduct occurs. Specific attributes of the reasonable person's counterpart, such as age, level of education, degree of experience, etc., are identified in various ways with those of the defendant under a body of subsidiary rules.

Using the modal formula for the counterpart relation, where **r** stands for the reasonable person, **d** for the defendant, and **u** for the possible world, the logical relationship established by the legal standard of negligence is as follows:

$$\mathbf{Crdu}$$

According to this expression the reasonable person is the defendant's counterpart at a possible world **u**.

Since law ascribes properties to the reasonable person which the defendant possesses in the actual world, we may represent this arrangement as follows:

$$\mathbf{O_1 \ldots O_n(d,w^*) \dashrightarrow O_1 \ldots O_n(r,u)}$$

This expression states that if **O** is a property (e.g., professional skill) which the defendant has in the actual world (**w***) then the reasonable person has that property **O** in a possible world **u.**

Negligence law asks the judge or jury to decide whether, given that the reasonable person is the defendant's counterpart with certain of defendant's attributes ($\mathbf{O_1 \ldots O_n}$), would the reasonable person have foreseen that such-and-such consequences would follow from an act. Thus, letting the expression **Fxy** stand for 'x foresees consequence y,' we may represent symbolically the propositions which the judge or jury must consider in entering a judgment with respect to the alleged negligence of the defendant **d**. The formula is:

$$\mathbf{[Crdu \ \& \ O_1 \ldots O_n(d,w^*) \dashrightarrow O_1 \ldots O_n(r,u)] \dashrightarrow F(ry,u)}$$

Notice that the knowledge of the reasonable person is evaluated at the possible world where the reasonable person exists, not at the actual world where the defendant exists.

What of the vagueness of 'negligence?' Because the factfinder must evaluate the thoughts and actions of a counterpart relative to those of the real-life defendant, the vagueness that accompanies the decision is exported from the actual world into a possible world. (Of course, the factfinder is *entering judgment* at the actual world.) The judgment itself is of a counterfactual nature *vis-a-vis* the acts or mental states of a merely possible being. The key question is: what *would* the reasonable person have done (or thought) in these circumstances?

Earlier a tolerance principle (TP) was constructed. It will be helpful to have a tolerance principle geared specifically for legal terms in fuzzy rules. This legal tolerance principle must reflect the common-sense intuition that if a term in a rule clearly applies to a given set of facts, then as factual situations with fewer and fewer of the relevant properties in common are considered (the 'hypotheticals game'), it becomes less and less possible for the term — and hence the precept — to apply to those facts. A principle of precept application tolerance (PAT) is given below:

(PAT) Necessarily, any given set of relevant facts F sufficient for the application of precept P could have arisen from a slightly different set of facts G, from any one set of facts from which it could have originated.

Here 'necessarily' means the tolerance remains in force even if particular laws of a legal system, or principles of international law, had been different from the way they actually are. There is no peculiar property of actual norms or the actual facts to which they have been applied that introduces the tolerance.

Stated formally, (PAT) contains a conditional statement attaching the antecedent and the consequent to the possibility operator. This statement denotes that if some state of affairs is a possible application for a precept, then some very slightly different state of affairs is also possible. Here the sense of 'possible' must be restricted from the broadly logical sense that it normally carries in modal logic. For purposes of (PAT) 'possibly P' means 'there are ways cases might have been adjudicated such that P.' Keeping this restriction in mind, the principle is formalized as:

$$[][\ P(F) \dashrightarrow\ P(G)]$$

P(F) represents 'precept P is held to apply to a set of legally or ethically relevant facts F.'

To see how the Sorites paradox is connected with (PAT), let $[\mathbf{w}_1 \ldots \mathbf{w}_n]$ be a sequence of worlds, and $[\mathbf{P}(\mathbf{F}_1 \ldots \mathbf{P}(\mathbf{F}_n)]$ be a sequence of precept-fact applications. Each $\mathbf{P}(\mathbf{F}_i)$ exists in $\mathbf{w}_i$. Assume that a pair of members $\mathbf{F}_i$, $\mathbf{F}_{i+1}$ are different from each other such that as **i** increases, the number of legally or ethically relevant attributes $\mathbf{F}_i$ has in common with $\mathbf{F}_1$ decreases until $\mathbf{F}_n$ is attained, which has *no* relevant facts in common with $\mathbf{F}_1$. The legally or ethically relevant facts singled out by $\mathbf{F_i}$ may be taken as those specified by the definiens of the precept definition for the operative term of art **T** in **P.**

IV

This framework establishes a model of possibilities permitted by (PAT). $\mathbf{W_2}$ is a world which realizes the possibility that $\mathbf{F_1}$ is constituted of certain facts — those which make up $\mathbf{F_2}$ — and the tolerance allows that $\mathbf{F_1} = \mathbf{F_2}$. Then, $\mathbf{w_3}$, which realizes the corresponding possibility for $\mathbf{F_2}$, also realizes a possibility for $\mathbf{F_1}$. Paradoxically, $\mathbf{F_n}$ consists of a completely different set of facts from $\mathbf{F_1}$. Suppose a multinational corporation manufactures and distributes cans of pesticide throughout the world. Distribution of the product in a developed country with high levels of literacy, a standard of 'due care' would dictate that the pesticide cans carry warning labels in the language of that country, even though a small percentage of the population may be illiterate. (A skull-and-crossbones might be a good idea, but is that symbol universally understood to signify poison?) Suppose there is a sequence of possible worlds in which the percentage of literate individuals decreases and the percentage of illiterate individuals increases. The sense in which the written warning label evidences 'due care' diminishes bit by bit. When we reach a possible world where there are no literate individuals, the degree of truth of a precept such as 'C exercises due care by providing warning labels on its pesticide cans' has reduced to 0.

There is a common accompaniment to precept-based vagueness not captured by (PAT). This second aspect of vagueness involves the sense in which saying 'A is short' means 'A is of *notably* slight height.' This sense of vagueness refers to underlying interests or values. The term 'notably' is a value term, whose meaning is not exhausted by factual considerations. This second aspect of vagueness implicates judgments of value or interest, and will be designated (V/I).

Judgments called for due to (V/I) often pose irresolvable disagreement. As a result, disputes about values and interests may appear to be as unsolvable as the hardest cases involving (TP) and (PAT) *supra*. In applying terms of value or interest some reference to human purposes is required, although the appropriate nature and scope of such underlying considerations are not precisely demarcated by the meanings of the terms. Thus, the special difficulty associated with making judgments under (V/I) is not coextensive with the problem of indeterminacy of vagueness associated with (PAT). Some disputes bound up with (V/I) do not involve problems of vagueness at all.

Although vagueness obscures the dividing line between a fetus and a person, the moral debate surrounding abortion would still exist even if a clear dividing line distinguished the fetus from the person. For those who believe that all human concepti are inviolable, the distinction between a fetus and a person is not morally relevant. Even if the vagueness of words was not at issue, the (V/I) dispute would persist.

An important characteristic of (V/I) judgments is that they can influence the truth value of the judgment that is itself in question. Whether an object's height is deemed 'notably slight' can be influenced by the extent to which people actually do tend to take notice of this increment of height in the customary course of making judgments that the height is 'short.' Many judicial decisions have the effect of declaring certain similarities and differences between factual states of affairs significant. In constitutional doctrine, a judgment that the personal sexual relationship between a married heterosexual couple (*Griswold v. Connecticut)* and an unmarried heterosexual couple (*Eisenstadt v. Baird*) is notably similar with regard to contraceptive laws exerts an influence as to which future states of affairs fall within the scope of rules governing the right of privacy.

How is the problem of (V/I) judgment to be dealt with? At least part of the solution lies in recognizing that, to the extent that deciding 'x is short' is founded on a judgment about whether x's slightness of height is notable or not, entering the judgment does not require the discovery nor the declaration of the exact semantic boundaries of 'short.' The peculiar difficulties associated with determining precise boundaries for 'short' do not prohibit entering judgment in all possible cases. When there is lack of agreement about (V/I) judgment calls, it gets harder to make decisions confidently and to give good reasons for coming down one way rather than another.

It may be necessary to just draw a line, declaring the boundaries of the property without justifying the exact routing and contour of the line inscribed as against other possible lines. However, it is not clear that judges and jurors are burdened with discovering or declaring definitive boundaries obscured by the vagueness of legal terms *simplicitur*. What they are doing instead, with respect to (V/I) problems, is entering a judgment of value in a particular case. This is not to say that the judgment is one that will be fixed in all possible worlds in which the rule is applied.

V

The province of drawing lines for all possible worlds of legally relevant fact situations is principally for the legislative, not the judicial branch. Making a decision in a particular case is, in effect, to lay down a rule for all possible cases in the sense that other cases *of the same kind* would have been decided in the same way as the case at hand. It is reasonable to think that other cases similar to the particular case will be decided in a similar fashion. But there remains a distinction between deciding a particular case by applying a pre-existing rule to it and formulating a new rule *ab initio*. This critical distinction tends to pass undetected due to the cumulative weight customarily accorded judicial decisionmaking (though not to decisions of juries) over time. The weight of precedent confers a unique disposition to establish patterns for an indefinite number of future cases on the basis of what is decided in a particular case. This causal influence gives the appearance of a rule to what are actually discrete judgments rendered in particular cases.

The difficulty associated with (V/I) judgments which must be entered in connection with vague terms is resolved by the recognition that it does not pose a threat that judges (or jurors) are making law — that is, formulating rules — merely by drawing boundaries to establish the contours of properties made unclear by the vagueness of the terms which denote them.

Principles of construction regulate the interpretation of texts containing vague language such as wills, contracts, and statutes. Moreover, judicial reasoning associated with case law appeals to general principles presupposed by a body of decisions and by the legal system as a whole. However, even with help from higher-level standards, all problems of legal interpretation are not resolved. Plausible arguments can often be advanced for either of two conflicting results. Nevertheless, there is good reason to suppose that deep interpretive problems remain compatible with, or perhaps even central to, a sophisticated conception of law.[16] This conception is due in part to the important role played by existing legal standards which preclude absolute discretion and arbitrariness in the formulation of a judicial decision. Further, legal interpretation is subject to a demand for argument based on reasons.

On the other hand, metaphysical problems of vagueness are intractable in a way that these interpretive problems are not. It is commonly thought that vagueness gives rise to hard-core undecidable cases. It is not as if the answer is to be found by a superhuman judgment based on an elaborate theoretical interpretive construct. Instead, as a matter of meaning, any possible answer is necessarily arbitrary and wrong. According to this view, there is something about the nature of language that prevents legal rules from attaining what is required of them. We expect judges and jurors to decide cases according to rules (the rule-of-law). Yet if no answer is even in principle possible, then any one answer is as good as any other. The presence of vagueness in rules seems to be inimical to the concept of the rule-of-law.

VI

In sum, the basis for the distinction between classical normative problems of legal interpretation and the special metaphysical problems of vagueness may be stated as follows. The problems of interpretation are always susceptible to some further reasoned argument and a call for justification of a kind that can ultimately be grounded in some more or less coherent background theory of political morality. The problems of vagueness, however, are logically isolated from this type of influence of reason, since nothing could possibly count as a reason for deciding one way or another.

The resolution of the Sorites paradox associated with (PAT) is based on the following idea. If an object or state of affairs has been authoritatively held to be within the scope of a given term of art, there is a set of properties possessed by that object or state of affairs which may be identified as the legally or ethically relevant properties grounding that judgment. As sets with properties that have fewer and fewer of the legally or ethically relevant characteristics are considered, it becomes less and less possible for the object or the state of affairs to be encompassed by the term of art and hence, fall within the meaning of the precept. What is needed is a schema representing *degrees of possibility*. If some particular object or phenomenon represents a possibility for the extension of a rule, then some very slightly different object or state of affairs is also a possibility for its extension.

An example will illustrate this idea. Imagine a connecting series of possible worlds in which we move from a paradigm case of an object to which a precept clearly applies to a paradigm case of an object to which the precept does not apply. Let the precept be **P**: 'No vehicles are allowed in the park.' Let the object in $\mathbf{w}_1$, where the precept clearly applies, be an automobile. The object in $\mathbf{w}_n$, where the precept clearly does not apply is, say, a baby stroller. If the definition of 'vehicle' for purposes of **P** is 'any dangerous conveyance,' then we may suppose that the set of relevant properties possessed by the automobile are those which make it a dangerous conveyance: its engine, steel body, heavy weight, etc.[17] We may suppose that there is a world $\mathbf{w}_k$ somewhere in between the two extremes which contains an object exhibiting some of the relevant properties of each of the two object in $\mathbf{w}_1$ and $\mathbf{w}_n$, for instance, a motorized baby buggy.

In terms of this example, if an automobile has more of the relevant properties which make it a 'dangerous conveyance' than a motorized baby buggy, then the automobile is a 'vehicle' to a greater degree than the buggy. Because the notion of satisfying a predicate is correlative to the idea of truth value of sentences, it may be said that the assertion that the automobile is a 'vehicle' possesses a greater degree of truth than the assertion that the motorized baby buggy is a 'vehicle.'

A degree-theoretic framework will assign degrees of truth, ranging from a value of 0, representing absolute falsehood, to 1, representing absolute truth. Referring back to the previous example, we assign the highest degree of truth to the proposition that 'an automobile is a 'vehicle' for purposes of **P**,' and the lowest degree of truth value to the proposition that 'a (non-motorized) baby carriage is a 'vehicle' for purposes of **P**.'

The degree-theoretic framework can be expressed formally to depict the underlying structure of the apparent paradox of vagueness. The structure defuses the threat of irrationality which so far has seemed to haunt the rule-of-law.

In systems of logic with only two values, the connective 'or' (**v**) operates to assume the higher of the values of disjunctive components. The following formula for disjunction (D) may be given for the degree of truth framework:

(D) Val(P v Q) = Max[Val(P), Val(Q)]

The table below reflects computations of values for this formula where 0 is assigned for absolute falsehood and 1 is assigned for absolute truth:

P	Q	P v Q
1(T)	1(T)	1(T)
1(T)	0(F)	1(T)
0(F)	1(T)	1(T)
0(F)	0(F)	0(F)

Simiarly, the connective 'and' (**&**), which serves to assume the lower of the values of the conjunctive elements, gives rise to the following formula for *conjuction* (C):

(C) Val(P & Q) = Min[Val(P), Val (Q)]

Again, a table may be constructed to show the different values:

P	Q	P v Q
1(T)	1(T)	1(T)
1(T)	0(F)	0(F)
0(F)	1(T)	0(F)
0(F)	0(F)	0(F)

The formula for the operator 'not' (-) expresses the degree to which the sentence that has been negated drops below the value of absolute truth (1). Thus, *negation* (N) is represented as follows:

(N) Val(-A) = 1 - Val(A)

The table below shows an application of (N) to the values 0 and 1:

P	-P
1(T)	0(F)
0(F)	1(T)

For implication, the most critical element in the argument connected with (S), it is clear that the formula needs to account for the difference in the degree of truth between the antecedent and the consequent. This aspect is captured by the following formulas (I):

(I) Val(P ---> Q) = 1 - [Val(P) - Val(Q)] if Val(P) > Val(Q)
Val(P ---> Q) = 1 if Val(P) $\leq$ Val(Q)

The table below shows how the degree of truth formula reflects the difference in truth value between the antecedent and consequent. When an antecedent has only a marginal degree of truth above the consequent, the conditional statement has just marginally less than absolute truth. This situation is shown with a replacement value of 0.9 for **P** and 0.8 for **Q**:

P	Q	P ---> Q
0.9	0.8	1 - [Val(0.9) - Val (0.8)] = 1 - 0.1 = 0.9

Similarly, if an antecedent is a good deal more true than a consequent, then the conditional statement becomes much less than absolutely true. This situation is shown with a replacement value of 0.9 for **P** and 0.2 for **Q**:

P	Q	P ---> Q
0.9	0.2	1 - [Val(0.9) - Val(0.2)] 1 - 0.7 = 0.3

The formulas (D), (C), (N), and (I) serve as a way of resolving the paradox of vagueness (S). To see why this is so, we may return to the example involving the term 'short' previously used in connection with (S) and (TP). Consider a series of individuals $A_1 \ldots A_n$. Each individual is slightly taller than the preceding one. Further, assume that the statement 'A_1 is 'short'' is completely true — its degree of truth is 1; and the statement A_n is 'short'' is completely false — its degree of truth is 0. In two-valued logic, the tolerance associated with 'short,' expressed by the principle (TP), means that the following conditional statement is true:

A_1 is 'short' ---> A_2 is 'short'
where A_1 = height H, and A_2 = height H + i or less

As demonstrated before, such conditional statements were used to construct the valid argument (SA). However, if (SA) is deployed to reach the (absurd) conclusion that some person A_n seven feet in height is 'short,' then it appears suspect. The principal virtue of the degree of truth model is that it shows more precisely what is occurring in each step of (SA).

In each stage of (SA) the degree of truth of the antecedent is slightly greater than that of the consequent. This occurs because each immediately preceding individual in the series $A_1 \ldots A_n$ is slightly shorter than the next succeeding individual. According to formula (C), each conditional statement in (SA) falls below absolute truth by a small degree. The degrees of truth possessed by each conditional statement in the sequence that makes of (SA) gradually approaches 0 truth value.

When the objects and states of affairs to which fuzzy precepts are to be applied are compared across possible worlds (as in the hypotheticals game), degrees of similarity are assessed in a variety of respects. In the discussion of the Sorites paradox, however, only one property — shortness — was held variable. But singling out only one feature for comparison in this way oversimplifies legal reality. Previously in this article it was noted that the vagueness associated with 'short' is uni-dimensional. The vagueness associated with most terms of art in fuzzy precepts is multi-dimensional. A state of affairs falling within the extension of a precept may be similar to another state of affairs with respect to one legally or ethically relevant property, but dissimilar with respect to another relevant property. Multi-dimensional vagueness may be handled under the degree theoretic framework as follows. First, an expanded model is constucted. If the expression of a single feature of similarity is given by a pair of numbers in the interval **[0, 1]**, then the expression of two features of similarity is provided by an expansion to:

$$[0, 1] \times [0, 1]$$

The expanded model derives from a component-wise extension of the relation 'less than or equal to.' Of course, it is not necessary that the number of aspects of similarity be limited to just two. Accordingly, the degree of truth model can accomodate **n** aspects of similarity with the following modification:

$$[0, 1]^n$$

Apart from its merit in giving an anatomy of a Sorites argument, the degree theoretic framework, as applied to (PAT), fits our intuition that vague transnational precepts carry various *degrees of weight* which come to bear importantly on the enterprise of analogical legal and ethical reasoning.

**Kevin T. Jackson is Professor of Philosophy at Fordham University.*

ENDNOTES

1. Many international declarations, treaties, and conventions also contain generalizable provisions which require, in many cases, elaborate interpretation to determine their applicability to nonsignatory nations and to factual circumstances not specified in the language of the documents. A large amount of interpretation is also involved in determining which, and to what extent, human rights initiatives impose legal and ethical obligations on certain nonstandard addressees of the rights, such as corporations and individuals. Thus, although the U.N. Charter states that all member nations shall promote basic freedoms without discrimination as to race, gender, language, or religion, is seems reasonable to take the human right to freedom from discrimination, especially in employment contexts, as properly addressed to corporations that are operating in the member nation-states.

2. I have argued elsewhere that an idealized jurist or moral philosopher — dubbed Grotius — instead of a multinational manager or executive, should be taken as the supreme authoritative interpreter for such obligations of multinational corporations. In light of the deep level of theoretical disagreement involved in many applications of the ethical algorithm, such an impartial global jurist appears to be better equipped to produce the best interpretations. If the corporation's own leaders are free to interpret their own obligations, they may tend to be unprincipled, self-serving, and inconsistent, and inclined to follow goals of inadequate justifications such as economic efficiency and maximization of wealth, instead of conforming to principles of justice, fairness, and due process. *See*, K. Jackson, 'Jurisprudence and the Interpretation of Precepts for International Business,' *Business Ethics Quarterly*, Volume IV, Number 3, July 1994.

3. T. Donaldson, 1989, *The Ethics of International Business*.

4. It is not clear that it can be definitively declared just what the home or host country's domestic legal and ethical standards are in hard cases involving pronounced intra-national dissensus. For instance, in areas such as capital punishment, abortion, affirmative action, gay and lesbian rights, etc. Donaldson's procedure incorrectly assumes that juridic interpreters will be able to identify a clear home norm competing with a clear host norm. If that were so, the only difficulty would be to determine which of the two alternative domestic standards is preferable. However, in hard domestic cases there is often room for reasonable disagreement over just what the law or community morality of an individual country is. In the United States, for example, there is a good deal of dispute about whether various kinds of affirmative action (such as hard quotas) are in line with the provisions of Title VII of the Civil Rights Act. These sorts of reasonable splits of opinion may result in an array of multi-faceted international conflicts when multiplied by a number of different countries with similar intra-national differences in interpretation.

5. *MacPherson v. Buick Motor Co.*, 1916, 217 *N.Y.* 382, 11 N.*E.* 1050.

6. *Chaplinsky v. New Hampshire*, 1942, 315 *U.S.* 568, 62 *S.Ct.* 766.

7. 115 *N.Y.* 506, 22 *N.E.* 188, 1889, grandson murders grandfather, but unable to inheret under the latter's will according to principle that noone should profit from their own wrongdoing.

8. Hilpinen, 1985, 'Normative Conflicts and Legal Reasoning,' eds. E. Bulygin, J. Gardies and I. Niiniluto, in *Man, Law and Modern Forms of Life*, 191.

9. Alston, 1967, 'Vagueness,' ed. P. Edwards, VIII *Encyclopedia of Philosophy*, 218.

10. W. Alston, 1964, *The Philosophy of Language*, 85.

11. The history of the argument is treated in Moline, 1969, 'Aristotle, Eubulides and the Sorites,' 78 *Mind,* 393-407. *See also,* Black, 1963, 'Reasoning with Loose Concepts,' II *Dialogue*, 1.

12. Jackson, 1985, 'Definition in Legal Reasoning,' 25 *Jurimetrics Journal,* 377.

13. *Id.* at 382-84.

14. C.L. Stevenson, 1944, *Ethics and Language*, 223.

15. *Id.*

16. This view is argued for in R. Dworkin, 1986, *Law's Empire*.

17. An accessibility relations, patterned after the concept of jurisdiction is assumed to ensure that each of the worlds $\mathbf{w}_1$ through $\mathbf{w}_n$ is subject to **R**. That is, in our example, if **R** exists in **w***, then $\mathbf{Acc(w^*, w_1 \ldots w_n)}$.

Chapter Eleven

Boyle's Lock'n'Key: Consent and Contract

Roberta Kevelson

I

Not surprisingly, even the Crits have taken their place in the bazaar of neo-conservatives, since that is the fate of all revolutionaries who survive and become symbolic signs and referent ideas. Their presence, incongruous among defunct dissenters, is especially a kind of oxymoron, because they are not part of the very inconsistencies and internal contradictions of so-called classical liberalist law which, as a group, they targeted. It is a flaw in the message of Critical Legal Theory that it chose to focus on the inconsistencies, 'repugnancies' and conflicts of law within liberalist law instead of riding the crest of indeterminacy, internal contradiction and legal paradox as a new wave: a turbulence welcomed and embraced. They have pointed to paradoxes in the law as through contradiction of law were not an opportunity, a structural aspect of law's capacity to evolve and transform itself in its representation of social values. The Critical Legal Studies Movement, in general, has attempted to touch consciences higher than the law, to suggest that at the core of the law is no conscience at all, but the hard, materialistic fact of legal property only. This legal factiveness of the idea of Property is, the Crits claim, a fiction fashioned by the status quo to conserve and save itself.

But there are new voices arguing strongly against assumptions held by spokespersons of the CLS group, and they want to show that Civil Rights and Property Rights cannot be understood except in relation to one another, that they are relational terms in Peirce's sense, just as 'child/parent'; 'student/teacher'; 'vendor/buyer' are relates only and are unthinkable other than relationally (Altman, 1990; *Critical Legal Studies: A Liberal Critique*; see also Riker, in Frandel and Dickman, eds, 1990;49-64; Kevelson, 1994). This emerging dissent against the position of Critical Legal Studies is a process of dissent in general, regardless of the subject material; it is a going-against-the-grain of any wood whatsoever. New criticism of the Crits is itself a continuum of a consent to dialogue, to interact and to oppose.

That skeletal dissent process, its logical bones, is the characteristic structure of a 'liberalistic law' as Locke gave it early expression modelled upon, as I see it, the image of his good friend and counterpoint, Robert Boyle: the lock'n'key icon underlying the relational concept becomes the dominant mark of Legal Realism following Holmes, and Legal Semiotics following Peirce.

Yet James Gordley for one (1991) argues that law has lost philosophical moorings. We have no longer (if we ever did have) a clear notion of the philosophical underpinnings of our modern contract doctrine, in commonlaw societies in particular.

At the outset I want to call attention to the fact that far more than a genealogy of law's philosophy is wanted, especially for contract and property. Significantly absent is a philosophical, theoretical appreciation of the role of contradiction and its congeners, incongruity and repugnancy. Indeed, the law is not a determinate and neat institution or text. But it is an artifice, a fiction, an artwork, and as such is indeterminate. All open systems may increase and indefinitely evolve in significance by such a process of dynamical interpretation. This is not a defect, as the CLS mavens present it. It is precisely this premise of fallibility, of sustained and complexly expanding paradox, that needs a new hard look from a prejudiced semiotic eye.

The invention of a new theory is the invention of a new kind of instrument. Peirce's theory of signs and theories of complex, dynamical systems at this edge of the millennium are becoming relates of a method of observation and a mode of explanation without precedent. Origins, or grounds of the emergence and initial development of an idea, is not the same as a repetition of that idea in some other field. But each 'appearance' constitutes a reinterpretation of a referent idea and a new dimension to its growing complexity. Therefore, if we see the Peircean idea of a semiotic development of thought interpreted, directly and indirectly, in other discourses, in other inquiries, we know that this new offshoot itself becomes an opportunity for occasions of chaos and instability and hence of change in a transforming and not merely incremental way. A qualitative change is just this: a transformation of a general idea. This process is essentially a dynamic transaction of meaning that is regarded as goods and values with respect to an encoded or consensually and contractually agreed upon medium such as money, as counters of various kinds. I will come back to this concept of transacting value through signs or mediation in the concluding part of this paper. In particular I will connect the legal notion of 'consent' with Hayekian views on the growing significance of values as a result of an ongoing exchange consensually held by consent of viewers or players. E.g., Hayek says that most 'relativistic positions on questions of history, culture, or ethics are derived from the erroneous interpretation of the theory of evolution,' which fails to grasp the principle of a provisional, non-relativistic set of referent principles, (Hayek, *Studies* . . . 1967/1980:38).

It is one thing to show that all value exchange is relational. It is quite another to assume that to go beyond the notion that our acts and ideas are relative with respect to their ability to evolve into new significance is to say that value is merely the expression of arbitrary power and will. From this viewpoint, and from Peirce's, a consensus is never the result of relativism, and neither is it the determination of an external authority upon members of a community. Rather, the capacity for self-determination — for self-governance and self-organization — pertains to choosing partners or relates in self-binding and contractual ways. Hayek's point is that all human values relate to *something*. While we may not see the relate to which a given value is relative, we correctly judge our values to be relational, (Hayek, *ibid*).

Every science builds on its substratum of theories. The law is no different in this respect, as Hayek suggests in his 1959 paper on 'The Logic of Scientific Discovery,' (p. 59): 'Observation is always *observation in the light of theories*.' This is not a nominalistic or constructivist position: it is a semiotics position which holds that a new idea emits a force and irradiation and thus makes disclosure of something new into a possibility. Discovery of the meaning or significance of phenomena come *after* the image in the mind, or the manifestation of the initial Quality or Icon. Thus the world viewed is not the world observed, but is the *occasion* for it only. The idea of consent, or the idea of a social contract, is theory that seeks to explain the phenomenon of interpersonal exchange and voluntary cooperation in whatever falls within the broad definition of human organization as a self-referring and self-determining empirical fact, (Hayek, *Studies*, 1967/1980, Ch. II, pp. 23-24). This is also pure Locke!

Frank Michelman is said to have spearheaded a new movement which is not in the path of CLS, nor is it 'liberal' (in either neo or 'classical' senses), but has been dubbed a 'civic republicanism' or revival/reinterpretation of ideas that have their roots in the closed Aristotelian cosmology. The objective of this revival is to reject the liberalist's premises, as the Crits have also done, and with this rejection to declare the old liberal and

Realist's 'pluralist presumptions' oppressive of the many and also punitive with respect to a genuine dialogic jurisprudence. Michelman rejects the authenticity of the old idea of the 'common good' as an idea which has outlived itself. But he retains nevertheless the shape of this idea as a kind of touchstone or useful referent, since so much social emotion is tied to it still, (Michelman, 'Law's Republic,' *Yale U. Press* 97 1988:1493; see also Stephen Feldman's repudiation of the position of the 'Civic Republicans,' because of the flaws in their discourse, and the weakness of their case as presented, (*Georgetown Law Journal*, 81 1993:2243-90).

According to Feldman's understanding of Michelman's argument true dialogue cannot result in any consent of a legitimate nature unless each and every member of the community takes part and none is coerced, manipulated, dominated or pressured by power forces in any way, (ibid:2245). Thus no absolute dialogue is ever possible one might well conclude. From Michelman's perspective *no consent can be or ever is legitimate*.

Here, too, as with the Critic Legal Theorists, an all or nothing totalitarian, and utopian perspective makes the actual society always inferior and defective compared with the *ideal* model. Instead of the actual being occasion for wonder and for celebration, actual human society viewed here is a shame, a failure, and an embarrassment; it is an example of unrelatedness and inhumanity. In short, this new republicanism, as its cousin CLT, is a kind of self-hatred, self-denial, and abjectivity, that masquerades in moral mummery, (this is not Feldman, but Kevelson).

Feldman *almost* puts his finger on the rotted core of these critiques of liberalism when he asserts, as did Peirce, that all arguments are fallible, that we begin with our prejudices, i.e., with the acceptance of ourselves in relation with our world. This is not truth. This is not axiomatic. This is not pure. But this is not escapist either and not cowardly and not ascetic. Feldman suggests that our prejudices do not spring full grown from the god's ear. But they are based on our communal experience: 'Prejudices derived from communal traditions . . . are prerequisites of communication and liberation . . . (they enable us to understand) . . . ' We understand in a commonsense fashion, an experiential mode that which we then may observe in principled manner, and shape into theory as one shapes clay, chisels stone, carves wood even against the grain, (see Feldman, above for analysis of Michelman and ilk, especially at 2245-48).

These New Republicans, like the Crits, reject not only the premises underlying liberalism, but they reject even more fervently the power forces and property holders that call the shots. Without digressing here to remark in any detail that the concept of Property so thoroughly rejected in these antiliberalist views is largely one kind of representation of the concept of legal property *only*, namely that concept of Property which traditionally refers to Real and other tangible goods, private and public, and which are exclusive with respect to the rights of the holder.

They seem not to want to consider Adolph Berle's still astute observation that 'legal property,' as representing Real Property, is transformed into the power of ideas by the middle to end of this twentieth century. Today power is, or may be, represented by the 'new property' (as Charles Reich noted several decades ago). Especially in our time power is representable by ideas as signs, i.e., by 'intellectual property' of all kinds. The intellectual property capable of bringing abut social change and political consequences on national and global scale is not unlike the old property allegedly despised by Crits and New Republicans alike. Their medium is intellectual goods and counters, but these are no less intended to effect and profoundly influence society than is territory and gold, now as in olden times. Intellectual Property is no less inaccessible, on any scale invented to measure it in distributable units, than the resources of a nationstate could have been, or could yet be, reduced to a finite amount and cut up into fair and equal parts, so that every member of the society conceivably may share in equal manner. Thereby consent and consensual participation in the goods of the society may be fully realized. But Intellectual Property is not assumed by either Crits or New Republicans to be part of the common store.

Feldman does not quite say this. Hayek has come close. But I say that the arguments for rejection of liberalist law are not only fallacious but are malicious. This malevolence is nothing other than a masked greed in the name of social morality. We call it *PC*!

Altman also has identified a fatal flaw in the CLT charges: this has to do with what he sees as their skewed judgment of a 'liberal conception of law,' (Altman, above, at page 105). The CLT's presupposition is that a 'liberal' legal system must be not only cleansed and purified of its internal inconsistencies, but its very structure is the cause of its internal rottenness. It must be eliminated and replaced with a system less prone to human foibles. So the Crits imply.

It is worth mentioning before going on to the next section that even Bentham's horror of the repugancies in the law was slight in comparison with the nihilism of the Crits. Bentham may have not grasped the logical relational structure represented by Boyle's image of consent, nor of Locke's corresponding theory, but as Ross Harrison points out so well in his study of Bentham, 1983, Bentham was unyielding on his affirmation of the interdependence of liberty and property and law: 'Property and law were born and die together,' Bentham said, (from the manuscripts housed at University College in London, Book 32: 151, cited in Harrison, pp 250-51).

In passing, Bentham clearly distinguished between tangible property and intellectual property, just as he distinguished between intellectual and practical actions as two kinds of motives and motive forces, (Bentham, *Principles of Morals and Legislation*, 1780/1948:97-98). He speaks of 'figurative' representations of the idea of 'motive' in the sense that Peirce would regard as a 'figure,' i.e., as a *rhetorical*, consequential force of an idea, (Bentham, above, at p.99).

II

It is useful to step to one side for a moment and to consider the possible repercussions of the fact that Bentham not only distinguished between tangible and intellectual property, but also strongly resisted the possibility that fictions in law derived from two mutually exclusive modes of the non-tangible, *imaginative* aspects of the law.

In particular, Bentham insists that the kind of legal fiction which functions to represent referents and precedents in the law which do not exist, but which are needed to effect a confidence in the law's stability, is different in kind from the legal fiction which presupposes an 'original' and actual social contract; such a presupposition is assumed as the ground for 'consent' in Locke's sense.

This is the worst kind of legal fiction; Bentham regards it as the 'pestilential breath of fiction,' especially in his commentaries on Blackstone's Commentaries, in which, ironically, the Lockean notion of a contractual 'consent' is affirmed.

One may not, Bentham argues, begin with anything short of a 'true premise,' in justifying legal principles. To do otherwise is to degrade the entire foundation upon which the Common Law rests: if a social contract is taken to be anything but an historical event, i.e., a factive event, 'any supposition that there is is merely fiction or fabulous,' therefore invalidates the entire argument of 'The Law,' (see discussion in Harrison 1983: 37-40; cited from Bentham's *Comment on the Commentaries*, in *New Collected Works*, eds. Burns and Hart, 1928).

Despite Bentham's enormous and much-declared indebtedness to Locke, it is from Locke that Blackstone appropriated, or misappropriated, the unforgivable 'fiction' of social consent. On the one hand, it is Locke that provides a method of 'making our ideas clear' (note, Peirce's reinterpretation of that notion for his own seminal 1870's essay with that title thinly paraphrased or disguised). Bentham, indeed, sees himself as following Locke's exemplary mode of making our ideas clear. It is Locke, rather than Descartes, he chooses as mentor even as he resists and rejects the very assumptions Locke holds in his advocation of hypotheticals in inquiry. Perhaps it is Locke's most important distinction between simple and complex qualities in ideas that Bentham fails to correctly grasp. But he is in good company, and for a very long time, at least as long as it takes Peirce to recast the problem in semiotic, mediational terms. This problem is discussed elsewhere.

Locke makes his distinctions in a way that closely parallels and represents Boyle's distinction between 'corporeal' and so-called 'simple ideas.' The former, which Bentham takes as a basis for grounding thinking and knowing in sensibility, fails to grasp the relational structure of Boyle's 'corporeality' which forms the basis of Locke's semiotic theory in the *Essay*. What takes place in Locke's development of sign-theory adapted by Peirce, as we know, is a most transparent mode of appropriation: Locke utilizes Boyle's notion of relational 'consensus' in the corporeal theory and translates it, first, into the *Essay* and then into the *Treatises*, and subsequently into other works as well.

The manner in which Locke makes critical and central use of Boyle's concept of relational community, as illustrated by the famous 'lock'n'key' image and model, is not quite in the way that Bentham speaks of paraphrase, or periphrasis. In Bentham's understanding, the process of periphrastic adaptation of an idea, from one context to another, is distinctly different from a figurative or rhetorical use of a phrase or idea. To Bentham, periphrasis preserves an original idea. It does not interpret it, in Bentham's sense. The 'original idea' is presumed to consist of abstract and unmodifiable truths. Therefore, it can be transplanted from discourse to discourse without losing any aspect of its 'truth,' (see Bentham's discussion of the idea of 'translation' in note 491, in *Fragment on Government* (1776) in *New Collected Works*, eds. Hart and Burns, *op cit*).

In point here is a radical difference between a Peircean semiotics that derives from Locke and from Boyle and in which the notion of an enduring essence is absent, and Bentham's notion of essences which, he wants to presume, persists unchanged from age to age, context to context, and from case to case in Law.

The crucial difference is that Bentham maintains a static notion of entities, or he wishes to. But Boyle, with his emphasis on relations *in some respects*, i.e., on *ad hoc-ness* — suggests an idea of community which exists for a purpose, dissolves, reforms in other respects, and yet maintains for each community *the symbol of consent*, as he presents the lock-and-key as a good fit. Bentham thinks in terms of substitution of elements on a constant grid or ground. But Locke, as Peirce after him, suggests a permutation, or translation, of a dynamic, meaning-altering process: an evolving, process of sign-interpretation, even and especially, with respect to 'consent' in community.

Perhaps the most difficult major assumption of a Peircean-pragmatic understanding of consent in community is its provisionality and its implicit denial of eternal compacts, eternal truths, agreements which once made are assumed to hold until the proverbial end of time. Pragmatism, in the sense that this method of inquiry was held and profoundly, rather than superficially, esteemed, is a rejection of the traditional 'quest for certainty' so well put by John Dewey (who occasionally met with Peirce in the same general 'pragmatists'' camp).

Such provisional judgements, held and acted on *as if* they were truths in the old, classic sense (in which the world was finished, defined, created) merely represent such absolute notions of truth. Provisionality *interprets* the old 'truth' even as Peirce's logic of possibility *interprets* the idea of the syllogistic argument (see Kevelson, 1987).

It is important to distinguish between a legi-sign, or provisional judgment — the ad hoc community that comes together out of common purpose and not merely mechanically, out of a kind of automated or programmed 'habit' — and the so-called signifiers with no signified as the structuralists tried to argue, after Barthes and company. The latter is *mere anarchy*.

The concept of consent in a Peircean semiotics is distinctly different from the antifoundationalism too often, and wrongly, associated with American Pragmatism and Peircean Semiotics. A provisional frame of reference does exist and does hold so long as it is certifiable, verifiable, useful, and is not a bulwark against open, free inquiry and discovery. Once the framework for consent is clearly seen as inadequate in the light of new discovery, new significant knowledge, new Reality in brief, this referential complex legisign must then be either reinterpreted if possible or de-composed if reformation and modification is not possible without totally deranging and disfiguring in procrastean fashion the original (i.e., currently established) leading principle.

Boyle's admiration for the emergent chemistry of his time was unmistakable, based largely on the emphasis of that chemistry toward experimentation; experimental efforts to establish links between theories, as opposed to constructing absolute theoretical explanations intended to explain once and for all the world and those ideas which partake of the 'corporeality' of this world.

Similarly, Locke's work, especially explicit in the *Conduct of the Understanding*, emphasizes the experimental nature of the philosophical method he describes, and the anti-dogmatist attitude which informs such inquiry.

Peirce also understood that the whole traditional substructure of exchange was in the process of revolutionizing an entire complex meaning of what the interpersonality and agreement were coming to signify. The enormous consequences of this great transformation of an idea is only now beginning to be observed in the sciences both hard and human, so-called. As Warren Samuels notes in his introduction to *New Horizons in Economic Thought* (1992), 'One of the sources of heterogeneity within neoclassicism is due precisely to the different positions which neoclassicists themselves take on fundamental questions: the nature and role of competition, statics versus evolutionary dynamics, undertainity, the nature and etiology of tastes and human choices, the relations or interrelations between individual and collective action . . . ' These are all at stake; the old rationality is clung to by neoclassical diehards, (at pages 2-6).

But the moving finger writes — said the poet and is an index — (not that of Omar Khayam, of course, but of Peirce) . . . and having writ moves on, . . . ' So do we, back to the future, to Locke & Co.

III

The idea of consent is enormously problematic. Although the bulk of existing literature on aspects of Locke's understanding of consent is vast, there are many, highly respected scholars who maintain that what Locke thought has little or nothing to do with the practical aspects of consent. Indeed, if there appears to be a significant absence of a philosophical substratum to contract law it may be because, as Dunn and others have remarked, the theory of relational obligation implicit in the term, 'Consent,' in Locke's work is quite different from the understanding of 'consent' as government mirroring or reflecting the 'psychological state of the governed.' This latter is in some respects Hobbesian, as discussed in a rich and inimitable fashion by Hannah Pitkin for example, (see Kevelson on this aspect of representation, 1988).

But according to Dunn, Locke's theory of consent is an explication, I take it, of a presupposed deontic logical structure which characterizes relations based on mutual consent, such as contracts and other binding agreements which law, *presumed by mainstream theorists to be deontic in structure*, enforces.

The law, from the perspective of consent as mutual obligations, is indeed a logic of commands, of duty and obligation, i.e., of such functions named by Hohfeld and others to represent the powers of property as relational forces. But the deontic structure is not primary, (Kevelson, 1987).

Occasions or opportunities for consent arise at three points, as Dunn presents Locke's concept: 1) at the point when an individual enters into a society to join it as a member; 2) when a member of a society elects or chooses someone as a representative in government procedures, i.e., chooses an agent as actor; and 3) when these agent/representatives actually make law, i.e., legislate. From this view of Locke, members of a society are not coerced into the dictates of the powerful and/or propertied, but can reverse powerlessness, in terms of active consent, into a living force at the second and third points of consent. Thus, in a democratic society, whoever has the vote has the power of effecting or disengaging the terms of consent. This is an interpretation of Locke at variance from many more usual views, e.g., Plamenetz and others, (see Dunn, 1967/1982, in Chappell (ed), 'Consent in the Political Theory of John Locke,' at pages 51-80, in Garland edition).

From Dunn's understanding questions of consent arise only with respect to issues concerning taxation, but not with respect to disputes over property. Locke seems to assume that the 'origin of property is independent of consent,' and only its transfer requires the reciprocity of consent. Consent is the possibility for political society in the first place, Dunn says; but it is also, as a means or mode, the method by which political society is a continuum that is evolving as a kind of exemplar, I suggest, of a permanence/change paradox.

I take this view of Locke's triadic consent by Dunn as close to my own understanding of consent as a referent sign, and Interpretant in Peirce's lexicon, for the evolved notion of a theory of contracts in law. The idea of contract holds even when agreement is nonperformable or impossible, or is a 'phantom,' as noted in Foster, ('Promise and Impossibility' in R.J. Davis and D. Park, eds., in *No Way: The Nature of the Impossible*, 1987:184-213, New York: W.H. Freeman & Co.).

In particular, the idea of a 'phantom' contract is worth a passing comment at the least, since it is evocative of the notion of 'trace' in both current biology theory and in linguistic theory. In semiotics as well, it is used to refer to cultural vestiges of customary practice which are no longer observable but which remain in evidence, e.g., in architecture, in modes of interpersonal conversation and turn-taking, and formulaicly, in institutionalized discourse such as legal discourse, (Kevelson 1990). In brief, a 'phantom' is a kind of implication, or as David Bohm has discussed in the context of chaos theory, an implicative force unfolding, becoming significant.

Foster reminds us that during Peirce's prime time, the late 19th century, a distinction was made in the United States between an impossible contract and one which was 'absurd' or 'highly improbable,' (Foster, above, pp. 190, 191).

The volatility, or instability of the course of definitive meaning of contract in law, is paralleled by the early years of the 20th century, with an 'absence of consensus' regarding the doctrine of contract law. Mid-century saw a crisis which still continues, regarding agreement on contracts in law. What seems to have happened during the turbulent development of the concept of contract as it moved from relatively simple, in a simpler society, to a more complex and assertively pluralistic society in the United States, was that the older, absolutist and rejected doctrine had become eclectically dis-ordered, with legislators selecting isolated pieces of the law that could be patched and fitted together, in 'bricolage' fashion. As a new 'editorialized' montage the face of the law recalled, and represented interpretively (with broad brush strokes and great license), various older contexts of the law of which the various pieces were once integral parts. But the older fabric of the law as a coherent whole bore small resemblance to the new composition. The ideas that were once major motifs, or themes of the law, such as Consent, Contract, Property, became almost embellishment, of nostalgia, sentiment, and conservatism as a fundamentalism.

Those responsible for making this patchwork claimed to be interpreting positive law in new ways, since the positive law retained an image of consent that members of society had actually willed *as* such consent. But in fact, since parties to a contract could claim on either side that they had not assumed certain obligations, nor did they intend such obligations to be predicated upon agreements of discrete and ad hoc relations, the domain of the idea of contract came to resemble a subject empty of predications and 'property' — as Pirandellan actors with no play, (Gordley, 1991:227-31).

Less than a decade ago Morton Horwitz advanced the notion — a Peircean kind of notion — that all complex sign-systems such as ideas, as legal systems, together with their respective subsystems, evolved as continua. This of course is in opposition to the now-classic but much contested Kuhnian view which rejects the continuum premise. In Horwitz' view the law of contracts underwent trauma and suffered, as a result, deep schisms. This rupture first began to occur, he says, as early as late 18th and beginning of the 19th centuries. In the referent notion of contract two parties fused, and by consent and agreement to mutual obligation, i.e., to interchange, they became a larger, i.e., more complex social relation. But by the middle of the 19th century this process had become so altered in its interpretation, and as a result of a succession of traumas, that contract came to represent a sloughing off of differences which formally distinguished parties, and came instead to stand for a reduction of such differences into a notion of agreement as of 'one mind.' The devolution is shocking: from increase into relationally more complex units, to decrease to more atomistic, ephemeral units of quasi-sameness. The oppositional, agonistic nature of consent and contract becomes shorn of its conflictual character and hence simplified, (Horwitz, above at pages 926-27).

What needs to be explored also is reversal from a process of non-linearity and complexity to one of linearity and simplicity. It matters enormously which premises we hold since one leads to greater freedom via instability and unpredictability, while the other has consequences of certainty, definition, determination. The way of the former has few supporters and little general appeal. But it is the former, dialogical course of the law of contract and its stopping places for consent to reinterpret, renew or revise itself, that requires active participants, and risk-takers with something to lose.

Earlier I spoke of two kinds of motivation, from Bentham's view of the law: one speculative and the other practical. In Peirce the practical and the speculative are but different perspectives, different modes of organization of the same idea. The impulse to both or either, derives from what he calls the 'Gnostic Instinct,' a curiosity which is biologically built into our questing modes of life. This 'gnostic instinct' is what draws people into relations in the first place, and effects such relations as satisfy this gnostic instinct *by consent*. This curiosity is, according to Peirce, 'the cause of all purely theoretical inquiry, and every discovery of science is a gratification of curiosity.' It is the force of semiotic inquiry regarded as the 'method of methods' or the adaptation and relational reciprocation of 'the methods of one science to the investigation of another,' (*CP* 7.66, c.1902).

IV

Boyle's illustration of the lock and key comes out of his inquiry into the experience of two physical 'qualities' or general systems — two coherent texts, in semiotic terms — coming together and bringing about a new unity. Boyle was a famous chemist even in his own time, and stood on a threshold that barely marked the boundary between alchemy and the new science of chemistry. Peirce, we know, was trained as a chemist, and he brings it into his curiosity about the process of ideas evolving, of becoming conjoined with other idea systems into new complex relations. All this background, that the alchemy before Paracelsus to the alchemy survives in Boyle as a trace, a phantom, an Interpretant Sign is a kind of consensus-sign.

The lock and key illustration suggests that this image of consent is not for a good fit only but is a *means*, as a theory is an instrumental means, to get from some place to some place else. It is a means of motion. This curiosity or gnostic instinct which underlies the quest of key and lock for each contract is for something else, *some possible to be realized as a consequence of consent*.

In Boyle's theory, keys and locks are not made for one another, but adjust to one another, *in some respect*. In Boyle's words, 'we must consider each body not barely as it is in itself an entire and distinct portion of matter, but as it is a part of the universe, and consequently placed among a great number and variety of other bodies, upon which it may act and by which it may be acted on in many ways (or upon many accounts . . .),' (*ibidem*).

It is different textures of each body capable of responding to divers contexts and bodies it meets which is the reason that agreement may be in some respects only, and not in a totality. In this sense I may add, consent is partisan, is partial, is *in some respects*. There is always something left over: some surplus. That which is the rest of a lock and that which is the rest of a key — of its metal, its position, its shape, its possessor — is not pertinent to any particular adaption of lock and key with respect to their purpose *as this relation*, (Boyle, from *Origins of Forms and Qualities*, 1666, in Stewart, M.A. (ed.) 19791-96).

Consent, from Boyle's thought, was intended to bring about a consequence. It is analogous to an idea as a synthesis of thought, i.e., a signification which has meaning to the extent that it *is* consequential. Thus, we may suggest that if 'consent,' as derived from Boyle and discussed in Locke and is critical in liberal law theory, is intended to bring about a result, *then a relation is its result*. Such relation in a civil or jural society is the actual experience which becomes represented by law in the form of the legal contract. A contract is a representation of consent. Both contract and consensus imply a referent set of shared principles which correspond to recognition between questors, each following what Peirce calls a 'gnostic instinct.'

Finally, since it is not practical to explore Boyle further in this context, I want to note that every semiotic inquiry begins on the basis of consent, since it is consent which links inquirers and brings about a relation between them. The occasion of consent becomes the possibility for meaning to evolve. As a basis of law it is the opportunity for cooperative and self-organizing societies. In science, at microscopic as well as human social levels, in the domains of physics and of chemistry, it emerges also as a function for self-determination, (Earley, 1989).

Peirce says that pragmatism is not a system of philosophy, but only a method of thinking. Yet it corresponds, he says, with some but not all of the major principles of British and Scottish Common Sense philosophy. How it is different is crucial to a grasp of Peirce's own invention of semiotics; but these differences must be taken up elsewhere.

What concerns the idea of consent and contract in law in this paper is twofold: 1) the fact that the criticism of liberalist law has not grasped the dynamical process of dialogue, consent and the medium of property in social exchange; 2) it has not grasped the notion of spontaneity, of curiosity, of the *value* of instability and inconsistency of liberal law.

Boyle's theory of emergent forms, of 'corpuscular philosophy,' had not worked its way out of mechanistic framework, but it set the scene for this new stage of legal theory to act upon. Boyle's lock 'n' key can be seen to have constituted a new framework which was deeply cultivated during the following eras, and especially by 19th century jurists. For example, Chauncy Wright, called by Peirce and others the father of pragmatism, traces his own development via Gray's Botany, Boyle's corpuscular theories, Locke's notion of consent, and ultimately through John Stuart Mill. Thus pragmatism, as a new method of growing ideas, saw light.

It is not a lineal process. At every stage it is a process based on agreement between principles, in *some respect*. Peirce has enormous respect for the achievements of Boyle, as he does for Locke. Of Boyle, Peirce says that it was his genius to see the consequential character of relations, of consents, as only simulating or representing divine design. But such relations are not determined, are not necessary, and are such artifices designed to signify the 'moment' of creative conjoining. And it is Hume, we know, who takes the notion of such consent a step further, to apply it to the notion of Justice as consensual artifice, (Kevelson 1993; some of Peirce's reference to Boyle, touched upon here, are in *CP* 5.62065; *CP* 6.11, 316, 360, 542; 13-17).

In closing, we may imagine an after-image of Boyle's lock 'n' key: — a kind of 'phantom' contract — like an ad hoc coded cardboard insert in the slot of a hotel door.

REFERENCES (selected)

Alexander, Peter, 1985, *Ideas, Qualities and Corpuscles: Locke and Boyle on the External World*, Cambridge: Cambridge University Press.

Altman, Andrew, 1990, *Critical Legal Studies: A Liberal Critique*, Princeton, New Jersey: Princeton University Press.

Bentham, Jeremy, 1780/1948, *The Principles of Morals and Legislation*, New York Hafner Publishing Co.

_____, 1928, 'A Fragment on Government' and 'A Comment on the Commentaries,' in *The Collected Works*, eds. Burns and Hart, Oxford: Oxford University Press.

Bohm, David, 1980, *Wholeness and the Implicate Order*, London: Routledge & Kegan Paul.

Boyle, Robert, 1666/1979, *Selected Philosophical Papers of Robert Boyle*, ed. M.A. Stewart, Manchester: Barnes & Noble, 1-96.

Chappell, Vera, ed. 1992, *John Locke: Theory of Knowledge*, Vol. 8, New York and London: Garland Publishing.

Collins, Hugh, 1986, *The Law of Contract*, London: Weidenfeld and Nicolson.

Dunn, J., 1967/1982, 'Consent in the Political Theory of John Locke,' in ed. V. Chappell, Westport, Connecticut: Garland Press, 51-80.

Earley, Joseph E., ed., 1989/1991, *Individuality and Cooperative Action*, Washington, D.C.: Georgetown University Press.

Eisele, C., 1979, *Studies in the Scientific and Mathematical Philosophy of Charles S. Peirce*, ed. R.M. Martin, Amsterdam: Mouton de Gruyter.

Feldman, S., 1993, 'Civic Republicans,' *Georgetown Law Journal* 81: 2243-90.

Foster, Thomas E., 1987, 'Promise and Impossibility,' in *No Way*, eds. R.J. Davis and D. Park, New York: W.H. Freeman and Co., 184-213.

Gordley, James, 1991, *The Philosophical Origins of Modern Contract Doctrine*, Oxford, Clarendon Press.

Green, Thomas Hill, 1874/1968, *Hume and Locke*, New York: Th. Y. Crowell.

Harrison, Ross, 1983, *Bentham*, London: Routledge and Kegan Paul.

Hayek, Friedrich, 1957/1959, *The Counter-Revolution of Science*, Indianapolis: Liberty Press.

_____, 1967/1978/1980, *New Studies in Philosophy, Politics, Economics and the History of Ideas*, Chicago: University of Chicago Press.

Kevelson, Roberta, 1987, Peirce's *Method of Methods*, Amsterdam: John Benjamins.

_____, 1988, *The Law as a System of Signs*, New York: Plenum.

_____, 1990, *Peirce, Praxis, Paradox*, Amsterdam, Mouton.

_____, 1993, *Peirce's Esthetics of Freedom*, New York: P. Lang.

_____, 1995, in press, *Peirce, Science, Signs*, Amsterdam: Rodopi Editions.

Kendall, Willmoore, 1959, *John Locke and the Doctrine of Majority-Rule*, Urbana: University of Illinois Press.

Locke, John, 1659/1789/1993, ed. D. Wooton, *Political Writings of John Locke*, New York: Penguin.

_____, 1690/1956, *An Essay Concerning Human Understanding*, Chicago, Henry Regnery.

_____, 1704/1993, *Of the Conduct of the Understanding*, Bristol: Thoemmes Press.

Mackie, J.L., 1976, *Problems from Locke*, Oxford: Oxford University Press.

Michelman, F., 1988, 'Law's Republic,' *Yale University Press* 97: 1493.

Peirce, Charles S., 1981-1986, *Writings of Charles S. Peirce*, I-IV, Chronological Edition, eds. M. Fisch, *et al*, Bloomington: Indiana University Press.

_____, 1931-1935; 1958, *Collected Papers*, eds. P. Weiss, Ch. Harthshorne, and A. Burks, Cambridge: Harvard University Press.

_____, Microfilm Edition of the manuscripts, 33 reels, with Annotated Catalogue by R. Robins, 1958, University of Massachusetts Press.

Plamenatz, J.P., 1938/1968, *Consent, Freedom and Political Obligation*, Oxford: Oxford University Press.

Samuels, W.J., ed. 1992, *New Horizons in Economic Thought*, Hants: Edward Elgar Publishing.

Chapter Twelve

Pragmatism and the Limits of Rationality

Jay Knaack*

I

This essay in Government, Economics and Semiotics is intended to provide a brief framework for interpreting the relations between Law, Politics and Economics. Traditional Pragmatism or Political Progressivism will be contrasted with more contemporary perspectives which are in the spirit of Pragmatism but reflect the impact of modern mass media on politics and economics. My own abbreviated versions of some modern insights will hopefully illustrate various claims that our behavior in these areas is really not rational or pragmatic. Indeed, contemporary analysts of public policy lead us to conclude that our economic, political and economic systems are not used as rational means to achieve rational outcomes, but are motivated by emotional and what Political Scientists call 'symbolic' significance.

The way in which I and others of my generation understood Pragmatism was as a theory of social reform in a world of constant change. Continuous and sometimes pretended attempts at reforming our institutions over the past one hundred years have left many people cynical while others remain optimistic that a more just and prosperous society can be brought about through law. Responsible critics of our economic, political and legal behavior still work within the spirit of rational reform, even when they show why and how reform efforts are so often impossible, self-defeating, or result in mere gestures that provide satisfaction without substance. After I introduce Pragmatism, I will review some criticisms of our standard political, legal and economic mythology.

Pragmatism, in my opinion, is important for understanding political life in the United States in the twentieth century. It is, I think, often claimed to be our favored political philosophy. It is home grown, optimistic, and practical. It also emphasizes inquiry and experiment and novel solutions for intractable problems. As a Philosophy, Pragmatism is generally held to be opposed to abstract theorizing, logic chopping and the offering of definitions that have nothing to do with experience. I believe that it was in this vein that C. S. Peirce proposed the then radical idea that theory grows out of practice, and not out of pure reasoning. He also believed that just as the world has evolved toward greater forms of order and control, our experience evolves toward a more perfected knowledge of the world. On his view, evolutionary process and historical progress were synonymous.[1]

Peirce's optimistic view was actually very idealistic, and was put into more practical sounding terms by his contemporary, John Dewey. Dewey believed that Democratic institutions, public education, free inquiry and freedom of speech together allow people to apply the techniques so successful in the physical sciences to the social sciences. Dewey continuously emphasized doing over knowing, and practice over theory.[2] Like Peirce, he opposed fixed ideas or the dead hand of outmoded tradition and beliefs which are inapplicable in the modern world. Dewey's idea was that the acquisition of scientific knowledge was possible by testing and modifying theory. The more applicable the theory, the better people could control and predict events in a world of economic and social change and insecurity. Now, he also claimed that scientific knowledge is a species of practical knowledge, related, for example, to technology which is developed by adapting means and ends in actual practice. He also viewed ethics as a practical activity, in which our valued goals or ideals and our practical means to achieve them can modify each other. As I understood him, for people to blindly pursue social ends without worrying about the means could lead to controlling people or denying them their freedom. On the other hand, pursuing certain means, like the law, can become dehumanizing ends in themselves which lead us to forget that they exist for the sake of socially valued ends. Without constant reflection on what we are doing, ethics and politics can become hopelessly closed, or matters of pure expediency. The middle path was to use social scientific research, open discussion and debate, and a democratic format for instituting progressive social experiments.

One problem with this theory, which has been illustrated by Murray Edelman, to whom I will return, is that ends and means, noble social goals and policy proposals, are used as bargaining chips in the competition for political power.[3] By the time that represented political interests become involved in debate, it becomes impossible to distinguish between what is supposed to be a social reform and the agendas of various special interests. Policy will be heavily compromised, and often those representing entrenched interests will resist reform or merely vote for token reforms. Secondly, the idea of using scientific method on social problems itself tends to define and limit social ends and means in unacceptable ways.[4] We may be faced with the possibility of social engineering, or of weighing social values against monetary costs. The principles of Pragmatism, in other words, can be used to rationalize and justify programs and legislation that are only nominally in the spirit of pragmatism or social progress. What we should like to consider to be objective and useful policies for advancing and protecting individual and collective goods and rights, can turn out to be heavily politicized and compromised by competing interests. The analogy between science and ethics can surely also lead people to mistakenly think that pragmatic ethics are those that are purely expedient and made to order.

II

Today the cause of reform is far from dead. Just within the past few years we have had, in keeping with this tradition, national debates over women's rights and the right to an abortion, over the complexion of the school and college curriculum, and over commercial marketing techniques that are claimed to adversely effect behavior. Currently, people are debating political correctness, or the censorship of slanderous and libelous forms of social reference that are racist or sexist, and cultural diversity, policies which encourage the acceptance of different ethnic groups. In a similar vein the media are full of news about debates over the reform of our national health and medical system, and an international trade agreement which is supposed to aid the economy. Also, I remember that within the past forty years, we have witnessed (in the press, and on television and in news magazines) repeated and on going attempts to reform political campaign financing, legislative process, the judiciary and criminal justice system, some of our financial institutions and laws, education, the welfare system, taxation, land use and pollution. It is hard to find anything that hasn't been proposed for reform for some reason or other. Today political candidates use the rhetoric of reform in order to get votes. They may, for example, claim that they are political outsiders, and because of that, they alone can reform politics and law which is dominated by vested interests or one sort of political ideology or another. The concept of 'reform' has been politically transformed from a radical program for social progress to a dull and expected political slogan. Television and televised news casts are surely worth mentioning as having contributed to this transformation and popular perception. The media, in the quest for exciting news focus on and blow up political controversy. (This does not preclude the fact that the media have also helped make us more aware of some social problems and economic and political crises).

I now wish to turn to the mass media, in particular television, which is commonly believed to have had an immense impact on political behavior and our interpretations of social and political reality. From a semiotic perspective, we may look upon news reporting in the mass media as an illustration of a redundant communications system which constructs its own messages, targets and tries to capture its own passive audience, and defines and justifies itself as the correct mirror of reality. However, in the process of defining reality in the terms chosen by its programmers and writers, these dramatizations and distortions provide material for new sorts of criticisms and analyses. For example, we traditionally, at least in theory, insisted on the separation of government and society, or law and economics, for the sake of liberty. But televised debates between economists and journalistic experts over federal fiscal policy, taxation, or budgeting may not always seem politically neutral. Indeed, economics is the primary topic of political debates, and debates about social issues usually turn into economic debates. This suggests that a very deep and possibly unwelcome relationship has developed between law, politics and economics. In news reports and political interviews it appears that a decision or policy in one area is sure to impact the other areas. Also, the media introduces the viewer to once closed legislative sessions and committee hearings, and to court room proceedings thousands of miles away. Television and monthly news magazines also introduce the viewer to people talking about their medical complaints, their legal complaints, psychological complaints and consumer complaints.[5] Also political news often consists in interviews in which elected officials engage in name calling and charges of impropriety against their opponent rather than in any meaningful discussion of the issues. Our younger generation, having grown up watching television, look rather incredulously upon the idea that we operate with any political, economic or legal philosophy at all. From the point of view generated by television, economic, political and legal terminology appear to be little more than tools used in the competition for political power. I think that the media tends to supplant the old regime of received wisdom and theory about political and economic life, with a continuous rhetorical clamor in which public policy is made and remade, built up and destroyed, all of which eventually becomes repetitious and boring, but not without serious effects on the electorate and political outcomes. Also, television newscasting may contribute to the popular perception that people feel that they are politically helpless or powerless, instead of economically self-reliant and politically independent.[6] Furthermore, television newscasts tend to support the idea that Politics, Law and Economics are not themselves coherent or rational systems and do not cohere with each other. Their coherence is suggested by newscasters and politicians, but there appears to be no deliberate coordination in fact. Similarly, Economics, Law and Politics do not seem to exist primarily to bring about rational results, but rather, are made to appear to do so because they provide people with temporary psychological and emotional gratification. Television is, of course, a private commercial enterprize, whose goal is to make profits by advertising commercial products. Similarly, political candidates and reformers can use television to advertise themselves and their own agendas. The parallel between the two is that both tend to promise the viewer results which are indispensable to their well being.

III

John Kenneth Galbraith is an economist who has not hesitated over the years to attack our collective habits of production, advertising and consumption.[7] (Thorstein Veblen, one of our other great economic critics, also attacked his own earlier version of 'consumerism' in an attempt to show that Economics is not based upon rational calculation).[8] One of Galbraith's main points is that the consumer has become the target of persuasive selling, and rather than being in command of the economic system, is a victim of it. The consumer rebellion he mentions in his 1972 Presidential address to the American Economics Association,[9] has since that time produced a constantly extended record of products liability suits and safety and engineering regulations. I will return to consumerism, after I review some of the main complaints made by Galbraith and others about the ways in which some people pretend, or try to convince themselves and others, that various laws regulating and licensing business and trade are rationally justified by supposedly fulfilling the true (though largely hidden) telos or purpose of the economic system, that is, to correct supply and demand. This mythology, as Galbraith calls it, is based upon the false supposition that consumers act in a perfectly rational way from a profit maximizing point of view. It can be used to justify irrational and unjust economic arrangements. But once properly understood, Galbraith believes that economics can be made rational from a constructive and just social point of view.

Galbraith's chief argument is that since the great economic depressions of the first half of the century and two world wars, governments everywhere have been forced to try to control economic life for the citizens. This is quite contrary to the premise of classical theory according to which governments are automatically suspect and irresponsible, and need to be separate for the sake of economic liberty and progress. The reason is that, for example, in the United States, government agencies and officials try to correct the well known and harmful excesses of the business cycle: chronic over-production, over-extended debt, unemployment and depression by initiating a variety of techniques. For example, one can mention price supports, wage supports (via union laws and minimum wage laws), massive government employment in its own bureaucracies and in education and the military, government indebtedness, and indirect control of consumption and production by manipulating taxes and interest rates and governmental expenditures.[10] This is sometimes called our own version of mass behavior modification. Hence, during every election and legislative session, proposed policies and laws usually center around economic issues. Government is in fact heavily involved in our economic life, and concurrently, economic interests are heavily represented and influential in the government

The cause of this is not hard to find. Industrialization and mass production, as Galbraith constantly reminds us, could not survive in a completely unprotected and competitive atmosphere where unmanipulated supply and demand determine outcomes. Industrialization requires long term investment, guaranteed returns, long term contracts with labor, suppliers and sellers, etc. Galbraith has dubbed this the planning system, dominated by a few giant firms or conglomerates which he calls an oligopoly, or joint monopoly. Planning requires that a firm be sure to produce and market what they can sell. Planning requires market research, identifying the targeted consumers, products research and design, advanced advertising and sales, estimates of start up costs and contracts for materials and labor, all in order to capture new investment. Furthermore, each firm has a good idea about what its competitors will be doing so that they compete with similar products for shares of the market they themselves jointly produce. The flow of investment and consumption is maintained by firms persuading the consumer to buy the product and offering easy financing, and by financial institutions offering easy financing for consumers and investors. Members of the government on the other hand use various indirect methods as outlined above to help various sectors which are politically perceived to be in trouble while it also maintains its own high employment rate and debt.

Politically, much of this economic activity is rationalized as means for maintaining a free and competitive economy. Galbraith continually chides the members of his own profession who invariably rationalize these activities as ways in which the market is supposedly reestablishing equilibrium between supply and demand. But indeed, if there was such a creature as a self-correcting market, then there would not be any need for economists, or laws and regulations for that matter. Classical economic theory can be used as an excuse for justifying quasi-monopolistic practices and inefficiencies which may have nothing to do with the health of the economic system or society. Political opponents can also claim that activities they dislike disrupt the free market, and use economic ideas like 'free trade' to justify special political and economic agendas. But if we actually tried to emulate a perfectly free system, we might end up in economic, social and political chaos.

IV

Now one popular theory that complimented Galbraith's was that the United States was ruled by a Power Elite.[11] The theory came from investigations intended to discover just who does rule the United States, since it did not appear that the usual Governmental branches and officers had any recognizable power to change, direct or coordinate anything. Furthermore, neither the consumer or the voter seemed to be sovereign, when in fact consumers were subject to the hard sell and few voters bothered voting. The idea was that some hidden committee or connected groups controlled the government behind the scenes, and that this committee or group could be identified and located. Once located, it could presumably be reformed or thrown into jail.

Candidates for membership in the elite were the chief officers of large firms and businesses, members of the law firms they hired, legislators whose campaigns they contributed to, and judges whose nomination they could influence.[12] This system was supposedly justified by the academics, who were its leading Ideologists. Hollywood movie stars and professional athletes used in advertisements were the ones who supposedly sold the public on the ideal personal benefits available to each person in the system, whether rich or poor.

However, the theory of the Power Elite was too general and vague, to account for civil rights legislation, health and pollution laws, and the power of groups which were not economically based or part of the economic establishment. The theory of Political Pluralism advanced the idea that a great variety of interest and political action groups compete to capture the law, some permanent, some formed for a special occasion or cause.[13] Television allows the candidates and special groups to make wide spread appeals on their own without any special or grass roots backing. As mentioned earlier, reform itself has also become a popular political slogan used to arouse voters. Today, rather than supposing candidates are hand picked by a political elite, it now appears that candidates choose themselves and also choose or seize upon popular issues in order to get votes. Candidates seek office not as a means to solve issues, but use issues as a means to gain office in order to gain influence for their own personal agendas or party.

But before I continue, it is important to note that consumption and consumerism, which are some of Galbraith's chief concerns, have become major issues in contemporary reformist thought and also for many Semioticians and other critics considered to be in the Post-Modern camp.[14] According to one theory, advertisers aim at arousing the viewer's unconscious sexual and social fears, suggesting that their products will overcome these fears. Also, after two or three generations of television viewing, it appears that people become socialized into being consumers, who will thoughtlessly buy and go into debt for goods which they do not particularly need or desire, but which they believe provide them with a sense of identity and security. There is therefore a parallel one can suggest between the images used in commercial advertising, and the creation of political images, which I will use to introduce my own brief exposition of the work of Murray Edelman.[15] He goes a good way toward exploding some of our myths about politics, especially in his analysis of the impact of the mass media. He also uses a good number of insights into rhetoric and the construction of meaning that have been developed by contemporary Semioticians.

V

Edelman's idea is not simply that politicians on television appear to be like good used car (or used horse) salesmen, but that politics itself has become a national media past time, a continually passing spectacle of crises and contentions, inflated by the politicians and the supporters of various causes, and by media reporters and writers as well. The intention of both is to capture viewers and to persuade them. Politicians therefore can be likened to television news marketing experts. Various issues and crises are tried out to see if they get any attention. Media opinion polls immediately try to gauge their popularity or lack of public interest from day to day. Hence, the candidate or debater can alter his or her approach and rhetoric, or change to some other issue or topic to keep voter interest.

Those who create the daily news programs selectively choose and edit what they take to be exciting events in order to get viewer attention. When politics is part of the news, politicians can choose to tell the media what they think voters will want to hear. The listeners are in a passive position in which they cannot respond or ask questions. This evidently encourages the making of quick and emotional, rather than deliberate or rational appeals. Politicians also aid the media in the construction of crises. The news also constructs political and social enemies and friends who are presumed to be causes or cures for crises.[16] Political rhetoric is also tailored to be ambiguous, according to Edelman, so that people who may have opposed views on some issue think the candidate is on their side. Politicians therefore use the media and appeals to crises in order to polarize voters and stir them up so that they will become politically active. Like the media which is always interested in creating an audience, the politician may stick with an issue for a while and abandon it when it no longer arouses interest or he or she may simply revive some other issue. The basic issues, such as unemployment, welfare reform, war, financial crises, political scandal, urban violence, prison over crowding and government irresponsibility, are common and well known, so that both news casters and politicians have no problem in explaining or communicating with their audience because they basically say what the audience already expects to hear. This suggests that the members of the audience will respond in predictable ways to key phrases and key issues. Politics, like the news, therefore, generates interest by parading well known and well tested attention getters.

The general impression of this analysis is that the news and politics are similar to old fashioned melodramas, in which the same old villains and heroes are dragged out, such as evil foreign dictators and corrupt political insiders who the candidate can easily attack. The candidate thereby also tries to make him or herself sound like an accomplished leader who can bring about change. Edelman says that this type of rhetoric creates a constant stream of threats and reassurances for the viewer. Politicians provide the illusion that they know what is going on and that they can correct the problem. But what this sort of rhetoric actually does, according Edelman, is to make the viewer acquiesce to the judgments of the politician, since the viewer is not acquainted with the larger issues which may appear to be highly complex and, in fact, incomprehensible. It also develops viewer dependency on the politicians who claim to be able to deal with such complexities that they themselves manufacture in fantasy and in reality, as in understanding governmental budgets and tax laws. Threats and reassurances also make the viewer suppose that the Political, Legal and Economic establishment is indispensable to their well being. The politician serves to connect the viewer to a conception of the world at large by the way in which the issues or crises are named or described. The politician also makes it appear that the world at large can be brought under control. In this way, politics and politicians keep alive people's interests, as well as the offices and political and legal structures which provide them with influence and incomes. In other words, continuous grandstand appeals to the media assure the political establishment that competition between various interest groups and peddling of influence can go on as usual. Politicians therefore become public symbols, representing various causes and particular Ideologies. Edelman argues that the television viewer, and politicians themselves, can become hypnotized and mystified by their own ideal constructs, which disguise and neutralize long standing and aggravating social problems.

Finally, it appears that policies created to solve social problems or to address aggravating issues often fail, or are simply used to divert funding to other things, because they are created by the representatives of established interests which are the causes of the problems in the first place. They themselves, in other words, maintain their existence and profits on the condition that they be able to keep perpetuating the same social problems and malfunctions.

VI

In conclusion, I will turn to the topic of the limits of rationality, which, along with works that show the limits of various moral theories, has become predominant in the past few years. Before I do so, however, I wish to add that many of us have wondered why we have come to rely more and more upon the courts to act upon important social problems. The reasons appear to be that no one group or Philosophy dominates any of our thousands of governments and special interest groups, and that the very people who once desired reform, are, or become, part of the economic and political establishment themselves, and therefore depend upon there being no serious reforms that might threaten their own strategic position.

Now I have tried to briefly outline some modern criticisms of our fixed ideas about Economics, Politics and Law, and I have also suggested that these criticisms are congruent with the general Pragmatic program for progressive reform. I believe that they will contribute to that important tradition. We should note that the best laid plans and most rational and workable policies for reform are bound to be deformed in the political process where they will be diluted, diverted or defeated. Even the Libertarian's idea of using classical economic theory to argue for liberty, rights and the absence of governmental presence appears to simply provide another list of rhetorical devices which can be used as weapons in political competition between various entrenched groups. However, it is worth looking at one sort of problem, which is quite different from the usual difficulties we have run into in well publicized projects like urban renewal, welfare programs, and prison reform. For example, it has been shown that people may rationally prefer the allocation of tax dollars and their own dollars for the sake of preventing disease or accidents.[17] However, if this were to consist in the transfer of monies, now used for crises intervention, then people would be bound to sit by without being able to rely upon expensive intervention measures in crises situations. Hence, they would be robbed of the moral satisfaction of helping others. So, while expensive measures for crises intervention are not economically rational, they are still important for 'symbolic' purposes. People can reassure themselves that something is being done for those in immediate need. Therefore, it may be more satisfying for voters in general to be able to act upon and pay for policies on a crises by crises basis. But this means that what gets taken care of, and when, and to what extent, is simply a matter of what may happen to come out of continual political jockeying.

**Jay Knaack is Professor of Philosophy at the University of West Florida.*

ENDNOTES

1. For an overview of Peirce and Dewey and some of their original critics, see Amelia Rorty, 1966, *Pragmatic Philosophy*, Garden City: Doubleday & Company, Inc.

2. John Dewey, 1929, The Gifford Lectures, published in 1960 as *The Quest For Certainty*, New York: G. P. Putnam's Sons.

3. Murray Edelman, 1988, *Constructing The Political Spectacle*, Chicago: University of Chicago Press.

4. Claudia Mills, 1992, *Values and Public Policy*, New York: Harcourt Brace Jovanovich College Publishers.

5. For example, see Robert Hughes, 1993, *Culture of Complaint, The Fraying of America*, New York: Oxford University Press.

6. An exposition of this problem can be found in Richard Sennett, 1977, *The Fall of Public Man*, New York: Alfred Knopf.

7. John Kenneth Galbraith, 1967, *The New Industrial State*, Boston: Houghton Mifflin Co. For an overview of Galbraith's many works, see David Reisman, 1980, *Galbraith and Market Capitalism*, New York: New York University Press. Also see for other relevant views: Leonard Silk, 1974, *Capitalism the Moving Target*, New York: Praeger Publishers.

8. Thorstein Veblen, 1899, *The Theory of the Leisure Class*, New York: The MacMillan Company.

9. John Kenneth Galbraith, 1972, published as 'Power and The Useful Economist' in Silk, *The Moving Target*, note 7.

10. For an overview, see Silk, *The Moving Target*, note 7. The classical historical and economic analysis is to be found in Karl Polanyi, 1957, *The Great Transformation*, Boston: Beacon Press.

11. C. Wright Mills, 1956, *The Power Elite*, New York: Oxford University Press.

12. For an illustration of related ideas, see G. William Domhoff, 1983, *Who Rules America Now?*, New York: Prentice-Hall, Inc.

13. For an illustration of related ideas, see Robert Dahl, 1961, *Who Governs?*, New Haven: Yale University Press.

14. Robert Bocock, 1993, *Consumption*, London: Routledge, 82-95.

15. Murray Edelman, *Constructing the Political Spectacle*, see note 3.

16. Stuart M. Kaminsky and Jeffrey H. Mahan, 1985, *American Television Genres*, Chicago: Nelson Hall. See 'Myth and History and Television News,' 165-176.

17. Claudia Mills and Douglas MacLean, 1992, 'Rethinking Rationality,' in Claudia Mills, *Values and Public Policy*, note 4.

Chapter Thirteen

Civil Codes and the Case of Quebec: Semiotic Musings around an *accent aigu*

Pierre Legrand*

I
Introduction

This essay is about civil codes and their meanings and, more specifically, about the newly-enacted Quebec civil code and its meanings. At one level, my paper partakes of a larger research interest in comparative legal culture. As regards the study at hand, my concern lies with a *culture juridique de survivance*, or a besieged legal culture. In Quebec, the legal, largely francophone, community perceives the legal culture in which it operates as being under attack from without — I have in mind the geographical proximity of English-speaking Canada and of the United States; and from within — I am referring to the historical fact of a substantial anglophone presence within Quebec itself. At another level, my research is an exercise in local knowledge aimed at assessing the merits of a particular legislative reaction to perceived threats from geography and history. Before I turn to the Quebec experience as such, however, I propose to develop some ideas about civil codes generally. I am especially concerned to illustrate their central character within the legal communities and societies they have served by focusing on aspects of their historical and philosophical significance.

II
Civil Codes

Law, like language, is an essential manifestation of social life and reveals the soul of a people: it is, through the values it institutionalizes and the institutional forms it adopts, a symbolic manifestation always bearing the mark of the native land. The history of each country is, so to speak, the history of its law.[1] In the way it provides for an intelligible and manageable order, law assuages a quest that communities have consistently pursued: 'The discovery or imposition of a cosmos on chaos has been a primarily theoretical and practical concern of all human groups.'[2] There are, of course, as many experiences of legal order as there are legal cultures. Indeed, comparative legal studies engages in a reflection on experiences of legal order and on the symbolic modes and interpretive performances through which legal orders are expressed, perceived, and accomplished by members of the legal and lay worlds. One of the most influential such experiences of legal order in Western history remains that of codification — a distinctive and enduring 'means of ordering reality' and a 'mode of perceiving, of construing, and potentially of controlling the social field.'[3]

The earliest collections of edicts, often the most ancient documents to have been preserved from civilizations that vanished as long as four thousand years ago, were not codes of law in the modern sense. Not only did they not evidence an attempt to present the totality of a territory's laws, but often they did not even carry legislative value. Moreover, they did not appear as a configuration of general statements partaking of a logical whole.[4] Accordingly, it is usually said that the first, and most significant, code for Western civilization remains Emperor Justinian's sixth-century collection of Roman laws, later to be known as the *Corpus Juris Civilis*. But, once again, the word 'code' is abused for the bulk of the Roman compilation — that part known as the *Digest* — consisted of an extensive casuistic patchwork offering literally hundreds upon hundreds of brief case studies and their solutions, all borrowed from the writings of jurisconsults. It is, however, accurate to say that a much smaller component of the *Corpus Juris Civilis*, known as the *Institutes* and meant as a student textbook, had little to do with the *Kategorienlehre* of the *Digest* and offered the salient elements that would nowadays be associated with a code of laws. Most characteristically, the *Institutes* sought to bring to light patterns of reality, to define them in terms of their abstract features, and to arrange them by reference to orders and genres.[5]

The *Institutes*, deriving their inspiration from the jurisconsult Gaius (who himself had borrowed from an earlier systematizer of Roman legal science, Scaevola), purported to represent the world as a system by organizing the reality exhaustively around the categories of persons, things, and actions (the latter term referring to the interactions between persons and things). It is the primacy thus given to the knowing subject using words capable of describing the world — the anthropomorphic focus of the *Institutes* — that allowed Kelley to assert that 'Justinian's system [. . .] was in effect the first system of social engineering.'[6] In other words, Roman jurists were acting on their unarticulated fundamental intuition that the world could be organized or harmonized, that one should, therefore, capture social interactions and represent them within the boundaries of written reason, and, finally, that such systematization was intrinsically useful. This deep conviction in the possibility of instituting an isomorphism between a cognitive system and the world it purports to encapsulate offers the early demonstration of a compelling phenomenon which continues to captivate: the faith of entire legal communities in the probative efficacy of propositional knowledge.

The end of the eleventh century witnessed an intellectual revival of the *Corpus Juris Civilis* as it became the subject of intensive scholarly study and provided the focus for the establishment of the first law schools in Northern Italy. No doubt helped by the fact that Justinian himself had created a climate of religiosity around his collection by explicitly conferring upon it divine status, the *Corpus Juris* was readily associated with the Holy Scriptures. Jurists asserted that Roman laws were but divine commands expressed through the mouth of princes. Over the next centuries, the *Corpus Juris Civilis* and the extensive doctrinal literature which it spawned in scholars searching for the immanent rationality of the Roman compilation progressively spread across most of Europe and eventually supplemented, or displaced, many of the local customs. In the process, that body of unenacted Roman law (which also comprised an important canon law component) became a kind of supereminent law common to most of Europe, a *jus commune*. The ever-growing ascendancy of Roman law, combined with the influence of humanist schools of thought privileging natural reason and mathematics, produced, in the seventeenth century, scholarly texts about law purporting to actualize and order the Roman compilation. The authors of these works aimed to optimalize the accessibility and, therefore, the usefulness of the Roman model for European States by 'domesticating' it. In this way, Roman law was stripped of its more technical aspects and was organized on the basis of general principles in accordance with natural reason. Doctrinal writers set themselves the task of expressing these great principles and of exposing them according to deductive logic so that the whole of the subject-matter would be self-evident.

While one can identify diverse reasons why the view of the world as a single determinate rationalizable order failed to seduce English lawyers to the same degree and why these accordingly resisted the quest for formal rationality, the traditional absence of an influential body of scholarship about the law in England, making English law *'ein Recht ohne Rechtswissenschaft*,'[7] must count as an important factor. The point is not, of course, that continental jurists were more credulous than others or that English lawyers were less concerned with the accuracy of their observations or with rationality. Rather, the English lawyers' gaze was not bound to things by the same intellectual system on account of the different epistemological framework within which they were already operating.[8]

Nationalistic fervour and authoritarian leaders subsequently channelled the body of scholarly work that had developed in continental Europe into the adoption of codes of laws known as 'civil codes,' the most influential and most celebrated of them — albeit not the earliest one for the Prussian civil code had preceded it by ten years — being the *Code civil des Français* promulgated into force in 1804 under the aegis of Napoleon. The French code was in many ways a product of the Revolution and had indeed been preceded by four drafts that had been prepared and rejected in the decade following 1789. The adoption of the French civil code heralded a move away from a situation which had been dominated by a mixture of sub-national, or local, customs and supra-national law (the *jus commune*) to a case where the code was being seen as an important symbol of *national* unity, whether political or legal, and as a formal affirmation of the doctrine of equality of all citizens before the law.

Throughout the nineteenth century, most jurisdictions in continental Europe enacted a civil code, and many ensured that their colonies did likewise. Interestingly, although some civil codes were imposed from outside — Napoleon was a particularly keen proselytizer — a number of jurisdictions willingly adopted external models (it is noteworthy that, by contrast, no jurisdiction has ever voluntarily imported the common law tradition). Others yet developed home-grown products. Looking back, one sees that '[d]uring the last hundred years and more, codification [. . .] has been the cardinal vehicle of law reform and unification of the national laws.'[9] Thus, Varga reports the findings of a UNESCO investigation published in 1957 and showing that the form called 'codification' existed in 67% of known legal systems and that each system included an average of six codes.[10] One is tempted to quote Michelet: *'C'est un important spectacle de voir les principaux symboles juridiques se reproduire chez tous les pays, à travers tous les âges.'*[11] In the process, the link between codification and the politico-legislative realm became firmly embedded. The perception of codification 'as an act of the deliberate and unfettered will of the ruler,'[12] as an act of power, has indeed led some authors to assert that 'codification is nothing but a means for the [S]tate to assert its domination by shaping and controlling the law.'[13] Mallieux would have concurred, he who presented the 1804 French code as *'un recueil d'ordres donnés par le maître de l'Etat.'*[14]

The importance of a civil code for a jurisdiction having adopted that form of legal ordering can hardly be exaggerated. As the leading English historian reminds us: 'do not suppose that a civil code merely settles legal details: those small rules which will interest none but lawyers.' Rather, it deals 'with the most vitally important of all human affairs.'[15] What makes a civil code so significant from the point of view of a given society is that it has as its object the various passages or events in the life of the citizen and that it seeks to apprehend the world of interactions, social or otherwise, between a citizen and his fellow citizens. A civil code, for instance, deals with acts of birth, the authority of parents over their children, adoption, marriage, divorce, ownership, inheritance, contracts (whether sale, lease, loan, or mortgage . . .), and accidents. As will have been apparent, one finds here the same organizational trilogy that had characterized Justinian's *Institutes*: persons, things, and actions. It must be emphasized that modern codes systematically adopt this general outline or a variation thereof. The similarity is all but coincidental for, as I have explained, the intellectual roots of contemporary codes can all be traced to Justinian's compilation through at least seven hundred years of scholarship about law. The web of relationships in which facts and events are placed as they are represented in terms of a code is not, therefore, the product of short-term experience alone: every code is an heirloom, the product of an incalculable sequence of generations.[16]

A code is a cosmology. It attests to an effort to totalize or to produce absolute knowledge inscribed in categories, typologies, and polarities. The architectonics of a code find their expression in a coherent structure which, in the case of the 1804 French *Code civil*, proceeds from books to titles to chapters to sections to sub-sections to articles. Through the series of pithy statements that are subsumed within this hierarchy of divisions, the code purports to offer a fully cohesive representation of the world as it has come to be experienced by members of the society where it is drafted or, possibly more accurately, as they would wish to experience it. With a code, the world is abstracted through a process of mental ordering: it is temporalized and spatialized. It is also ordered; the provisions of a code being numbered consecutively in an uninterrupted sequence — the French code, for instance, beginning with article 1 and concluding with article 2283. In this sense, therefore, it does not seem excessive to assert that a civil code is a legal fiction since it represents a moulding or shaping of the world, 'the crafting of a narrative.'[17] Indeed, the latin *fictio* refers to 'creation' just as it connotes 'simulation.'

The result is an exhaustive and autarkic text. The code is exhaustive in the sense that it is without gaps as regards those fields of law it embraces. Within its general ambit, a code, in other words, is never silent. Even when an issue arises which it does not explicitly address, the code makes provision for how such an issue must be addressed. The autarky of the code, for its part, arises from the related idea that all of the basic law pertaining to those fields of law covered by the code is to be found in the code and not elsewhere and, moreover, that all of the code's provisions hide an underlying and fundamental unity. This is not to say, of course, that the code cannot accommodate legislative interventions outside its confines. Indeed, such measures are adopted daily in practically every jurisdiction where a civil code is in force. But, these statutes and regulations claim only adjectival status in the sense that, irrespective of their substantive importance, their application assumes, explicitly or not, the existence of the primary body of principles, doctrines, and rules to be found in the civil code. Moreover, when a statute or regulation is silent on a given issue, the interpreter naturally falls back on the civil code which, therefore, always acts as the legal substratum of the legal order: it is *incontournable*.

The virtues of exhaustivity and autarky claimed by civil codes show how the ascription of the label 'code' to a legislative intervention is hardly sufficient to turn a statute or regulation into a *code*. An illustration may be helpful. Article 1-103 of the American *Uniform Commercial Code* makes the point that the application of the Code turns not only on the provisions of the Code itself but also on a body of law — the common law and the law of equity — which, given its historical role within American law, cannot be regarded as being of adjectival character. In other words, there exists, in the case of the American *Uniform Commercial Code*, a body of law that is of basic or fundamental character, that is necessary for the application of the Code, and that is to be found outside the Code itself. The *Uniform Commercial Code* is clearly not autarkic. For this reason, it is, therefore, not a *code* in the traditional sense.

These remarks would be incomplete without at least some brief consideration being given to the matter of form.[18] Blanché notes that abstraction, through the formulaic expressions retained by the code, implies generalization.[19] One could add that codification also entails a stabilization and permanentization of the legal vocabulary. A code, thus, appears as a canonized form; indeed, Weber could write of the French civil code (with pardonable exaggeration) that many of its epigrammatic and monumental sentences 'ha[d] become parts of common parlance in the manner of ancient legal proverbs.'[20] Clearly, its systematicity and the prescriptive power of its lapidary provisions confer to a civil code a singular persuasive strength that captures the imagination of its interpretive community in whose eyes it readily appears as intangible and incontestable.

For all jurisdictions having fostered a civil code, the field of law — known as the 'civil law' — that is subsumed under the institutional trilogy has consistently remained by far the most significant branch within the legal order. Again, this assumption of centrality by the civil law, and by the civil code which is the civil law's cornerstone, finds its origins in the days when it was the focus of Justinian's compilation in the sixth century. In France, for instance, the civil code acts as a citizen's constitution,[21] and is arguably a more powerful legal symbol than the formal Constitution itself.[22] Perhaps the relative significance of the civil code may be measured by the fact that, although France has experienced fifteen Constitutions since 1789, the 1804 code remains: *les Constitutions passent, le Code reste*. It is in the civil code, for instance, that one finds a proclamation of the right to private ownership and its corollary, a prohibition against expropriation without compensation. Likewise, it is the civil code that asserts the binding character of contracts and the integrity of the human person.

The hypertrophy of the civil law as compared to other fields — such as criminal law or constitutional law — reflects itself in the heightened status of teachers, practitioners, and judges operating within the intellectual confines of the civil code and the civil law, in the structure of the legal studies curriculum (where, for instance, a first-year 'Introduction to Legal Studies' is, effectively, an 'Introduction to the Civil Law'), and in the prestige attached to scholarship about the civil code and the civil law in general. Indeed, one author assimilates those branches of the law that do not partake of the civil law to 'an illegitimate child.'[23] To say that the *mentalité* prevailing in jurisdictions governed by a civil code is emphatically dominated by that code is, therefore, an understatement: in all things, the jurist initially reasons from the legal and social perspective embodied in the code. In other words, once there is the civil code, there is in place a scientific (or scientistic?) construction of the world. This structure becomes the only source of knowledge within the legal and lay communities. He who is able to mobilize the 'scientificity,' or appearance of scientificity, thus established, who is able to enlist its strength or power or efficacy, finds his discourse admitted by the audience (within or outside the legal community) pre-disposed as it is to accept the superiority of these arguments. In law as elsewhere, scientificity is legitimacy. In civil law jurisdictions, the civil code is the fountain-head of legitimacy.[24] In this way, it must be seen that codification is more than an opaque object through which events are perceived: it is a form of action determining how we talk, think, and conceive. It affects what we experience.

It is not unusual for authors, even today, to make reference to the 'sanctity' of the code and to allude to the 'reverence' which it commands. Such, indeed, is the power of civil codes over the collective consciousness that jurists from territories where a code is to be found will readily say that they live in codified jurisdictions, even though the code covers part of their law only. In this way, it can be seen that civil codes help to delineate a legal identity (and, indeed, a national identity). The civil code's 'power to fascinate, its hold over us and thus the images and figures through which it defines a destiny' remains unabated.[25]

Given that codification has proved such a determining intellectual phenomenon in legal history — the enduring system of thought that is the institutional trilogy of persons, things, and actions has been compared in consequence to that other, linguistic, trilogy of subject, object, and verb[26] — and because a civil code carries such primordial significance within a given legal culture in terms of the crucial role it plays in defining the *mentalité* of a whole community of jurists (and, indeed, non-jurists), one readily understands how the adoption of a new civil code represents a momentous event for any jurisdiction — not least for Quebec, and indeed for Canada as a whole to the extent that Quebec's is the only Canadian legal system partaking of the civilian heritage. Against this background, I now wish to turn to the Quebec experience itself, and to appraise it in the light of the civilian *Weltanschauung* as it has ripened over the centuries.

III
The Case of Quebec

I have referred to the way in which a civil code aims to capture the world. One can picture a civil code as the precipitate or residue following upon a large-scale distillation process of the fundamental values of a society at a particular point in time. In this sense, a civil code encapsulates, if selectively, a society's *acquis expérientiel,* or body of experience. Codification encodes experiences. Because codification is but the outward manifestation of an implicit structure of attitude and reference, it is a reflection of a given legal culture and of a given legal *mentalité*. A civil code wishes to be the collective memory of a given legal culture. A code is, therefore, a memorial — or, as the case may be, a counter-memorial — to the past. This enterprise of domestication affords a code a means of controlling the world. But, there is at least one other sense in which codification is an act of control: through the structure it develops, the categories it establishes, and the formulations it retains, a code purports to dictate an agenda. In other words, a code, in one of these recurrent loops, features an instrumentalist dimension: constituted by the culture of which it is but one of the artefacts, the civil code purports to constitute it in its turn.[27] The code provides a framework within which it expects people to live their lives. In the insightful imagery of Greimas, *'[l]e législateur [. . .] vise un objet juridique, qui est [. . .] l'instauration et le maintien d'une certaine culture juridique, c'est-à-dire, de 'bonnes manières juridiques' (comme il existe des 'manières' de table, de conversation, etc.). L'ordre instauré par le droit est, d'une certaine façon, le règne du convenable.* '[28] The idea of a civil code as a State-sponsored code of conduct — the reason indeed why Montesquieu opposed codification[29] — emerges in an unmistakable way from a Quebec Ministry of Justice commentary accompanying the coming into force of the new code. The cover of that book proudly announces the 1994 civil code, replacing the 1866 version and the 1981 interim edition, as representing *'un mouvement de société,'* or 'a social shift.' The directive connotation of this expression is clear: law, once again, has assumed the role of a 'steering medium.'[30]

My insistence on inscribing the civil code within a broader political agenda will surprise many colleagues within the legal community, especially in a jurisdiction like Quebec where mainstream positivistic thinking continues to assume, somewhat reflexively, that a code is written under the banner of apoliticism concerned as it is with the technical and arcane matters of the law. But one must, of course, take a broader view of the issue. As we know, culture derives from historical experience. So do the forms that culture embraces, such as codification. A civil code, bringing together the private law of a given jurisdiction, is not a simple act of accumulation and acquisition that would have taken place over the years or centuries and resolved itself into a formulaic phrasing of legal problems and solutions. It would be absurdly reductionist to see codification as the mere formulation of codified rules. What accretion of elements we see is supported by impressive ideological formations. Codification is an incorporative cultural form. Just as culture is a source of identity, codes are a source of identity. From a semiotic point of view, for instance, a given culture consists in a hierarchy of particular communication systems.[31] All these systems are signifying systems. They operate by relying on one another: they are in constant interaction (one can think of the economic, the legal, the social, etc.). None of the signifying systems can count on a mechanism that would allow it to be born and to develop in an isolated manner. This fact means that if one is to envisage one of these systems — say, the legal as evidenced in a civil code — one cannot study it in isolation without taking into account all the relations which it holds with the other signifying systems of the whole. Concretely speaking, for instance, the examination of the code-as-civil-law cannot be detached from the consideration of the code-as-political-message.[32]

Codification, as I have noted, is the rewriting of an original text, the original text being the existing world. All rewritings reflect an ideology and, as such, manipulate what it is that they are rewriting. Codification is a simple example of such manipulation, undertaken in the service of power. Indeed, it can be asserted of the code what Benveniste said of language, which is that '*[il] reproduit le monde, mais en le soumettant à son organisation propre.*'[33] In its positive aspect, the code can foster the development of a legal system, of society. Thus, it introduces new concepts, generates new connexions, allows for new insights, stimulates innovation. It affords an example of the shaping power of one culture (the code) on another (the existing world). In its negative aspect, codification-as-rewriting can repress initiative, distort, and constrain. As a cultural phenomenon, the code is a prison, a reconstruction of the universe through which we now see and understand the world. It is a representation of the world, having moved away from it. As a style of cognitive approach, as a discursive organization of meaning, the code thus paradoxically does two things at once: it gives us a view of the world and, acting as a mediator in our perception of the world, blinds our relationship to the world, our understanding of the world. Nowhere indeed is this blinding effect more apparent than in the recent Quebec variation on the theme of civil codification.

Having established that a civil code fulfils both mnemonic and programmatic functions,[34] I wish to insist on the latter feature (which is, in any event, also linked to memory: through its programme, the code wishes to institute a new memory). Making reference to the 1994 Quebec civil code, I propose to address one programmatic dimension in particular: that of the treatment of the anglophone minority established in Quebec since 1763 which, today, constitutes approximately 10% of the population and continues to play a leading role in the cultural, educational, and financial spheres. This point refers to the threat 'from within' as it is understood by the largely francophone Quebec legal community and which I mentioned at the beginning of this essay. I take as the baseline of my argument a remark by Lotman concerning the 'semantic mobility' of cultural texts like the civil code. Lotman notes that "the same text may give different information to its various 'users'."[35] I want to focus on the information the code as a disseminatory device gives to someone who is sensitized to the treatment of linguistic minorities. Interestingly, the code is silent on the issue. What, then, is the focus of my enquiry? The answer lies not in what the text explicitly says, but rather in what it does not say or says only by implication. The object of my observations is the negative space of the civil code, that is, what is left outside the explicit code, that about which nothing is expressly said. I argue that this negative space defines the code just as much as what is to be found explicitly within it.[36]

The brief historical conspectus of codification that I developed above alludes to at least two symbolic features of codes which have indeed been largely constant:

1. civil codes as symbols of legal or political unity;
2. civil codes as symbols of formal equality — the equality of all citizens before the law.[37]

Far from propounding unity and fostering equality, the new Quebec code, drawing on the aura that attaches to civil codification, institutionalizes the value of exclusion. A brief semiotic excursus will show the potent impact of the formalization and officialization of exclusion by the Quebec code on the local legal community and eventually on Quebec society as a whole, that is, on its interpretive community and beyond.

Carbonnier aptly refers to a civil code as a *'livre-symbole.'*[38] The code is itself a sign and is, moreover, a compendium of many of the most relevant signs in the eyes of a legal community. As symbol, the code holds a semiotic capital — an idea which is developed by one of the most famous admirers of the French *Code civil.*[39] Whether Stendhal, for he is the writer in point, would have regarded himself as a semiotician is an open question. What is clear, however, is that he made at least two observations which contemporary semiotics would not disavow. In his *Racine et Shakespeare*, he first noted that *'[l]'influence des signes sur la faculté de penser est extrême.'*[40] He added: *'L'effet de tous nos signes, quels qu'ils soient, n'est pas seulement de communiquer nos idées, comme l'ont dit jusqu'à ce jour les auteurs de toutes nos vieilles grammaires. La propriété la plus importante des signes est: 1° de nous aider à combiner nos idées élémentaires et à en former des idées composées, et 2° de nous aider à fixer ces composés dans notre mémoire.'*[41] In other words, says Stendhal, one must recognize that signs are never devoid of attempts to persuade: through the symbol that it is, a text such as a civil code affects the way we think, the way we form ideas, and the way we remember these ideas. The Quebec code, as it appears to the Quebec legal community (and to Quebec society), is an invitation to think the world in a way which bears little relation to the world as it is to be found in Quebec and as it has been found there for more than two centuries. It urges the Quebec legal community to think through the new legal order instituted by the code, one without any meaningful anglophone presence. The code promotes the idea of the anglophone minority being denied any significant role within the new legal order. How did we get there?

Quebec having been allowed by the British conquerors, in 1774, to keep its civil law of French origin, the 1866 civil code mediated a polarized society: the francophone majority were farmers, the anglophone minority were financiers. *Jus conquestus!* But the 1866 code also dictated a dialogical society: Quebec civil law was extracted from French law, mostly, and from English law, also — the result of nearly one hundred years of British rule. The dual filiation was clear, both as to form and substance. The dialogue was enshrined in the code itself in another way: both the French and English versions of each provision appeared side by side. Indeed, the code was drafted in French and English simultaneously, some of the drafters being francophones and others being anglophones and all being bilingual. No provision was drafted in one language then to be translated in another: all provisions were intrinsically bilingual. None of the two versions was official, both were official: the meaning of one version was to be ascertained by reference to the other. So said the code itself in one of its most famous articles. The message was clear: Quebec is a mixed jurisdiction, and meaningful coexistence for the two linguistic communities must imply meaningful dialogue.

For the last forty years, more actively so since 1980, the Quebec government has formed the project to do away with the 1866 code and to enlist the new code in a programme of political affirmation by the French-speaking constituency in Quebec, a clear minority within Canada and a clear majority within Quebec itself. The powerful imagery of the code as an embodiment of 'the law' ought to proclaim to the rest of Canada and to the population of Quebec itself — along with the symbolism generated by the provincial flag, the provincial colours, the provincial bird, and the provincial motto — that Quebec had at long last reached adulthood. It could now be itself, it no longer needed to be 'mixed.' It no longer required French or English law to point the way. The Quebec government is, therefore, able to erase the humiliating symbol of a code made for a peasant society, infeodated to French humanism and English pragmatism. It is official (the code has spoken): Quebec francophones are no longer to be confined to the earth: *humiliatio*, *humilis*, *humus*: earth, that is, the peasantry. Let us erase the age of subordination from the collective memory, proclaims the Quebec government. In this way, while the signifier that is the new code is the outcome, or the ultimate term, of a linguistic system (its product), it also acts as the starting-point of a mythical system (the march towards political self-determination).

The government's aim is to efface the 1866 civil code from the collective memory. The 1866 code had become what the Quebec government no longer wants Quebec to be: it was un-autonomous in its formal and substantive dependence on other legal (political) cultures and it was un-unilingual in its assertion of French and English as the languages of codification. It had achieved, in other words, what the Quebec government no longer wants to do: it had connected with the past and conflated the past with the present, it had taken the past beyond its pastness and given it a presence. The Quebec government now seeks to negate the past through the denial of an anglophone reality in Quebec history.

The new code is called the *Code civil du Québec*. It is also called the *Civil Code of Québec*. By virtue of Canadian law (Canadian law is made in Ottawa, outside of Quebec), Quebec must release both language versions and make them both official. But note the *accent aigu* in both designations: the English title is spelt in French! The code, as a symbol of the political agenda of a nationalist government, reflects an antecedent decision to mould the civil law so that the law can be used to assert the political rights of Quebec's French-speaking majority. In other words, the code, as a signifier conventionally chosen, refers back to the signified conventionally determined beforehand.

Because of its political connotation, the code is, more than ever (and possibly more than has been the case in other civil law jurisdictions historically), the constitution of Quebec (although, technically, it subordinates itself to Quebec's *Charter of Human Rights and Freedoms* — an 'ordinary' statute). If Quebec cannot have a formal, or public law, Constitution because Canadian law will not allow it, it will, *faute de mieux*, have a private law constitution. Constitution? *Cum* — *statuere*: stand together. Together? Here is the myth, the mystification, the lie. The idea of the new code is for the minority within Canada to exclude the minority within Quebec. In the past, codes such as the Swiss or the German civil codes have had their prestige established in the light of their technical value. They were lacking the dramatic aura which accompanied the coming into force of the French civil code in 1804. But the new Quebec code wants drama because the francophone majority feels the political situation to be dramatic: it will, thus, be the code of closure. It will close itself to Quebec's anglophone population. While the code denotes commonality ('let us stand together'), it connotes discrepant experiences (the anglophone and the francophone lives) and excludes one of them from its ambit. The *non-dit* of the code is that this common project is not for anglophones (unless, of course, they wish to operate in French!). Moreover, like Napoleon with the 1804 French code, Quebec will use its new code as a symbol of foreign policy; it will substitute the threat to separate from a foreign land (Canada) for the Napoleonic threat to conquer foreign lands.

Unlike Justinian's compilation or Napoleon's code, the Quebec code does not seek to remind us of a history that was accomplished, but proclaims a history to be accomplished. In this way, the code is so obviously the consequence of a political decision: it was, indeed, drafted by a select group of anonymous civil servants (another break with the past as the civil law has traditionally entrusted the preparation of its codes to scholars or, eventually, to practitioners or judges). The rhetoric of the new code is clear. The idea is not to preserve the legal memory as much as to establish it. The decision was taken that the legal memory of the Quebec community would be interrupted. The new code is an *anti-mémoire*. This fact explains why the government produced a commentary proclaiming the sources of practically each of the 3,170 provisions of the code to be within Quebec law — clear evidence to the contrary notwithstanding (another way, of course, in which the new code is the code of exclusion and the code of closure: fearing the threat 'from without,' to which I referred at the beginning of this essay, the code engages in a defensive celebration of particularism). The reinvention of memory fostered by the code also explains why the codifier did not publish the French and English versions of the new code side by side. The message is unmistakable: let the English version, published *à part*, be confined to relative oblivion. In this way, its role in the interpretation of the code, that is, in the *life* of the code, will, hopefully, prove negligible. It should help that the quality of the English is verifiably poor on account of the fact that it was prepared by francophones who are not trained in the law (quality is also a sign!). It should help, also, that the 'official' commentary published by the government is available in French only. Thus, whether the code is analyzed from the internal relational organization of the discourse — that is, in its syntactic dimension — or from a pragmatic angle, that is, from the point of view of its mode of insertion in a socio-political context, the epilogue is inescapable. Embracing a distinctly impoverished version of legal positivism, the new code regards itself as purely self-authenticating. It also sees itself as unilingual. The age of dialogism is gone. The reduction of pluralism is acknowledged in the civil code itself, the 'peristyle' of the legal order.[42]

IV
Conclusion

A civil code, like other texts that are also explicit means of communication, reveals the superposition of many strata of significance and calls for many levels of reading. A surface reading of the new Quebec civil code suggests that Quebec's private law is renewed. A deep reading shows that Quebec's political programme is renewed. The code may be, like all codes before it, a substantive compromise. But a political compromise it is not: yes to Quebec francophones, no to Quebec anglophones. The new code aspires to become the new *doxa*. But in so doing it acts in a paradoxical way: the common practice of civilian codifications has been to seek to achieve unity and equality rather than exclusion. Consider the French, German, Italian, or Spanish experiences, for instance. The code constitutes a *savoir* and operates a distinction between the *connaissances sanctionnées* (what knowledge the code authorizes) and the *connaissances périmées* (what knowledge the code regards as obsolete).[43] As a printed and, therefore, in the eyes of the reader, a complete, closed, and definitive text, the code informs the legal community in Quebec that, in functional terms, one is to regard the use of English to interpret the code and to give life to the code as obsolete. Some law publishers have understood this point only too well: although they publish the French and English versions in parallel — *marché oblige* — the English typescript was initially only 25% of the size of the French one.

It is not in doubt that the symbolic order helps to generate the social order we live by. Yet, we know that the discontinuities the Quebec government seeks to achieve through its new code need not automatically succeed (although, even if it were to fail, the fact that the discriminatory crusade had even been attempted would nonetheless cast a long shadow over the enterprise of codification). Not every effacement of collective memory is endorsed by an interpretive community. Bitterness keeps memory alive. Betrayal sharpens memory. What life will this sign that is the *Civil Code of Québec* have in social life? It is, of course, unclear that the code will have any meaningful life beyond the legal community. Will the civil code capture the popular imagination and become, beyond the collective legal memory, part of the collective memory *tout court*. The key lies in the diffusion of the sign that is the code. Dissemination can take many forms all concurring towards enhanced visibility with a view to achieving a penetration of the collective mind. But even within the legal community itself — the interpretive community — the new canon or the sacred text — may yet fail. The sign may yet be rejected. Conversation may yet be wanted. Civilization may yet prevail over the new civil law. Any contracting parties may, after all, choose not to be governed by the new code — as allowed by the code itself at article 3111!

As event and as book, the new code seeks, from 1 January 1994, to be the new *lieu de mémoire* of the Quebec legal community and of Quebec society. Does it deserve to be? As the text of the code challenges the *tissu social*, it loses its ecumenical function — the anglophone minority is told that it cannot *inhabit* the code. Can the code still claim to be the grammar of the law (*grammatikê* = culture, erudition)? We cannot say that the code is non-significant. We can only hope, somewhat wistfully perhaps, that it will prove *insignificant*: the ideal social order that the new Quebec code promotes must be rejected because it rests on exclusion. A quotation from the literary critic Northrop Frye, used by Howes before me, appears particularly apt: 'A society enriches itself by what it includes; it defines itself by what it excludes.'[44] But the last meditation is the French philosopher Alain's: '*Exclus du droit? Ce n'est pas si simple. Il n'y a pas intérêt à exclure jamais personne absolument.*'[45]

**Pierre Legrand is Professor of Comparative Legal Culture at Tilburg University.*

ENDNOTES

1. L.-A. Warnkoenig, 1826, *Introduction à l'étude du droit romain*, trans. L. Etienne, Mons: Leroux, 30.

2. M.K. Green, 1994, 'Codes of Civilization and Codes of Culture,' in *Codes and Customs*, ed. R. Kevelson, New York: Peter Lang, 93. See also G. Tarde, 1994, *Les transformations du droit*, Paris: Berg, 30-31 [originally published in 1893].

3. D.R. Kelley, 1990, *The Human Measure [:] Social Thought in the Western Legal Tradition*, Cambridge, Mass.: Harvard University Press, 49.

4. E. Cohen, 1993, *The Crossroads of Justice [:] Law and Culture in Late Medieval France,* Leiden: Brill, 4-7.

5. See generally, on the intellectual genesis of modern classification, M. Foucault, 1966, *Les mots et les choses*, Paris: Gallimard, 137-76.

6. Kelley, *supra*, note 3, 53.

7. J.W. Jones, 1940, *Historical Introduction to the Theory of Law*, Oxford: Oxford University Press, 1, not. 1 ['a law without legal science'].

8. I am adapting a thought by Foucault, *supra*, note 5, 55.

9. H.E. Yntema, 1949, 'The Jurisprudence of Codification,' in *David Dudley Field [.] Centenary Essays*, ed. A. Reppy, New York: New York University School of Law, 251.

10. C. Varga, 1991, *Codification as a Socio-Historical Phenomenon*, Budapest: Akadémiai Kiadó, 18.

11. J. Michelet, 1973, 'Origines du droit français cherchées dans les symboles et formules du droit universel,' in *Oeuvres complètes*, t. III: *1832-1839*, ed. P. Viallaneix, Paris: Flammarion, 640 [originally published in 1837] ('It is an important sight to witness the main legal symbols reproducing themselves in all countries, across the ages').

12. F.A. Hayek, 1982, *Law, Legislation and Liberty*, t. I: *Rules and Order*, London: Routledge & Kegan Paul, 84.

13. Varga, *supra*, note 10, 334.

14. F. Mallieux, 1908, *L'exégèse des codes et la nature du raisonnement juridique*, Paris: Giard, 9 ['a collection of orders given by the Master of the State']. *Cf.* W.T. Scott, 1992, 'Codification,' in *Law and the Human Sciences [:] Fifth Round Table on Law and Semiotics*, ed. R. Kevelson, New York: Peter Lang, 429: 'the central concept is that of control.'

15. F.W. Maitland, 1911, 'The Making of the German Civil Code,' in *The Collected Papers of Frederic William Maitland*, t. III, ed. H.A.L. Fisher, Cambridge: Cambridge University Press, 481.

16. I very closely paraphrase observations on language by N. Elias, 1991, *The Symbol Theory*, London: Sage, 129.

17. N.Z. Davis, 1987, *Fiction in the Archives*, Stanford: Stanford University Press, 3.

18. I have addressed the matter at greater length elsewhere: P. Legrand, 1993, 'Civil Law Codification in Quebec: A Case of Decivilianization,' 1 *Zeitschrift für Europaïsches Privatrecht* 574.

19. R. Blanché, 1955, *L'axiomatique*, Paris: Presses universitaires de France, 76.

20. M. Weber, 1978, *Economy and Society*, t. II, eds. G. Roth & C. Wittich, Berkeley: University of California Press, 865 [originally published in German in 1922].

21. See, on the 'constitutional' status of the French civil code, J. Carbonnier, 1986, 'Le Code civil,' in *Les lieux de mémoire*, t. II: *La Nation*, vol. 2, ed. P. Nora, Paris: Gallimard, 308-09; B. Rudden, 1989, 'Soviet Civil Law,' 15 *Review of Socialist Law* 33 [now '*Review of Central and East European Law*'].

22. See, for a reflection on Dutch legal culture as offering another example of a civilian legal culture where the Constitution is not central to the political tradition and carries limited symbolic prominence, W.J. Witteveen, 1993, 'The Symbolic Constitution,' in *Constitutional Review [:] Theoretical and Comparative Perspectives*, ed. B. van Roermund, Deventer: Kluwer, 94 & 100.

23. J.W. Van Doren, 1993, 'Things Fall Apart, or Modern Legal Mythology in the Civil Law Tradition,' 2 *Widener Journal of Public Law* 447, 466.

24. A. Bernard & Y. Poirmeur, 1993, 'Doctrine civiliste et production normative,' in *La doctrine juridique*, Paris: Presses universitaires de France, 131-32.

25. P. Goodrich, 1992, 'Poor Illiterate Reason: History, Nationalism and Common Law,' 1 *Social & Legal Studies* 7, 9.

26. Kelley, *supra*, note 3, 9. *Cf.* S. Herman & D. Hoskins, 1980, 'Perspectives on Code Structure: Historical Experience, Modern Formats, and Policy Considerations,' 54 *Tulane Law Review* 987, 994-95: 'Gaius and Justinian subscribed to a view of society as a civil drama that develops successively the actors (persons), the stage set (things), and the dramatic action (modes of acquisition).'

27. See E. Morin, 1984, 'Epistémologie de la complexité,' *Revue de la recherche juridique* 47, 60 & 74, where the author introduces the idea of 'organizational recursion' as an instance of the complex thought processes that are a feature of modernity.

28. A.J. Greimas, 1976, *Sémiotique et sciences sociales*, Paris: Seuil, 111 [emphasis original] ("The legislator aims for a legal objective which is the institution and the upholding of a certain legal culture, that is, of 'good legal manners' (in the way there are table or conversation 'manners', etc.). The order instituted by the law is, in a certain way, the rule of the suitable.")

29. Montesquieu, 1951, 'De l'esprit des lois,' in *Oeuvres complètes*, t. II, ed. R. Caillois, Paris: Gallimard, part VI, XXIX, cc. 17-19 [originally published in 1748].

30. J. Habermas, 1987, *The Theory of Communicative Action*, t. II: *Lifeworld and System: A Critique of Functionalist Reason*, trans. T. McCarthy, Cambridge: Polity, 365 [originally published in German in 1981].

31. See P. Guiraud, 1973, *La sémiologie*, 2d ed., Paris: Presses universitaires de France, 27.

32. L. Francoeur, 1992, 'La série culturelle: structure, valeur et fonction,' in *La culture inventée*, eds. P. Lanthier & G. Rousseau, Quebec: Institut québécois de recherche sur la culture, 61.

33. E. Benveniste, 1966, *Problèmes de linguistique générale*, t. I, Paris: Gallimard, 25 ['it reproduces the world, but by subjecting it to its own organization'].

34. See, for the introduction of culture as 'memory' and 'programme,' Francoeur, *supra*, note 32, 62-63.

35. J. Lotman, 1973, 'Different cultures, different codes,' *Times Literary Supplement*, 12 October, 1214, col. 2.

36. See, for the idea of 'negative space,' D.R. Hofstadter, 1989, *Gödel, Escher, Bach: An Eternal Golden Braid*, New York: Vintage, 63.

37. But *cf.* M. Green, 1992, 'Law, Forms of Life, and Metaphysical Metaphors,' in *Law and the Human Sciences [:] Fifth Round Table on Law and Semiotics*, ed. R. Kevelson, New York: Peter Lang, 154: 'Laws, since they are general, cannot take account of the concrete differences and circumstances of individuals and thus will always be a source of oppression.'

38. Carbonnier, *supra*, note 21, 305 ['a book-symbol'].

39. See Stendhal, 1934, *Correspondance*, t. X: *1836-1842*, ed. H. Martineau, Paris: Le Divan, 277: 'En composant la *Chartreuse*, pour prendre le ton, je lisais de temps en temps quelques pages du Code civil' [letter to H. de Balzac from Civita-Vecchia dated 30 October 1840] ('While writing the *Chartreuse*, in order to find the tone, I would read from time to time a few pages from the civil code.')

40. Stendhal, 1925, *Racine et Shakspeare* [sic], t. II, ed. P. Martino, Paris: Champion, 64 [originally published in 1823 and 1825] ('the influence of signs on the ability to think is extreme.')

41. *Id.*, 74 ['The effect of all our signs, whatever they are, is not only to communicate our ideas, as the authors of all our old grammars have said up until now. The most important property of signs is: 1° to help us to combine our elementary ideas and to form compound ideas, and 2° to help us to fix these compounds into our memory.']

42. Tronchet, one of the codifiers of the 1804 French civil code, spoke of it as 'le péristyle de la législation française': Locré, 1827, *La législation civile, commerciale et criminelle de la France*, t. I, Paris: Treuttel & Würtz, 395 ['the peristyle of French legislation'].

43. G. Canguilhem, 1983, *Etudes d'histoire et de philosophie des sciences*, 5th ed., Paris: Vrin, 13.

44. N. Frye, 1973, *The Critical Path: An Essay on the Social Context of Literary Criticism*, 2d ed., Bloomington: Indiana University Press, 105, cited by D. Howes, 1988, 'Dialogical Jurisprudence,' in *Canadian Perspectives on Law & Society [.] Issues in Legal History*, eds. W.W. Pue & B. Wright, Ottawa: Carleton University Press, 71.

45. Alain, 1958, 'Histoire de mes pensées,' in *Id.*, *Les arts et les dieux*, Paris: Gallimard, 47 ['Excluded from the law? It is not that simple. There is no interest in ever excluding someone absolutely'].

Chapter Fourteen

Seals, Oaths and the Primacy of Ritual

J. Ralph Lindgren*

I

Until recently semiotics was thoroughly modernist. One key aspect of that is the cognitivist perspective from which semiotics was traditionally approached. Within that perspective what is believed is regarded as primitive and what is done is treated as behavior scripted by belief. Signs are understood from the cognitivist perspective as anything that can be taken by someone as standing for anything else and semiosis is regarded as an encoding process. This being given, the task of semiotic analysis was portrayed as one of showing how the more potent signs in our environment are best decoded. C. S. Peirce, of course, was one of the masters at doing just that.

In the past few decades the cognitivist orientation has been increasingly displaced by various forms of non-cognitivism in a variety of disciplines. The key feature of that orientation is the conviction that practice is regarded as primitive and belief as derivative. From this perspective, semiosis is fundamentally a ritual process by which stereotyped behaviors come to be coordinated in support of communication. Instead of portraying signs as enacted beliefs, non-cognitivism recommends regarding them as coordinated behavioral patterns that recur over a range of circumstances.

Three years ago I pointed out how the substitution of an approach that gives primacy, not to knowledge or myth, but to ritual or practice, enabled scholars in religion studies to shed fresh and useful light on the early Pythagoreans, the oldest living traditions to consciously focus on systems of signs as the ultimate basis of meaning (Lindgren, 1992:233-53). I suggested there that semiotics could benefit by approaching sign systems from a non-cognitive perspective. In what follows I offer further support for that proposal.

This paper is divided into three sections. The first two trace the history of two legal signs in the West, viz., the seal and the oath. Both of these signs function in that area of law that deals with evidence, i.e., with those signs that are accepted as proof of other signs. At one time seals and oaths were accepted as complete proofs, as sufficient evidence for claims of authenticity and truthfulness. Although today their roles are somewhat different, they are still essential in some circumstances. The final section is devoted to showing that the continuing role of these signs over the past six millennia is illuminated better from a non-cognitivist than from a cognitivist perspective.

II
The Seal

Two of the meanings of the verb 'seal' are of interest here: sealing to close or secure and sealing to authenticate. The former practice is slightly more ancient. The earliest practice of sealing, predating even the invention of writing, consisted in securing the contents of jars, baskets, caves, burial chambers and the like. Before the invention of locks, this was accomplished either by shaping clay over the stopper or lid or by fastening the opening with a cord and pressing clay around the knot. In each method the clay was then impressed with a distinctive mark. Cylinder seals, stamps and signets were commonly used for that purpose until Roman times.

To the extent that sealing actually deterred unauthorized intrusions, it appears to have worked by means of a threat of magically induced consequences. This is particularly likely where religious symbols were impressed on the clay medium. These marks of divine authority are thought to have excited awe and reverence in the population generally. A second consequence of sealing was to afford assurance to the receiver of the containers' contents. So long as the seal remained intact, those who opened these containers were assured that the contents had not been altered since being deposited. The intact seal, as it were, attested to the genuineness of the containers' contents.

Sealing to authenticate appears to have originated from the practice of sealing in order to close or secure. It involves the practice of impressing or affixing an emblem to an instrument, such as a document or scale, as proof of its authenticity or accuracy. Under this practice, a sealed instrument is self-authenticating in the sense that its truth or accuracy requires no further proof than that it was 'sealed and delivered' (Blackstone, 1775-79:II, 306). In this section, the history of sealing to authenticate will be sketched over three eras: ancient, medieval and present.

The practice of sealing to authenticate was widely used in antiquity. Sir Henry Maine insisted that its earliest appearance in jurisprudence was in the Roman law regarding wills (Maine, 1861:210). This was clearly mistaken. The oldest form of seal yet discovered, the cylinder seal, first appeared in Mesopotamia during the late fourth millennium B.C.E. It was apparently used then as a method of identifying property and protecting against theft.

Seals functioned in several ways in the early second millennium *Code of Hammurabi*. Judges that altered a decision that had been recorded on a sealed document were subject to impeachment (*Code of Hammurabi*, sec. 5, in Pritchard, 1969:166). Traders who carelessly failed to obtain sealed receipts for the money paid to a merchant were not entitled to have those funds credited to their accounts (*Code of Hammurabi*, sec. 99-107, in Pritchard, 1969:170). No member of a man's family may challenge his arrangements to leave a piece of property to his wife, son or daughter, if he does so by means of a sealed document (*Code of Hammurabi*, sec. 173, in Pritchard, 1969:172-74).

The seal was in use among the ancient Israelites, and is mentioned frequently in the Hebrew and Christian Bible. In the book of *Jeremiah* we find an account of a sale of land in which the seal figured in a central way (Falk, 1964:71).

> So I took the evidence of the purchase, both that which was sealed according to the law and custom, and that which was open: And I gave the evidence of purchase unto Baruch the son of Neriah, the son of Maaseiah, in the sight of Hanameel that subscribed the book of the purchase, before all the Jews that sat in the court of the prison (*Jeremiah* 32:9-12).

In other biblical passages we find caves being sealed to direct that no one should enter. Thus, the prophet Daniel was sealed in the lion's den. '[T]he king sealed it with his own signet, and with the signet of his lords; that the purpose might not be changed concerning Daniel.' *Daniel* 6:17. Similarly, to prevent the followers of Jesus from stealing his body from the sepulchre, Pilate ordered the Pharisees to: 'Go your way, make it as sure as you can. So they went, and made the sepulchre sure, sealing the stone, and setting a watch' (*Matthew* 27:66).

Perhaps the most compelling evidence in the *Bible* that a sealed instrument is self-authenticating is found in the *First Book of Kings*. The passage also shows that the person whose seal was used was strictly liable for the consequences of its use. Hearing from Ahab, her husband, that his offer to purchase a vineyard from one Naboth was rejected, Jezebel consoled Ahab and boasted that she would effect the transaction.

> So she wrote letters in Ahab's name, and sealed them with his seal, and sent the letters unto the elders and to the nobles that were in his city, dwelling with Naboth. And she wrote in the letters, saying, Proclaim a fast, and set Naboth on high among the people: And set two men, sons of Belial, before him, to bear witness against him, saying Thou didst blaspheme God and the king. And then carry him out, and stone him, that he may die.

The elders and nobles followed the instructions of the letters, but when Jezebel brought Ahab to possess the vineyard, they were intercepted by the prophet Elijah who brought word of God's condemnation of Ahab. Ahab was held responsible for the treachery even though the letters were written and his seal imposed without his authorization (1 *Kings* 21:9-22).

The role of the seal in English common law reached its zenith during the late middle ages. Historians generally agree that the seal was not indigenous to English jurisprudence, but instead derived from Roman Law, introduced from the continent with the invasion of William the Conqueror during the Twelfth Century C.E. (Blackstone, 1775-79:II, 305; Pollock and Maitland, 1899:I 94, II 223; Plucknett, 1956:631). Once it arrived on English shores, however, it was developed mainly in two contexts, deeds and contracts.

The practice of transferring land by deed derived from the pre-conquest practice of transferring land at the direction of royal charters. Charters were considered valid during the Anglo-Saxon period if issued by the King or an appropriate official. The *Magna Charta* is a late example of this practice. After the transition to the use of deeds, however, the seal of the executing party was required. Throughout the middle ages, 'it remained the law that no deed was valid without a seal' (Plucknett, 1956:612).

The second context in which the seal played an important role in English common law was that of contracts. As in Roman law, the form of an agreement can be sufficient to make it enforceable at law. As early as the twelveth century a contract or a covenant under seal was strictly binding.

> Now when anyone in court puts in as proof of his debt a charter made by the other party or some ancestor of his, the other party either acknowledges the charter or does not. If the debtor does not acknowledge the charter, he may deny or contradict it in two ways: either by admitting in court that the seal is his but denying that the charter was made by, or with the consent of, himself or his ancestor, or by denying completely both seal and charter.

> In the first case, where he acknowledges the seal publicly in court, he is strictly bound to warrant the charter and to observe without question the agreement set out in the charter as it is contained therein; and he should blame his own poor custody if he suffers damage because his seal was poorly kept (Glanvill, 1965:X, 12. Also see Pollock and Maitland, 1899:II, 220).

By the sixteenth century judges had framed the motto: 'a seal imports a consideration.' However, historians generally agree that this was a confusion. Agreements under seal need only be delivered to be valid. No consideration needs be shown. Pollock and Maitland pointed out instance after instance in which people were obligated by their seals even though they were applied without their knowledge or permission (Pollock and Maitland, 1899:I, 508; II, 536). Furthermore, as Plucknett noted, 'sealed contracts were enforceable centuries before the doctrine of consideration came into existence' (Plucknett, 1956:634).

Contracts under seal, then, are not one form of ordinary contract, but a distinct form. The consensus view is that in English common law, as in Roman law, two types of contract or agreement must be distinguished. As Holdsworth put it, 'in English law the two formalities are needed for making an agreement actionable are either a writing under seal, or a consideration. . . .' (Holdsworth, 1937:VIII, 80).

Commercial instruments were an increasingly common form of contract under seal by the fifteenth century. The bond illustrates this. It is an instrument under seal that was developed under the Italian law merchant. 'At common law, a bond was a writing, sealed and delivered, binding the obligor to pay a sum of money. If not under seal, it was not a bond' (Corbin, 1952:Sec. 258). Developed by merchants to expedite trade, these instruments made debts payable to the bearer rather than, as had been the practice under Roman law, to the creditor. The seal played an essential role in the development of bonds and other negotiable instruments since the creditor was usually not available to attest to the authenticity of the document (Plucknett, 1956:665-69. See, generally, Holdsworth, 1937:VIII, 113-76).

Just as the motivation to honor a sealed container during ancient times was supplied by the fear of magical consequences suggested by the inscriptions on the seals, so also in the middle ages reverence for a seal fostered acceptance of sealed instruments at face value. Corbin observed that the awe inspired by the sheer formality of ceremonies surrounding the use of a seal was sufficient to motivate acceptance (Corbin, 1952:Sec. 240).

In remarking about the self-proving dimension of the seal in the common law of England, Pollock and Maitland echoed that sentiment and also remarked how strict sealed obligations were in medieval England. '[A] deep seated reverence for a seal served to adjourn some difficult questions which otherwise must have come before the king's courts. A natural person is bound by his seal; he has himself to blame if some one else, at all events some one whom he has trusted, puts his seal to a bad use' (Pollock and Maitland, 1899:I, 508).

The status of the seal in our day is complex. Two types of seal are recognized: public credit seals and private credit seals. Public credit seals are kept and used by public officials to authenticate their official acts. These include the seals of states, the federal government, foreign and domestic courts and certain public officials such as notaries public. Public credit seals prove themselves in the sense that the authenticity of documents that bear appropriate public seals is established without the need for witnesses. For example, the seal of a notary public, once shown to be genuine, is sufficient to establish that the signatures on a document are authentic.

Seals of private credit are treated differently in different jurisdictions. About half the states have enacted statutes that abolish the common law distinction between sealed and unsealed documents and require that all be treated as unsealed. These statutes, along with the Uniform Commercial Code, have gone a long way toward requiring witnesses for the authentication of all private documents. In these states the distinction between formal and informal contracts remains in tact. Corbin described that distinction as follows:

> The most important difference between a formal and an informal contract at common law lies in the fact that a formal contract can be made operative by sealing and delivery. Neither a consideration, as now defined, nor subsequent action in reliance is necessary in order to make the sealed promise enforceable (Corbin, 1952:Sec. 252).

Another change widely reflected in current law derives from adjustments that have been traced to the influence of the Christian Church on English common law (Berman, 1983:345). Unlike the ancient and medieval practice, modern law makes available a defense of fraud in the execution of a seal. Thus, Corbin observed, 'one man cannot bind another by attaching a seal without authority, any more than he can bind him by forging his signature' (Corbin, 1952:Sec. 242). As we have seen, this has not always been the case.

III
The Oath

Black's Law Dictionary defines an oath as 'any attestation by which a person signifies that he is bound in conscience to perform an act faithfully and truthfully, e.g., President's oath on entering office.' An oath is distinguished from a vow. A vow is merely a personal promise, whereas an oath is a promise made before an authority figure. By swearing an oath a person not only undertakes an obligation, but also becomes liable to sanctions imposed by that authority.

Traditionally, an oath has been a religious act, invoking the penalty of divine retribution should the obligation undertaken be violated. As such, oath-taking appears to be rooted in the even more primitive practice of the curse, except, in the case of the oath, the ritual invocation of divine punishment is conditional and self-directed (Falk, 1964:60-61). Thus, Corbin observed:

> In earlier centuries, men who feared ghosts were asked to swear by the ghosts of their ancestors. In making promises, those who feared and worshiped an awful Deity pledged their faith, or called God to witness, or made the sign of the cross. The small boys of today no doubt feel the weight of an awful sanction when they say 'I cross my heart [and hope] to die' (Corbin, 1952:Sec. 240).

An oath is self-endorsing in the sense that it establishes that the person making it is under obligation to perform the sworn duty faithfully and truthfully. No further evidence is needed that the duty is voluntarily undertaken than that the oath is duly sworn. In this way, oaths are solemn undertakings. Some even mark turning points in the history of a people. Thus, the people of Israel were constituted as a people by an oath.

> That thou shouldest enter into covenant with the Lord thy God, and into his oath, which the Lord thy God maketh with thee this day: That he may establish thee today for a people unto himself, and that he may be unto thee a God, as he has said unto thee, and as he hath sworn unto thy fathers, to Abraham, to Isaac, and to Jacob (*Deuteronomy* 29:12-13).

Oath taking in legal contexts is of very ancient origins. Over the millennia it has undergone a variety of changes. In this section the history of oath-taking will be sketched over three eras: ancient, medieval and present.

In the ancient era legal disputes were regularly resolved by the use of witnesses or documentary evidence. Witnesses swore oaths assuring the judges of the truth of their statements. Thus, in a mid-second millennium *Edict of Ammisaduqa*, a debtor could prevail in a dispute over the wording in a loan agreement if he produced 'his witnesses to the wording of the document which the lender had denied, and they shall speak their testimony before god,' (*Edict of Ammisaduqa*, sec. 7, in Pritchard, 1968:527).

If, however, witnesses and documentary evidence were unavailable, the disputes were often resolved by the parties themselves swearing an oath. One such instance is related in a fourth millennia Sumerian legal text. 'Lugalemahe bought a slave for four shekels of silver. The witnesses are dead. Therefore, if Lugalemahe swears to it, he can keep the slave,' quoted in Boecker, 1980:24.

Another practice, common throughout the ancient near east, was to permit a bailee to escape liability by swearing that he had done nothing wrong. Thus, in *The Laws of Eshnunna*, early in the second millennium, a man who accepted a deposit which later turned up missing, could avoid replacing the lost property if he 'swear him an oath in the gate of Tishpak [the main god of Eshnunna] saying: 'Together with your property my property was lost; I have done nothing improper or fraudulent.' If he swears him such an oath, he shall have no claim against him,' (*Code of Hammurabi* Sec. 103-03, 120, 227, in Pritchard, 1968:163. Also see: *Exodus* 22:7-9).

Throughout the ancient near east, people accused of wrongs against the person could often exculpate themselves by taking oaths. Under the *Code of Hammurabi*, as well as ancient Jewish law, a wife who was accused by her husband of adultery, but was not caught *in flagrante delicto*, could escape punishment by swearing to her innocence, (*Code of Hammurabi*, sec. 131, in Pritchard, 1968:171, *Numbers* 18-19).

Oaths played key roles in Roman law as well. Justinian reported that oaths were used to settle disputes over the existence of oral testamentary trusts. These were noticed by Maine and mistakenly thought to be the earliest appearance of legally recognized oaths.

> . . . [I]f a testator charges his heir with a trust to transfer the whole inheritance or some specific thing, and the trust cannot be proved by writing or by the evidence of five witnesses . . . the alleged beneficiary, having previously sworn to his own good faith, may put the heir upon his oath: whereupon the heir may be compelled to swear that no trust was even charged upon him, or, in default, to transfer the inheritance or the specific thing, as the case may be, in order that the last wishes of the testator . . . may not be defeated (*Institutes of Justinian*, 1913:II. 23.12).

In ancient times, oaths were not only recognized by the different legal systems, but penalties for perjury were regularly provided. In late third millennium Sumer, witnesses who perjured themselves were subject to fines of fifteen shekels of silver, (*The Law of Ur-Nammu*, sec. 25, in Pritchard, 1968:525). The *Code of Hammurabi* prescribed a penalty of death for anyone who gives false testimony in a capital case, (*Code of Hammurabi*, sec. 3, in Pritchard, 1968:166). In Israel, false testimony was considered so grave an offense that its proscription was included in the Decalog: 'You shall not bear false witness against your neighbor' (*Exodus* 20:13). Two types of penalties were provided in ancient Israel for those who violated that injunction (Dorff and Rosett, 1988:70-71). According to one, they were to be required to restore 120% of what anyone lost because of their false testimony and besides, they were to make a 'guilt offering' with the priest (*Leviticus* 5:20-26). According to the other, the magistrate was required to apply the principle of *lex talionis*. 'You shall do to him as he schemed to do to his fellows. . . . Nor must you show pity: life for life, eye for eye, tooth for tooth, hand for hand, foot for foot' (*Deuteronomy* 9:16-21).

In all these examples of oaths we observe two aspects, viz., the undertaking of an obligation and the invocation of deities. The latter aspect was often incorporated into the practice of oath-taking quite indirectly. Oaths were often sworn in holy places, such as temples, in the presence of sacred objects, such as cult artifact, administered by priests, or sworn in a god's name (*Deuteronomy 6:13).* The reference to the divine in oath-taking, whether direct or indirect, served to assure others of the oath-taker's commitment to performing upon the obligation thereby undertaken. The profession of regard to a deity which the oath-taker reverenced, however, was not the central feature of the oath. Rather, the oath is a solemn act of undertaking an obligation. In these examples of oath-taking, the divine appears to have served to officiate over such pledges. This point was emphasized by Cicero.

> Where an oath is involved, our attention should not be focused on fear of possible punishment but on the essence of taking the oath itself. An oath is a sacred and binding undertaking; and what you promise as an obligation, with God as witness, as it were, you must honor. At that point it does not involve the wrath of the gods, which does not exist, but it involves justice and trust. Ennius, you remember, wrote a famous line: 'A nourishing Trust, fitted with wings, and the oath of Jupiter!' (Cicero, 1974:Book III, Sec. 104)

The treatment of the oath under the common law of England derived from Germanic influences present in its Anglo-Saxon heritage. In pre-conquest Britain, the oath figured importantly with the ordeal in settling disputes among and within the tribes. Those with grievances swore out complaints before the elders. Those accused swore out their defence. These oaths were, Plucknett conjectured, the earliest form of pleading (Plucknett, 1956:400). After these 'fore-oaths' the decision was made as to who would be permitted to enter an oath of proof. Proof in Anglo-Saxon Britain was not concerned with establishing the facts in particular cases.

> Oath was the primary mode of proof, an oath going not to the truth of specific fact, but to the justice of the claim or defence as a whole. The number of persons required to swear varied according to the nature of the case and the rank of the persons concerned. Inasmuch as the oath, if duly made, was conclusive, what we now call the burden of proof was rather a benefit than otherwise under ancient Germanic procedure (Pollock and Maitland, 1899:I, 39).

Just as oaths in ancient times referred to the divine as witness, so also in Anglo-Saxon Britain the oath had a supernatural dimension. As with the ancients, the Germanic tribes initially found that sufficient.

> [E]ven when the proof is to consist merely of oaths, a supernatural element is present. The swearer satisfies human justice by taking the oath. If he has sworn falsely, he is exposed to the wrath of God and in some subsequent proceeding may perhaps be convicted of perjury. . . (Pollock and Maitland, 1899:II, 600).

By the late twelveth century, oaths were replacing battle as the preferred means of deciding disputes. Thus, Glanvill reported that the Grand Assize 'requires the oaths of at least twelve men.'

> When twelve knights who are all certain of the truth of the matter appear to make the recognition, then the assize shall proceed to declare which of the

> parties, demandant or tenant, has the greater right in the land claimed (Glanvill, 1965:II. 18).

The importance of oath-taking was further reinforced in the thirteenth century in the Great Charters issued by the English kings. For example, the Great Charter of King John pledged that: 'A free man shall not be amerced . . . but by the oath of honest men of the vicinage,' (Magna Charta, 1839:Chap. XX).

The Anglo-Saxons were unsure of whether perjury ought to be punished. 'Will it not be interfering with the gods?' (Pollock and Maitland, 1899:II, 541). By the end of the twelveth century Glanvill reported that the royal constitution provided for severe penalties for jurors convicted of perjury (Glanvill, 1965:II, 19). Harold Berman suggests that the law of perjury underwent development at that time due to the influence of the Christian Church that asserted its interest in perjury as a sin.

> Christianity had an important effect on judicial proof by oaths, since the swearing of oaths began [by the eleventh century C.E.] to take Christian forms and was supported by ecclesiastical sanctions. Oaths were administered by priests in churches, at altars, on relics, and through appeals to divine sanctions against falsehood; and false swearing was subject to discipline through ecclesiastical penances (Berman, 1983:65).

During the middle ages, perjury on the part of witnesses was dealt with by the Church through the jurisdiction of the Chancery. The lay courts focused mainly on juror perjury. In those times a jury verdict could be reversed by another jury twice its size. When that happened, the verdict of the original jury was regarded as false and the jurors who returned that verdict were guilty of perjury and subject to heavy fines and imprisonment. During the twelfth and thirteenth century, Pollock and Maitland report, 'the law seems to have no procedure which directly strives to distinguish among untrue verdicts those which are sworn with a knowledge of their falsehood,' (Pollock and Maitland, 1899:II, 542).

At present, as in earlier eras, oaths are used in a variety of contexts. Today, the judicial oath is the central case of oaths in law. These attest to the truth of testimony introduced in judicial proceedings. They are ordinarily discussed in the same terms as are familiar from earlier eras.

> An oath is a declaration of the truth of a statement, which may be either written or oral. . . . In its strict sense the term refers to an attestation that is coupled

> with an invocation to the Supreme Being to witness the words of the attesting party and to visit him or her with judgment if the words be false (Skojec, 1989:1047).

In contrast to the ancient and medieval era, oaths are no longer regarded as conclusive proof of the sworn statement, but only as a necessary prerequisite to giving testimony. Courts will accept testimony only if the witness swears to it. McCormick distinguished two functions of the rule that testimony not be admitted unless taken under oath. 'As a ceremonial and religious symbol it may induce in the witness a feeling of special obligation to speak the truth, and also it may impress upon the witness the danger of criminal punishment for perjury. . . .' (McCormick, 1972:582). These, of course, have been the distinctive aspects of oath-taking all along.

A second difference between present practice and previous eras relates to the capacity to swear an oath. At common law and in the ancient era, belief in a divine being who avenges false swearing was a prerequisite of the capacity to swear an oath. Those who were affiliated with recognized religions could meet that test, but those who belonged to other religions, or who were atheists or agnostics, could not. In our day that incapacity has been eliminated (McCormick, 1972:141-2). Courts now accept the testimony even of those who do not believe in a supreme being. All that is required is that each witness affirms that he or she is bound in conscience to speak the truth (Skojec, 1989:1048-49).

IV
Conclusions

From a cognitive perspective, what can be said about the seal and the oath? On this view the practice of sealing for authenticity and oath-taking must be portrayed as expressing the beliefs of those who engage in these practices. Much can be said for approaching practices in each era from that perspective. With ample access to relevant cultural information, we can ask and answer the question as to what the Sumerians and medieval English had in mind as they invoked the seal as proof of the validity of documents, as to what the Hebrews of old and Americans of the present think they are up to when they testify under oath.

However, what the cognitive approach will not illuminate is the survival of these practices over the past six millennia. The reasoning here is straight-forward. If the practices of affixing seals to documents and of oath-taking had changed to accommodate changing patterns of belief, the cognitive perspective could suffice to explain that change. However, that isn't what happened. We have seen in the first two sections of this paper that these practices remained basically intact while the belief structures relating to them underwent radical changes. For example, the oath was initially used to call down a divine curse on the oath-taker should he not perform on the obligation thereby undertaken. In our day, oaths are indiscernible from mere affirmation of the obligation to tell the truth, an utterance that need not even mention the divinity, much less invoke its curse. From a cognitive perspective the inheritance of these practices can only be discounted as the product of powerful superstition.

The changing patterns of belief that have attended the seal and the oath over the millennia poses no special challenge for the non-cognitive perspective. If anything, the variety of beliefs that have been thought compatible with these rituals shows their richness and versatility, rather than their irrationality. How, then, does the non-cognitive approach illuminate these practices?

From the non-cognitivist perspective semiosis is the process whereby some phenomena are linked with others, such that the former can be taken by someone as standing [in] for the latter. The distinctive aspect of this approach to semiosis is the proposal that this linkage is best seen as a coordination accomplished by ritual practices.

In previous papers to these workshops I sketched several ways in which this occurs. For ease of discussion, consider the example of communication. Of course the cognitivist conviction that communication amounts to the encoding, transfer and decoding of messages is utterly rejected. Instead, non-cognitivism proposes that we regard communication as the coordination of stereotyped display and response patterns. This coordination can be accomplished in either of two ways, depending upon whether the phenomena to be linked are causally related to the survival of the sponsoring population. In the case of animal communication, they are causally related. Those animals that do not respond to threatening displays by predators are considerably less likely to survive as a species than are those animals that do so respond. The more general point here is that semiotic linkages often result from natural selection (Lindgren, 1992:245-46).

Phenomena linked through semiosis, however, need not be causally related. As indicated in my discussion of money two years ago, causally unrelated phenomena are frequently linked by ritual practices such as commercial exchanges. There the linkage is established by conventional rituals in which causally unrelated phenomena are substituted for one another (Lindgren, 1993:293-95).

The coordination established by seals and oaths is between the performance by the person who attaches the seal or takes the oath and the judicial interpretation given those performances. For example, for most of their careers, seals were taken as sufficient to prove the authenticity of documents and oaths as sufficient to establish the truthfulness of the oath-taker.

The semiotic process by which this coordination occurred might be construed either as a result of natural selection, similar to that of animal communication, or as conventional, like money. Until quite recently, the former analysis was preferred. Consider the case of oaths. For millennia oath-takers were thought to be causally motivated to tell the truth by fear of retribution at the hands of the god by whom they swore. This belief suggested to many that those who swore falsely would be selected against by a just god.

With the merging of the oath and the affirmation, that gloss on the oath has given way to another that represents it simply as a solemn device whereby the oath-taker publicly undertakes an obligation. Here there is no hint of a causal connection between the affirmation and a truthful performance. What is present here, as with money, is a common need for some settled practice that established the existence of an obligation to tell the truth and at least one device that, because of its salience, is accepted by the population as the way that will be accomplished. In this respect, oaths and seals are accepted at face value in much the same way as is money, not because there is a causal connection that is noticed, but simply because it is the prevailing convention.

**J. Ralph Lindgren is Clara H. Stewardson Professor of Philosophy at Lehigh University.*

Author's Note:

Over the past few decades a non-cognitivist approach to semiotics has increasingly been asserted. Instead of viewing knowledge as primitive and action as behavior scripted by knowledge, thus portraying semiosis as an encoding and decoding process, this approach accords primacy to practice and views belief as derivative. On that view, semiosis is a process of ritualization by which stereotyped behaviors come to be coordinated over a wide range of circumstances.

This paper adds further evidence in favor of the non-cognitivist approach to legal semiotics. It focuses on two signs in the law of evidence, the seal and the oath. A review of their usage over the past six millennia shows that their ritual functions continued intact long after belief structures associated with their usage came and went several times over. Whereas these discontinuities pose no special challenge for a non-cognitive approach, they are quite inconvenient for a cognitivist approach to semiotics.

REFERENCES

Berman, Harold J., 1983, *Law and Revolution: The Formation of the Western Legal Tradition*, Cambridge, Massachusetts: Harvard University Press.

Blackstone, William, 1775-79, *Commentaries on the Laws of England*, 4 vols., Oxford: Clarendon Press.

Boecker, Hans Jochen, 1980, *Law and the Administration of Justice in the Old Testament and Ancient East*, Minneapolis, Minnesota: Augsburg Publishing House.

Cicero, 1974, *De Officiis/On Duties*, Edinger transl., New York: Bobbs-Merrill Co.

Corbin, Arthur L., 1952, *Corbin on Contracts*, One Volume Edition, St. Paul, Minnesota: West Publishing Co.

Dorff, Elliot N. and Arthur Rosett, 1988, *A Living Tree: The Roots and Growth of Jewish Law*, Albany, New York: State University of New York Press.

Falk, Ze'ev W., 1964, *Hebrew Law in Biblical Times*, Jerusalem: Wahrmann Books.

Glanvill, 1965, *The Treatise on the Laws and Customs of the Realm of England Commonly Called Glanvill*, ed. G. D. G. Hall, London: Nelson.

Holdsworth, William, 1937, *A History of English Law*, Vol. 8., London: Nethuen & Co., Ltd.

Institutes of Justinian, 1913, Moyle transl., 5th ed., Oxford: Clarendon Press.

Lindgren, J. Ralph., 1992, 'Semiosis as Ritual,' ed. R. Kevelson, *Law and the Human Sciences*, New York: Peter Lang, 233-254.

_____, 1993, 'The Emergence of Signs: The Seminal Convention of Money,' ed. R. Kevelson, *Flux, Complexity, and Illusion*, New York: Peter Lang, 283-298.

Magna Charta, 1839, London: Major and Jennings.

McCormick, 1972, *McCormick's Handbook on the Law of Evidence*, 2d ed., by E. W. Cleary, St. Paul, Minnesota: West Publishing Co.

Maine, Henry S., 1861, *Ancient Law*, London: John Murray.

Plucknett, Theodore F. T., 1956, *A Concise History of the Common Law*, 5th Ed., Boston: Little, Brown and Co.

Pollock, Frederick and Frederick W. Maitland, 1899, *The History of English Law Before the Time of Edward I*, 2d ed., 2 vols., Boston: Little, Brown and Co.

Pritchard, James B., 1969, *Ancient Near Eastern Texts Relating to the Old Testament*, 3d ed., Princeton, New Jersey: Princeton University Press.

Skojec, Sheila A., 1989, 'Oath and Affirmation,' 58 *Am Jur* 2d 1043, 1047.

Chapter Fifteen

Evolution and 19th Century Legal Pragmatism: Darwin and Holmes

Alfred S. Neely*

I
One of the Faces of Holmes

Justice Oliver Wendell Holmes, Jr. 'has . . . been all things to all commentators.'[1] One of Holmes' many faces is that of the iconoclast, and as much dismantler as builder of systems. This is a role Holmes played on broad fronts. He has been described, for instance, as:

> first and foremost, a late nineteenth century intellectual radical. He was concerned with smashing existing fixed systems of the universe and substituting a fluid one. *The Common Law* was his most telling work — it was critical of the quasi-religious formalistic logic of his time and supportive of two fluid organizing concepts, history and community values.[2]

My purpose here is to examine one facet of Holmes as iconoclast.

My approach is to focus on a small story in the history of ideas. Its objects are two disparate figures — a naturalist and a jurist. In particular, the inquiry is how the science of Charles Darwin came to influence Holmes' jurisprudence. My concern is not so much the nature of Darwin's influence, but rather the manner of the influence, and how Holmes saw it and accepted it. What I am interested in concerning Holmes and Darwin in the 19th century, in the parlance of Presidential politics in the 20th, is — what did Holmes know, when did he know it, and how did he come by it? The goal is some insight, albeit narrow, into the revolutionary quality of the epistemology of the legal pragmatism evidenced in Holmes.

II
The Darwinian Revolution and 19th Century Thought

Charles Darwin's *On the Origin of Species by Means of Natural Selection or the Preservation of Favored Races in the Struggle for Life* appeared in 1859. It has been described as 'the most influential book since Newton's *Principia*.'[3] It represents a true turning point. As one observer noted: 'For historians of science, the 'Darwinian Revolution' has always ranked alongside the 'Copernican Revolution' as one of those episodes in which a new scientific theory symbolizes a wholesale change in cultural values.'[4] In similar vein, its significance also has been recognized in the more particularized world of American law. Justice Felix Frankfurter's description of the event is typical: '[B]etween Story and Langdell there occurred one of the decisive ideas in the history of thought — the publication in 1859 of the Origin of Species.'[5] More recently another characterized this work as 'the determining influence on American law during the remainder of the [19th] century' in which '[e]volution would soon become the school in which law itself was to be learned . . . .'[6]

Darwinian evolution stood in sharp contrast to that which it challenged. It proceeded on the premise that the world is the outgrowth of natural forces playing out over long reaches of time.[7] Evolution was thus process, the product and promise of change. Beyond its evolutionary component, Darwinism contained a second basic proposition, that of natural selection as evolution's driving force.[8] Darwin's promise of change, however, did not carry a promise of progress to a better end.[9]

III
Darwin's Imprint in Holmes

Darwin's presence in Holmes' thought is undeniable. The opening paragraph in Holmes' 1881 book, *The Common Law*, is an early and perhaps most famous point of origins.

> The life of the law has not been logic: it has been experience. The felt necessities of the time, the prevalent moral and political theories, intuitions of public policy, avowed or unconscious, even the prejudices which judges share with their fellow-men, have had a good deal more to do than the syllogism in determining the rules by which men should be governed. The law embodies the story of a nation's development through many centuries, and it cannot be dealt with as if it contained only the axioms and corollaries of a book of mathematics. In order to know what

> it is, we must know what it has been, and what it tends to become. We must alternately consult history and existing theories of legislation. But the most difficult labor will be to understand the combination of the two into new products at every stage. The substance of the law at any given time pretty nearly corresponds as far as it goes, with what is then understood to be convenient; but its form and machinery, and the degree to which it is able to work out desired results, depend very much on its past.

These evolutionary themes repeat. Holmes observed, for example, that the law 'is forever adopting new principles from life at one end, and it always retains old ones from history at the other, which have not yet been absorbed or sloughed off. It will become entirely consistent only when it ceases to grow.' One sees them again in his famous parallel of the cat's clavicle: '[J]ust as the clavicle in the cat only tells of the existence of some earlier creature to which a collar-bone was useful, precedents survive in the law long after the use they once served is at an end and the reason for them has been forgotten.'[10]

Holmes' 1899 address to the New York State Bar Association, *Law in Science and Science in Law*, yields similar artifacts. For example, in discussing why plighting of troth did not make the journey from ecclesiastical to secular courts, he described the occurrence as 'a lively example of the struggle for life among competing ideas, and of the ultimate victory and survival of the strongest.' Holmes believed '[w]e have evolution in . . . conscious thought and action no less than in lower organic stages . . . .'[11] And the evidence is in Holmes' judicial record as well: 'I think the strike a lawful instrument in the universal struggle of life . . . .'[12]

Holmes' evolutionary world, as Darwin's, was not one of design, known ends or notions of progress. Holmes wrote in 1925: 'I don't know that causes produce equivalent effects — or whether the cosmos is merely having a transitory whim of orderly sequence, but discoveries are made on the assumptions of continuity &c. and therefore those assumptions seem best for practical purposes. Chauncey Wright long ago pointed out to me the impossibility of assuming necessity as an ultimate cosmic fact. I don't know anything about ultimate or absolute truth and all the rest follows.'[13]

IV
The Darwin\Holmes Link — According to Holmes

The philosopher Morris R. Cohen was one of Holmes' many correspondents. In one exchange Holmes commented to the effect 'that of all the intellectual gaps between generations the gap between his own and his father's appeared to him the widest,' and Cohen asked 'whether this intellectual shift might be ascribed to Voltaire.'[14] Holmes responded:

> Oh no — it was not Voltaire — it was the influence of the scientific way of looking at the world — that made the change to which I referred. My father was brought up scientifically — i.e. he studied medicine in France — and I was not. Yet there was with him as with most of his generation a certain softness of attitude towards the interstitial miracle — the phenomenon without phenomenal antecedents, that I did not feel. The difference was in the air, although perhaps only the few of my time felt it. The Origin of the Species I think came out while I was in college — H. Spencer had announced his intention to put the universe in our pockets — I hadn't read either of them to be sure, but as I say it was in the air. I did read Buckle — now almost forgotten — but making a noise in his day, but I could refer to no book as the specific cause — I never have read much of Voltaire and probably at that time had read nothing.[15]

By Holmes' account he did not turn to Darwin until 1907,[16] and at that late date his purpose was principally edification. As he wrote in 1909, 'I regard pretty much everything, and especially the greatest things, in the way of books, as dead in fifty, nowadays in twenty years. The seeds of thought germinated and produce later seeds. The old structures are remodelled and have electric lights put in. One of the proofs that a word contains living thoughts is that it kills itself. . . I read Montesquieu simply to admire his genius . . . [T]o read the great men of the past was the last achievement of a studious life.'[17]

V
The Darwin\Holmes Link — Is Holmes to be Taken at His Word?

One of the many great challenges with Holmes is accepting him on his own terms, by his own lights, and at his own word. One reason for this difficulty is that this seldom leaves one with tightly drawn distinctions, neatly tied parcels, and a minimum of loose ends. Holmes may have found his Darwin 'in the air,' but not surprisingly his commentators have tended to search for more specific explanations of the Darwin so clear in Holmes. Various possibilities have been suggested.

His first official biographer and one of his last law clerks, Mark DeWolfe Howe, thought Holmes found his Darwin in Herbert Spencer, the great popularizer of the term 'evolution.' Holmes read Spencer's *Social Statics* and *First Principles* in 1863 while recovering from his third round of Civil War wounds.[18] E. Donald Elliott was of similar view.[19] Herbert Hovencamp, on another hand, thought the answer to the 'perplexing question' of how Darwin influenced Holmes was in Holmes' reading of the Darwinian cultural anthropologist Edward B. Tylor, whose 1871 book, *Primitive Culture*, was cited in Holmes' *The Common Law*.[20]

Others have not been so insistent about identifying definitive lineage of Darwin in Holmes. Philip P. Wiener agreed that Darwin was 'in the air,' and that Holmes did not have to read him. Conversation and correspondence, teachers and friends were among the sources, honed by Holmes' war experience, from which Holmes took his Darwin. For Weiner the important thing is that we know Holmes did get it.[21]

Holmes' most recent biographer, G. Edward White, seems generally in agreement with Wiener. He sees Darwin in Holmes' record.[22] However, he raises another possibility, that Holmes took his Darwin from neither the air, Spencer, Tylor nor any other derivative source, but instead directly from Darwin. Perhaps Holmes read Darwin surreptitiously and long before the 1907 date he admitted, and was unwilling, even incapable of giving it any more recognition than in broad stroke and in passing.[23] White notes, without commentary, Holmes' claim '[d]espite the presence of a marked copy of an 1860 edition of *The Origin of the Species* in Holmes' library. . . .'[24] This possibility, that Holmes' failure to give direct attribution and credit to Darwin's influence was a lie, might be explained as a product of his inclinations not to share credit and recognize intellectual debts. White observes, for example, that although Holmes' early work was to an important extent derivative of the work of others, . . . the derivative aspects of his early scholarship are not readily discerned because Holmes was loathe to acknowledge influences on and antecedents of his work, and fiercely protective of contributions he regarded as original to him, even when their originality was perhaps cloudier than he claimed.'[25]

This, however, does not ring true in this instance. Although Holmes may not be known for modesty in style or ambition, he was capable of putting himself in limited place and perspective: 'It makes one realize that apercus, one's own or of others, that seemed to indicate a new point of view were but particles in a current.'[26] Furthermore, Holmes was open, lavish and frequent in otherwise recognizing the uniqueness and greatness of Darwin and his contribution to modern thought. Holmes' words in 1895 in praise of Spencer evidence even greater respect for Darwin: 'H. Spencer you English never quite do justice to . . . He is dull. He writes an ugly uncharming style, his ideals are those of a lower middle class British Philistine. And yet after all abatements I doubt if any writer of English except Darwin has done so much to affect our whole way of thinking about the universe.'[27]

Another possibility is that Holmes did not need to learn his Darwin from Darwin. His sense of the harsh realities of evolutionary struggle might have been more vividly taken from his experiences on the battlefields of the Civil War. As he said years later, looking back on his wartime experience, '[f]or my own part, I believe that the struggle for life is the order of the world, at which it is vain to repine.'[28]

Still another explanation of Holmes' casualness might be that he simply did not care enough to trace his own thoughts among the intellectual currents of his day. Some have suggested, for example, that Holmes' much celebrated stance of judicial restraint was a product of neither 'humility' nor praiseworthy 'skepticism,' but rather was to be understood 'in Holmes' fatalism, in his attitude toward power, and finally in his detachment . . . To a remarkable degree, Holmes simply did not care.'[29] In this light, the question of where he got his Darwin might have seemed trivial in the face of his own profound sense of the inevitability of the unknown and the unknowable, '[t]hat the universe has in it more than we understand, that the private soldiers have not been told the plan of campaign, or even that there is one. . . .'[30]

VI

A Way of Knowing — 'The difference was in the air. . . .'

It may be, however, that the answer is not so much in secondhand sources, intellectual arrogance, apathy, carelessness or outright deception. Perhaps Holmes really can be taken on his own terms, by his own lights, and at his own word. The answer may be in his manner of thinking, his ways of knowing, his sense of which questions were important and deserved serious and careful answers, and which less so. Holmes' protege, friend and proselytizer, Justice Frankfurter, points a way.

> You damned sociologists, you historians who want to get it all nice and fine on paper, you haven't learned how much in this world is determined by non-syllogistic reasoning, or without conscious exploration of a problem with a view

> to reaching a logical conclusion. You fellows haven't learned that. You think that we're just rationalistic — not merely reasonable, but rationalistic — automata of a logical process.[31]

For Frankfurter the 'impalpables' of a thing might be the most significant route to understanding, and the historian's failure to recognize this his greatest shortcoming: 'I should think you historians fail, as much as you fail in anything, in recapturing that impalpable thing, what was in the air. That's the most important thing in understanding events — the things that aren't written down because everybody takes them for granted.'[32] Frankfurter believed this to be so with Darwin and Holmes: '[T]he *Zeitgeist* moved also through O.W. Holmes, Jr. He came to maturity when Darwin had upset men's most ancient beliefs. The evolutionary doctrines worked as ferment beyond their immediate scope.'[33] What Frankfurter provides is a setting in which one can better understand why a Holmes could comfortably explain that his Darwin 'was in the air.'

The picture becomes more complete and Holmes' explanation more understandable when its philosophic underpinnings are considered. This requires a view of Holmes as more than iconoclast and a dismantler of systems, one which sees him as in fact offering a substitute, namely the American philosophy of pragmatism as it emerged and developed in the late nineteenth century. Holmes himself might not have conceded the intellectual link, at least not always and not openly. Pragmatism sometimes ranked with the federal antitrust law, the Sherman Act of 1890, in Holmes' pantheon of humbugs.[34] As he wrote to Pollock in 1908, 'I think pragmatism an amusing humbug — like most of William James's speculations . . . .'[35] Others have seen it differently, and placed Holmes within pragmatism's mainstream.[36]

Actually Holmes himself was less harsh and often complimentary in his views on other principals of pragmatism such as John Dewey and Charles Sanders Peirce. These two crystallized and brought pragmatism to its status as a special and uniquely American philosophy. Concerning Dewey, Holmes wrote:

> I read John Dewey, *Human Nature and Conduct*, a book that I find hard to characterize. It is like shavings of jade — subtle — sometimes epigrammatic — emancipated — seeing the world and man as fluid — an immense advance upon any book there was when I was younger — yet somehow not quite seeming to

> arrive anywhere — and not feeling to me quite as new as it is civilized. I seem to have known the fundamentals before.[37]

Holmes' experience with Dewey's *Experience and Nature* was similarly positive and difficult: 'It makes on me an impression like Walt Whitman, of being symphonic, and of having more life and experience in his head than most writers, philosophers or others. He writes badly and creates more difficulty by his style than by his thought.'[38]

Holmes also had genuine respect for Peirce, although his praise was not unqualified. As he wrote to Harold Laski, 'Peirce thinks his ultimates are cosmic ultimates, whereas I think they couldn't be assumed to be more than his intellectual limitations.'[39] In that regard Holmes viewed himself a diametric opposite: 'I don't believe or know anything about absolute truth.'[40] But when it came to Peirce's effect, Holmes was fully generous and suggests his own sense of the mysterious, often hidden paths by which great ideas take hold and bring about change. Again, Holmes to Laski:

> [L]ast night came *Chance, Love and Logic* by Charles S. Peirce with introduction by Cohen and supplemented by Dewey. Averse as I am to improvement right now I at once read Cohen's masterly little discourse and I think I must read the book at once. It suggests an image. More than ten years ago we had a flower bed on the bank in front of the house — including certain poppies that my wife's father gave her with the warning that she never would get rid of them. The bed was obliterated as I have intimated ten or more years ago — but a few days back my wife had some turf turned up to allow some creeping roses to expand and lo! up came the old poppies — the seeds must have been waiting their time. So these obscure geniuses drop a few seeds that no one notices and when they are dead their seeds sprout and blossom into one's most valued flowers. How much more impressive than 'our most highly gifted men.'[41]

It seems that Holmes' debunking of pragmatism was more personal to James than particular to pragmatism itself.

In fact, the pragmatism Holmes sometimes denied seems evident in and relevant to his comment on Darwin. Dewey's description of the contours of pragmatism is helpful in seeing this:

> Pragmatism . . . presents itself as an extension of historical empiricism, but with this fundamental difference, that it does not insist upon antecedent phenomena but upon consequent phenomena; not upon the precedents but upon the possibilities of

action. And this change in point of view is almost revolutionary in its consequences.[42]

Thus, when Holmes tells that 'it was in the air,' he also relates that for him effect is more important than attribution. It seems that for Holmes it is more than adequate explanation that it is 'in the air.' That is all one need know. Anything more, although interesting, is superfluous. Or, in Dewey's terms, 'antecedent phenomena' are of minor importance, unlike 'consequent phenomena,' which are key.

This manner of difference is evident elsewhere in Holmes. For example, in 1910 he wrote Sir Frederick Pollock concerning his recent reading of the French mathematician and physicist Poincare. Holmes had been bothered by Poincare's mathematics, a subject in which Holmes freely admitted his own shortcomings.[43] This, alone, would lead many to disqualify themselves from taking insight from premises beyond their understanding. That was not so with Holmes: '[B]ut I said to myself that if the premises and conclusion are above the table and you accept both it doesn't matter so much by what particular wheels underneath the writer brings out the result.'[44] This could be taken as intellectual arrogance. But instead it might reflect the method of one who valued the sensibilities and reality of the final result far more than the logic of the syllogism that produced it.

The same may be seen in Holmes as judge. It seems that '[w]hen Holmes was in the process of writing opinions . . . , he would ask his secretaries to find him citations, preferably from his previous opinions . . . .'[45] The implication is that he was not driven by doctrines of precedent and *stare decisis* where it was most expected, in the process of judging. This might be taken as evidence of judicial sloth, intellectual arrogance or worse. Or perhaps this is just another illustration of Holmes' pragmatic sense that precise attribution of sources and authorities was just not necessary and important enough to go out of one's way to mention. In that context it does not surprise that he was casual in explaining the origins of his intellectual debt to Darwin.

'The difference was in the air' was all the answer Holmes needed, and he was not inclined to worry the matter at the instigation, or for the benefit, of others. For Holmes it was just not very important where he got his Darwin. What was important to him was that he got it, and that its insights were available in addressing the future. In this was the hand of the pragmatist who 'will pay whatever attention to the past is required by good strategy.'[46] Also in this one sees the hand of the iconoclast, altering the 19th century sense of which questions are the important questions, and how one should address and answer them.

**Alfred S. Neely is Professor of Law at the University of Missouri-Columbia.*

ENDNOTES

1. G. Edward White, 1986, 'Looking at Holmes in the Mirror,' 4 *Law and Hist. Rev.* 439, 440.

2. G. Edward White, 1971, 'The Rise and Fall of Justice Holmes,' 39 *U. Chi. L. Rev.* 51, 74.

3. Alan Cromer, 1993, *Uncommon Sense: The Heretical Nature of Science,* 39.

4. Peter J. Bowler, 1984, *Evolution: The History of an Idea,* 1.

5. Felix Frankfurter, 1930, 'The Conditions For, and the Aims and Methods of Legal Research,' 15 *Iowa L. Rev.*, 129, 132.

6. Bernard Schwartz, 1993, *Main Currents in American Legal Thought,* 282.

7. Bowler, *supra* note 4, at 4.

8. Cromer, *supra* note 3, at 39-40.

9. Bowler, *supra* note 4, at 184-85. Both Darwin and Herbert Spencer saw the process as 'open-ended,' although Darwin did not subscribe to Spencer's notion that progress would inevitably and necessarily 'advance toward higher levels of organization.' *Id.* at 9.

10. Oliver Wendell Holmes, Jr., 1881, *The Common Law* 1, 36, 35.

11. Oliver Wendell Holmes, Jr., 1899, 'Law in Science and Science in Law,' 12 *Harv. L. Rev.*, 443, 449, 447.

12. E.g., *Plant v. Woods*, 176 Mass. 492, 505, 1900, dissenting J. Holmes.

13. Oliver Wendell Holmes, Jr., ed. Mark DeWolfe Howe, 1953 to Harold J. Laski, July 23, 1924, in 2 *Holmes-Laski Letters,* 634.

14. 'The Holmes-[Morris R.] Cohen Correspondence,' ed. Felix S. Cohen, 1948, in 9 *J. Hist. Ideas,* 14 n.27, editor's description of likely content of missing exchange.

15. Letter from Oliver W. Holmes, Jr., to Morris R. Cohen, Feb. 5, 1919, *id.* at 14-15. Henry Thomas Buckle's *History of Civilization* appeared in 1857. He presented history as a science and developed the proposition that order is the offspring of chance.

16. Mark DeWolfe Howe, 1957, *Justice Oliver Wendell Holmes: The Shaping Years 1841-1870*, citing Letter from Oliver Wendell Holmes, Jr. to Clara Sherwood Stevens, April 28, 1907.

17. Letter from Oliver Wendell Holmes, Jr. to Canon Patrick A. Sheehan, July 17, 1909, ed. D. Burton, 1976, in *Holmes-Sheehan Correspondence*, 27, 28.

18. Howe, *supra* note 16, at 156.

19. E. Donald Elliott, 1984, 'Holmes and Evolution: Legal Process As Artificial Intelligence,' 13 *J. Legal Stud.*, 113.

20. Herbert Hovencamp, 1985, 'Evolutionary Models in Jurisprudence' 64 *Texas L. Rev.*, 645, 649.

21. Philip P. Wiener, 1949, *Evolution and the Founders of Pragmatism* 172-85, Harper Torchbooks 1965.

22. G. Edward White, 1993, *Justice Oliver Wendell Holmes: Law and the Inner Self*, 41, 129, 146-52.

23. Howe noted that Holmes did not read Darwin until 1907. Howe, *supra* note 16, at 156, citing Letter from Oliver Wendell Holmes, Jr. to Clara Sherwood Stevens, April 28, 1907.

24. White, *supra* note 22, at 500 n.183.

25. *Id.* at 113; also at 115, 126-27, 205-25.

26. Letter from Oliver Wendell Holmes, Jr. to Sir Frederick Pollock, Mar. 1, 1918, ed. Mark DeWolfe Howe, 1941, in 1 *Holmes-Pollock Letters: The Correspondence of Mr. Justice Holmes and Sir Frederick Pollock* 1874-1932, at 261.

27. Letter from Oliver Wendell Holmes, Jr. to Lady Pollock, July 2, 1895, in 1 *Holmes-Pollock Letters*, *supra* note 26, at 57-58.

28. Oliver Wendell Holmes, Jr., 'The Soldier's Faith,' ed. M. Lerner, 1943, reprinted in *The Mind and Faith of Justice Holmes*, 18, 20.

29. Yosal Rogat, 1964, 'The Judge As Spectator,' 31 *U. Chi. L. Rev.*, 213, 254-55.

30. Oliver W. Holmes, Jr., 1918-19, 'Natural Law,' 32 *Harv. L. Rev.*, 40, 43.

31. *Felix Frankfurter Reminisces*, 1960, recorded in talks with Dr. Harlan B. Phillips, 10.

32. *Id.* at 57.

33. Felix Frankfurter, 1931, 'The Early Writings of O. W. Holmes, Jr.,' *Harv. L. Rev.*, 717, 722.

34. *See* Alfred S. Neely, 1993, 'A Humbug Based on Economic Ignorance and Incompetence' — Antitrust In the Eyes of Justice Holmes,' *Utah L. Rev.*, 1.

35. Letter from Oliver Wendell Holmes, Jr. to Sir Frederick Pollock, June 17, 1908, in 1 *Holmes-Pollock Letters*, *supra* note 26, at 138-39.

36. See Thomas C. Grey, 1989, 'Holmes and Legal Pragmatism,' 41 *Stan. L. Rev.* 787, 788; Catherine W. Hantzis, 1988, 'Legal Innovation within the Wider Intellectual Tradition: The Pragmatism of Oliver Wendell Holmes, Jr.,' 82 *Nw. U. L. Rev.* 541, 594-95; Marcia J. Speziale, 1981, 'Oliver Wendell Holmes, Jr., William James, Theodore Roosevelt and the Strenuous Life,' 13 *Conn. L. Rev.* 663, 671; Note, 1975, 'Holmes, Peirce and Legal Pragmatism,' 84 *Yale L. J.* 1123; Jan Vetter, 1983, 'The Evolution of Holmes: Holmes and Evolution,' eds. M. Konvitz and G. Kennedy, 1960, in *Holmes and the Common Law: A Century Later* 9, Cf. *The American Pragmatists.*

    Some see Holmes as something quite different. See H. L. Pohlman, 1984, *Justice Oliver Wendell Holmes and Utilitarian Jurisprudence* 163-64; Robert W. Gordon, 1982, 'Holmes' *Common Law* as Legal and Social Science,' 10 *Hofstra L. Rev.* 719, 722-32; Patrick J. Kelley, 1990, 'Was Holmes a Pragmatist? Reflections on a New Twist to an Old Argument,' 14 *S. Ill. U. L. J.* 427; G. Edward White, 1986, 'Looking at Homes in the Mirror,' 4 *Law and Hist. Rev.* 439, 448-49. Others see Holmes as simultaneously a pragmatist in legal outlook and anything but in personal philosophy. Jeremy Cohen, 1989, 'Congress Shall Make No Law: Oliver Wendell Holmes,' *The First Amendment and Judicial Decision Making* 60, quoting Henry Steele Commager, 1950, *The American Mind.*

37. Letter from Oliver Wendell Holmes, Jr. to Harold J. Laski, June 14, 1922, in 1 *Holmes-Laski Letters*, *supra* note 13, at 431.

38. Letter from Oliver Wendell Holmes, Jr. to John C. H. Wu, Dec. 5, 1926, ed. Central Book Co., 1947, in *Justice Holmes To Doctor Wu: An Intimate Correspondence*, 1921-1932, 40.

39. Letter from Oliver Wendell Holmes, Jr. to Harold J. Laski, Sept. 21, 1923, in 1 *Holmes-Laski Letters*, *supra* note 13, at 541.

40. Letter from Oliver Wendell Holmes, Jr. to John C. H. Wu, June 16, 1923, in *Justice Holmes to Dr. Wu: An Intimate Correspondence*, 1921-1932, *supra* note 38, at 13.

41. Letter from Oliver Wendell Holmes, Jr. to Harold J. Laski, Sept. 11, 1923, in 1 *Holmes-Laski Letters*, *supra* note 13, at 537, 537-38.

42. John Dewey, 1982, 'The Development of American Pragmatism,' in *American Pragmatism: The Classic Writings*, 23, 32-33.

43. Letter from Oliver Wendell Holmes, Jr. to Sir Frederick Pollock, Sept. 1, 1910, in 1 *Holmes-Pollock Letters*, *supra* note 26, at 166. See Letter from Oliver W. Holmes, Jr., to Morris R. Cohen, Sept. 10, 1918, 'The Holmes-[Morris R.] Cohen Correspondence,' *supra*

note 14, at 12; 'I wish I knew their beastly language, as I feel helpless when they sail off on the aeroplane of their calculus.'

44. Letter from Oliver Wendell Holmes, Jr. to Sir Frederick Pollock, Sept. 1, 1910, in 1 *Holmes-Pollock Letters*, *supra* note 26, at 166.

45. White, *supra* note 22, at 313. Furthermore, 'he was far more concerned with stylistic elegance and pithiness than with technical legal analysis and exegesis.' *Id.* at 410.

46. Ronald Dworkin, 1986, *Law's Empire,* 162.

Chapter Sixteen

From Racket to Natural Law: The Permutation of Smuggling into Free Trade

William Pencak*

I

Defending new trade regulations passed in 1764 by the British Parliament for the North American colonies, Thomas Whately, secretary and advisor to Prime Minister George Grenville, invoked the principles of mercantilism. These had guided all the European powers in the administration of their empires. 'It is the policy of every nation to prohibit all foreign trade with their plantations,' he wrote. If the colonies' 'most valuable commodities' were not 'exported either to Great Britain or to British plantations' and allowed to benefit 'any other country . . . , they would destroy the very purpose of their establishment, and the Mother Country would be ruined by the prosperity of her colonies.'[1]

In mercantilist thought, economic and military well-being were indissolubly linked. Dependencies were obliged to send their cash crops to the land which ruled them. This reduced their price, and limited the outflow of gold and silver to the colonies. More importantly, it obliged other nations desiring, say, tobacco or sugar, to buy from the Mother Country, paying its prices and duties, and increasing its wealth. Moreover, colonial trade was supposed to be carried only in British or British colonial ships, and the colonies were to be supplied with manufactured goods only from Britain or, if of foreign origin, second-hand via Britain. Mercantilism, successfully practiced, would increase British industry, train sailors and provide ships useful in war, and bring in hard cash, essential for building and paying a formidable army and navy. Even Adam Smith, following his defence of a free exchange of foreign commodities, excepted the Navigation Acts: 'As defence, however, is of much more importance than opulence, the act of navigation is, perhaps, the wisest of all the commercial regulations of England.'[2]

Did the American colonies on the eve of the Revolution think so? Faced with the obvious fact that the British navy protected their ships in wartime, that British arms conquered Canada on their behalf, and that they benefited from bounties encouraging production of indigo and tar, pitch, and turpentine, it seems the colonies could not easily deny the protecting aegis under which they too flourished. Speaking with William Pitt shortly before he left England in 1775, Benjamin Franklin recounted 'that, having more than once travelled almost from one end of the continent to the other, and kept a great variety of company, eating, drinking, and conversing with them freely . . . , as to the Navigation Act, the main material part of it, that of carrying on trade in British or plantation bottoms, excluding foreign ships from our ports, and navigating with three quarters British seaman, was as acceptable to us as it could be to Britain.'[3] 'If the trade of the colonies is protected by the British navy,' wrote Samuel Adams in 1772, 'there may possibly be from them [the Navigation Acts] inferred a just right in the parliament of Great Britain to restrain them from carrying on their trade to the injury of the trade of Great Britain.'[4]

And yet there is a subtext, a criticism of the Navigation Acts in the very statements in which the colonies profess to acquiesce in them. For example, having asserted to Pitt the *general* acceptability of the Navigation Acts, Franklin goes on to qualify it with so many exceptions that he is leaving Britain very little indeed. 'We were not even against regulations of the general commerce by Parliament, provided such regulations were *bona fide* for the *whole empire*, not for the small advantage of one part to the great injury of another.' Franklin assumes the colonies competent to judge the good of the whole and set their interests above those of other parts of the empire, which he deems 'small.' What are his specific instances? 'Obliging our ships to call in England with our wine and fruit, from Portugal or Spain' to ensure duties were paid; 'the restraints on our manufactures, in the woolen and hat making branches, the prohibiting of slitting mills, steels works, etc.' In last-minute negotiations to determine if England and the colonies could reach an agreement, Franklin added as hardships 'obliging us to land some of our commodities in England before we could carry them to foreign markets, and forbidding our importation of some goods directly from foreign countries, . . . and a greater loss to us than gain to Britain, and therefore proper to be repealed.' Franklin recognized that 'as Britain had deemed it an equivalent for her protection, we had never applied, or proposed to apply, for such a repeal.' In other words, he stated that the colonies had generously borne disproportional 'hardship' but would not suggest repealing the laws which produced it, thereby shifting the onus of blame from colonies who refused to pay even indirectly for military protection to a Mother Country which foolishly and unjustly favored the interest of one part of the empire over another. The interests of colonies and England are placed on a level of equality. So are Parliament's and the colonial legislatures' law-making power. Franklin proposes as a solution that 'since the power of Parliament to make' the acts of trade 'was now disputed, that they should be re-enacted in all the colonies, which would demonstrate their consent to them.'[5] Franklin's last utterance is perhaps intentionally ambiguous. Is he assuring his British auditors that all the colonies will indeed assent to the Navigation Acts voluntarily, or is he only saying they will be passed by those colonies which in fact consent to do so?

Again, turning to Samuel Adams's remarks of 1772, he adds to his statement granting that '*possibly*' the Navigation Acts are justified in return for protection: 'It may be the wisdom of the colonies, under present circumstances to acquiesce in *reasonable* restrictions' on their commerce, for after all '*power* she [England] undoubtedly has to enforce her acts of trade.' Adams underlined these words. The implication is that the colonists may judge what is '*reasonable*' and what is not, and that in any case the Navigation Acts do not benefit the whole empire, but are an exertion of '*power*' by one part of it over another: these are 'her' acts of trade, not 'ours.'

II

Similar qualifications appear in other colonial expressions which seem to support the Navigation Acts while only objecting to the new taxes and means of customs enforcement of the 1760s and 70s. John Dickinson's famous *Letters of a Pennsylvania Farmer* begins grandly that 'the Parliament unquestionably possesses a legal authority to *regulate* the trade of Great Britain and all her colonies. Such an authority is essential to the relation between a mother country and her colonies, and necessary for the common good of all.' But Dickinson then goes on to make 'the common good of all' as he and the colonists see it the test of the legality of Parliamentary legislation. He sweepingly grants that before the Stamp Act of 1765 'every statute' was 'always imposed with design to restrain the commerce of one part, that was unjurious to another, and thus promote the general welfare.'[6] By approving the Navigation Acts in this manner Dickinson gives the colonies the residual power to deny them, or any law, should it prove in their judgment injurious to the whole as they define it.

Thomas Jefferson followed this line of reasoning as well. 'The Navigation Act, therefore, becomes a proper subject of treaty between the two nations. . . . We will consider the restrictions on our commerce, now actually existing, as compensations, yielded by us for the protection and privileges we actually enjoy, only trusting that if Great Britain on a revisal of these restrictions, is sensible that some of them are useless to her and oppressive to us, she will repeal them.'[7] Regarding Mother Country and colonies as two equivalent 'nations' bound together only where it suited their mutual convenience, Jefferson made the colonies the judge not only of what oppressed them, which was plausible, but of what was useless to England, which was not. He thus tried to drape the mantle of true justice over any colonial rejection of the Navigation Acts.

III

It was only one step from selective rejection of restrictions on trade to denial England possessed any right at all to regulate colonial commerce. As a prelude to the economic argument, those who took this position had to show that the colonies were not obligated at all to England for protecting them. A weaker and more plausible version of this case was put forward by John Adams, who wrote that Britain only protected America 'for her own interest, because all the profits of our trade centered in her lap,' thereby implying the Mother Country was prospectively rewarded for her assistance.[8] Even British participation in the Seven Years' War was suspect. 'It was of no less consequence to Great Britain than it was to the colonies that these should not be overrun and conquered by the French,' maintained Oxenbridge Thacher in 1764. He also insisted that while 'the colonies are no particular gainers by these acquisitions,' especially Canada, which resulted from the war, as the new territory was not added to them, 'Great Britain gaineth immeasurably.'[9] John Adams added: 'But it ought to be remembered that her name, not her purse, nor her fleet, ever protected us until' the war of the 1750s. Even then, the 'annual millions from America enabled her to do so.' Adams and Thacher here reinforced an argument put forward as early as 1721 by Massachusetts' agent in Britain, Jeremiah Dummer, who argued 'it were no difficult task to prove that London has risen out of the plantations. . . . Tis to them we owe our vast fleets of merchants ships, and consequently the increase of our seamen, and improvement of our navigation . . . to make the figure we do at present, and have done for near a century past, in all parts of the commercial world.'[10]

James Otis of Massachusetts was an especially strong proponent of the case that England was indebted to the colonies, rather than the reverse. He stressed their military exertions in the common cause: 'The province of the Massachusetts, I believe, has expended more men and money in war since the year 1620, when a few families first landed at Plymouth, in proportion to their abilities than the three kingdoms [of England, Scotland, and Ireland] together. The same, I believe, may be truly affirmed of many of the other colonies.' Yet in the same pamphlet, *The Rights of the British Colonies Asserted and Proved*, Otis asserted that the Navigation Act 'is a good act, so are all that exclude foreign manufactures from the plantations.'[11]

However, Otis wrote and spoke differently when his words did not reveal his identity or extend beyond Boston. He not only dismissed the distinction between internal taxes such as the Stamp Act and external ones on trade as meaningless, he insisted that any regulation which increased prices or decreased profits for colonials was every bit as much a tax, and hence deserving of resistance, as the most blatant duty. Almost every law passed by Britain involving colonial trade laid 'some grievous restriction on American commerce which consequently imposes a *real*, though no *direct* tax.' Britain was 'the monopolizer of all the commodities of the colonies, who in return are obliged to take her manufactures and commodities at her own price, not being allowed to trade at any other market.' Adopting in anonymous newspaper articles the pseudonym 'Hampden' writing to John Pym — thereby suggesting to his countrymen that they suffered under grievances equal to those which provoked the English Civil War of the 1640s — Otis went on: 'What American peasant before the late regulations ever dreamt his dearly bought coarse coat . . . was taxed half its cost to maintain those who live and die in the ease, luxury, and prodigality of Great Britain? Now they know.'[12] Speaking to a Boston Town Meeting on May 5, 1766, Otis drew the logical conclusion: 'The merchants were great fools, if they submitted any longer to the laws restraining their trade, which ought to be free.'[13]

Otis finally articulated what Massachusetts and its fellow-colonies had been practicing since their inception: that free trading, known ignominiously as 'smuggling,' was both legitimate and good, whereas confining the colonists' trade to England and her dominions was technically legal but unjust and unnatural. This honesty was unusual, since the

Americans usually tried to achieve respectability in British eyes by defending the Navigation Acts, in heavily qualified form, to be sure. In fact, the colonists became livid when denounced by loyalists and the British as 'smugglers.' Mercy Otis Warren highly resented that 'they represented the mercantile body in America as a set of smugglers, forever breaking over the laws of trade and of society.'[14] 'Novanglus' John Adams replied to 'Massachusettensis' Daniel Leonard's charges linking the smuggler and the Whig — 'the smuggler received protection from the Whig, and he in his turn received support from the smuggler' — by arguing the Tories were the most notorious smugglers of all: 'If I were to let myself into secret history, I could tell very diverting stories of smuggling Tories in New York and Boston. Massachusettensis is quarreling with some of his best friends.'[15]

Adams thereby legitimated smuggling by arguing that even the Tories were doing it. But this was only one of many justifications. If the colonists went out of their way to look for loopholes as to why they could selectively reject the Navigations Acts, they were equally imaginative in finding excuses for smuggling. Custom granted legitimacy: the *Boston Newsletter* noted that the trade 'is now so well established' that even the British High Court of Admiralty ruled 'that every British subject had an undoubted right of purchasing French produce in every neutral port in America, or Europe' provided 'the appellants swore they had not corresponded directly with the French.'[16] Also, it was unfair to enforce the acts of trade in certain places — Boston had especially zealous customs officers in Charles Paxton and Thomas Lechmere — and not in others. Even Governor Francis Bernard agreed that 'it is very hard that the merchants of this province, who desire at least as much favor as any other of the continent, should be restrained in their trade while their neighbors are allowed to carry on an unbounded trade with any part of the world they please.' He especially complained of 'the open and barefaced disregard of the laws of trade which is now carried on by the most dangerous practices in Rhode Island.'[17]

IV

Besides being novel and unfair, enforcement of the Navigation Acts was seen as destructive of the colonial economy. 'We are ultimately . . . yielding large supplies to the revenues of the Mother Country, while we are laboring for a very moderate subsistence for ourselves,' lamented the Boston Society for Encouraging Trade and Commerce, an organization of merchants formed to oppose restrictions on commerce. 'But if our trade be curtailed in its most profitable branch . . . it will scarce be possible for us to earn our bread.'[18] That 'most profitable branch' must have been the smuggling of foreign sugar and molasses, for the protest was directed against the Revenue Act of 1764 which legalized importation of these items, as it was impossible to stop the trade, but placed a heavy duty on them.

The obvious partiality of trade regulations to the influential West India planters provided another excuse for their evasion. The Molasses Act of 1733 had been explicitly passed, as its opening words read, because 'the welfare and prosperity of your Majesty's sugar colonies in America are of the greatest consequence and importance to the trade, navigation, and strength of this kingdom,' and over the objections of adherents of the mainland colonies.[19] Sir John Barnard had in fact predicted that laying a prohibitive tariff on foreign molasses would compel the French to manufacture more easily transported rum themselves, 'and sell it in a smuggling way to our fishing vessels': 'They would have a stolen market for it in the British dominions, and an open market in all other parts of the world.'[20] In their December 1763 description of the 'State of Trade,' Boston's merchant community protested that if a sugar or molasses tax were actually enforced, 'the whole fishery must be infallibly broke up.' Charging that 'this act was procured by the interest of the West India planters with no other view than to enrich themselves,' they defended smuggling as essential for New England's prosperity: 'It is plain that our [British and West Indies] islands are able neither to supply us with what we want from them, nor to take from us what lumber and fish we are obliged to export.'[21] If in their putative support of the Navigation Acts the colonists gave lip service to the notion these laws existed for the good of the whole empire, when confronted with specific instances they clearly indicated that the acts favored other parts of the empire over themselves. Tory Daniel Leonard, 'Massachusettensis's,' argument in favor of the acts that 'to prevent one part of the empire being enriched at the expence and . . . impoverishing of another, checks, restrictions, and sometimes absolute prohibitions are necessary' rang hollow indeed to those who thought themselves impoverished by the acts of trade.[22]

V

The Tea Act of 1773, which Britain cleverly designed to undercut smuggling by selling large quantities of surplus East India Company Tea through loyalist merchants at lower prices than the smugglers could match, did not lead to a direct defence of smuggling, but rather to claims that a monopoly seller of this important commodity threatened a healthy economy. An anonymous writer in the *Boston Gazette* predicted that one monopoly foreshadowed others. The East India Company would soon establish sales 'in every other article of trade,' to be followed by 'all the great manufacturing houses in England: So that they could not fail to engross, in a little time, the whole trade of this great and extensive continent.'[23] Smuggling was both a right and a duty, a means of preventing North America from being degraded to the level of British India, and an essential concomitant of political freedom and personal independence. As another anonymous columnist explained, 'The very establishment of exclusive trading companies is an infringement of that distinguished petition of the free Briton [through] which from time immemorial he had forced his sovereign to recognize his right to a FREE TRADE.'[24] At last, the implied yet avoided major premise of the impact of British commercial legislation on the colonies was directly articulated.

Thus, smuggling was not smuggling at all, a point the colonists had sometimes made explicitly. William Cooper, Secretary of the Boston Town Meeting and a smuggler himself, wrote that 'what has been called an illicit trade has been winked at by all former administrations, it being eventually more profitable to Britain than the colonies . . . Our trade with the Spanish Main and Spanish and French West Indies, as also the Mediterranean, furnished us with large remittances for the British merchants.'[25] The colonies really contributed to British prosperity not so much by enabling the resale of colonial commodities to bring specie into the Treasury's coffer, but by acquiring such specie themselves through a world-wide illegal trade that enabled the colonies to demand British manufactures.

Even Cadwallader Colden, future loyalist and lieutenant-governor of New York, opposed enforcement of the Navigation Acts for this reason in a letter to William Pitt: 'The Northern colonies cannot pay for their consumption of British manufactures by their own produce, exported only to the British colonies. . . . The consumption of British manufactures in the Northern colonies increases in proportion to their ability to purchase them, and nothing can make the Northern colonies interfere with the British manufactures, but their poverty or inability to purchase.' Colden expressed his wish that 'a mutual intercourse in trade be obtained between the British and Spanish colonies,' for it would be 'highly advantageous to Great Britain' as well. He hinted in the conclusion of his letter that Pitt should not blame him if he had trouble enforcing new or existing trade regulations: 'It is difficult to prosecute with success against the bent of the people, while they are under the prejudice to think that the Sugar Islands have gained a preference inconsistent with the true interest of their Mother Country.'[26]

Smuggling was not only salutary, it was even impossible to define. 'It would puzzle any reasonable person to properly define what smuggling is in North America,' argued an anonymous Bostonian. 'The critical situation of these provinces are such, that without making the most of our whole produce, and having a free vent, it will be impossible to keep up our credit with the mother country.'[27] It seemed that what was necessary for community survival could not bear the odious name of 'smuggling' even if it were illegal. Another writer insisted that 'punishments are devised on the most unjust pretence that smuggling is a general, national crime.' In fact, trade regulations 'restrain people from the free use of their own property, and . . . turn the course of business into . . . unnatural channels.'[28] Just as the laws of nature and the natural rights of man served the colonists well when they defended their rebellion against the right of Parliament to legislate for them, the abstract, natural rights of people to trade freely and use their property as they wished, could be upheld as 'higher' laws and 'inalienable' rights in opposition to unjust, illegitimate statutory law which violated them. Just as the colonial 'mob' was no illegal gathering, or 'mob' at all, but the body of the people defending natural rights to life, liberty, and property against usurpations,[29] the 'smuggler' was no smuggler at all, but the equally heroic upholder of the natural rights to property and free trade. The colonists inadvertently discovered these rights while searching for ways to justify their violation of laws restricting their trade.

Adam Smith, on the contrary, discovered the 'natural' law of free trade in a quest to show how British mercantilism in fact worked in reverse, to benefit the colonies at the Mother Country's expense. His nine-hundred-page *An Inquiry into the Nature and Causes of the Wealth of Nations* was a would-be British Declaration of Independence, also published in 1776, explaining why Britain should rid itself voluntarily of its costly and obstreperous provinces. The work builds to this final peroration: 'If any of the provinces of the British empire cannot be made to contribute towards the support of the whole empire, it is surely time that Great Britain should free herself from the expence of defending those provinces in time of war, and of supporting any part of their civil and military establishment in time of peace.' Smith terms the colonies 'appendages, a sort of splendid and showy equipage'; the rulers of Britain have 'amused the people with the imagination that they possessed a great empire on the other side of the Atlantic' when in fact 'it has hitherto existed in the imagination' only (899-900).[30] If smuggling were not smuggling for the colonists, the empire was no empire for Smith.

Whereas the colonists argued that even the watered-down mercantilism they endured robbed them for the benefit of the British Isles, Smith countered that it constituted the unearned subsidization of the colonies by the home government. British North America was the most prosperous place on earth, Smith wrote, using language that could have been borrowed from his friend Benjamin Franklin's 1751 pamphlet *Observations Concerning the Increase of Mankind, Peopling of Countries, etc.* 'The most decisive mark of the prosperity of any country is the increase of the number of its inhabitants. In Great Britain, and most other European countries, they are not supposed to double in less than five-hundred years' (70). In the colonies, they were doubling every twenty-five.[31]

Smith stressed that this prosperity was the result of an indulgent empire's neglect, rather than any virtue on the part of colonists. For the most part until the 1760s England had the good sense to leave them to their own devices: 'The colonies owe to the policy of Europe the education and great views of their active and enterprising founders,' but 'the greatest and most important of them, so far as concerns their national government, owe to it scarcely anything else' (556). 'Folly,' 'injustice,' and 'disorder,' not the 'wisdom and policy' of Europe, 'peopled and cultivated America' (555).

In fact, Smith was critical of several aspects of the colonists' behavior. They had such an abundance of land and farm animals that they wasted them: we can 'with difficulty discover there the character of the English nation, so well skilled in all the different branches of agriculture' (223). Smith here cites Swedish Professor of Economy Peter Kalm's *Travels into North America*, published in 1770. Smith objected to the fact colonies were able to print up paper money and let it depreciate as 'tyrannical' — the 'scheme of fraudulent debtors to cheat their [British] creditors' (310-311) and to escape taxes to pay for their defence. He regarded 'speculation' as to whether taxes could be made uniform throughout the empire as 'a new Utopia, less amusing certainly, but not more useless and chimerical than the old one' (886-887). He questioned whether the Americans would even accept equal Parliamentary representation since the 'genius of the British constitution . . . protects and governs North America,' unlike the far richer 'oppressed' yet 'depopulated' East Indies where the full effects of mercantilism could be seen (73).

Smith was glad that England's mercantilism worked badly, for this unintended approximation of free trade was the cause of both colonial and imperial prosperity (551). Yet he found even an attenuated mercantilism deleterious. In fact, he devoted many more pages to the negative effects of trade regulation on England than he did to the colonies. The main harm mercantilism inflicted on its perpetrators was the diversion of capital to colonial staples from more productive endeavors. Smith concluded, after a lengthy discussion so even the thick-headed would see the colonies as a drain and a subsidy to small groups of sugar planters or the East India Company (557-573), that 'the monopoly of the colony trade . . . has rendered the whole state of industry and commerce more precarious and less secure than if their produce had been accommodated to a greater variety of markets' (573). Ironically, Smith may here have been engaging in a little intellectual mercantilism himself. His argument appeared in volume two of Massachusetts' former Governor Thomas Hutchinson's *The History of the Colony and Province of Massachusetts-Bay*, a work published in London in 1768, Smith cited it elsewhere to support his discussion of colonial currency (893), thus showing that he read it, but he did not credit Hutchinson's far more significant discussion of capital theory.[32]

VI

Despite their differing assessments of who mercantilism injured the most, Smith agreed with his colonial counterparts that North America's real value lay in the largely illegal trade, or smuggling, which enabled the colonies to acquire the wealth that created a demand for British manufactures: 'The enormous expense of the Great War [of 1754-1763] . . . must have been chiefly defrayed,' Smith deduced, 'not by the export of gold and silver, but by that of British commodities' (411). Even defence was better served by free trade than by the hoarding of specie. And whence came demand for these commodities? Thanks to 'the discovery of America . . . the productive powers of labor were improved, and its produce increased in all the different countries of Europe, together with the real wealth of the inhabitants.' 'By opening a more extensive market for whatever part of the produce of their labor may exceed the home consumption,' the colonies encouraged Britain 'to improve its productive powers, and to augment its annual produce to the utmost, and thereby to increase the real revenue and wealth of the society' (415-416).

Smith referred to 'nature' and 'natural' on many occasions to give his notion of free trade the validity of universal law. America adhered to 'the natural course of things' where capital was directed first to agriculture, then to manufactures, and 'last of all to foreign commerce.' Yet the interference of European governments reversed 'the natural order of things' there into an 'unnatural and retrograde' one (360). Similarly, monopoly forced toward the colonial trade a 'much greater proportion of the capital of Great Britain than what would have naturally gone to it,' thereby breaking the 'natural balance which would otherwise have taken place among all the different branches of British industry' (570). Still, 'the natural good effects of the colony trade more than counterbalance to Great Britain the bad effects of the monopoly' (574). Smith's repeated use of the word 'natural' at times assumed the form of an incantation. In one paragraph, Smith linked the phrases 'in its natural and free state' with 'the colony trade' in four consecutive sentences to demonstrate the superiority of an empire of free trade over one of mercantilism (576). America owed its prosperity to its closer conformity than Europe to a natural law; Smith is in effect defining the 'pursuit of happiness' Thomas Jefferson considered one of the rights granted to man by 'Nature and Nature's God' in the same year of 1776 as the 'natural' right to free commercial activity.

Although Smith considered the colonies a needless drain on the British treasury, he used them as his most important exhibit to show that lands which already were approximating free trade and ruled their people with minimal interference prospered best. He stressed that the annual cost of governing North America was under L65,000 a year before the 'present disturbances . . . an ever-memorable example at how small an expence three millions of people may not only be governed but well governed' (541). Smith despaired that England would have the intelligence to 'voluntarily give up all authority over her colonies, and leave them to elect their own magistrates, to enact their own laws, and to make peace and war as they might think proper.' Such an enlightened measure 'never was, and never will be adopted by any nation in the world,' he predicted (582).

Yet only six years after the publication of *The Wealth of Nations*, Smith's dream came true. Disgusted with the enormous cost of a war that, after all, began over the issue of raising a revenue from North America, that had led to the ignominious surrenders of Burgoyne and Cornwallis, and had started a world war with France and Spain, the British Parliament handed Lord North the only 'no confidence' vote given to any government between the Glorious Revolution of 1688 and 1832. The new Prime Minister, Sir William Petty, the Earl of Shelburne, cognizant not only of Smith's writings but of Josiah Tucker's in a similar vein, agreed with Smith that by ridding itself of the colonies, 'Great Britain would not only be immediately freed from the whole annual expence of the peace establishment of the colonies, but might settle with them such a treaty of commerce as would effectually secure to her a free trade, more advantageous to the great body of the people, though less so the merchants, than the monopoly which she at present enjoys. By thus parting good friends, the natural affection of the colonies to the mother country . . . would quickly revive. It might dispose them not only to respect, for whole centuries together, that treaty of commerce which they had concluded with us at parting, but to favor us in war as well as in trade, and instead of turbulent and factious subjects, to become our most faithful, affectionate, and generous allies' (582).[33]

With four versions of his great work published by 1784 (xxiv-xxii), Smith lived to see his vision come through in part. Although the colonies obtained independence the previous year, Shelburne was quickly ousted and replaced by William Pitt the Younger, who instituted commercial retaliation against the new United States.[34] But in the transformation of smuggling into free trade, of the dominant paradigm of economic thought from mercantilism to laissez-faire capitalism, we can note the humble beginnings of a new economic order, take pride that American praxis became the basis of the world's economic theory, and observe with at least a little unease that our Founding Fathers, by defining subversive and illegal economic practices as just and legitimate, set a precedent we can only hope will not be cited too frequently.

Two final postscripts: Smith was ultimately right about the United States and Britain becoming friends. But if we apply his theory to decolonization since World War II, we can only sit in the middle of a process not yet completed, and wonder whether the gap between the First and former colonial worlds will only grow wider as nations enjoy the privileges of trade with underdeveloped countries without the inconveniences of governing them. Will a planet increasingly united by commerce ultimately lead to greater prosperity for all nations with the intelligence and industry to trade as freely as they dare? Or will a new mercantilism emerge to protect nations, markets, and workers from foreign competition? In either case, our new configuration has yet to find an Adam Smith.

**William Pencak is Professor of History at Penn State.*

ENDNOTES

1. [Thomas Whately], 1765, *The Regulations Lately Made Concerning the Colonies, and the Taxes Imposed Upon Them, Considered*, London, 88-89.

2. Adam Smith, 1937, *An Inquiry into the Nature and Causes of the Wealth of Nations*, ed. Edward Cannan, New York, 431.

3. A. H. Smyth, ed., 1905-07, *Writings of Benjamin Franklin*, New York, 6: 323.

4. Harry A. Cushing, ed., 1904-06, *Writings of Samuel Adams*, New York, 2: 322-26.

5. Smyth, ed., *Writings of Benjamin Franklin*, 6: 331-32.

6. John Dickinson, 1768, *Letters from a Pennsylvania Farmer*, Philadelphia, 7-8.

7. Andrew A. Liscomb, ed., 1905, *Writings of Thomas Jefferson*, Washington, 17: 126-28.

8. Bernard Mason, ed., 1972, *The American Colonial Crisis: The Daniel Leonard-John Adams Letters to the Press, 1774-1775*, New York, 129.

9. Oxenbridge Thacher, 1965, *Sentiments of a British American*, reprinted in Bernard Bailyn, ed., *Pamphlets of the American Revolution, 1750-1765*, Cambridge, 492.

10. Mason, ed., 1721, *Colonial Crisis*, 129; Jeremiah Dummer, *A Defense of the New-England Charters*, London, 38.

11. James Otis, *The Rights of the British Colonists Asserted and Proved*, reprinted in Bailyn, ed., *Pamphlets of the American Revolution, 1750-1765*, 455, 461.

12. *Boston Gazette*, December 9, 1765, December 23, 1765, Harbottle Dorr identifies Otis as the writer in his marginalia on the newspaper, Dorr Papers, Massachusetts Historical Society.

13. *Boston Evening-Post*, May 19, 1766; Thomas Hutchinson to Thomas Pownall, May 11, 1766, Massachusetts Archives 26: 231, typescript at Massachusetts Historical Society.

14. Mercy Otis Warren, 1805, *History of the Rise, Progress, and Termination of the American Revolution*, Boston, 1: 39-40.

15. Mason, ed., *Colonial Crisis*, 180.

16. *Boston Newsletter*, October 1, 1760.

17. Francis Bernard to William Pitt, October 5, 1761, Bernard Papers 9: 229-232, Houghton Library, Harvard University.

18. *Boston Gazette*, May 28, 1764.

19. William MacDonald, ed., 1904, *Select Charters and Other Documents Illustrative of American History*, New York and London, 248.

20. Leo Stock, ed., 1924, *Proceedings and Debates of the British Parliament Respecting North America*, Washington, 4: 184-85.

21. Colonial Society of Massachusetts, *Publications* 19, 389-90.

22. Mason, ed., *Colonial Crisis*, 23.

23. *Boston Gazette*, November 1, 1773.

24. *Massachusetts Spy*, October 14, 1773.

25. William Cooper to John Boylston, November 7, 1768, Boylston Papers, Massachusetts Historical Society.

26. Cadwallader Colden to William Pitt, December 27, 1760, Colden Papers, New York Public Library.

27. *Boston Evening Post*, January 7, 1765.

28. *Ibid.*, June 17, 1765.

29. Pauline Maier, 1972, *From Resistance to Revolution: Colonial Radicals and the Development of American Opposition to Britain, 1765-1776*, New York, 3-5.

30. Page numbers in parentheses, for the rest of this essay are to the edition of Smith's *Wealth of Nations* cited in note 2.

31. In 1751, Franklin wrote, point #10: 'But in proportion to the increase of the colonies, a vast demand is growing for British manufactures, a glorious market wholly in the power of Britain, in which foreigners cannot interfere, which will increase. . . . Therefore Britain should not too much restrain manufactures in new colonies.' Point #11: 'There are supposed to be now upwards of one million English souls in North America (though 'tis thought scarce 80,000 have been brought over

the sea), and yet perhaps there is not one the fewer in Britain, but rather many more, on account of the employment the colonies afford to manufacture at home. This million, doubling, suppose but once in 25 years, will, in another century, be more than the people of Engalnd. . . . What an accession of power to the British empire by sea as well as land! What increase of trade and navigation! What numbers of ships and seamen!'

31. Franklin and Smith were friends: see Esmond Wright, 1986, *Franklin of Philadelphia*, Cambridge, 125, 158, 181.

32. See Lawrence S. Mayo's edition of Hutchinson's *History*, Cambridge, 1936, 2: 338-343, for a nearly identical argument.

33. Vincent T. Harlow, 1952, *The Founding of the Second British Empire, 1763-1793*, London, 1: 203-210, 308-311.

34. *Ibid*, 1: 485-492.

Author's Note: Eighteenth century works published in America cited in this essay may be found in Clifford K. Shipton, ed., *Early American Imprints*, 1620-1800 (Worcester, 1959), a microfilm collection.

Chapter Seventeen

Legal Semiotics and Normative Imposition in an African Context: The Case of the San/Bushmen

B. D. D. Radipati*

I
Introduction

This essay addresses an essentially European pursuit into legal theory from an African perspective and with an African orientation. In particular, it seeks to find a linkage between a (legal) sign system, imposed law and the San/Bushmen status under municipal law (principally of some specified countries in Southern Africa) and international law. Admittedly, the present attempt is exceptional, for this triadic connection has never been a subject of inquiry in the past. Given this, a brief statement regarding the backdrop from which the essay will proceed, is apposite.

II
Legal Semiotics

Because semiotics (or semiology) is the science that studies the life of signs within society, law, as a social phenomenon has been perceived as possessing a sign-content. Indeed, England's most celebrated jurist, Jeremy Bentham (1748-1832), defined law as an assemblage of *signs* declarative of a volution concerned or adopted by the sovereign in a state, concerning the conduct to be observed in a certain cause by a certain person or class of persons, who in the case in question are or are supposed to be subject to his power. A derivative of this is the construct 'legal semiotics' or legal semiology which in a 1985 study, Goodrich advanced a fairly convincing definition thereof, thus:

> The notion or, more optimistically, the putative discipline of legal semiotics refers to a broad and frequently ill-defined tradition of legal analysis and doctrine rather than to any specific or homogeneous body of theory. In this

> very diffuse sense, the semiotics of law studies law as a signifying system or in its signifying aspects; that is, it endeavours to systematically comment upon the linguistic, textual, communicational, symbolic and rhetorical facets of legal regulation.[1]

That said, a remarkable discernment about legal semiotics has even now been made. It is that the latter is a distinct area of semiotic inquiry and that it has the following subdivisions: (a) relations between law and legal systems; (b) relations between legal discourse and legal practice; (c) exchange of signs between official legal actors and non-official members of the general public; (d) sign structure of inquests and trials; (e) inter-systemic communication between codes of legality and codes of legitimacy; (f) relations between the laws of logic and the logic of laws; and (g) a comparativst semiotic perspective on legal cultures.[2]

In view of this, and since the primary focus of this essay is on the interaction between legal semiotics and imposed law, the first- and last-mentioned subdivisions will largely inform the succeeding discussion. But a slight degression to what constitutes the last-mentioned subdivision should assist in the comprehension of the matters that appear *infra*.

III
Normative Imposition

Normative imposition (or imposed law) is generally understood as involving alien origins of law. More pointedly, imposition means being forced to conform with a norm or order not compatible with one's interests or values. Other views on this prevail, of course. For there are some who view imposed law as a tool, together with political trickery and economic might, to dominate a resentful, disprinted and debilitated population. Still others consider the lack of 'democractic consensus' as the pre-eminent quirk of imposed law.

Kidder, in an earlier discussion,[3] has given an admirable, if largely critical account of theories of normative imposition, and little purpose would be served in re-chroncling all that here. However, one point which he makes and which merits repetition here, is that the disruption of established indegenous social patterns, including their systems of authority and dominance, is a consequence of any introduction of external law.[4] Indeed, the said disruption cannot be attributed solely to Euro-centric normative imposition, for massive dislocations seem to characterise all instances where foreign norms or order are or is thrust upon others. The terrible experiences of the San/Bushmen whereby the latter are subjected to both Batswana and Euro-centric norms and order are a fitting archetype here. Thus, imposed law can exist in all societies, even in those where the 'foreign element' is not European. Anyhow, because there is no society in which a single legal system is operative but rather that every society is constituted by a network of legal systems — subsystems that conflict and vie with one another for position, influence and dominant power,[5] — normative imposition is possible even in nations that exist as a single (race) entity as long as there is a differentation in culture and norms. In Southern Africa nowhere is this more stark than in Botswana, Namibia, Angola, Zambia and Zimbabwe. It is for this reason that one can legitimately talk of both externally and internally imposed law. And it is this general point that will underpin the analysis immediately below.

IV
Triadic Connection

This part of the essay attempts to find a nexus between semiotics, law and normative imposition, in so far as this triadic combination impacts on the San/Bushmen. In view of this, the following factual background should serve as a convenient departure point.

That the San/Bushmen are the indigenous or longest term inhabitants of Botswana, Namibia and to some smaller extent Angola, Zambia and Zimbabwe is indubitable. Consider that recent archeological data show that for at least 30,000 years these people were the sole inhabitants of the countries referred to above. Since their initial contact first with the Khoikhoi some 4,000 years back, then with the Bantu-speakers and finally with the Dutch colonists up to the present, the San/Bushmen, have, needless to mention, been subjected to unwarranted bigotry, discrimination, scorn and humiliation.

This is aptly illustrated by the late novelist, Bessie Head, herself a victim of racial prejudice in both South Africa, her country of birth, and Botswana, her adopted home. In *Maru*,[6] she observes:

> And if the white man thought that Asians were a low, filthy nation, Asians could smile with relief — at least they were not Africans. And if the white man thought Africans were a low, filthy nation, Africans in Southern Africa could still smile — at least they were not Bushmen . . .

> Of all things that are said of oppressed people, the worst things are said and done to the Bushmen.[7]

That then is the short, sad tale of the San/Bushmen. The offshots thereof remain to be teased out.

Since 1945, the protection of indigenous people[8] has been a very prominent item on the political agenda of actors under international law. Three strands of activity can be identified. First, the International Labour Organisation has focused attention on the problem of indigenous workers as a result of stimulus from various Latin-American states. This culminated in conventions adopted in 1957 and 1989 on the Protection of Indigenous and other Tribal and Semi-Tribal Populations in Independent Countries. Second, the United Nations Human Rights Sub-commission on the Prevention of Discrimination and Protection of Minorities has seized the question of indigenous people. The consequence thereof was the appointment in 1972, of a special rapporteur on the problem of discrimination against indigenous populations, José Martinez Cobo, who presented a final report in 1983. In 1982 the Sub-commission inaugurated a Working Group on Indigenous Populations. The present schedule of this team focuses on the preparation of a draft Universal Declaration on the Rights of Indigenous Peoples. It submitted a first revised text of the draft in 1989. Work on a second revised text is proceeding. Additionally, in 1985, the General Assembly of the United Nations set up the United Nations Fund for Indigenous Populations to assist representatives of indigenous organisations and communities to participate in the activities of the Working Group. At the 1989 session of the Working Group, indigenous people were represented by delegations from far afield. It is of note that the San/Bushmen were unrepresented thereat. That aside, it is telling that the United Nations designated and celebrated the year 1993 as the year of indigenous people. Lastly, the third strand of activity has been the work done in respect of indigenous people by non-governmental organisations in different parts of the world.[9] That the San/Bushmen, among other indigenous people were and continue to be the target and beneficiaries of these benevolant acts is a matter beyond controversy.

A. *What of developments at the municipal level?*

Significantly, most, if not all, the constitutions of the countries in which the subject of the present discourse, *viz* the San/Bushmen live, expressly guarantee and protect the rights and freedoms of all citizens (inclusive of the

San/Bushmen)[10] irrespective of race, colour, creed, ethnic origin and social standing. Thus, the legal basis for equality amongst the entire citizenry in the said countries is present, and an infraction thereof is justiciable. But constitutional provisions are known to be just that, and without implementation or an informed civic society, they soon denegerate into meaningless words contained in scraps of paper that gather dust on bookshelves. The attainment of promises embodied in constitutional provisions therefore lies less in the content of constitutions and more in the execution of relevant governmental policy. Conceivably, this is more applicable to an exceptionally marginalised community such as that of the San/Bushmen, than with any. A natural successor to this contemplation is a brief scrutiny of the institutional response of some of the governments of Southern Africa to the plight of the San/Bushmen.

In 1974, the government of the Republic of Botswana instituted a special programme called the Bushman Development Programme. The objects of the programme were and still are (a) the facilitation of social integration of the marginalised section of the population into the mainstream of the society and (b) the development of rural settlements to a level that is comparable with that of other rural villages in the country by providing the necessary social services to improve the living conditions in those settlements. In 1978, the programme was re-defined and re-named the Remote Area Development Programme as it was no longer targeted specifically for the San/Bushmen in the Ghanzi district of Botswana, but rather for any marginalised community anywhere in the country[11].

It is noteworthy for comparative purposes that whilst the government of the Republic of Botswana has not and continues not to recognise the San/Bushmen as a distinct society demanding special attention and has persistently refused, even at present, to accord the said community the status of indigenous people in defiance of international convention, Namibia has done just the opposite. It has singled out the San/Bushmen as a specifically disadvantaged community and has conferred upon them the distinction of indigenous people. Of course this somewhat insignificant contrast in the treatment of the San/Bushmen by the governments of the two countries should not be read as denying the existence of their collaboration in matters relating to the welfare of the San/Bushmen. For by now, two regional conferences on development programmes for the San/Bushmen have already been held in both countries. And in September 1993, the University of Botswana hosted a workshop which sought to address a number of issues pertaining to the San/Bushmen research. It was attended, among others, by visitors from Namibia and South Africa. It should thus be obvious that the life and experiences of the San/Bushmen have come to occupy centre-stage at both the international and municipal planes.

That aside, at issue here is an attempt (already expressed above), to discern a connection between semiotics, law and normative imposition in so far as the same impact on the San/Bushmen. The following discussion proceeds from the proposition, so often advanced by Sanders,[12] that in San/Bushmen society, there is a minimum of law. It is apparent that the said society never felt a need to formulate a concept of law, as the same (i.e. law) is apprehended in Western jurisprudence, since as it has been perceived:

> Among the [San]/Bushmen, law goes on in the hearts and heads of people. It does not have a technical existence of its own, but forms part of a general way of life in terms of which the community constitutes an economic, moral and religious entity. Justice is seen to reside in harmony and accommodation. Hence [San]/Bushmen law is basically consensus law, and disputes are settled informally, in a style which stresses conciliation and restoration.[13]

It being a matter of great regret that the San/Bushmen apprehension of law can never be fully articulated by reference to contemporary society's linguistic ideology, recourse has, of late, been had to the society's rock art as a possible source of the depiction of their law. Arising from this, a rather rudimentary inventory of the San/Bushmen law has been drawn from recent ethnographic studies and it seems to endorse, fairly strongly, the viewpoint that in the said society, law exists as values, rules and processes for external conduct which are treated by a community as obligatory.[14] Of course such values, rules and processes neither exist as a system, nor as a distinct entity governing San/Bushmen interaction and conduct, as might be the case in other societies.

In view of the present brief, this is noteworthy since the concern here is with how the appearance of law is essential to an understanding of its values, rules and processes. Because San/Bushman society is egalitarian and ekes out a living in the most spartan way, its law as exhibited on rocks is limited and is inclined to emphasise societal cohesion and consensus-seeking. This notwithstanding, the law that actually governs the daily lives of the San/Bushmen is the African customary law and Euro-centric law. This is the internally and externally imposed law that was referred to above, and the

San/Bushmen experience affords a remarkable instance thereof in an African context. And as a confirmation of the conventional disruptive nature of normative imposition — a thesis previously advanced — this imposed law has tended to cause massive dislocations to the said society's indigenous culture. But the San/Bushmen have been forced to comply with it, largely out of lack of choice, docility and habit rather than because of moral conscience,[15] for there is no doubt that they would rather live under circumstances that comport with their own culture than under those that do not.

Such is the terrible fate of any society that is subjected to imposed law, whether African or otherwise. And such is the connection that is seen to exist between semiotics, law and normative imposition and how the triadic connection bears upon the San/Bushmen of Southern Africa.

**B.D.D. Radipati lectures on law at Vista University.*

ENDNOTES

1. Peter Goodrich, 1985, 'Language, text and sign in the history of legal doctrine,' eds. Domenico Carzo and Bernard S. Jackson, *Semiotics, Law and Social Science*, 95.

2. Roberta Kevelson, 1982, 'Comparative Legal Cultures and Semiotics: An Introduction,' 1 *American Journal of Semiotics* 63 at 65.

   But even so, there are some general assumptions held by legal semiotics, and the same must be recited here for they will tend more or less to inform the succeeding discourse. They are that (i) there is no ideal legal system in any society, there are only relations between legal subsystems which conflict for the position of ascendancy (ii) legal acts include decisions, commands and requests, and rules; there are both verbal and non-verbal legal acts, but all acts are presumed to derive from a verbal infracture; (iii) assumption of authority, often implied but deleted in explicit acts, characterises traditional presumptions of trust and legitimacy; (iv) co-existing legal subsystems re-inforce as much as they conflict at times with each other; in order to understand not only the dialogue between opposing and/or complementary subsystems one needs intersystemic bridge laws; and (v) the system of logic which predominates in any given society is a referrent model, or sign for contextual social structures and cultural institutions: *ibid* at 69-70.

3. Robert L Kidder, 1979, 'Toward an integrated theory of imposed law,' eds. Sandra B. Burman and Barbara E. Harrel-Bond, *The Imposition of Law,* 289.

4. *Ibid* at 296.

5. Lawrence Friedman, 1975, *The Legal System*, cited in Roberta Kevelson *op cit* note 2 at 68.

6. Bessie Head, 1971, *Maru* (African Writers Series 101).

7. *Ibid* at 11.

8. This term has come to characterise reference to such communities as the San/Bushmen of Southern Africa and native Americans of North America, among others, particularly since the publication of the tentative definition proposed by the Special Rapporteur of the Sub-Commission of the United Nations Human Rights Commission, José Martinez Cobo. It reads thus:

> 'Indigenous communities, peoples and communities are those which, having a historical continuity with pre-colonial societies that developed on their territories, consider themselves distinct from other sectors of the society now prevailing in those territories, or parts of them.'

   Brownlie makes the following three comments about the definition. First, the approach places much emphasis on antecedence, and the general result is that, apart from the factor of priority of settlement, there is little or nothing to distinguish an indigenous people from any other ethnic group. Second, a particular attribute of certain types of traditional aboriginal culture is its vulnerability in the face of economic individualism and entrepreneurial pressure. Third, this definition has laid emphasis on the criterion that indigenous peoples form non-dominant sectors of society: Ian Brownlie, 1992, *Treaties and Indigenous Peoples*, The Robb Lectures 1991, 60.

9. This helpful historical account is a recitation of what appears in Brownlie *supra* at 56-58 and the writer's indebtedness thereto is hereby expressly acknowledged.

10. An excellent dramatisation of the Botswana San/Bushmen's full and equal citizenship is shown in the case *S v Baoke*, High Court of Botswana, Criminal Trial No. 32 of 1978, 23 November 1978, unreported, on file with the author.

11. Sidsel Saugestad, 'Botswana: The Inconvenient Indigenous Peoples,' No. 2, 1993, *International Work Group for Indigenous Affairs Newsletter*, 36-41; C. J. Butale, Botswana's Minister of Local Government, Lands and Housing, official opening speech at the second regional conference on development programmes for Africa's San/Bushmen populations held in Gaborone, Botswana on 11-13 October, 1993, on file with the author.

12. A. J. G. M. Sanders, 1989, 'The Bushmen of Botswana — From Desert Dwellers to World Citizens,' 4 *Law and Anthropology* 107; 'The Law of the Bushmen as Reflected in their Rock Art,' Unpublished paper, 1993, on file with the author.

13. Sanders, 1993, *ibid* at 3.

14. *Idem.*

15. More on this see Sally M. A. Lloyd Bostock, 'Explaining Compliance with Imposed Law,' eds. Sandra B. Burman and Barbara E. Harrel-bond, 1979, *The Imposition of Law*, 9.

AUTHOR'S COMMENTS ON SELECTED BIBLIOGRAPHY

On Peircean treatment of the inter-relation of law, economics and politics against referrent legal systems of value, see Roberta Kevelson, *The Law as a System of Signs*, New York: Plenum Press, 1988.

On the various approaches to legal semotics, see eds. Domenico Carzo and Bernard S. Jackson, *Semotics, Law and Social Science*, Gangemi Editore and *Liverpool Law Review*, 1985.

On how structural semiotics provides crucial insights into law, see Bernard S. Jackson, *Law, Fact and Narrative Coherence*, Liverpool: Deborah Charles Publications, 1988.

On a systematic analysis of the relationship between contemporary semiotic theory and modern jusiprudence, see Bernard S. Jackson, *Semiotics and Legal Theory*, London: Routledge and Kegan Paul, 1985. A review of this book appears in Anthony Beck, 'The Semiology of Law' (1987) 7 *Oxford Journal of Legal Studies* 475.

On cultural objects as signification, see Anthony Giddens, *Social Theory and Modern Sociology*, Cambridge: Polity Press, 1987, 100-102.

On how the San/Bushmen cultural heritage should be preserved by educational programmes, see J. Tsonope, 'Education and Culture,' a paper presented to the Second Regional Conference on Development Programmes for the San/Bushmen held in Gaborone, Botswana on 11-13 October, 1993, on file with the author.

On the San/Bushmen linguistics, see Rainer Vossen, 'Studying the Linguistic and Ethono-History of the Khoe-Speaking (Central Khoisan) Peoples of Botswana-Research in Progress,' 1984, 16 *Botswana Notes and Records* 19; Rainer Vossen *et al*, 'Khoe Linguistic Relationship Reconsidered,' 1988, 20 *Botswana Notes and Records* 61.

On how English law has been adapted in Africa, see Kenneth Roberts-Wray, 1960, 'The Adaptation of Imported Law in Africa,' 4 *Journal of African Law* 66.

On whether there should be a semiotic anthoropological approach to law, see Irene P Winner, 'Is There an Anthropological Approach to Law?' in ed. Roberta Kevelson, *Law and the Human Sciences*, New York: Peter Lang Publishing Inc, 1992, Chapter 25.

On traditionalism and normative imposition in Swaziland, see Peter N. Takirambudde, 1983, 'External Law and Social Structure in an African Context: An Essay About Normative Imposition and Survival in Swaziland,' 16 *Comparative and International Law Journal of Southern Africa* 209.

Chapter Eighteen

Speech as a Universal Right: International Law and the Case of Salman Rushdie

Bruce L. Rockwood*

> 'Everyone has the right to freedom of opinion and expression; this right includes freedom to hold opinions without interference and to seek, receive and impart information and ideas through any media and regardless of frontiers.' Article 19, Universal Declaration of Human Rights, UN General Assembly Resolution 217 (III 1948).

I

The international legal order is a system of sovereign states,[1] each of which is treated as a 'subject' of international law, entitled to its own legal and cultural system.[2] Traditionally, only states have existed as 'legal persons' in the international legal system, and individuals, whether citizens of sovereign states, refugees, or stateless persons, have been treated as 'objects' of the international system. States operate within a framework of general international norms and rules aimed at promoting peace and stability, noninterference, and mutual recognition.[3]

Since the end of the Cold War, the stability of the international order enforced by the pressures of a bipolar world has diminished. The Soviet Union, Yugoslavia, and Czechoslovakia have all broken up into smaller states more closely linked to the ethnic or national identities of their populations, and pressures for further splintering of these and other states are continuing. States of the 'Third World,' such as Algeria,[4] India, Angola, Rwanda, and The Sudan, are torn by ethnic, religious, and ideological violence and civil wars. While the first non-racial elections in South Africa were held from April 26 to April 29, 1994, the future of that troubled land is uncertain, and torn by racial and tribal tensions.

In the turmoil of this period, one source of controversy is the scope and meaning of the concept of human rights.[5] Human rights in the western tradition has been a concept which focused on individual, as opposed to group, rights; and emphasized civil and political, as opposed to economic and social, rights.[6] In the western tradition, the individual has a right to speak, vote, and seek change, but no right to any particular outcome or economic status in society. In contrast, some non-western societies are said to place a greater value on group or communitarian rights. For example, M.M. Slaughter argues:[7]

> Whereas the Western liberal tradition places priority on individual autonomy, the Islamic tradition presents a communitarian view in which the concept of the self is realized collectively in the community of Islam and is defined through traditions and concepts of honor. The concept of the autonomous self requires the free speech principle; the socially situated self of Islamic society necessarily rejects free speech in favor of prohibitions against insult and defamation.

A diagram of this distinction might look like this:

	INDIVIDUAL RIGHTS	**GROUP RIGHTS**
CIVIL AND POLITICAL RIGHTS	**To speak, to vote; religious freedom.**	**Proportional representation; autonomous regions. Group religious rights.**
ECONOMIC AND SOCIAL RIGHTS	**Education and training for economic opportunity. Private property.**	**Housing; right to development. Land use regulation.**
	Health care and a clean environment: these could arguably be viewed as both individual and group rights.	

Figure 1

Without the constraints of the bi-polar Cold War era, countries and peoples have felt free to act on deferred agendas, whether health care in the United States, or ethnic cleansing as in the former Yugoslavia. Advocates of human rights as universal norms, rather than finding themselves empowered by the demise of Cold War excuses for ignoring human rights violations by 'friendly' countries, instead find themselves increasingly stonewalled by the argument that such rights, although embodied in treaties and customary international law, are archaic holdovers of an imperial or colonial era, and do not take into account the cultural and legal traditions of non-western states which are now a majority of the states in the international system.[8]

The validity of this critique under international law, particularly of its use in opposition to rights of freedom of speech and expression, and also in regard to its challenge to the very idea of the universality of human rights norms,[9] is the subject of this paper. International law, human rights, and the law and literature movement[10] interconnect in the case of author Salman Rushdie, who remains to this day under a death sentence pronounced by Iran for the crime of publishing a book which offends some believers.[11] Thus his case can provide a focal point for this discussion.[12]

This approach reflects the author's cultural perspective that freedom of speech is a fundamental right under United States law, even apart from its treatment under international law.[13] The First Amendment contains the main insights that assure the legal protection of individuals *and* groups in the United States.[14] Debate about the scope of free speech is common in the United States, from campus speech codes to the ruling of the United States Supreme Court that biased intent can be used to increase the penalty in criminal cases.[15] Yet the insight that free speech is central is not limited to the United States, but is reflected in such agreements as The European Convention on Human Rights and Fundamental Freedoms, whose Article 10 provides:[16]

> (1) Everyone has the right to freedom of expression. This right shall include freedom to hold opinions and to receive and impart information and ideas without interference by public authority and regardless of frontiers. . . .

Global commerce in speech, embodied in multinational publishing companies, entertainment media, broadcasting, and the internet has created an indivisible world community that cannot avoid acting on the view that speech is a fundamental right. Justice Robert Jackson's comment about the scope of Congress's power to regulate interstate commerce applies here:[17]

> If it is interstate commerce that feels the pinch, it does not matter how local the operation that applies the squeeze.

The law of every developed country, and not merely the United States and Britain, clearly guarantees Rushdie the right to write, to publish, and to seek to influence public opinion through the free play of ideas. The corollary is that, in an interdependent world where communications is a key to the global economy, the right that supports Rushdie within the United States must, of necessity, support him in every other country. In condemning Rushdie, Iran seems to claim the right to punish a 'speech-act' under its criminal code through a broad assertion of universal jurisdiction, even when the book is not published in her territory, and when actual enforcement of her laws and cultural values would violate the territorial sovereignty and jurisdiction of the United States, the United Kingdom, or wherever Rushdie or his interpreters and publishers are found. Such a sweeping assertion of what, in its more moderate guise, is sometimes called the 'effects doctrine,' would have devastating implications for the autonomy, cultural integrity, and creative rights of the citizens of all countries, and cannot be acknowledged or assented to by any civilized nation which is a member of the international legal system. The distinction is reflected in the following diagram:

	EXTERNAL EVENT	**DOMESTIC IMPACT**
LEGITIMATE EXERCISE OF DOMESTIC JURISDICTION 'Effects Doctrine'	**Plan drug smuggling; Fix commodity prices; Share markets.**	**Drug use & crime; Prices rise illegally; Monopolies.**
ILLEGITIMATE EXERCISE OF DOMESTIC JURISDICTION 'Universal Jurisdiction'	**Publish a book critical of a foreign sovereign, or viewed as blasphemous by a religion, or advocating a scientific view, such as evolution, rejected by some religion or group.**	**Ideas forbidden at home are published abroad, and may influence domestic climate of opinion due to permeability of borders (satellite t.v.; internet; mail; media).**

Figure 2

Conduct abroad that has *concrete* effects within the territory is, in this view, subject to the territorial jurisdiction of the country where the effects occur, when the defendant comes within the territory impacted.[18] But conduct abroad that has only *symbolic* effects within the territory, should *not* be subject to territorial jurisdiction even if the defendant comes within the territory impacted.[19] And it certainly is not subject to the extraterritorial assertion of jurisdiction, direct or indirect, without the consent of the state where the enforcing state seeks to assert its enforcement jurisdiction.

When do 'effects' become sufficiently 'concrete' to move beyond mere 'symbolic' effects? When the impact of the conduct abroad has measurable results on markets, prices, health (use of illegal drugs), and not when the impacts are either entirely introspective or spiritual, or when, if physical and violent, such as with rioting, there is a significant, responsible intervening factor such as public condemnation and incitement by secular or religious authority. In short, if, but for the intervening cause of domestic political and religious leaders pointing out and condemning Rushdie's book, and inciting the public to riot, no such rioting were to occur, then the foreign conduct would not be the true cause of the domestic effect at all.[20] Price fixing abroad causes prices to rise within the territory, but incitement to riot by anti-Rushdie opportunists within Iran, India, and other countries, caused the mob violence in response to Rushdie, not Rushdie or his work.

'Free speech is the whole thing, the whole ball game. Free speech is life itself,' Rushdie said at Columbia,[21] and it is because he is right that is so important that the international legal system respond more aggressively on his behalf.[22]

To fit this analysis within the framework of human rights norms established in the last century, note first that 'Public International Law' has also been called 'The Law of Nations,' 'Transnational Law,' or 'The Law of War and Peace,' but never 'The Law of Peoples.' People have arrived relatively late as actors in the arena of public international law, and are still primarily viewed as 'objects' rather than 'subjects' of the international legal order. Individuals ordinarily lack standing to pursue legal remedies in international forums.[23] Thus, the rules of law applied in analyzing the legality of the fatwa against Rushdie reflect rules of a system which focuses on injury to states as such, and not on injuries to individuals. The argument on behalf of Rushdie must really be an argument on behalf of any state whose sovereignty is infringed by an attack on the life, liberty or property of Rushdie. The injury to the state is what is subject to international redress, and not the injury to Rushdie as such.

Second, injury to *speech* itself is arguably an injury to the state as well as any assault on Rushdie might be, not because a state may have something like the American First Amendment as part of its domestic law, but because preventing persons protected by a state, whether citizens or not, from speaking or publishing, is an infringement on the exclusive territorial sovereignty of the state. States may limit the speech of their own nationals and residents by a variety of standards, but they cannot permit external interference with domestic standards without risk of severe consequences for their independence and sovereign equality, as provided for in so many international conventions and covenants.[24]

Third, since World War II international practices and conventions have emerged which give standing and protection to individuals within the international system. Such treaties as the International Covenant on Economic, Social and Cultural Rights, the International Covenant on Civil and Political Rights, and the Convention on the Prevention and Punishment of the Crime of Genocide,[25] all have contributed to the gradual expansion of human rights law.

Fourth, after World War II the old Colonial Empires were given up, sometimes relatively peacefully as with India, although with the incredible suffering of the partition, which was not coincidentally linked to sectarian strife. Others were given up after prolonged war, as with the French in Indo-China and Algeria.[26] Most of Africa and Asia quickly followed, and with the independence of these states came the rapid expansion of the United Nations Organization (UNO), the emergence of the Third World, and the rise of demands from former colonies for a 'New International Economic Order.'[27] This era of independence was consciously viewed on all sides as subject to the rules of the new UN system, and the norms of customary international law which favored both the independence of nations, and the recognition by these new nations of their roles within the existing, if expanding, international legal order. The subsequent assertion of alternative perspectives on the nature, sources, origin, and binding nature of traditional rules of public international law[28] does not undermine the binding nature of this international reality. Each of these nations was and is deemed by the international legal system to have acquiesced to being bound by and subject to the rules of customary public international law and conventions to which they adhere (such as the UN Charter) as a part of their initiation into the international system.

Some of the new nations argued that customary public international law was derived from the customs, usages and practices of ex-Colonial powers and their Western allies, and not legitimate. 'Why should old norms be binding on us when we played no part in their creation?' But they (and we) are all born into a world we did not make, and we have to live by its rules, even as we seek to improve them.

In the 1970's developing countries were vigorous in asserting their total sovereignty over their economic resources. The UN General Assembly Resolution called the 'Charter of Economic Rights and Duties of States,'[29] holds in Chapter II, Article 1:

> Every State has the sovereign and inalienable right to choose its economic system as well as its political, social and cultural systems in accordance with the will of its own people, without outside interference, coercion or threat in any form whatsoever.

These states emphasized their sovereignty and equality among nations, and their opposition to any interference in their internal affairs.

A second thread in this analysis, based on the original ideals of the League of Nations as well as the United Nations, is support for universal norms protecting all peoples and all persons in their own basic, fundamental and universal rights. One sees this in the Universal Declaration of Human Rights,[30] and in such more specific and binding Conventions as the International Covenant on Civil and Political Rights.[31] Part I, Article 1 of that Convention states:

> 1. All peoples have the right of self-determination. By virtue of that right they freely determine their political status and freely pursue their economic, social and cultural development.

Part II, Article 6.1 of that same Convention notes that 'Every human being has the inherent right to life. This right shall be protected by law. No one shall be arbitrarily deprived of his life.' As Iran subscribes to this Convention, one can argue that this provision requires a showing that the death sentence on Rushdie be 'not arbitrary.' Further, Rushdie did apologize and seek forgiveness, and many scholars argue that the teachings of Islamic law on this point permit mercy and cancellation of the fatwa, even assuming it was lawful in the first place.[32] Article 6.4 of the Convention states that 'Anyone sentenced to death shall have the right to seek pardon or commutation of the sentence. Amnesty, pardon or commutation of the sentence of death may be granted in all cases.' Clearly the norms of international law are as or more advanced than those of the United States.[33]

These international law norms may be derivative of the Western, former colonial powers, but they have been subscribed to in principal by most of the Third World as they became independent. Their application in practice may be inadequate. For example, Article 17.1 of this Convention holds that 'No one shall be subjected to arbitrary or unlawful interference with his privacy, family, home or correspondence, nor to unlawful attacks on his honour and reputation,' which would seem to include being assassinated for writing or translating a book, or being the victim of a mob in your own home or country, or when you travel in a country which is a party to the Convention.

Article 18.1 of the Convention calls for 'freedom of thought, conscience and religion,' without 'coercion which would impair his freedom to have or to adopt a religion or belief of his choice.' Arguably Mr. Rushdie would have this right, whether one interprets his writings as rejection of religion in general, or critical of a religion without indicating rejection of the idea of having a belief as such.

However, Article 18.3 notes that 'Freedom to manifest one's religion or beliefs may be subject only to such limitations as are prescribed by law and are necessary to protect public safety, order, health, or morals or the fundamental rights and freedoms of others.' This could be read narrowly to permit banning a book only when it threatens to cause an imminent breach of the peace, as might well be the case in a country such as India. Or it might be read broadly by an outraged Iran seeking to vindicate its religious views on a barbarian world through a broad assertion of universal jurisdiction over anything causing 'effects' within Iran. Almost anything can be 'prescribed by law' if a state wishes to do so. Almost anything can be deemed 'necessary.' Clearly, Article 18.3 does not provide much protection for Rushdie.

Article 19 of the Convention protects freedom of expression and communication, but notes in paragraph 3 that 'The exercise of the rights provided for (above) carries with it special duties and responsibilities,' and therefore may be restricted if done so 'by law' and if 'necessary' to protect the 'rights or reputations of others' or to protect 'public health or morals.' Such language can be read narrowly, but it appears to create a large loophole for a leader such as the Ayatollah seeking to take advantage of its terms.[34]

These citations demonstrate the tensions built into international human rights law noted in Figure 1: (A) between group and individual rights, and

(B) between liberty or civil and political rights, and economic or subsistence rights. People will disagree which rights are more basic, or which rights are in some sense a prerequisite for the exercise of all other rights. Some nations will argue there is a right to development that supplants all other rights, and that the needs of the group must outweigh the needs of individuals, such as students, protestors, and advocates of minority rights.

Nonetheless, there is an emerging consensus on the importance of all human rights as norms which govern and check the international behavior of states. In fact, the tension between advocates of group rights and those of individual rights may, in some sense, be a tactic, aimed at diverting attention from the real objections of those who control the power in authoritarian states and are simply unwilling to relinquish it. The protestations of the military government of Haiti in recent months smell of this rationale. These norms disturb authoritarian states because they operate not only in states dealings with each other, but in each state's dealings with its *own* people.[35]

This trend in some ways counters the first trend noted above, since while the UN and its members all affirm principles of noninterference and mutual recognition, the very idea of human rights norms as universal standards implies a right to act to intervene in the 'sovereign internal affairs' of other, recalcitrant states. The only way to reconcile this is to develop a balancing test much like that used in procedural due process analysis in American case law. What is the nature of the liberty or property interest at stake for the individuals who feel threatened? What interests are at stake for the group or state which opposes them? How central are the competing concerns to, on the one hand, the core rights of individuals under various UN General Assembly Resolutions, conventions, and customary public international law; and, on the other hand, to the fundamental notions of territorial sovereignty and independence long advocated by the same international system? From such an analysis certain procedural protections as well as substantive results can be obtained. Notice of objection to publication of a book in India, followed by prohibition of its import and sale after riots have occurred, is a measured response of reasonable scope; a death warrant to be executed abroad in the absence of publication within the territory is not. Most legal systems of the world are familiar with the concept that certain rights must be balanced against each other, so it is only a question of finding a formula that is appropriate for doing so in this case.

Sometimes such an analysis may lead to international intervention that is claimed to be for humanitarian purposes, with or without the sanction of a regional or international organization. The December, 1989 U.S. invasion of Panama, referred to as 'Operation Just Cause' by President Bush, was much criticized at the time, despite our claims that we were restoring democracy and arresting a drug dealer. Tanzania's intervention against Idi Amin in Uganda, and Vietnam's ouster of the Khmer Rouge from Cambodia, are more widely viewed as good examples. The gradual engagement of the UN and the U.S. in Somalia and Bosnia are examples where balancing has become trickier, and more open to debate. The presence of former President Carter and other foreign observers monitoring elections around the world in recent years illustrates an emerging consensus that domestic politics are more a matter of international concern than the Third World would have admitted during the height of the demands for a 'New International Order' in the mid-1970's.

A third trend which has emerged with the growth of the interdependence of nations has been remarked on widely since the early 1970's.[36] Called 'Globalization,' it deemphasizes the role of the State. Issues, businesses, crises, problems: everything is international now. Pollution is no respecter of national boundaries. Ozone depletion, global warming, past and future energy shortages, multinational corporations, all pose global problems seeking global solutions. The problems of the environment clash with the problems of trade and sustainable development, but always in a global context.

As a result, since there is no global government, we see a continuing trend of states to resort to pursuing their own formerly domestic legal objectives through extraterritorial legal action against non-resident aliens for acts taken abroad which have effects within the complaining state, through broad interpretations of the effects doctrine, or use of protective, universal or enforcement jurisdiction. A Hong Kong resident in the U.S. executes insider trades through a bank affiliate in Hong Kong. A Panamanian dictator is indicted for drug trafficking, as are scores of past and present Mexican officials. The U.S. and Europe seek to extend the reach of their antitrust laws to foreign conduct having 'effects' within the country.

To sum up current international legal theory and practice, depending upon the issue, incident, or occasion, a state — *any state* — may claim:

(1) Absolute control over its internal affairs and freedom from external interference over internal affairs, with internal being defined by the state for itself.

(2) The right to apply international norms to its neighbors conduct towards their own people (we like to *export* democracy, while we used to say the Soviets sought to *impose* communism).

(3) The right to apply its own domestic or municipal law to the acts of foreigners abroad.

STATE OPTIONS.
Figure 3

This is rather starkly drawn, but if we may take it as a rough model for much contemporary public international law thinking, then the Rushdie affair raises some interesting questions. For example, if, under the relevant version of Islamic Law applicable in Iran, Rushdie's book merely by its existence on the planet constitutes an act of unforgivable blasphemy at the level of a capital offense, would not the Ayatollah have the same right to apply his law extraterritorially under the theory of 'protective jurisdiction' as the United States claimed when it first indicted Noriega, the de facto head of a foreign state, and again when it invaded his country and took him prisoner? The United States did this when it seized by trick an Arab airline hijacker at sea in the Mediterranean and brought him to the U.S. for trial.

Further, if a culturally diverse and fragmented state like India suffers riots and loss of life and thus harm to the rights of large segments of 'an entire people,' would that not give India some right of action under international norms, customs, treaties and so forth for damages or other remedies? There might be a reason to blame Indian officials for mishandling the riots, or for blaming political agitators for encouraging the riots to spread, but this might only reduce or spread liability, much as principles of 'joint and several liability' have developed in American tort law. Perhaps India can sue the publishers in the countries that publish the book, for damages caused by its ultimate distribution in India, which resulted in unavoidable protests and clashes. See again Articles 18 and 19 of the International Covenant on Civil and Political Rights discussed above.

Conversely, is not the act of threatening death, or calling for destruction of the book, interfering in the sovereign, internal affairs of those states which choose to publish it? See Article 6 of the same Convention. That is, isn't it possible, under international law, to argue that the act of publishing

The Satanic Verses is both, in a sense, protected by international law, and in another sense, condemned by it? Or, to make a lesser claim, isn't it clear that existing norms and rules of public international law can be employed to advantage by all parties to this dispute even if we in the West think the issue is clearly well settled by law? And are threats to kill a foreigner abroad as such normally considered illegal (at least where they are credible) under international law when made this way, even by a head of state?

We live in a diverse world where mutual respect and tolerance is a sometime thing, and where our own very First Principles — our First Amendment in the United States, for example — may sometimes need to be reexamined, explained, and defended. Many of us may accept Justice Holmes' case as very convincing:

> But when men have realized that time has upset many fighting faiths, they may come to believe even more than they believe the very foundations of their own conduct that the ultimate good desired is better reached by free trade in ideas — that the best test of truth is the power of the thought to get itself accepted in the competition of the market, and that truth is the only ground upon which their wishes safely can be carried out. That at any rate is the theory of our Constitution.[37]

But we have to recognize that it was, after all, a *dissent*, and that Holmes also ruled earlier that free speech 'would not protect a man in falsely shouting fire in a theatre and causing a panic.'[38]

How then can one defend the publication of Rushdie's book, and freedom of speech generally, against the claim that in the view of one faith it is 'false,' and that, being published at all is the same as falsely yelling fire and causing a panic? Perhaps the answer, to draw an analogy to a recent and controversial review of Catherine MacKinnon's *Only Words*,[39] is to draw a distinction between writing about the possibility, and then considering what would happen if you did so, falsely, the next time you went to the cinema. Should you be arrested for writing about it, the same as if you had actually done so? The 'general principles of law recognized by civilized nations' (ICJ Statute, Art. 38(1)(c)) clearly reject this notion.

Professor D'Amato argues that 'freedom of speech is the most fundamental human right because it acts as a check, through ridicule and exposure as well as debate, upon the tendency toward governmental excess and runaway power accumulation.'[40] And Professor Shue, in his defense of basic rights as including economic and social as well as civil and political rights, argues that speech rights are not something that can be traded away for a little more bread, since the right to organize and demand one's rights using speech may be a prerequisite for getting any bread at all.[41] These are arguments for defense of speech in general, and not for defense of Rushdie's novel in particular. It is easy for a Western civil libertarian to see the slippery slope from regulating or punishing certain speech to loss of free speech altogether. It may not be obvious or persuasive to a believer from another cultural and legal tradition. Still, if one considers the context of *The Satanic Verses* in the sequence of Rushdie's earlier and more clearly historical-political works, it is easy to make the case that his book is as much a political satire on the current regime in Iran as it is a satire on Islam.[42] Rather than acting out of religious scruple, the government of Iran has merely thrown up the traditional smoke screen to distract us from its real offense — criticism of the Islamic Revolutionary State. The argument is clear, but obviously is not of the sort that will convert the religious zealots in Iran.

An approach to lowering tensions and getting a settlement to end the fatwa against Rushdie might be to seek to communicate to all other cultures, including Islamic ones, the centrality of the First Amendment of the U.S. Constitution to our society, and the extremely narrow grounds for limiting speech rights in the United States in the light of our culture, history and legal tradition.[43] The Constitution, Bill of Rights and the Flag are potent symbols to many Americans and have much the same impact as the Islamic faith has in an Islamic society. Perhaps a mutual respect for our respective sacred symbols would lead to a recognition in Iran that nothing further could be gained for them by maintaining the fatwa.

Unfortunately, many Americans' commitment to the First Amendment as a key symbol has faded in recent years, in favor of broad restrictions aimed at disfavored speech, be it called hate speech or pornography, or demands for politically correct dialogue in textbooks and classrooms. Thus an attempt to draw comparisons between our respective key symbols might backfire. The outrage of the Iranian government over Rushdie's book, the angry mobs in India, and the protesting Muslims in London who object to a peculiarly British law that prohibits blasphemy only against the established Anglican Church,[44] is mirrored in the debate over a 'flag burning' amendment to the First Amendment here. Many Americans appear willing to limit speech with the same fanaticism we tend to expect when we read another article about Iran.

Despite the difficulty, seeking greater understanding of the things we care most strongly about is vital, if we wish to achieve an international accommodation that protects those in any society who seek to pursue a traditional or religious way of life, while protecting the speech and cultural rights of those who are non-believers. The problem is, as the current crises in Algeria and Bosnia show, what to do when people of any faith want to live and let live, but are faced with fanatics who will not brook any kind of difference within the society: secular versus fundamentalist in Algeria, Catholic, Orthodox and Muslim in Bosnia.

Westerners know little about Islamic Law.[45] Islamic law and legal procedures, Islam's diverse literary and cultural traditions of tolerance and diversity are no more well known here than the U.S. Constitution is known in Teheran or Damascus.[46] Writers, scholars and students in the Islamic world have suffered more from this debate than we have in the West, since it has polarized opinion in their communities about work they themselves wish to do. Most Muslim countries do not support the Ayatollah, particularly in respect to the death sentence.[47]

Much of Western culture has been hostile to the Islamic world in the past, when not simply ignorant of its history, law, literature and culture. After World War II the Islamic nations shared in the independence movements of the era, and in the cultural defensiveness reflected in such experiences as the debate over the UNESCO Press Code proposal.[48] There was the controversy over the television docu-drama, 'Death of a Princess,' which threatened to disrupt U.S.-Saudi relations for a while.[49] The best response is education, through the schools and through conferences sponsored by the UN and other organizations. The emerging peace settlement between Israel and the PLO makes this both more imperative, and more dangerous, as efforts to foster trust may attract fanatics interested in destroying all hope by violence. Even so, efforts must be renewed to work with Muslim religious leaders to get the widest possible support for withdrawal of the Rushdie fatwa.

The people of the U.S. should study their own First Amendment traditions more closely, since if they cannot understand the logic of their own right to free speech and explain it to a foreigner, how likely is it they are going to be able to persuade the world that the strong support of free speech ought to be a fundamental human right under international law? A view of these legal principles emphasizing tolerance and solidarity, rather than barriers, differences and confrontation, may be the best approach to reconciling the problems of basic rights and liberties in the context of a pluralist world.[50]

Finally, it proves too much for critics in Third World countries to claim they are not bound by agreements made between their predecessors and the former colonial powers, or by the customary rules of another era. To accept that argument would imply that any agreement made today could be objected to on the same or some similar basis tomorrow. Instead, we must acknowledge that we all have predecessors, just as we all have parents and, whether or not we have children, we all have successors whom we teach by precept and by example. Each generation, and every state, must work within the framework it inherits, and shape that framework to meet the needs of the present and future. It is merely a debating point that a country was once a colony, and not a telling point about the legitimacy or binding effect of universal norms. International human rights norms have been articulated for some time, reflect a widespread consensus, and include the individual right to free expression as a central concept.

**Bruce L. Rockwood is Professor of Business Law at Bloomsburg University.*

ENDNOTES

1. The degree to which sovereignty remains a meaningful concept is subject to debate. See: *1994 Proceedings of the 88th Annual Meeting of the American Society of International Law 'The Transformation of Sovereignty,'* Washington, D.C., 1995.

2. One problem facing international law is the meaning of the right of cultural self-determination within established states for the same rights of minority groups and individuals within those nations. Do peoples as such have this right, regardless of the impact of the exercise of such rights upon the states within which they exist? The June, 1993 World Conference on Human Rights at Vienna, Austria produced the 'Vienna Declaration and Programme of Action' which, in Article I(2) provided: 'All peoples have the right of self-determination. By virtue of that right they freely determine their political status, and freely pursue their economic, social and cultural development.' *World Conference on Human Rights, United Nations*, New York, 1993, p. 29. Cf. the problem of Bosnia-Hercegovina, where rights articulated in terms of groups rather than individuals have lead to so much violence.

3. See: the UN Charter and many other international agreements; J.G. Starke, Q.C., *An Introduction to International Law*, 10th edition, London:Butterworths, 1989. Professor Reisman notes: 'Make no mistake about it. International law is a woefully bad system: it does not work well and when it does work, it produces and distributes

values in ways that should offend all but the morally defective. Yet it is the only international legal system we have on an interdependent planet where some system of international law is inescapable.' Michael Reisman, 'The Teaching of International Law in the Eighties,' *International Lawyer* 20, no.3, Summer, 1986:987.

4. Daniel Singer, 'Algeria Slides into Civil War,' *Nation*, 21 Feb. 94, 1.

5. Rhoda E. Howard, 'Human Rights and the Necessity for Cultural Change,' and Vinay Lal, 'The Imperialism of Human Rights,' in VIII *Focus on Law Studies* #1, (Fall, 1992) 4-11; Jeremy Waldron, 'Minority Cultures and the Cosmopolitan Alternative,' 25 *Univ. of Michigan Journal of Law Reform* #3&4, 1992:751.

6. See: panel discussion among Louis Henkin, Abdullahi An-Naim, Anne Bayefsky, and Mark L. Schneider, 'An International Human Rights Agenda for the End of the Century: New Human Rights?' 1994 *Proceedings of the American Society of International Law*, Washington, D.C., 1995.

7. M.M. Slaughter, 'The Salman Rushdie Affair: Apostasy, Honor, and Freedom of Speech,' 79 *Virginia Law Review*, 1993:153, 155.

8. China's objection to the now abandoned attempt of the United States to link most-favored-nation trading status with human rights progress is one example.

9. P. Shenon, 'Indonesia Moves to Stifle Criticism, Both at Home and Abroad,' *New York Times*, 29 June 94, A13, c 1; J. Darnton, 'Group Finds Widespread Rights Violations Continuing in World,' Amnesty International Annual Report, *New York Times*, 7 July 94, A13, c 1.

10. Bruce L. Rockwood, 1993, 'Law and Other Stories,' Chapter XIX ed. R. Kevelson, *Flux, Complexity, and Illusion*, New York: Peter Lang; Bruce L. Rockwood, 'Telling Stories in School: Law and Literature as an Approach to the Business Law Curriculum,' IX *Focus on Law Studies* No.1, Fall, 1993:9-10.

11. Salman Rushdie, 1988, *The Satanic Verses*, New York: Viking Press. See: 'Witness for Freedom,' *New York Times*, 14 Dec. 1991, p 22, col. 1; Leslie H. Gelb, 'Rushdie's Death Foretold,' *New York Times*, 29 Dec. 1991, Sect. 4, p E9, col. 6; Julian Barnes, 'Letter From London: Staying Alive,' *New Yorker*, 21 Feb. 94, 99. The precedent continues to be applied in other cases: 'Egyptian Writer Jailed for Blasphemy,' (Case of Alaa Hamid) *Bloomsburg (Pa.) Press-Enterprise*, 28 Dec. 1991, p 23; 'Anti-Fundamentalist Writer Is Shot to Death in Lebanon,' *New York Times*, 16 Jan. 1992, p A8, c.3; Chris Hedges, 'Mobilizing Against Pop Music and Other Horrors,' *New York Times*, 21 July 1993, p A4, c. 3; Taslima Nasrin, 'Sentenced to Death,' *New York Times*, 30 November 1993, p A25, c. 1; 'France Fears Fallout From Algerian Turmoil,' *New York Times*, 21 December 1993, p23 c.1.; 'Algerian Teacher and Son Killed at School,' *New York Times*, March 6, 1994, p 10, c. 4.

12. Salman Rushdie, 1992, *Imaginary Homelands: Essays and Criticism 1981-1991*, New York: Granta/Penguin Books; 'Our Lives Teach Us Who We Are,' *Chronicle of Higher Education*, 8 Jan. 1992, p B5, c.2; 'A Four Year Death Sentence, and Counting,' *New York Times*, 7 Feb. 1993, Section 4, p E21, c.2.

13. But see: Nat Hentoff, 1993, *Free Speech for Me -- But Not For Thee*, New York: Harper Perennial; Stanley Fish, 1994, *There's No Such Thing As Free Speech . . . And It's A Good Thing Too*, New York: Oxford.

14. See, W. Michael Reisman, 'The New International Holy Alliance and the Struggle to Appropriate and Censor General Cultural Symbols,' in 'Speech, Religious Discrimination, and Blasphemy' Panel, April 7, 1989, 1989 *Proceedings of the 83rd Annual Meeting of the American Society of International Law*, Washington, D.C. 435-439; Aryeh Neier, 'Watching Rights,' *Nation*, 5 July 1993, pp. 7-8.

15. 'Comment: Bad Motives,' *New Yorker*, 21 June 1993, pp. 4-6. Defense of free speech often makes strange allies: 'Senate Approves Longer Sentences for Hate Crimes,' *New York Times*, 5 Nov. 1993, p. A20, c.1. 'U.S. Had More Than 7,000 Hate Crimes in '93, F.B.I. Head Says,' *New York Times*, 6 June 94, A16, c 3.

16. See the exegesis of this section in Eric Barendt, 1987, *Freedom of Speech*, Oxford: Clarendon Press.

17. J. Lieberman and G. Siedel, 1992, *Business Law and the Legal Environment*, Orlando: HBJ/The Dryden Press, 17.

18. See: *United States v. Humberto Alvarez-Machain*, 60 U.S.L.W. 4523, U.S. June 15, 1992, No.91-712; 'Agore: International Kidnapping,' *American Journal of International Law* 86 no.4, October, 1992:736.

19. In the case of common law defamation this may be debated, but the view that jurisdiction to enforce is based upon jurisdiction to prescribe suggests that the authority to punish defamation ought to lie with the state where the publication occurred, and not be extended to the hypothetical whole world where news of the publication may subsequently spread. cf. 'The Cutting Case,' Letter, Secretary of State of the United States to the U.S. Ambassador to Mexico, Department of State, Washington, D.C., November 1, 1887., published in [1887] Foreign Relations of the United States 751 (1888). See also, *Rivard v. United States*, 375 F.2d 882 (USCA, 5th Cir., 1967). *The Restatement, Third, of the Foreign Relations Law of the United States* (Philadelphia: American Law Institute, 1987), Section 402, provides: 'Subject to Section 403, a state has jurisdiction to prescribe law with respect to ... (c) conduct outside its territory that has or is intended to have substantial effect within its territory.' Section 402(3) further provides that a state has jurisdiction to prescribe rules of law with respect to 'conduct outside its territory by persons not its nationals that is directed against the security of the state or against a limited class of other state interests.' cf *United States v. Rodriguez*, 182 F.Supp. 479 (S.D.Cal.1960); *United States v. Pizzarusso*, 388 F.2d 8 (USCA, 2nd Cir., 1968). Such expansive readings of authority may appeal to a state that is seeking to vigorously assert itself internationally, but they risk creating reciprocal precedents

which, if widely applied, would undermine territorial jurisdiction in the long run. Iran for example might well argue that its condemnation of Rushdie was aimed at protecting the security of its Islamic Republic. Most states, on balance, would agree with the sounder view of Justice Marshall, 'The jurisdiction of the nation within its own territory is necessarily exclusive and absolute. It is susceptible of no limitation not imposed by itself. Any restriction upon it, deriving validity from an external source, would imply a diminution of its sovereignty to the extent of the restriction, and an investment of that sovereignty to the same extent in that power which could impose such restriction.' *The Schooner Exchange v. McFaddon*, 11 U.S. (7 Cranch) 116, 136 (U.S. Supreme Court, 1812). Singapore from time to time excludes the *Economist* or the *Wall Street Journal* from its shores when it objects to their editorial conduct, and the U.S. and U.K. do not file diplomatic protests. If Singapore were to send police officials abroad to cane their editors for the 'effects of their editorials and news reports upon business interests in Singapore,' however, that would be another matter. The same is true with respect to Rushdie.

20. Cf. the 'last clear chance doctrine,' discussed by Judge Harry Friendly in *In Re Kinsman Transit*, 338 F.2d. 708 (U.S.C.A., 2nd Cir., 1964).

21. Rushdie, 'Our Lives Teach,' 8 Jan. 1992, p B5, c 1, *supra*, Note 13.

22. 'The International Committee for the Defense of Salman Rushdie and His Publishers invited some 60 authors to write public letters to Mr. Rushdie responding to one of the most extreme examples of censorship in modern times.' These letters collected in *The Rushdie Letters*, published by the Univ. of Nebraska Press in March, 1993. *Chronicle of Higher Education*, 27 Jan. 1993, p A10, c.2; S. Heller, 'MLA Asks, Have Scholars Done Enough on Behalf of Salman Rushdie,' *Chronicle of Higher Education*, 12 Jan. 1994, pA 13, c 3.

23. Anthony D'Amato, 'Perspectives: International Human Rights at the Close of the Twentieth Century,' *International Lawyer* 22 no.1, Spring, 1988:167; Anthony D'Amato, Chair, Panel on 'New Customary Law: Taking Human Rights Seriously?' 1993 *Proceedings of the 87th Annual Meeting of the American Society of International Law*, Washington, D.C., 1994:229.

24. See,for example, the following documents in Louis Henkin, et al., eds., 1993, *Basic Documents Supplement to International Law Cases and Materials*, American Casebook Series, St. Paul, MN: West Publishing Co.; The Preamble to the UN Charter, and Article 1 of the Charter, pp 1-2; Article 4 of the Convention on the Rights and Duties of States, p 30; Article I of the Conference on Security and Cooperation in Europe, Final Act (Helsinki Accords), p 263; Article 4(a) of UN G.A. Resolution 3201 (XXIX 1974), the Declaration on the Establishment of a New International Economic Order, p. 520.

25. *Ibid.*, at pp. 146, 151 and 163 respectively.

26. See Albert Camus, 1989, *The Stranger*, trans. Matthew Ward, New York: Vintage Books; and Albert Camus, 1968, 'The Guest,' eds. Edward Mitchell and Rainer Schulte, *Continental Short Stories*, New York: W.W.Norton, 106.

27. See, for example, Jan Tinbergen, 1976, *RIO: Reshaping the International Order: A Report to the Club of Rome*, New York: E.P. Dutton.

28. Anand, 'International Organizations and the Functioning of International Law,' *Indian Journal of International Law* 24, 1984:51.

29. G.A. Res. 3281 (XXIX 1974), 14 *I.L.M.* 251 (1975); *supra*, Note 18, at p. 511.

30. *Supra*, Note 25, at p. 143.

31. Adopted and Opened for Signature, Ratification and Accession by General Assembly Resolution 2200A (XXI) of Dec. 16, 1966. U.N. Gen.Ass. Off.Rec., 21st Sess., Supp. No.16 (A/6316), p. 52, and *supra*, Note 19.

32. Ved P. Nanda, 1994, 'Islam and International Human Rights Law: Selected Aspects,' 1993 *Proceedings of the 87th Annual Meeting of the American Society of International Law*, Washington, D.C., p. 327; Abdullahi Ahmed An-Na'im, 1990, *Toward an Islamic Reformation: Civil Liberties, Human Rights and International Law*, Syracuse, New York: Syracuse University Press, 1990.

33. Consider the support for capital punishment in the United States at a time in world history it is on decline almost everywhere else.

34. The Vienna Convention on the Law of Treaties recognizes in Article 53, 64 and 71 that preemptory norms of *jus cogens* from which 'no derogation is permitted' do exist as a check on rogue nations. Genocide is prohibited by this concept. *Supra*, Note 25, p. 98. If it is unlikely that a universal right to publish books offensive to religious or ethnic groups without prior restraint will be considered to be a preemptory norm anytime soon, arguably there is a core right of speech so fundamental to international discourse that the ICJ ought to recognize it as a norm, and use it to prohibit state spon- sored attacks on writers such as the fatwa on Salman Rushdie.

35. Consider the implementation of the Conference on Security and Cooperation in Europe (CSCE) Final Act, which lead to the establishment of Helsinki Watch, Americas Watch and other human rights monitoring organizations; the Carter Human Rights Policy; Amnesty International and other NGO's; the Inter-American Court of Human Rights and the European Court of Human Rights.

36. Miriam Camps, 1974, *The Management of Interdependence*, New York: Council on Foreign Relations.

37. *Abrams v United States*, 250 U.S. 627, 630 (1919), Holmes *dissenting*. This case is analyzed in Lee C. Bollinger, 1986, *The Tolerant Society*, New York: Oxford University Press, pp. 1-23.

38. *Schenck v United States*, 249 U.S. 47, 52 (1919).

39. C. Romano, 'Between the Motion and the Act,' Review of: *Only Words* by C. MacKinnon; *Democracy and the Problem of Free Speech* by C.Sunstein; and *The Invention of Pornography* by L. Hunt in *Nation* 15 Nov. 1994, 563-570.

40. *Supra*, Note 24, 'Perspectives,' at pp. 176-177.

41. Henry Shue, 1980, *Basic Rights: Subsistence, Affluence and U.S. Foreign Policy*, Princeton, New Jersey: Princeton University Press, pp. 5-9, 30-31, 91-93.

42. See 'Salman Rushdie: Two Brown Men, Falling Hard,' and 'The Hit Men,' in John Leonard, 1993, *The Last Innocent White Man in America, and Other Writings* (New York: The New Press, 249.

43. Despite the dispute over First Amendment protections for 'Flag Burners,' constitutional faith still burns brightly for many Americans. S. Levinson, 1988, *Constitutional Faith*, Princeton, New Jersey: Princeton University Press.

44. 'Blasphemy: Offence confined to Christianity,' *R. v. Bow Street Magistrate's Court*, ex p. Choudhury, 1990 *Crim.L.R.* 711 (1990).

45. N.R. Keddie, 'Arguments for Islam,' Review of: *Islam and Democracy: Fear of the Modern World*, by Fatima Mernissi; *The Islamic Threat: Myth or Reality?* by John L. Esposito; *Passion and Politics: The Turbulent World of the Arabs* by Sandra Mackey, *New York Times Book Review*, 13 December 1992, p. 7, c 1.

46. M.Bradbury, 'The Man With a Story for Everything,' Review of *Damascus Nights*, by Rafik Schami, *New York Times Book Review*, 7 November 1993, p. 13, c 1.

47. Most Islamic nations have rejected the death sentence imposed by Iran. 'Iran View Opposed by Muslim Nations, 46 Countries Do Not Support Rushdie Death Threat,' *New York Times*, 17 March 1989, p. A8, c.6.

48. Barber, 'UNESCO:Threat to Press Freedom,' and Mergui, 'UNESCO: The State and The Media,' in *Index On Censorship* 10 no.1, Feb., 1981.

49. Richard Goldstein, 'Did PBS Try to Kill 'Death of a Princess',' *Village Voice*, 2 June 1980.

50. See: Milner S. Ball, 1985, *Lying Down Together: Law, Metaphor and Theology*, Madison: The University of Wisconsin Press; Lee C. Bollinger, 1988, *The Tolerant Society*, New York: Oxford University Press.

Chapter Nineteen

The Literary Fraud: An Intractable Problem for Law and Semiotics*

W.T. Scott**

I
Introduction

In an earlier paper at these Round Table gatherings (Scott 1989) I raised some issues concerning fakes and forgeries, and make no apology for returning to these concerns now. As we will see, making sense of the artistic fake, especially the literary examples, plunges us into the essential semiotic and legal questions: of originality; of authorship/ownership; of value; of authenticity; and, of course, of fiction and of truth.

Many disciplinary groupings and individuals are centrally-concerned with the trustworthiness of apparently-meaningful representations. Psychiatrists come to mind — they appear to be *very* concerned about trustworthiness — but the list is a long one. It contains, arguably, any form of scholarship whereby we go, in the move familiar to semioticians, from the manifest to the latent, from the evident and palpable to an understanding of what lies under or within. Whatever our understanding is, it is always ours, what is significant to us, as private but also as social beings. By reason of that latter fact, if for no other, we are not condemned to solipsism and/or uncontrollable idiosyncrasy in our understanding of what is going within and without, as is frequently implied or asserted by many enthusiasts of the postmodern temper. At the very least, we can make sense together within a particular normative social order, using the forms of discourse and text-types it provides for its members, with which we have been familiarised and become more or less proficient.

Semioticians are also familiar with the fact that what is evident and palpable, immediately available to the senses may, over and above rarely being the terminus for our attentions, be misleading. The animal and plant worlds are full of deceit. Camouflage is an example, one which we in the human, social world, mercifully retain, as tact or deodorants exemplify.

Lies, however motivated, provide a large and diverse class of deliberately-misleading 'meaningful representations.' Contained within this category are the sorts of phenomena of interest in this paper, literary fakes and forgeries.

I will attempt to show that these particular sorts of deceit present intractable problems for legal process, for legal semiotics, and for literary analysis. This is not to say we cannot offer some useful concepts that may help us somewhat in our various forms of 'evaluation.' However, the main argument will be that satisfying strict criteria with regard to the key terms listed in the opening paragraph above is rarely possible.

As a result, I will argue, those with an interest in the value — commercial and aesthetic — of 'cultural' texts always face irreducible difficulties. Commercial value has something to do with origination of texts, especially with ownership of the copyright to what is, in nontrivial and demonstrable respects, an original text. This, for reasons we will discuss below, often underwrites aesthetic value in Western cultures, which, if esteemed highly by those trusted in such judgements, in return boosts commercial value. The trust which the makers of such judgements need, for their part, to place in those offering texts to the market can, as we will see, be abused in ways that may elude scrutiny and, if detected, radically undermine what sense we have of genuine worth inherent in the valued artefacts of our cultures. Even if we merely suspect that our libraries and museums are full of undetected fakes and forgeries, the damage is done.

After some theoretical preliminaries, I will try to illustrate the main points by recounting the tales of two famous literary forgeries, which are connected by more than the fact that the key figures all have Scottish names.

II
A Hierarchy of Texts

The fact that all texts are thirds, in Peircian terms, semiotic forms mediating contents somehow for someone is reason enough for caution about the place of truth and related concepts, even when we consider very '*literal*' texts conveying information about the real, palpable world. Manuals and guidebooks are possible examples. Even here, however, many users of texts need to be constantly reminded that what they are dealing with is not the real thing, but a representation of some aspects of whatever the text is about, to foreground that deceptively-innocent but extraordinarily-difficult preposition.

When what is being faithfully represented (i.e., accurately, lucidly and enduringly represented) is *conceptual,* and unamenable to ostensive support for interpretive purposes, for example, the wishes of the authors of the American Constitution, we are in deeper difficulty. However, as Peirce, and more recently Eco (Eco, 1990), remind us, we have not reached impossibility, merely difficulty. By various hermeneutic means we can get reasonable approximations to what was probably meant at the time. What that means to us now is another, but not necessarily different, in part or in whole, matter. To take an analogy from Linguistics, speakers of languages, especially languages with known histories and accumulated texts, written and/or spoken, usually deal quite easily with the differences among etymological ('original' ?), literal, conventional, and intended meanings, for individual words and larger constructions. Using language involves making such judgements about what our interlocutors seem to have in mind, even when the message reaches us from long ago and far away in geographic and/or cultural space.

We are still on the right side of impossibility when we encounter texts which are offered and taken as '*fictional.*' Here, the users of the text know or suspect that, however realistic or archetypal or ennobling the subject matter, however credible the attitudes, opinions and beliefs woven into the text, we are in the domain of artifice and artificiality, of inauthenticity. The claim that, by ignoring our disbelief, we are able to engage with Higher Truths as only the imaginative arts can display them, merely shifts the locus of the bogus to our mundane reality, used as the vehicle through which we glimpse the Ideal and to which we return inspired and empowered. However, the morality of perhaps merely pleasuring ourselves in invented imitations of objects, events and experiences, for escapist reasons, is of long-standing concern. Even exemplary, moralistic tales, such as parables, allegories and fables, with their transparent iconicity and didactic payload, may be read just as stories, for fun.

Plato's attack on the so-called 'natural-sign' arts, in Book 10 of *The Republic*, is obviously important here. For Plato, even material objects are themselves mere approximations to the abstract forms, hence representing the pseudo-real is to drive us deeper into illusion, not closer to the real. However, his obsession with an overwhelmingly visual epistemology, and with representation as imitation — as iconic in semiotic terms — fails to engage satisfactorily with linguistic texts. These are constructed from signs that operate symbolically (arbitrarily and conventionally) and, moreover, are experienced by doubly-inward means: we have to get into a book and to do so have to unravel/re-weave the patterns of form and content laid down there for us by the author(s).

A further level, and level of difficulty for the evaluators of texts, awaits. It may be argued that invented, imaginative *texts of real literary value* embody the highest of Higher Truth, that of Art. The aesthetic integrity of the text is manifested by the overwhelmingly internal features of content and form mentioned above, studied within literary aesthetics and most succinctly captured in Jakobson's famous 'poetic' function of language (Jakobson, (1958)1960). Briefly, the text is as much about itself and its embodiment of what is technically possible, as it is about the real or ideal world beyond the text. In Peircean terms, it is monadic, being, not meaning.

We have additional assurance that we are in the presence of great art when we can identify and delimit the text, that is, when we can attend to a specific construction as an integral whole. For that to be possible the text should be a definitive whole, not one of many competing versions, or part of a series without starting or finishing points.

We are greatly helped in establishing such particularity (not only in texts with claims to the Higher Truths of Art) if we can identify an original author. Best of all is a holograph MS or whatever, signed or otherwise authenticated as the definitive, final and only text launched forth into the world from the master's hand. Thereafter, its subtleties of content and form will manifest themselves in response to the competent reader's careful forensic efforts, by means of which we can experience vicariously the fruits of imaginations and intelligences richer than our own.

III
Collapsing the Hierarchy

The above makes a good story, but it is one that many scholars now query. It has, to adopt the post-modernist ploy of reading for absences, many omissions.

For example, our preoccupation with the unique and original object may be seen in a less innocent light: as the purest outcome of capitalism — the monadic artwork is by definition, monopolistic — and/or as an elitist recoil from industrial capitalism, with its limitless capacity for mass-reproducing identical artefacts. On the latter argument, even books would be subject to this constant pressure to supply the marketplace with the authentically-new (which, is, of course, what so-called newspapers, the one-day bestsellers that now rival books in wordcount at least, provide). Only fundamentalists dream of a world with one book that everyone reads all the time.

The essentially collaborationist view taken in the previous section of the triadic author-text-reader relationship is another problem in these distempered times. Derrida's determination to resist any such contract, with its assumption of a joint search for shared, conclusive meaning, is the best-known expression of a deeply-disabling attitude to our capacity for creating shared understanding, let alone for making art that might be considered valuable from various perspectives.

If interpretation of texts, all texts, never comes to rest, even for an individual, but consists merely of our being decanted to yet another discursive formation, with each interpretive apprehension settled-upon just momentarily, and only because we compliantly endorse the underlying master narrative, then the consequences are indeed dire for any attempt to stabilise a text, quite apart from settle its meanings.

Pessimism becomes near-unavoidable if we complete our brief foray into the varieties of textual types by considering some fictional texts whose authors renege on the assumptions described in the more positive account of texts above.

We know that no ostensibly creative text can be perfectly original in form and content if only because it must appear to be a (particular type of) text when we encounter it (Peircean firstness). Also, it must be 'about' something, and trigger associations that we can contextualise (secondness) as well as represent something special in and of itself to someone somehow (thirdness).

However, the inevitable compromises with perfect originality (an impossible notion) go much further, well beyond the complex allusiveness of form and content that interanimates the many texts of our many cultures. There is always 'influence' and 'intertextuality,' in many forms, sometimes very prominently so. A translation, for example, is less original, presumably, than 'the original,' even if it involves substantial re-working. But it is usually offered to the reader in good faith, for whatever sort of translation it is said to be, such as close or free. Many European writers of the eighteenth century made a virtue and an art form of a very free form of translation/reworking, 'the imitation.' (The example has particular relevance for later sections of this paper.) These were often imitations of works in another language, presumed to be familiar to the cultivated readers for whom they were written, or whom they wrote, to adopt the more fashionable view of textual relationships which stresses the ways in which authors manipulate readers into specific intepretive performances. Consider also parody, pastiche and plagiarism and, finally, the subject matter of this paper, hoaxes, fakes and forgeries. In these latter cases of sub-optimal originality, the good faith between text and text, and between author and reader which the honest translator or parodist offers, has been compromised, or reversed altogether.

Given the closeness of the visual arts to the rewards of the market place, and other factors such as their amenability to 'restoration' or 'embellishment,' a rich discourse has developed among experts and dealers for classifying varieties and degrees of inauthenticity hence, often, aesthetic value (hence market value): *school of* and *attrib* are relatively innocent as are *after*, *in the manner of*, *imitation*, *fascimile*, *duplicate*, *copy*, *study for and version*. Even artistic illusion and other sorts of tricks played by textmakers on their consumers do not violate the basic, good faith, contract.

However, *fake*, *forgery*, *counterfeit*, *hoax*, *delusion*, *practical joke*, *charade*, *scam*, *confidence trick* and all the other forms of 'passing-off' do. In these, some form of bad faith, some unacceptable deception and inauthenticity, is involved There is harm done to those who buy, in various senses of that word, fakes or forgeries.

It is no defence to argue that what the faker is providing is an iconic representation less of the real artefacts than of whatever notions about these exist in the minds of those who are taken in. Derivative and unimaginative hack work also sets out to give purchasers what they want by imitating their preconceptions of what constitutes good art, but that is above board, and offensive only to those who know and can afford better. Van Meegeren's work, for example is, with hindsight, obviously of its time, and 'wrong.' Even the fact that it fooled philistine and not-so-philistine Nazis does not exculpate the work as bad art, or vindicate the worker as a man of conscience. He cheated, (see Danto, 1981:43).

Here we encounter directly the fundamental problems raised at the outset, particularly of authentication. Not only are aesthetic texts, however fact-based and representational, fictional, on various levels of signification, not only are they woven into and out of a web of other texts, in addition, what they are offered *as* on the surface is rarely what they turn out to be 'about.' They all cheat, some more outrageously and, in terms of some set of contractual conventions operating among the participants in these semiotic and communicative acts, more unethically than others.

Much of what we value is taken on trust, accepted at face value for what it appears to be, especially if those who should know are satisfied that all is above board. Even the most eminent experts make mistakes, however, as the case of the Hitler Diaries illustrates. As has been pointed out by various commentators, even if the diaries had been authenticated, we would have been little closer to the truth, given Hitler's well-documented (*sic!*) propensity for plain lies, and numerous other deviations from the facts. As Haywood puts it:

> Had the Diaries been genuine, they would be 'genuine fiction' rather than 'fictional fiction.' The dividing line between the genuine and the spurious, the acceptable and unacceptable, is often thinner than might be thought. These points (are) particularly relevant . . . when we look at the early novel, a genre which combined a new-found ability to render experience realistically with authorial disavowal and the passing off of fiction as genuine documents: memoirs, letters, and even diaries (Haywood, 1987:5).

(See, as an alternative to the analyses offered above and in anticipation of the concluding remarks of this section, John Searle's still-useful distinction between two other polarities or continua in textual studies, the serious v. fictional, and the figurative v. literal, in Searle, 1979.)

In concluding this deliberately simplified survey of some of the issues and terms, and in preparation for considering the two cases of literary forgery, it is worth laying-out, albeit in stark form, two of the parameters within which discussion of textual authenticity are often conducted.

INTERNAL EVIDENCE

FORM CONTENT

EXTERNAL EVIDENCE

If we begin top-left, stylistic evidence, for example, is often used to help determine authorship, hence authenticity and, possibly, integrity, of texts. At the time of writing, there is in Britain considerable controversy over the use in major trials of a word-count based system for establishing whether or not a written statement is by a single author, (see Canter, 1992; Holmes, 1993).

Bottom-left, if we can compare a suspect text with authenticated material, most obviously holograph material but also stylistic features of many sorts, then our assessment of authorship is the surer.

Top-right, features of content such as major and minor thematic patterns and discontinuities, anachronisms, borrowings and so on are relevant in questions of originality and/or authenticity. Bottom-right, comparison and contrast with other material or information deemed trustworthy and relevant provide supporting evidence for the hunches or judgements formed in the other quartiles.

One important factor about artistic fakes and forgeries in particular arises when we consider external evidence in the most general sense of the cultural conditions from which or into which a suspect text is launched. Human gullibility, like trust itself, is always with us, but in certain social and economic circumstances the cultural conditions themselves create a space which almost demands to be filled. A good example is that of the British art forger Tom Keating. He became a folk hero by being sucked almost accidentally into the overheated, greed-driven world of the 1970s art dealer, a species he despised and enjoyed hoaxing. (He was less happy when other artists began to produce forgeries of his forgeries for a market which had retaliated by coming to value genuine Tom Keating forgeries.)

IV
The Ossian Controversy

The cultural context which assisted the creation of the first group of forgeries I will consider, the Ossian poems of James MacPherson, need to be briefly described.

The poems appeared less than twenty years after the end of a Civil War in Britain. The Northern, Highland elements in Scottish life and culture had rebelled several times in the first half of the 18th Century against effective annexation/colonisation by the English. Many Lowland Scots were sympathetic, but most were not and participated in the rout of what was, nonetheless, felt to be the authentic, disappearing culture of a small, humiliated country.

Many of the great dichotomies and contradictions of the modern world were being created and mobilised in this process: primitive-progressive; authentic-synthetic; rural/agricultural — urban/industrial; ignorance/

superstition — education/enlightenment; innocent poetic dreams — calculated rational schemes . . . and so on.

In other parts of Europe, there was a similar sense of rapid development towards what we now recognise as the modern, industrial world-nation states and empires, with 'administrations' ruling out to boundaries from centres of power, exploiting the technologies of early capitalism. The process was exciting and dramatic to be sure, but frightening and destructive as well. In Scotland, where the creator of Jekyll and Hyde later emerged, the dynamic socio-economic acceleration into modernity, was especially energetic, the dichotomies and contradictions particularly powerful.

Among the urban intelligentsia, struggling to cope with both the shameful loss of national identity and esteem caused by the disaster of the war, maudlin nostalgia for a more noble, much older world of Celtic legend and myth became fashionable. Elegaic melancholy, it has been argued, functioned as a form of mourning, and as a variant on the vogue for sentimentality, for Lowland Scots. It has never gone away, but in the later 1750s it had created a great receptivity towards certain relics and ruins from which some pride and self-esteem might be salvaged. In modern terms, there was a market place looking for commodities, in particular for cultural commodities that would authenticate the ancient, ideally Homeric, cultural credentials of the nation, however divided, disgraced and declined.

James MacPherson was a young clergyman and aspiring poet born and brought up in the Gaelic speaking North (where he had witnessed the traumatic aftermath of the last battle of the Civil War) when he met with some other young literati in the Autumn of 1759. At that gathering he translated some ancient verses from the Gaelic, akin to some lines he had published a few years earlier, to modest acclaim. His companions urged him to recall and write down more. In 1760, *Fragments of Ancient Poetry Collected in the Highlands of Scotland and Translated from the Gaelic or Erse Language* was published in Edinburgh, and a second edition was published in the same year.

MacPherson had every reason to anticipate scepticism, even given that the work is a translation, therefore difficult to evaluate for the non-Gaelic speaking audience he had in mind. The opening remarks to the second edition, written by his great promoter the writer and academic Hugh Blair, get straight to the point:

> The public may depend on the following fragments as genuine remains of ancient Scottish poetry. The date of their composition cannot be exactly ascertained. Tradition, in the country in which they were written, refers them to an area of the most remote antiquity. . . . - the diction, in the original, is very obsolete; and differs widely from the style of such poems as have been written in the same language two or three centuries ago, (MacPherson 1760(1970):iv).

He goes on to assist readers curious as to their origins in time with a reference to the low prestige of Christianity 'in a fragment of the same poems which the translator has seen' (*ibid* iv) which might help to give a rough date.

Connoisseurs of literary fakes then and since picked up two clues. Most poems of the sort he prints are oral yet he says they were written. More importantly, the origin is shrouded in mystery, here a place and a time remote and unidentifiable enough to disable comparison between authenticated materials and the material being passed-off.

A third clue that the man was, in Scots-Irish colloquial speech, an 'artist' comes with this infamous come-on advertisement:

> -there is reason to hope that one work of considerable length, and which deserves to be styled an heroic poem, might be recovered and translated, if encouragement were given to such an understanding (*ibid*:vi).

It was, indeed, given and MacPherson set off to the remote areas of the Highlands and Islands of Scotland, the Romantic fringe of Europe, gathering material. From this fieldwork, allegedly, came the volumes *Fingal* in 1762 and, a year later, *Temora*. Both of these were published in London, significantly, where the translator was by then a celebrity despite the strong whiff of scandal that surrounded him because of doubts as to the authenticity of the material. Samuel Johnson, characteristically, denounced him from the start, but many others, including later sceptics such as David Hume, were sufficiently bewitched by the curiously atmospheric prose poems to put their doubts aside.

Hugh Blair, who had been one of the small group who originally encouraged MacPherson to publish the *Fragments*, published, in 1763, a dissertation aimed at proving the authenticity of the poems. In a move of great interest to the forensically-inclined, he wrote to David Hume, for advice on how to go about this. Hume's response, in two letters of September 19 and October 6, 1763, is still interesting today.

He says, circumspectly, of the poems:

> I often hear them totally rejected, with disdain and indignation, as a palpable and impudent forgery, (in Mackenzie, 1805:4).

He goes on to give another piece of evidence often associated with forgers facing accusation, and, potentially, an indexical sign of guilt in this case.

> The absurd pride and caprice of MacPherson himself, who scorns . . . to falsify anybody that doubts his veracity, has tended much to confirm this general scepticism (*ibid*:5).

As to method, Hume recommends that 'proofs must not be arguments, but testimonies' (*ibid*:6) by which latter term he probably means hard empirical evidence, as the two sorts of examples which he goes on to give suggest.

Firstly, MacPherson claimed that much of the poetry had been transcribed and then translated from an ancient manuscript book which he had discovered mouldering among the rafters of a great Highland family, the Clan Ranalds, whose home he had visited on his fieldtrip of 1760-1.

Hume recommends that Blair should get hold of this book (reputedly in the possession of MacPherson who was, at the time of his death, about to be sued for its return by the Clan Ranald heirs).

Having authenticated it, presumably by reference to the real owners, Blair should then do a systematic comparison between its contents and the contents of the books published by MacPherson. The Gaelic originals and MacPherson's should be 'the same,' presumably with regard to formal/stylistic features as well as content. The 1760 Preface already quoted from above had already been helpful on this point, with the assurance that 'The translation is extremely literal. Even the arrangement of the words in the original has been imitated,' (MacPherson, 1760(1970):vi).

Secondly, as these materials originated in the oral tradition and have no single historical entry point and original form, Blair should seek evidence that at least similar poems are and long have been recited among the population. It would not be enough for one responsible person or more than one to affirm that this is the case. Transcripts, signed, witnessed, dated, etc, should be obtained and compared with MacPherson's material. At some point, a cumulative proof of authenticity might be declared.

Despite the doubts, The Ossian Poems swiftly developed cult status right across Europe and also in the USA. Goethe and Napoleon were two passionate admirers, as was Jefferson. Indeed, Ossianism, as it became, has been described as 'the great Romantic drama of the conquest of the European mind by Gaeldom,' (Bush, 1952:171).

By the later years of the 18th Century, the controversy as the authenticity of the poems was a considerable embarrassment to a generation less personally scarred by the aftermath of Civil War, more successfully colonised, but still eager to find an authentic basis for a distinctive Scottish cultural inheritance.

In order to settle the matter, the now respectable Highland Society instituted in 1797, a major inquiry, broadly incorporating the advice of David Hume as the Chair of the Inquiry, Henry Mackenzie, acknowledged when the Report was finally published in 1805, (Mackenzie 1805:11). The inquiry took a long time because it involved a remarkably social survey. A questionnaire, no less, was distributed very widely, one of the earliest perhaps on record. (see Appendix 1 here.)

Despite absolving itself from adjudicating on the authenticity of the poems (in the opening sentence of the Report) the conclusion drawn from the results of the survey, given on page 152, is of interest:

> the Committee has not been able to obtain any one poem the same in title and tenor with the poems published by him (MacPherson).

However, as they carefully explain (p. 12 ff) there are many reasons why corroborative evidence would no longer be available a generation on from the first publication.

Cultural circumstances were, in any case, changing. The Ossian poems originally (*sic!*) appeared not long before the publishing industry developed the techniques of relatively cheap mass production, and mass marketing, which are now familiar to us.

The impact of industrialised mass production on the creation of art objects generally was, by the early 19th century, radically affecting the notions of originality and authenticity that we now regard as the norm.

As Orvell has argued:

> Whereas the earlier period saw the machines as an agent for demonstrating luxury and diffusing high culture through imitations of elite forms, the 20th century culture of authenticity was based, conversely, on a functionalist ethos that sought to elevate the vernacular into the realm of high culture, (Orvell, 1989:xvi).

The glorification of the new and the different, of the created rather than the recreated, re-cycled, or adapted, is, arguably, directly related to the limitless capacity of industrial production. Infinite quantities of infinite varieties of commodities are possible, and new lines of merchandise needed by producers competing for new markets or for market share. In such a system, ownership of, or rights to, whatever original is being replicated is important, and easier to establish when there is a single distinctive original and a single source, an author who authorises the text.

As already noted, these considerations directly affect the commercial value of aesthetic objects, which may or may not be affected by the aesthetic value accorded to them by those whose opinions carry weight.

In arriving at these opinions, it may be argued that the genesis of a text is irrelevant, even when the object has been exposed as fraudulent in the sense that how it came into existence has been misrepresented to us.

Sir Walter Scott put the issue neatly, in a letter written in 1805, discussing the Ossian poems:

> - the question of their authenticity ought not to be confounded with that of their literary merit, yet scepticism on that head takes away their claim for indulgence as the productions of a barbarous and remote age; and — it destroys that feeling of reality which we should otherwise combine with our sentiments of admiration, (Scott, quoted in Lockhart, 1855:128).

He goes on to describe the poems as 'an absolute tissue of forgeries.' Yet he maintains that, despite knowing this and despite the lost 'feeling of reality' in his sense of the world conjured up by the poems, 'in the real attributes of poetry, MacPherson's version is far superior to any I ever saw of the fragments which he seems to have used' (*ibid*:128).

Others have been less charitable, insisting that provenance in all respects is important in evaluating any object of interest, especially art objects because, as Dutton and others argue, we need to know what sort of achievement is embodied in the object before us.

For Dutton:

> The significant opposition is not between forged and original but between correctly represented artistic performance and misrepresented artistic performance, (Dutton, 1975:312).

Part of that correct representation involves providing information about the work's origins, in particular about the author's or publisher's role. As Arthur Danto, among many, has pointed out, the accidental production of something that might be considered aesthetically valuable (for example, *objets trouvés*) disqualifies the object from the status work of art. That always involves work and art, for reassurance about which we go outside the work itself, to whom it is '*by*' and/or to what it is 'about' and/or *how* it was *achieved*. A piano recital recorded at slower speeds than in a live performance, over several sessions, is evidently a different sort of achievement than the real thing, done in real time. The possibilities for re-working material now available via so-called multimedia systems have recently generated many similar problematic cases of putative artworks highly relevant to the key concerns of this paper: originality, authorship, value, representation, fiction, reality, truthfulness, and truth.

In MacPherson's case, there seems little doubt that he created original and aesthetically valuable works that embody fragments from many sources, by no means only traditional oral verse and song, (as he himself pointed out), as well as large quantities of parody invented by him, (as he failed to point out). However, the literary (and cultural) value he claimed for them depended on the lie that he had merely translated them from texts whose purported context of origin was the crucial factor in conferring value. In other, semiotic-legal words, he misrepresented them. If he had published a pastiche of ancient Scots and Irish oral poetry, his efforts would have fared very differently, commercially as well as culturally, both at the time of publication and since, despite the persistence of opinions such the following from a more recent editor:

> of this there can be no question: that the ancient poetry, the antique spirit, breathes throughout this eighteenth century restoration and gives it enduring life, charm and all the spell of cosmic imagination, (Sharp, 1926: xxiv).

We have already referred to the fact that trust informs text-author and text-reader relationships. In most acts of communication, among the enabling reciprocal assumptions is the understanding that what is offered is offered in good faith by the person offering it, i.e. that *they* believe what they know *we* are surmising about the text. Grice's sincerity maxim refers to the same extraordinary fact about most of the transactions we engage in, including our engagement with most texts. We trust them and the people who provide them, not only the self-proclaimed authors but others around them, such as publishers and art dealers whose endorsements we generally accept as principal constituents of the interpretive framework we deploy.

V
The Ern Malley Hoax

The second literary scam which I will discuss appeared in the world by very different means. The *Ern Malley Affair* (the title of Michael Heyward's excellent book on the subject) was not a fraud perpetrated on the public but a hoax, aimed at discrediting the leading champion of serious avant-garde writing in Australia during the Second World War. The victim was a fashionable young poet, Max Harris, who also edited a literary magazine entitled Angry Penguins. The perpetrators were two other young poets, James McAuley and Harold Stewart, who had been drafted into what seems to have been a dirty tricks department in the wartime Australian Army. Their unit was presided over by a maverick, prankster, practical joker and general misfit, who encouraged Stewart and McAuley's contempt for all sorts of pretentiousness and self-serving seriousness.

In essence, what they did was to compose, over an eight-to-ten hour period, a number of poems, over 420 lines in total, or approximately one poem per half hour. They did this by various means, including plagiarism and parody of their own and other poems or, for example, taking every seventh word from a source poem. Using whatever was on their desks that day (including a report on the drainage of mosquito breeding grounds) they lifted words and phrases at random, made lists of them 'then wove them into nonsensical sentences,' (Stewart and McAuley in Haywood 1993:138). Their only rules of composition were: that there should be no coherent theme; that no technical finesse be shown, in fact, quite the reverse; that the style should not only imitate the target, Max Harris, but also other leading figures in the then firmament of Anglophone poetry. One trick in passing off the poems was to present them as the output of a dead man (aged 25, just like Keats) whose uneducated and uncomprehending sister was merely seeking an opinion from a leading figure in the literary world as to their worth. (Writing her letters, which included inventing a biography for the poet and concocting, brilliantly, style for the sister, took far more time than writing the poems!)

As they explained later:

> What we wished to find out was: Can those who write, and those who praise so lavishly, this kind of writing tell the real product from consciously and deliberately concocted nonsense?, (in Haywood 1993:138).

Harris was tremendously impressed by the poems, and, significantly, was convinced that the first truly world-class exponent of literary modernism to emerge from what was then a remote and unselfconfident cultural milieu had been discovered. Once again, the effect of specific cultural conditions upon the gullibility, or, at least, the readiness to believe in the authenticity of an artefact, of key recipients was an important factor.

Harris's enthusiasm for the poems was unswerving, even after all details of the true genesis and purpose of the poems were revealed. His argument was, from the outset and afterwards, that the hoaxers wrote better than they knew, for the spirit of the age was in them despite their avowed antipathy to that spirit. Almost half a century later, Robert Hughes seems half-persuaded by this, the main argument offered by those who defended the literary worth of the poems, in arguing that 'they proved the validity of surrealist procedures: that in letting down their guard, opening themselves to free association and chance, McAuley and Stewart had reached inspiration by the side door of parody,' (Hughes, in Heyward 1993:Introduction, xix-xx).

The authors, at least at that time, were in no doubt that the process of production which they had described rendered the poems worthless. They dismissed them as not even of psychological interest, written as they were by two minds each operating very deliberately as well as cross-cutting the others free-association, insofar as there was any presence for that key energizer of the surreal style. Even a memorable line such as 'The emotions are not skilled workers,' — bogusly attributed to Lenin — are condemned as phony, not only as attributed, but as an idea.

They justified their hoax as 'a serious literary experiment' (*ibid*:137) motivated not by malice to Harris but by the desire to prove that 'a literary fashion can become so hypnotically powerful that it can suspend the operation of critical intelligence in quite a large number of people' (*ibid*:139).

This is cautionary enough for all those with an interest in determining the authenticity and aesthetic value of texts, literary and other. (The perpetrators were preparing to ensnare the leading art critic, Herbert Reed, for whom they had put together a series of Ern Malley collages, when they were forced to go public in response to mounting suspicion and rumour!)

For legal semioticians, a hilarious epilogue provides yet more grounds for pessimism in the face of these meta-fictions, while reminding us yet again that the cultural context in which aesthetic and legal judgements are made is always a factor in cases such as these.

The Ern Malley controversy did more than make serious intellectual points about a literary fashion, about literary fashions generally, and about the vulnerability of the seemingly-priviliged interpreter/intermediary in cultural transmission. It also had the effect of stirring-up rather more philistine prejudices, particularly against the decadent features of Modernism as the avant-garde in the arts was generally called. Reactionary public figures, and bodies such as Catholic Action, took a closer interest in the situation after a libel case was threatened against Harris following a virulent review article published by him while the Malley controversy was at its height. Harris had to publish an obsequious apology to the well-connected target of his pontifications. A third humiliation approached, this time at the hands of those who considered themselves the guardians of public decency.

Shortly after the threatended libel action, in the Autumn of 1944, Harris, as the publisher of the Malley poems, was prosecuted on grounds of their obscenity. The case went to trial before a magistrate.

Neither of the by then self-confessed authors was present, or called, at the proceedings, which is an interesting fact in itself. A highlight among the evidence was the report of the policeman who had conducted the original interrogation of Harris. Possessed of an *extremely* literal mind, the detective had taken the martyred publisher through the Malley poems, line by line. Heyward reproduces some of the more bizarre, but depressingly plausible, examples of textual exegesis entered into the record from the detective's notebooks, (Heyward 1993:186 ff.). Despite his attempt to dodge the challenge by insisting on the role of the reader in deciding the interpretation of such freely-signifying texts, Harris was forced to rebut the detective's interpretations of particular phrases by offering his own, knowing full well that everyone knew that the poems had been produced so as to be as meaningless as possible. The detective's determination to find a morally-offensive interpretation remains impressive, but no more than the live re-run conducted by the Crown Prosecutor, who also scrutinised the poems line by line.

The summing-up by the magistrate is a masterpiece of incoherence. He condemns as 'ludicrous' the 'solemn and serious attempt to interpret seriously poems which may have been written in a far from serious spirit' (Heyward, 1993:208), dismisses any possibility of a satisfactory meaning being arrived-at, yet settles for exactly that as and where it suits the charge of moral ofensiveness.

The upshot was that the poems were found to be indecent, not obscene (as were other contributions to the same issue of Harris journal).

VI
Conclusion

As Grafton's interesting study shows (Grafton, 1990), creativity (essential to our modern notion of aesthetic value) and duplicity are inextricably linked. Both affect, or infect, at least to some degree, the different forms of authenticity that literary and other texts embody. A famous example is James Joyce's *A Portrait of the Artist as a Young Man*, a multiply-ironic novel which he referred to as a lying autobiography. This is a work where even the most determinedly unco-operative reader has to concede that the aesthetic possibilities of the novel as a genre are fully stretched, and the Higher Truths of Art available for contemplation, albeit in ways that deliberately and above all artfully flout the real-world, biographical and other, truths that provided Joyce's raw material. In addition to inventions, distortions and lies, he also incorporates parody, pastiche and plagiarism.

The point of art is, of course, to be artificial, sometimes brazenly, at other times contriving to conceal that what we are experiencing inhabits a different ontological plane from that of the real world. The artwork is real enough in itself, as a certain kind of conceptual structure emerging from and entering into cultural contexts that are also real, even if our only grasp of them is by means of other texts, representational forms whose contents we create and recreate in the conduct of our lives.

The main conclusion here is that, as social beings, we can never escape our dependence on the varieties of sincerity offered to us by others, always in texts of some sort. Therefore, particularly at moments — personal and/or cultural — when there is a powerful will to believe, such that trust tends towards gullibility and/or unperceived misinterpretation, the fraudulent will regularly defeat our forensic skills. That is no reason for abandoning these skills, and their inculcation in each generation, for the more we realise that the various levels of reality and sincerity we contend with are not only various but layered and texted, the more we need our hermeneutic instruments in order to minimise the occasions when our trust in texts and their publishers is, in fact, abused.

The final words here are the opening words of Eco's excellent survey of the difficult terrain we have been traversing:

> It seems that in natural language everybody knows what a fake, a forgery, or a false document is. At most, one admits that it is frequently difficult to recognise a forgery as such, but one relies on experts, that is, on those who are able to recognise forgeries simply because they know how to tell the difference between a fake and its original.
>
> As a matter of fact, the definitions of such terms as 'fake,' 'forgery,' 'pseudepigrapha,' 'falsification,' 'facsimile,' 'counterfeiting,' 'spurious,' 'pseudo,' 'apocryphal' and others are rather controversial. It is reasonable to suspect that many difficulties in defining these terms are due to the difficulty in defining the very notion of 'original' or 'real object,' (Eco 1990:174).

* *This work was supported by a Carnegie Grant.*

** *W.T. Scott is Professor of Language and Media at Glasgow Caledonian University.*

REFERENCES

Burwick, Frederick and Pape Walter, eds., 1990, *Aesthetic Illusion: Theoretical and Historical Approaches*, Berlin, New York: Walter de Gruyter.

Cantor, David, 1992, 'An Evaluation of the 'CUSUM' Stylistic Analysis of Confessions,' *Expert Evidence*, vol. 1, No. 2:93-99.

Danto, Arthur C., 1981, *The Transfiguration of the Commonplace*, Cambridge, Massachusetts: Harvard University Press.

Dutton, Dennis, 1975, 'Artistic Crimes: The Problem of Forgery in the Arts,' *British Journal of Aesthetics*, Vol. 19:302-314.

Eco, U., 1986, *Faith in Fakes*, London: Secker and Warburg.

_____, 1990, *The Limits of Interpretation*, Bloomington/Indianapolis: Indiana University Press.

_____, 1992, *Interpretation and Overinterpretation*, Cambridge: Cambridge University Press.

Grafton, Anthony, 1990, *Forgers and Critics: Creativity and Duplicity*, London: Juliet Gardner Books, Collins and Brown.

Heywood, Michael, 1987, *Faking It: Art and the Politics of Forgery*, Brighton, Sussex: The Harvester Press.

_____, 1993, *The Ern Malley Affair*, London: Faber and Faber.

Holmes, David, 1993, Authorship Attribution, Research Report No. 1, Department of Mathematical Science, University of the West of England, Bristol, England.

Insh, George P., 1952, *The Scottish Jacobite Movement: A study in economic and social forces*, Edinburgh: The Moray Press.

Jakobson, Roman, 1958, 1960, 'Concluding Statement: Linguistics and Poetics,' ed. T.A. Sebeok, *Style in Language*, Cambridge, MIT Press, 350-377.

Jones, Mark, ed., 1990, *Fake? The Art of Deception*, London: British Museum Publications.

Kurz, Otto, 1948, *Fakes: a handbook for students and collectors*, London: Faber and Faber.

Lockhart, John G., 1855, *Memoirs of the Life of Sir Walter Scott*, new edition, Edinburgh: Robert Cadell.

Mackenzie, Henry, 1805, *Report of the Commission of the Highland Society of Scotland Appointed to inquire into the nature and authenticity of the Poems of Ossian*, Edinburgh: Constable and Co.

MacPherson, James, 1760, 1970, *Fragments of Ancient Poetry Collected in the Highlands of Scotland and translated from the Gaelic or Erse Language*, Facsimile of Second Edition, Edinburgh: The Mercat Press.

_____, 1926, *The Poems of Ossian Translated by James MacPherson*, with Notes and with an Introduction by William Sharp, Edinburgh: John Grant.

Orvell, Miles, 1989, *'Introduction' to the Real Thing: Imitation and Authenticity in American Culture, 1880-1940*, Chapel Hill and London: University of North Carolina Press.

Scott, William T., 1989, 'In Search of the Truly Fake: Aspects of Iconicity and Deceit,' ed. R. Kevelson, *Law and Semiotics*, Vol. 2:307-319, New York: Plenum Press.

Searle, John, 1979, 'The Logical Status of Fictional Discourse,' in *Expression and Meaning*, Cambridge: University Press.

APPENDIX 1

EXTRACT from the "Report of the Committee of the Highland Society of Scotland appointed to Inquire into the Nature and Authenticity of the POEMS OF OSSIAN drawn up, according to the directions of the committee by HENRY MACKENZIE, Esq., its convenor or chairman with a COPIOUS INDEX containing some of the principal documents on which the report is founded"

In execution of the bufinefs affigned it, your Committee conceived it to be foreign to its duty to enter into any elaborate argument or difcuffion on the authenticity of thofe poems, or to examine, with critical or hiftorical labour, the opinions of different writers who have made this matter a fubject of controverfy. It conceived the purpofe of its nomination to be, to employ the influence of the Society, and the extenfive communication which it poffeffes with every part of the Highlands, in collecting what materials or information it was ftill practicable to collect, regarding the authenticity and nature of the poems afcribed to Offian, and particularly of that celebrated collection publifhed by Mr James Macpherfon.

For the purpofe above mentioned, the Committee, foon after its appointment, circulated the following fet of Queries, through fuch parts of the Highlands and Iflands, and among fuch perfons refident there, as feemed moft likely to afford the information required.

QUERIES

I Have you ever heard repeated or fung, any of the poems afcribed to Offian, tranflated and published by Mr Macpherfon? By whom have you heard them fo repeated, and at what time or times? Did you ever commit any of them to writing, or can you remember them fo well as now to fet them down? In either of thefe cafes, be fo good to fend the Gaelic original to the Committee.

II The fame anfwer is requefted concerning any other ancient poems of the fame kind, and relating to the fame traditionary perfons or ftories with thofe in Mr Macpherfon's collection.

III Are any of the perfons, from whom you heard any fuch poems, now alive? Or are there, in your part of the country, any perfons who remember and can repeat or recite fuch poems? If there are, be fo good to examine them as to the manner of their getting or learning fuch compofitions; and fet down, as accurately as poffible, fuch as they can now repeat or recite; and tranfmit fuch their account, and fuch compofitions as they repeat, to the Committee.

IV If there are, in your neighbourhood, any perfons from whom Mr Macpherfon received any poems, inquire particularly what the poems were which he fo received, the manner in which he received them, and how he wrote them down; fhew thofe perfons, if you have an opportunity, his tranflation of fuch poems, and defire them to fay if the tranflation is exact and literal; or, if it differs, in what it differs from the poems, as they repeated them to Mr Macpherfon, and can now recollect them.

V Be fo good to procure every information you conveniently can, with regard to the traditionary belief, in the country in which you live, concerning the hiftory of Fingal and his followers, and that of Offian and his poems; particularly concerning thofe ftories and poems publifhed by Mr Macpherfon, and the heroes mentioned in them. Tranfmit any fuch account, and any proverbial or traditionary expreffion in the original Gaelic, relating to the fubject, to the Committee.

VI In all the above inquiries, or any that may occur to in elucidation of this fubject, he is requefted by the Committee to make the inquiry, and to take down the anfwers, with as much impartiality and precifion as poffible, in the fame manner as if it were a legal queftion, and the proof to be inveftigated with a legal ftrictnefs.

(Report to the Highland Society, 1805: 1-3)

Chapter Twenty

Customary Law as Common Law

Leon Sheleff*

I

The role of custom is basic to an understanding of the development of the common law; it also lies, paradoxically perhaps, at the heart of the problematics in according recognition to the customary practices of tribal communities that came into contact with the representative authorities of the common law in the furthest reaches of the British Empire.

Both major European legal systems, the common law and the European civil law, have spread widely throughout the world, partly through imposed law as a result of conquest and annexation, partly as a result of deliberate reception of the law. The latter aspect is particularly noticeable in the case of the civil law system, since a number of countries, outside of Europe, and which had not been subject to colonial rule, voluntarily adopted certain aspects of the legal system of dominant European countries. Countries such as Japan, China, Thailand, Ethiopia and Turkey drew extensively upon the codes of European countries, mainly France and Germany, as an anticipated means of accelerating their economic and technological development.[1] The existence of codes in civil law countries certainly facilitated the process of reception of a foreign legal system. It is much easier to attempt reception of a legal system, when its central factor is a code; far more difficult when it is based on custom.

A central factor in a Civil Law system is the dominant role of a written code, which is presumed to provide certainty and comprehensiveness, with the role of the judge being to apply the law, while having little discretion for the judicial law-making that so characterizes the common law system.[2]

II

Indeed one of the main differentiating factors between the two major legal systems is the role of the judge, and the degree of activism that each system assigns to them. In the common law, the judge is a meaningful partner in the creation of legal norms. Judicial precedent is a recognized component of the legal system; and an essential factor in this aspect is the role of custom, with judges examining and evaluating the customary practices of the inhabitants of the realm, in order to decide whether or not to grant them the primatur of legal recognition. Historically, the origins of the common law were in the pronouncement of those customs that the king's courts held to be of general validity — that is, customs that were common to all of the realm, in contrast to the local customs of a particular area, that were slowly superseded.

In its initial stages, it was the customary law that formed the basis of the emerging common law system, and it was only gradually that statutes of Parliament came to be recognized as an important part of the law; in fact the original role of Parliament was as an advisory body (similar to the European Parliament of today); later it even had a judicial function that was almost of parallel significance to its legislative capacity (still noted in the leading role of the House of Lords at the apex of the judicial hierarchy). Until the end of the Seventeenth Century, the legislative function of parliament was of negligible import: its major role was not to make law but to declare law, a role more judicial than legislative.

But even so, even as the Parliament increasingly took over the task of legislation, the traditional structure and culture of the legal system remained, for the most part, as it had been — with the courts continuing to play an important role in the formation of the law through their role in interpretation.[3]

In fulfilling such a role, judges are not presumed to be acting in an arbitrary or idiosyncratic manner, neither laying down the law as an oracle, nor furthering their own individual beliefs or interests; rather they are considered as giving expression to the sentiments of the people, seeking to dispense justice in terms of standards and criteria that are acceptable to the community.

It is specifically this reasoning that is at the heart of the reluctance to set out codes, which tend to minimize the impact of evolving beliefs and practices. Indeed, as Guido Calabresi has pointed out, the increased role of statutory law in common law countries, poses serious problems for the capacity of the law to reflect changing social and cultural conditions, or even to fulfil its traditional role of judicial law-making; and he suggests means by which the role of the courts could be revived — for instance in declaring laws to be in disuse.[4]

It was the constrictive impact of codes on the possibility of continued natural evolution that led Carl von Savigny to battle so vigorously (yet in the final analysis, so unsuccessfully) against the movement to adopt a code for Germany.[5] His historical approach to the law was much more in line with the reality of the English common law than it was with the more rigid pattern of law in the civil law countries.

Paradoxically, the converse was also true; the positivistic approach to jurisprudence, so characteristic of English jurisprudence, was far more apt and relevant for the continental civil law system than it was for the English legal system, upon which it was ostensibly based. Indeed, given the problematics of judge-made law for a positivistic position, John Austin and others provided a basically false and fictitious picture of the role of the judge as only pronouncing the law, and not actually helping to make the law.[6] In fact, Max Weber referred to the difficulties that he had with the English legal system as it did not quite fit into his own model of a 'rational' modern law.[7]

A leading English historian of the law, Brian Simpson,[8] has strongly criticized the Austinian approach, and pointed out the inevitable inconsistencies that flow therefrom.[9] He suggests that the positivistic approach describes the judicial function in terms that have very little connection with the manner in which judges operate, and with the essential framework within which the law is interpreted. Thus Simpson raises a query: 'If, however, we abandon the positivist conception of the common law, in terms of what other conception can the institution be more realistically depicted?'[10] According to him, 'Positivists take as their basic model of law an enacted code, but a better starting-point, if we are concerned with the common law, is the traditional notion of the common law as custom which was standard form in the older writers.'[11] Simpson refers here to significant figures in the history of the common law, such as Hale and Blackstone, and he claims that their presentation of the law was in essence far more accurate than the rationalizations of later writers, such as Jeremy Bentham. And so he concludes: 'We need . . . to conceive of the common law as a system of customary law and recognize that such systems may embrace complex theoretical notions which both serve to explain and justify past practice . . . and provide a guide to future conduct.'[12]

Such an approach to the common law would certainly allow for greater sensitivity to the fluid nature of customs, and so there would be more consciousness of change in the law, and of the development of newer doctrines, instead of the routinized perception and rote pronouncement of custom as being of immemorial usage.

III

Peter Stein, in his study of the evolution of law,[13] quotes from an early nineteenth century document, written to the chancellor as a plea against England adopting a code, which, according to the writer would be to confine the law and inhibit its healthy future transformation. Thus,

> The first link of the great chain of law is formed by custom, and usage, and the adoption of those rules which instinctive expediency suggests . . . laws are nationally individual, and are as characteristically peculiar to the people, amongst whom they arise, as their religion, or language. And although their origin may sometimes be lost in the remoteness of tradition, yet it is based upon the most stable foundation — the spontaneous acknowledgement of the nation.[14]

The task, then, of those involved in the law, whether in the legislature or the judiciary, is to give concrete expression to the wishes of the people — in a sense, to make democracy work by ensuring that the rules of law will be constantly attuned to the people's desires. 'It is the genius of the people that gives birth to, and animates the system, which is elucidated, and technically arranged by the lawyers.'[15] He concludes: 'The course of jurisprudence is never stationary; it is either on the ebb, or on the flow . . . the law of many nations is a part of the character of the people.'[16]

It is true that over the years statute has played an increasingly important role in common law countries; further, that certain aspects of the law have been comprehensively presented in the form of codes or consolidating acts. Indeed, model codes have been drawn up in the United States in order to encourage consistency among the states, especially noted in the key areas, for a federal state, of commercial and criminal law. But while the term code is used, these are not in essence true codes, in the full sense of the word as used in civil law countries, as being a unified and single document, covering all, or almost all, areas of the law in an integrative and inter-related manner. This, the common law countries have failed to do, and so continue to work within a legal culture that is still basically oriented to the flexible development of the law in which judges help make the law, and do so in terms of their understanding of an evolving society.

IV

On this basis it is clear that custom lies at the heart of the common law system — and it is this historical tradition, still pertinent today, that facilitates a meaningful appreciation of customary law, as it is practised by various population groups, such as tribes, struggling to maintain their integrity in their contacts with the larger culture, sometimes an alien culture.

James Zion has suggested that the best way to present the law of the American Indians is as Common Law — as a law, that is, that in its structure bears much resemblance to the framework within which the common law itself developed.[17]

In this context, the historical debate as to whether or not the tribes, in various parts of the far-flung British empire, had a legal system, or whether they were controlled 'merely' by custom, is indicative of myopic thinking of the worst order, or a lack of knowledge of the historical development of the law, or of a deliberate denigration of the societies — or a combination of these factors.

For, if it was true that 'custom was king', as many were wont to state, why should that, in any way, detract from its role as law, as many were wont to argue, or raise questions as to whether or not there was a stable political order. It was only after pioneering work by legal anthropologists such as Malinowski, Hoebel and Gluckman[18] that grudging recognition was given to the fact that custom was not so-called 'king', but was, in fact, 'law' — a theoretical concession that was made easier by the desire to grant recognition of a minimum degree of order, as understood by the West, so as to allow for indirect rule, which in some places, (particularly where there were large population groups under the control of minimum colonial forces, as in Africa) was crucial for the purposes of effective control.[19]

The fact is that there was no need to show, as Hoebel tried to do,[20] that the customs of the tribes that he examined could be explained within a sophisticated jurisprudential system, as set out by Hohfeld.[21] The legitimacy of customary law did not require such a static explanation; its legitimacy, as the basis for law, was a natural outcome of the very development of the English Common Law. The parallels were not then just in the ultimate framework of the law *a la* Hohfeld, but in the manner in which the law was formed, accepted and respected.

In this sense, customary law was akin to the common law and the validity of custom could only be denied by ignoring the very nature of the Common Law itself. Part of the reason for this may lie not just in an ethnocentric approach to the habits of tribal, and presumably less-civilized, people, but to the fallacies as to law being propagated by a narrow positivistic doctrine of jurisprudence, one which was itself out of touch with its own legal system.

But some of the frictions of positivistic jurisprudence continued to affect the manner in which custom was perceived, even after it had been given a certain amount of legitimacy. The customs of indigenous peoples in various parts of the British empire were accepted not on their own terms, but within the context of custom as perceived within a positivistic spectrum. Thus the qualities that were attributed to custom, in terms of the Common Law, were now also associated with the custom of tribes, namely of being of immemorial usage, a static approach to custom that had been adopted by the Common Law judges (partly perhaps as to answer to the logic of positivism). A custom could only be accepted as law if its origins were unknown, and so an arbitrary data in the 12th century, 1189, was declared as being the presumptive moment in time when all recognized customs were in effect.[22] This was a legal fiction that worked quite well for the English Common Law, (and even then not always, as the parallel system of equity to rectify faults in the law proves) but was to have a stultifying impact on the tribal common law — at least as perceived by those governmental authorities that were prepared to concede legitimacy. For it led almost inevitably to the tribal customs being regarded as of long usage, and indeed of tribal society being seen as static, not susceptible to change. Those changes that were noted were often attributed to the influence of Western society ignoring the fact that change and progress were inherent in tribal society, and were of the essence of custom itself, as well as ignoring the fact that tribal societies nearly always maintained some degree of contact with other local societies whose influence could also often lead to change.

V

The predominant view of custom as static was to have far-reaching implications on the attitudes to custom in a modern world dedicated to change and progress.

Any attempt to relate to customary law must, it seems to me, come to terms with the impact of jurisprudential thinking on the manner in which custom is incorporated into a legal system — whether as being of immemorial use and therefore static, or whether as being part of a living group, reflecting changing mores, responding to changing circumstances, flexible enough to adopt to changing needs.

The manner in which customary law is perceived is of vital import for the possibility of creating a framework of legal pluralism. A perception of custom as some formalized relic of a backward people will lead to certain inescapable consequences: that customs can only be recognized if they are of long-standing usage, and once recognized, cannot be changed; or alternatively that they are not acceptable by the standards of the dominant culture and thus must be totally eradicated; or where several such customs exist, that the whole system must be rejected without any opportunity for the customs to respond dynamically to the changing environment, including those changes which are triggered by the impact of another culture which may also well be the dominant culture.

Those kinds of issues are not unique to customary law. One of the classic legal debates in the United States relates to the manner in which the constitution should be interpreted — whether in terms of a strict constructionist approach that hues close to the presumed intent of the framers, or whether in terms of a living document that is easily adaptable to the continuous development of a vibrant society.

Thus for instance, a leading constitutional scholar, Raoul Berger,[23] has argued forcefully in favor of the retention of capital punishment, without reference even to the substantive current criminological and philosophical debate, as the death penalty was in effect at the time of the constitutional convention. In direct contrast is the approach that examines penal policy in the light of what the Supreme Court defined as the 'evolving standards of decency,'[24] a theoretical framework initially applied to punishment in general, and then activated specifically in terms of the death penalty.

It is clear that in the modern world any approach that sees custom — particularly of another culture — in static terms, dooms that very culture to stagnation and ultimately rejection by imposing on it a rigidity which is generally by no means inherent in its nature. It also makes for a reluctance to grant recognition *ab initio*, or where recognition is granted, to impose other norms upon it, instead of allowing for a natural and gradual growth.

VI

It is quite possible that tribal customs that seem to be incongruous in the modern age will gradually be eased out by the members of the tribe themselves as their contacts with other cultures make them aware of alternative modes, or even where changing economic and social conditions make it increasingly difficult to practise the old customs. Polygamy becomes difficult to maintain in the light of pressures on the availability of land, bride-price becomes difficult to pay in a cash economy and in any case takes on the appearance more and more of dowry, witchcraft loses some of its influence as medical knowledge is extended. On the other hand, respect for nature, originally the result possibly of fear for its overpowering might, takes on enduring qualities that not only survive outer pressures but may present an intrinsic attraction to others desperately trying to re-define their own attitudes to the environment, and searching for a viable ethological ethnic. But one way or the other it is the people themselves who must contend with the issues of how to maintain their customs in a living culture.

Custom is an important source of law for all legal systems, and of the modern systems, particularly for the common law system. An awareness of its flexible nature is essential for its vitality and for the continuing viability of the culture.

It is possible that anthropologists are partly to blame for the inaccuracies that often attach to the customary law. Often even when stressing the nature of custom as law, they would tend to describe it as an inflexible framework, basically as it was at the time of the research. Very few anthropologists probed to determine how the customs have developed over time. Often where changes are noticed, particularly as a result of a return to the tribal community after the passage of time, these changes will be attributed to the influence of the dominant culture, part of a process of acculturation, instead of noting how much of the change is self-engendered, part of the ongoing history of the particular tribe, part of its essential resilience and capacity to adapt according to changing circumstances and changing needs.

For a full appreciation of the obligatory nature of custom and for its role in determining the need for custom in any legal system, it is advisable to note the role of custom in general in any legal system, including those that are recorded in writing and considered as sophisticated and complex. Thus leading textbooks in jurisprudence refer to custom in terms that make it not just perfectly compatible with the needs of a modern legal system, but also of manifest positive benefit. Thus George Paton writes of custom being 'useful to the lawyers and codifier,' as it 'provides the material out of which law can be fashioned' and 'psychologically, it is easier to secure reverance for a code if it claims to be based on customs immemorially observed and this is true even though historically the claim cannot substantiated'. He goes on to argue that custom having the force of law is based on 'the recognition that there is authority behind it.'[25]

However a more acute sensitivity to the role of custom in legal systems will emerge not only from such formal definitions or even from a reminder of the historical development of the common law itself, but also from a jurisprudential perspective that takes due accord of the manner in which law is used in the real world that allows for the obligatory nature of rules, that have been neither enacted by statute nor pronounced as precedent by the judiciary.

Sociological jurisprudence has always argued for the need for law to be attuned to social reality and to develop in terms of relevant social policy. But going beyond this approach are schools of thought that place special emphasis on the law in its extra-legal and extra-judicial manifestations.

VII

There are several theoretical perspectives in jurisprudence that place the emphasis in law not on the statute book or judicial precedent, but on the rules and norms that people lay down in the course of their everyday lives. It is these rules that determine, for so many people, the nature of the rights and obligations *vis-a-vis* their neighbors. Most people do not examine the minutiae of the law, or seek the aid of a legal expert to resolve a particular issue. They rely on the prevailing norms that exist in their community, or their profession, or in a particular field of endeavour. Basically they seek to enforce their rights in terms of those customary practices and patterns of behavior that have developed in response to similar kinds of problems in the past. Eugen Ehrlich has referred to this aspect of legal and social life as the living law.[26] Similarly, the theorists of the Scandinavian school of legal realism have suggested that legal rules are no more than particular form of general social norms, and should be understood in that light.

From the perspective of historical jurisprudence it is here that the key norms of a society are being forged and in an ideal situation. Law will in the long run give formal recognition to such practices, and in essence a recognition to the customs of the people. Savigny writes: 'in the general consciousness of a people lives positive law and hence we have to call it people's law . . . it is the spirit of a people living and working in common in all the individuals, which gives birth to positive law.'[27]

There are also advanced cultures such as in China and Japan where every effort is made to avoid litigation and legalistic solutions for what are generally considered to be social and human problems. Slowly overall normative systems emerge, such as the Guri in Japan, to describe how individuals resolve their differences without recourse to the formal legal system.

In recent years many efforts have been made to emphasize the positive role of alternative dispute resolution in the modern world; indeed, part of the attraction of this phenomenon is as a reaction to the frustrations of the expense, the procrastination, the uncertainties and the tension associated with the formal legal system. In this kind of context customary law becomes merely one aspect of a larger movement that seeks flexibility in both the procedural and substantive aspects of the law.

The truth is that the common law was originally of this type. Its origins were through processes very similar to that being described in some of the less dominant, yet nonetheless extremely important, theories in jurisprudence. In reality, this is still the essence of the common law, a factor that makes for a greater understanding of a customary law system.

Customary law, then, should be seen as part of a larger jurisprudential reality, as similar in many respects to the common law itself, as an expression of law-making that seeks to retain a close link between obligatory norms and popular sentiment, that makes for a fluid normative system, that is attuned to changing circumstances, and that allows for particularistic considerations within a pluralistic legal base.

Custom, then, far from being a problematic aspect of tribal life in the context of the modern world, becomes an integral aspect of a legal system, not an artificial addition reluctantly conceded, but an essential component of a meaningful law that is willingly accepted by the citizenry, because it is deeply embedded in their consciousness as a living part of their culture.

Furthermore, it is not inherently inferior to law. Peter Goodrich, in stressing the importance of custom, takes issue with Hart's somewhat condescending attitude to custom, an attitude in which custom is seen as the precursor of the later and more perfect law. Goodrich suggests, on the contrary, that far from law being the 'inheritor of custom,' as claimed by Hart, or the pinnacle of legal development replacing 'non-legal or customary order,'[28] it is destructive of those orders. Focusing specifically on the consequences of imperial expansion, Goodrich writes that:

> Colonization of territories invariably brought with it a . . . degree of Western legal order: centralized courts and enforcement agencies, rules and formal methods of adjudication were imposed upon non-legal cultures in the interests

> of domination, exploitation and administrative expediency. It is salutary . . . . to recall that the Western tradition of law is the product of a very specific, localized yet imperialistic culture and that it has never been the indigenous tradition of more then one small but highly expansionist group of European cultures.[29]

Goodrich goes on to argue that

> To the cultural relativity of legal order should be added its historical and social limitations . . . . Law is an essential aspect of the modern Western political tradition and of the ideology of government; it justifies authority and makes it appear natural, but as it is studied and reported it is of limited practical significance. Custom surrounds the law and lives within it; corporate self-regulation, shared expectations and specific local and ethnic practices are as likely if not more likely to prevent or resolve disputes or disorder than the centralized, bureaucratic and highly expensive legal administration.[30]

However Goodrich also suggests that the meaning of custom has been transformed, referring in the common law system not so much to the customary practices of the people but specific types of habitual activity of specialized groups (e.g. professions), as 'selected, interpreted and applied by the privileged class of experts in the law.'[31]

It is this development that has tended to undermine the more general law of custom, which is the essence of customary law. However, as ideas of legal pluralism spread and as customary law gains greater respect and recognition, it is possible that there may be a re-assessment of the common law itself, a renewed appreciation of the role of custom both in its historical development, and its natural potentialities as an integral part of the legal system.

* *Leon Sheleff is Professor of Law at Tel-Aviv University.*

ENDNOTES

1. As an example, for the situation in Japan see Yosiyuki Noda, 1976, *Introduction to Japanese Law*, Tokyo: University of Tokyo Press, Ch. 3, 'Reception of Western Law,' 41-64.

2. For a good description of the civil law, see Merriman, 1969, *The Civil Law Tradition: An Introduction to the Legal System*. For a comparison of the civil law

and common law systems, see Rene David, 1980, *English Law and French Law,* London: Stevens and Son.

3. See, for instance, R.G. van Caenegem, 1988, *The Birth of the English Common Law,* Cambridge: Cambridge University Press.

4. Guido Calabresi,1982, *A Common Law for the Age of Statutes.*

5. For good critical analysis, see discussion by R.M. Dias, 1985, *Jurisprudence,* London: Butterworths, Ch. 18, 'Historical and Anthropological Approaches,' 379-394.

6. John Austin, 1954, *The Province of Jurisprudence Determined*, 5th ed., London: Weidenfeld and Nicolson.

7. See my discussion of this issue in *Social Cohesion and Legal Coercion: Beyond Weber, Durkheim and Marx*, unpublished manuscript.

8. Brian Simpson, 1986, 'The Common Law and Legal Theory,' ed. William Twining, *Legal Theory and Common Law*, Oxford: Blackwell.

9. *Ibid.*, 8.

10. *Ibid.*, 18.

11. *Ibid.*, 18.

12. *Ibid.*, 18.

13. Peter Stein, 1980, *Legal Evolution: The Story of an Idea*, Cambridge: Cambridge University Press.

14. See *Ibid.*, 72. The quotation is from Letter to the Lord High Chancellor of Great Britain on the Expediency of the Proposal to form a New Civil Code for England - written by John Reddie.

15. *Ibid.*, 73.

16. *Ibid.*, 74.

17. James Zion, 1988, 'Searching for Indian Common Law,' eds. B. Morse and G. Woodman, *Indigenous Law and the State*, Faris Publications.

18. For representative examples of the work of these anthropologists, see Bronislaw Malinowski, 1949, *Crime and Custom in Savage Society*, London: Routledge and Paul; E.A. Hoebel, 1954, *The Law of Primitive Man,* Cambridge, Mass.: Harvard University Press; and Max Gluckman, 1954, *Judicial Process among the Barotse,* Manchester University Press.

19. See H.F. Morris and J.S. Reed, 1972, *Indirect Rule and the Search for Justice*, Oxford: Clarendon Press.

20. See also his joint work with the jurist Karl Llewellyn, 1941, *The Cheyenne Way -- Conflict and Case Law in Primitive Jurisprudence*, Norman: University of Oklahoma Press.

21. W.N. Hohfeld, 1923, *Fundamental Legal Conceptions as Applied in Judicial Reasoning*. See also his two articles — of the same name and similar content as they originally appeared in *Yale Law Journal*, Vol. 23 (1913), p. 16, and Vol. 26 (1917), p. 710.

22. The year 1189 was an arbitrary date — based apparently on an analogy with the 'limitation period fixed by the State of Westminster of 1275, for bringing writs.' See Lord Llyod, 1959, *Introduction to Jurisprudence*, London: Stevens and Sons, 340.

23. Raoul Berger, 1982, *Death Penalties: The Supreme Court's Obstacle Course*, Cambridge: Harvard University Press.

24. See *Trop v Dulles*, 356 U.S. 86 (1958). For general discussion see my *Ultimate Penalties: Capital Punishment, Life Imprisonment, Physical Torture*, Columbus: The Ohio State University, 1987.

25. George Paton, 1972, *A Textbook of Jurisprudence*, Oxford: Clarendon Press, 192.

26. Eugen Ehrlich, *Fundamental Principles of the Sociology of Law.*

27. Carl von Savigny, 1840, *System of Modern Roman Law*, 342

28. Peter Goodrich, 1986, *Reading the Law: A Critical Introduction*, London: Basil Blackwell, 63-64. The reference is to H.L.A. Hart, 1961, *The Concept of Law*, Oxford: Oxford University Press, 63-64.

29. *Ibid.*, 64.

30. *Ibid.*, 64.

31. *Ibid.*, 64.

Chapter Twenty-One

Land Usage as Privileged Discourse in Anglo-Australian Law

Helen Endre-Stacy*

The Mabo decision of the Australian High Court in 1992 finally ended the application of terra nullius to the Australian legal system. The High Court decision is, of course, of enormous legal importance. But the High Court judgement is only part of the discourse. It is one type or instance of Mabo-ness. The High Court judgement is not important so much for what it says about native title, but what it tells us about the role of the law, and particularly the High Court, in the generation of discourse in Australian society and culture. Aiming to resolve legal conflict, this legal text is also a site and moment of social change.

I
Introduction

'Conflict is nothing but the moral state of difference,' Roland Barthes, *The Pleasures of the Text*, 1973

The language of law and the system in which it operates act together to mediate the goals and intentions of judges as authors of legal texts. The meaning system in *Mabo* contributes to its cultural one-sided-ness, weaving a tangled web of human experience that is mediated by language. The dialogical, ideological and subjectivity-constituting nature of the *Mabo* language creates a rich social text. Although the range of acceptable interpretations may be limited (after all, the properties of the legal text always impose their own restrictions), this judgement does not speak to the narrow community of readers that an Australian High Court judgment ordinarily speaks to.

This paper considers how far the *Mabo* decision has concealed or displaced the metasoma that initially brought the matter before law. The uncritical reader has a large stake in believing that the decision exemplifies 'justice,' or, at very least, one that is coherent and defensible. I want to consider if the legal text has displaced the hierarchies involved, given that the decision rests upon those same hierarchies for its authority.

The two written majority judgements,[1] particularly the joint judgment of Deanne and Gaudron J.J., have called on 'context' to help in their understanding of how *terra nullius* came to be wrongfully applied to Australia from 1788. This appeal to context has enlarged the arena of the legal problems in issue, concomitantly bringing disputes about what is 'relevant' context. Those who disagree with the decision (and there are many) argue that the High Court judges have extended the context to included matters not 'relevant' to the legal issue.[2] *Mabo* is the iterability of the common law system of precedent writ large — the extent of context is *always* contestable. The radical indeterminacy of the common law system lies in this contest of what is, or is not, a relevant determining factor to the legal issue at hand.

The majority judgements discussed here set themselves the task of consolidating relevant context so that a new start can be made. The unspoken aim is to (finally) understand what the law *really* is, thereby '. . . eliminating the mass of prior writings and placing one in a position of sublime simplicity . . .'[3] Yet, at the same time, it seems more likely that the High Court decision simply confirms legislative and social moves towards racial equality for Australian Aboriginal and Torres Strait Islanders that have been underway in Australia since the early 1970s. The *Mabo* decision comes after almost twenty years of social, legislative and common law shifts in equality rights for Australian Aboriginal people.[4] This period began with federal and state legislation recognising Aboriginal cultural artefacts, limited forms of land rights, and then racial discrimination with the advent of the federal *Racial Discrimination Act* 1975.[5]

The majority judgements of Brennan, Gaudron and Deane J.J. in *Mabo* demonstrate the role of High Court judgement/text in this process of cultural reacclimatisation. Brennan J.'s judgment and the joint judgement of Gaudron and Deane J.J. are exercises in conflict resolution. Both judgements identify a problem, examine the circumstances surrounding its existence and its influence in the broader operation of the common law, and then suggest a remedy to that problem.[6]

More significantly, the decision demonstrates the inseparability of law, history, politics and aesthetics. The majority judgements of Brennan, Gaudron and Deane J.J. are more that neatly presented legal texts. They recast our national stories. Contextualised in Australian society, the *Mabo* decision continues a process of articulating new conceptions of the Real.[7] Ironically, the narrowness and specificity of the judgments means that the legal text is more an act of closure of an emergent and socially challenging concept. It acts to *contain* social disruption through constructing Real legal history at last. The *disruptive* effects of *Mabo* lie mostly outside law, in the mass media and through Aboriginal and Torres Strait Islander and white (mostly conservative) groups who have reinterpreted the formal legal effects of *Mabo*.[8]

II
The High Court's Decision

Eddie Mabo was a member of the Meriam people of the three Murray Islands in the Torres Strait that lies between the northern-most tip of Queensland and Papua New Guinea. The largest island is Mer (Murray Island) and the total land area of all three islands is about 9 square kilometres. In May 1982, Eddie Mabo and four other Torres Strait Islanders began an action in the High Court of Australia seeking confirmation of their traditional land rights, claiming that the islands had been continuously inhabited and exclusively possessed by the Meriam people. They gave evidence that the Meriam people lived in permanent communities with their own social and political organisation, although conceded that the British Crown (in the form of the then-colony of Queensland) became sovereign of the Islands upon their annexure in 1879. They claimed continued enjoyment of their land rights, and claimed further that these land rights had not been validly extinguished by the sovereign (Queen Victoria) in the late 1800's, or subsequently. They sought recognition of these land rights from the Australian High Court.

In its decision,[9] the High Court formally rejected that Australia (not just the Murray Islands) was *terra nullius* at the time of white settlement in 1788, holding that Aboriginal people were already in occupation of the land known as the English colony of New South Wales.[10] The Crown had gained radical title to the land of Australia on settlement, but this did not extinguish existing native title.[11] In relation to Eddie Mabo's claim,[12] the High Court found that the Murray Islanders had retained their local customs and traditions and that they were entitled to possession, occupation, use and enjoyment of their land.[13] In coming to its decision, the High Court relied upon three discursive salients: white observations of the presence of Murray

Islander people from the beginning of white settlement, secondly, on-going recognition of forms of Islander self-government and autonomy (as evidenced by legislative texts and authoritative reports) and finally, symbols of a land tenure system in use on the Murray Islands.

The land tenure the High Court considered in *Mabo* was that *specifically* practiced by the Meriam people of the Torres Strait Islands, who are Melanesian people with a lifestyle based upon Island agricultural cultivations and fishing. The Meriam people of the Murray Islands have a land tradition that is *indetifiably* based upon individual ownership and sedentary food cultivation. The spiritual nature of their relationship to the land is less clear, and was not argued before the High Court. In the Queensland Supreme Court decision of *Mabo* (where the findings of fact were made), and which handed down the decision subsequently appealed before the High Court, Moynihan J. had held that this relationship was *not* religious or spiritual.[14] Consequently, the High Court in *Mabo* did not (could not) consider the religious or spiritual aspect of Aboriginal and Torres Strait Islander connection with the land.[15]

Mainland Australian Aboriginal people, on the other hand, had a more (though not excessively) nomadic lifestyle, adapted to different climatic and geographic conditions.[16] There can be no doubt that *mainland* Aboriginal peoples' relationship to the land is fundamental to their spiritual traditions. In 1977 in *Milirrpum,* it was judicially noted that Aboriginal dreaming laws formed a subtle and elaborate system of laws.[17] Australian Aboriginal Dreaming laws impose eternal moral obligations collectively on a group. The Dreaming laws say that the earth surface is an enduring physical record of the earth as the original mother of everything. Dreaming laws derived from the earth provide the principles of order that govern relationships between Aboriginal people and between people and the natural world. Their kinship with nature provides the symbolic code for human conduct; the earth is the teacher and is revered as holding the wisdom for humanity. And yet it seems clear that, also for the Meriam people, the *emphasis*, the *ethos* is more on the community than Western systems of land tenure.[18]

III
Legal Discourse as Narrative and Discourse

Both majority judgements show an impulse to narrativise in a sense of making a lucid story out of the material available. The introductory paragraph of Gaudron and Deane J.J. resonates with the 'once upon a time . . .' introduction in tales of myth and fantasy:

> [T]he starting point lies in the second half of the nineteenth century with the establishment of the Colony of New South Wales.[19]

The story is told in terms of intrusion and hostility. A sense of chronology is established by expressions like '[a]s time passed,'[20] '[t]hroughout the rest of the century'[21] 'only seven years later.'[22]

A feel for those earlier frontier times is established on the idea of the white settlers lack of knowledge and understanding of indigenous culture. Initial lack of knowledge is not, however, compensated for by later perceptions. The judgement disapprovingly cites the writer who described the Aboriginal inhabitants in 1893 in terms of their 'treachery' and 'savage ideas.' This is juxtaposed to Cook's 1770 description of the Aborigines as benign and '. . . liv(ing) in tranquillity.'[23] Isaacs J.'s 1913 judgement is dismissed because of his 'refus(al) to recognise' an early treaty with local Aboriginal groups. The judgement reinscribes the noble savage myth as a justificatory rationale for its re-narrativisation.

Other cases standing as Australian legal precedent are also implicated in this history of oppression. They are dismissed for their conspiratorial part in the 'white expropriation,'[24] the 'obliteration or near obliteration of the Aborigines,'[25] and the:

> . . . conflagration of oppression and conflict which was, over the following century, to spread across the continent to dispossess, degrade and devastate the Aboriginal peoples and leave a legacy of unutterable shame.[26]

Brennan J.'s judgement is more restrained prose than Gaudron and Deane J.J.'s, but is more solidly based on appeal to logos: on fact and deductive reasoning, rather than on appeals to emotion. Certainly, Brennan J. speaks of dispossession and injustice, but in contrast to Gaudron and Deane J.J., such terms work as descriptors rather than as arguments in themselves.[27] The basis of Brennan's J. narrative is resolution of conflict. As with so many finely honed tales, he starts at the 'beginning' and finishes at the 'end.' The teleological impulse that drives his retelling of 'settlement' warns the reader that the judgement will progress from the context of his initial statement 'The Meriam people were in occupation of the Islands for generations before the first European contact,' to a declaration of their present status.

The reader can sense that this will be a nicely wrapped story. Although the dispossession of original inhabitants is now a part of Australian history: it 'underwrote the development of the nation,'[28] it is still possible, by abandoning *terra nullius* and the theory of absolute Crown ownership, 'to bring the law into conformity with Australian history.'[29] Brennan J. moves smoothly through an account of the life of indigenous Australians before and upon the arrival of Europeans, establishing a pre-history to the present story. From there, the text moves on to the acts of dispossession, discussion of the legal effects of dispossession, and an exploration of recent impediments and possible remedies. Finally, we reach the outline of remaining rights and entitlements.[30]

IV
Identity in the Discourse (ii) or (i)

Mabo is rich with unstated assumptions. They are part of the legal discourse and function as boundaries or constraints, and also to dismantle the taken-for-grantedness of Aboriginal and Torres Strait Islander oppression. To express the story of native title and the common law, the common law has re-asserted its capacity to speak both of and for that native title. The taken-for-grantedness of the authority of the speaker,[31] each Justice's articulation of their position regarding the common law so far, and referral of the Queensland Supreme Court decision on appeal to the High Court together emphasise the importance and status of the High Court judgments. High Court judges in Australia are probably the only people who can speak with such authority in informing the reader of what issues are the most important. After all, the only 'discipline' that can reach them is to have their judgment overturned by a subsequent act of parliament.

The High Court in *Mabo* utilised three dialectics of reconstruction. Each of them implicates the European historical enterprise of epoches and categorisation through essentialist attributes that arise through location within a pre-given category. Firstly, it asks (very briefly) what Aboriginal and Torres Strait Islander culture was before 1788; secondly, what the effects of the mix of Aboriginal and Torres Strait Islander culture have been in the intervening years, and, finally, what the present position is.

Brennan J. begins his judgement by expressing the issue in terms of its social ramifications. His definition of the contested issue as 'ownership' of land in the Murray Islands underscores the cultural importance of this decision. Although he initially and pointedly limits his observations to the Murray Islands, Brennan J.'s decision is influenced by a broader concern. He asks whether the law could be construed as if Queen Victoria has expropriated land that had been occupied for centuries by its indigenous population, without these people even knowing of it. Particular legal effects inhere in this statement of the issue: important legal consequences of 'knowledge,' entitlement through long and established usage, and the very concept of ownership itself.[32]

The final matter considered by Brennan J. is the application of the international law of settled territories. The foundational principle here is precedent.[33] He cites legal decisions that support universal and absolute beneficial ownership of all land vesting in the Crown. There is little ambiguity in his evaluation of these cases:

> According to the cases, the common law itself took from indigenous inhabitants any right to occupy their traditional land, exposed them to deprivation of the religious, cultural and economic sustenance which the land provides, vested the land effectively in the control of the Imperial authorities without any right to compensation and made the indigenous inhabitants intruders in their own homes and mendicants for a place to live. Judged by any civilised standard, such a law is unjust and its claim to be part of the common law to be applied in contemporary Australia must be questioned. The Court must now determine whether, by the common law of this country, the rights and interests of the Meriam people of today are to be determined on the footing that their ancestors lost their traditional rights and interests in the land of the Murray Islands on 1 August 1879.[34]

This statement signals his *purpose* in investigating legal precedent. The unspoken assumption is that the common law itself (omnipresent and omnibenevolent) could not possibly reduce indigenous people to 'mendicants.' Because any legal problem must emanate from legal decisions, they are open to being distinguished on 'new' facts. Brennan J.'s investigation seeks out the red herrings and the factual 'mistakes' of the past, 'declaring' the true or Real position, but with appropriate self-discipline:

> . . . this Court is not free to adopt rules that accord with contemporary notions of justice and human rights if their adoption would fracture the skeleton of principle which gives the body of our law its shape and internal consistency.[35]

And to reinforce the importance of the law and this skeleton of principle, Brennan tells the reader that 'the peace and order of Australian society is built on the legal system.'[36]

At first reading, the decision of Deane J.J. and Gaudron appears to be less restricted than Brennan's legal formalism. Brennan's is a case-by-case analysis, representing objective rigour and an 'obvious' conclusion.[37] The psychic motor for both judgements, however, is the same, to tell the 'one true story.'[38] Common to both judgements is the impression that the discourse did not come from the Justices, although it may have flowed out of their pens, or maybe scrolled itself across their pc screen. Statements like 'The common law of this country recognises a form of native title. . .' (Mason C.J. and McHugh J. say in their short judgement agreeing with Brennan J.),[39] or 'It may be assumed that the Meriam people knew nothing of the events of Westminster . . .' (Brennan J.)[40] are all disembodied and curiously detached.

Even Deanne J.J. and Gaudron, who most explicitly and emotively departed from the 'old' legal view of *terra nullius*, do this in a way that leaves individuals peripheral to legal propositions. Principles and process are the central focus and fulcrum. The law, and nothing else, was 'what done it' to indigenous Australians (that is, killed, enslaved and dispossessed them). The focus is upon law as an entity, not upon law as the production of individuals:

> Inevitably, *one is compelled to acknowledge* the role played, in the dispossession and oppression of the Aborigines, by *the two propositions* that the territory of New South Wales was, in 1788, *terra nullius* in the sense of unoccupied or uninhabited for legal purposes . . . The official endorsement, by administrative practices and in judgements of the courts, of *those two propositions* provided the environment in which the Aboriginal people of the continent came to be treated as a different and lower form of life whose very existence could be ignored for the purpose of determining the legal right to occupy and use their traditional homelands.[41] (emphasis added)

The implication is that the legal order of the last 204 years has been an anomaly perpetrated by two wayward legal principles.[42] 'Those two propositions' have a life of their own. 'They' have presented themselves and 'we' (in the past) have simply applied them. 'They' explain it all. There is no 'we' or 'what' that produced the 'they.' 'We' (in the past) were somehow out to lunch when the 'they' were being formed. The law is the subject, not an 'I' or a 'we.' It has been erroneous law that dispossessed Aboriginal people for white settlement because, in law, the land was 'empty.'

Their rhetoric is constructed to avoid an explication of *who* is 'doing' the law.' The drive in the judgement is to retain the view of law and legal judgement soundly within the aesthetic of the common law as an evolutionary and autonomous creature, imbued with a will and life of its own. Judge-made law has articulated where legal rationale places 'us' in that common law process, and then tidies up a particular point that (now) seems out of place and deviant. Ironically, for a decision that implies gross lack of legal and procedural intelligence in Australia's white history, the High Court's judgment draws its authority and legitimacy from the legal and procedural aesthetic code.[43] For example, Brennan J.'s reiteration of the integrity of the common law is delivered in apocalyptic and warning terms:

> It must be acknowledged that, to state the common law in this way involves the overruling of cases which have held the contrary. To maintain the authority of those cases would destroy the equality of all Australian citizens before the law.[44]

Unsurprisingly, the Court does not express a legal 'problem' in such a way that it may not be legally resolved. Any threat to the integrity of the common law is neutralised. Brennan J.'s discussion of the legal remedies available is a formality of articulating and limiting rights.[45] It rests upon his unspoken premise that the common law already recognises, and has *always* recognised, these rights. They are there, waiting to be 'discovered' or 'declared.'

The objects in *Mabo* have a similar transcendental and anonymous lack of presence. The judgements are a lengthy investigation of the extent of Crown title over land. The legal questions are land law questions, with an emphasis upon preliminary jurisdictional issues about the consequences of England's annexation of Australia as a colony.[46] Although the majority judgments refer to the doctrine of *terra nullius* acting as a form of racial discrimination,[47] and to dispossession of tribal land being a past injustice that constitutes 'the darkest aspect of the history of this nation,'[48] the victims of this discrimination are abstract and somehow anterior to language. They are not infants (forcibly taken to white institutions) and adults (used as servant labour) and they have no gender (women used for sex). The pre-white settlement history of the objects of this 'dark . . . history' is contained in five pages of a 217 page judgement.[49] The *aesthetics* of legal judgement-writing have obliterated any articulation of the present and the future of the objects of the judgement.[50]

In this way, *Mabo* stylistically reproduces the High Court's 1974 decision to overturn the common law entitlement of a husband to rape his wife.[51] Just as a raped wife's perception is the same under two antithetical legal rules, in *Mabo*, Murray Islander social organisation (that which guides use and tenure of land) has remained the same, but the common law has stretched to accommodate a different perception of the same 'facts.' Indeed, it was central to the majority decision in *Mabo* that the facts *had* remained the same, as this demonstrated the Islanders continuing connection with the land. The formalist approach would uphold an old rule that is 'anachronistic and offensive.'[52] The implication here is that it is methodologically viable, but not humanely desirable, that the courts should apply strict precedent. Significantly, in respect of both the common law rape in marriage rule and the doctrine of *terra nullius*, the High Court ultimately relied upon *its own readiness* to concede to an alternative legal approach.[53]

V
Textual Intersections: Law and Justice

The difference between Brennan J. and Deanne J.J. and Guadron's approach lies principally in their intersections of law and justice. For Gaudron and Deane J.J., justice comes through overturning *terra nullius*; for Brennan J., justice lies in restoring the efficacy of the common law. This difference in approach underlies their different expression of the legal questions at stake. The *similarity* in both judgements is that the system of operation and the authority of the law remain intact. Both judgements on this are clear — Crown sovereignty is not an issue that the Court may question.

In Brennan J.'s judgement, the findings of Moynihan J. in the lower court provided a factual account of an organised system of native land ownership (an equivalent of land tenure) on the Murray Islands, and recognises the interaction of this system of land ownership with early colonial Queensland's administration.[54] The term 'administration' is important, because Brennan J. is concerned to establish the nature of indigenous life on the Murray Islands prior to annexation to Queensland in 1878 (under Letters Patent from Queen Victoria). This allows him to reframe the legal question in the following terms: 'given this indigenous system was in existence, what were the consequences upon annexation?'

Brennan J. therefore enters into the main body of his judgement having already found that the Murray Islanders had an identifiable social 'organisation' which encompassed elements of work, sanction, organised activity, exchange, social life and rituals associated with marriage and death.[55]

All are facets of life recognisable by Western legal systems, and requisite to recognition and acceptance within that system.[56] This section clearly signals the recognition of a *prima facie* system of land ownership:

> The people who were in occupation of these Islands before first European contact and who have continued to occupy those Islands to the present day are known as the Meriam people. . . . Anthropological records and research show that the present inhabitants of the Islands are descended from the people described in early European reports. The component of foreign ancestry among the present population is small compared with most communities living in the Torres Strait. The Meriam people of today retain a strong sense of affiliation with their forebears and with the society and culture of earlier times. They have a strong sense of identity with their Islands. The plaintiffs are members of the Meriam people.[57]

This does two things He cites those 'facts' that show Murray Islanders' links to their land, and, secondly, he alerts the reader to the special nature of this particular case. Taking an inferential walk forward in the text at this point, the reader is alerted that Eddie Mabo's claim may be allowed to stand, but that there may be limits imposed upon its applicability to other Aboriginal and Torres Strait Islander claims to land tenure. This inference is confirmed by statements that conclude this first section of his judgement. Having been through the 'facts' of early indigenous occupation, Brennan J. formulates a legal question out of the issue: what were the effects of annexation on this form of ownership, and did annexation give the Crown 'absolute ownership of, legal possession of and exclusive power to confer title to, all land in the Murray Islands?'[58] Brennan notes that if annexation *did* pass exclusive title to the Crown:

> . . . the Queen took the land occupied by Meriam people on 1 August 1879 without their knowing of the expropriation; they were no longer entitled without the consent of the Crown to continue to occupy the land they had occupied for centuries past.[59]

Clearly, at this point, the reader is faced with the prospect of a challenge to the strict legal position on this issue. Framing the legal question this way allows the reader to anticipate an answer that says 'surely not.' Reading the subtext, Brennan J.'s task is formulated thus: given that the Meriam people did in fact 'own' their land to all intents and purposes at the time of Crown annexation, and given that asserting *total* Crown ownership upon annexation to Queensland in 1879 would render them no longer entitled to these clearly evidenced rights, what approach must the law take so as to legally recognise native title?

Brennan J.'s task is one of reconciliation of an instance of injustice within a legal system that aspires to equitable outcomes. The tension is clear — *something* has to go. The structure of his judgement from here is logical and straightforward, especially as the colonial declaration of sovereignty has been firmly placed beyond judicial examination by the Court. Brennan J. simply considers the direct effect of annexation. This leads to a three-pronged discussion: the concept of *terra nullius*,[60] the conclusion that the application of *terra nullius* was a misjudgment of the facts,[61] and how the legal system stands its ground in face of earlier misjudgment of the 'facts.' Brennan J. distinguishes all the arguments for *absolute* Crown ownership put by the respondents (the government of the State of Queensland) on the basis that native title can run with each of their arguments.[62] Native title is not inconsistent with their existence — it is not the principles which need to be abandoned, merely the interpretation of previous judicial decisions.

At the end of this section, Brennan J. concludes that pre-existing native title can still run as a burden on the Crown's radical title. Dispossession was never effected by common law acts of sovereignty, it seems, but only by subsequent acts of colonial or state government parliaments. He considers *terra nullius* again:

> As the basis of the theory is false in fact and unacceptable in our society, there is a choice of legal principle to be made in the present case. This Court can either apply the existing authorities and proceed to inquire whether the Meriam people are higher 'in the scale of social organization' than the Australian Aborigines whose claims were 'utterly disregarded' by the existing authorities

> or the Court can overrule the existing authorities, discarding the distinction between inhabited colonies that were *terra nullius* and those which were not.[63]

Of course, there is no choice. And since '[a] common law doctrine founded on unjust discrimination in the enjoyment of civil and political rights demands reconsideration,' Brennan J. reconsiders. He concludes that 'the common law of Australia rejects the notion' of absolute Crown ownership and finds that the antecedent rights of the indigenous inhabitants run as a burden on the Crown's title.[64]

Gaudron and Deane J.J. take a different approach to the act of colonisation and implementation of the common law. After restating the common law on the differences between conquered, ceded and settled colonies for English citizens occupying new territory, their Honours state that, in the case of a settled territory:

> . . . [t]he common law so introduced was adjusted in accordance with the principle that, in settled colonies, only so much of it was introduced as was 'reasonably applicable to the circumstances of the Colony. This left room for the continued operation of some local laws or customs among the native people and even the incorporation of some of those laws and customs as part of the common law.[65]

There is already an indication to the reader of Deanne J.J. and Gaudron's potential solution: recognition of existing rights within the common law system, while retaining the status of a settled colony. This is reinforced several pages later. They say:

> Obviously, where the pre-existing native interest was 'of a kind unknown to English law', its recognition and protection under the law of a newly settled British Colony would require an adjustment either of the interest itself or of the common law: either a transformation of the interest into a kind known to the common law or a modification of the common law to accommodate the new kind of interest.[66]

Deanne J.J. and Gaudron's ultimate decision modifies enough of the common law to recognise 'a communal native title,'[67] not of itself a common law entity, but one which, upon *Mabo*, becomes one. They undertake a lengthy (almost thirty page)[68] examination of precedents from New Zealand, Canada and Papua New Guinea to suggest that the common law *can* accommodate a system of recognised occupation and use. They affirm that native title may run with common law, without relying on traditional English concepts of individual proprietary ownership.[69]

Ultimately, they declare that native title is not a 'mere equity.' Even if such rights were not enforced by native inhabitants because they did not know they had these rights, or because of lack of legal access, this did not mean that the common law rights did not exist! The common law had (naturally, somehow) acted to preserve these rights, meaning that where the Crown had extinguished them without compensation, this was wrongful. Against this background, Deanne J.J. and Gaudron introduce[70] the line of legal precedent that deny an interest in land to indigenous inhabitants.[71] They find that 're-examination compels their rejection.'[72]

This approach clears the way for Deanne J.J. and Gaudron to consider the facts of this case under the subheading of 'the dispossession of the original inhabitants.'[73] The two legal principles to have caused this dispossession, described as 'the darkest aspect of the history of this nation'[74] are *terra nullius* and, secondly, the principle of full legal and beneficial ownership vesting in the Crown.[75] They reject *both* on the basis that native title can run with the common law, and that the application of *terra nullius* to these facts is insupportable.

As a rhetorical strategy primarily based on an appeal to pathos, Gaudron and Deane J.J.'s progression to the next segment (tellingly titled 'Should the propositions supported by the Australian cases and past practice be accepted?') is a brilliant move. Their question is the legal expression of the larger cultural question that grips contemporary Australia — 'should we continue to support the 'obliteration' and 'devastation' of Aboriginal rights?' The legal and cultural questions are equally impossible to answer in the affirmative. Deanne J.J. and Gaudron answer this question in only one paragraph and one that is almost self-evident.[76] If there were any doubt, however, it is dispelled in the first few words of the paragraph: 'If this were any ordinary case. . .' (page 100). Something which looms as large as the property law of the country is not something to be easily dismissed, yet the 'unique' status of this case imposes upon the Court a 'duty' to re-examine the two fundamental propositions under consideration. The magnitude of the issue persuades them to break with the tradition of legal precedent.[77]

But is this a break with tradition? In the final piece to their judgement that contains the exploration and declaration of the nature of the rights of native title, their use of 'unrestrained language' that is 'unusually emotive' for a High Court judgement is explained in cautionary terms.[78] The nature of the 'challenge' and the question of a break with tradition is dubious.

> [l]ong acceptance of legal propositions, particularly legal propositions relating to real property, can of itself impart legitimacy and preclude challenge.[79]

VI
Outcomes: *Mabo* -ness as an Interpretive Strategy

The *Mabo* decision has instigated enormous public and political debate in Australia about the relationship between indigenous Australians and white Australians. It has also catalysed debate about the role of the High Court. *Mabo* is heuristic in its self-conscious re-formulation of contemporary attitudes between differing, and often-times clashing, cultural beliefs. In articulating how 'we Australians' think about Anglo-Saxon and indigenous approaches to land tenure, it constructs how 'we' think about judicial articulations of 'how we think.' This new subjective 'we' still relies on the objective Other: the dispossessed Aborigine. This new sense of 'we' and 'how we think' is new in an ontological sense. It is a new way of conceiving our past 204 years and also a new way of conceiving our highest judicial institution.

In framing this shift in understanding,[80] the High Court has assumed a panoptic vision of Australian society — reaching into the past and drawing upon Australia's place in the international human rights community, so as to position contemporary Australian truths. The 'natural' contexts of the last 200-odd years of Australian history are, ineluctably, always, selections made by the High Court judges from the range of *identified* contexts. The remarkable aspect of the *Mabo* decision is that its choice of contexts has extended well beyond the usual constraints of legal adjudication.[81] *Mabo* 'the dispute' between two cultures is a statement of difference. *Mabo* 'the decision' of the High Court is a discussion of desire. It seeks to remove difference through identifying cultural similarities in land and property practices.

But there can be no question that this *legally* conservative High Court decision has had a de-stabilising effect. These have arisen in a variety of ways as the judgement continues to enter into many discourses outside legal discourse. *Re*-interpretation of the legal consequences of the judgement has ensured sustained high levels of public and political interest in 'the *Mabo* issue' through the mass-media. Grossly inflated interpretations by white conservative groups of the legal consequences of *Mabo* has instigated anxiety and has generated its own subversion.[82]

Additionally, a plain English book of *Mabo* is a re-formulation of the legal judgement that extends accessibility to the decision well beyond the usual legal audience.[83] In this sense, the *Mabo* decision is creating a dialogue extending well beyond the legal system. It is a dialogue that is expressly engaging political and cultural ideology, even though the judgement itself is written in an impersonal expository form. Like many decisions of senior appellate courts, *Mabo* demonstrates the instability of the legal linguistic code.

Subversion has occurred at a deeper level through the High Court's rejection of *terra nullius* to the Murray Islands and to mainland Australia. Australian Aboriginal and Torres Strait Islander people have always known that *terra nullius* has been a large category error within the anglo-Australian legal system — a system that has been mute before in justice to indigenous Australians in almost every other respect. White Australia has been less conscious of the legal error of *terra nullius*, but this clear identification by the High Court potentially de-stabilises every aspect of the legal system. How is one to know if the foundations of the system are not built on several, rather than merely one, flawed assumption?[84]

At the same time, the High Court deliberately closed off its questions — the point of closure within the decision lies at the point were the Murray Islanders practices can be identified within the dominant (Anglo-Australian) system of land tenure. Closure comes at the coast of the small Murray Islands; closure comes at the marginally expanded definition of property boundaries, newly signified by trees, rocks and village dwellings; legal closure occurs at the specific facts and circumstances of this appeal to the High Court.

VII
Conclusion

The signal absence in *Mabo* is any attempt by the High Court to understand an *Aboriginal or Torres Strait Islander* cultural concept of self. Aboriginal Dreaming paints a vision of community and interdependence that is different to the liberal view of the autonomous self.[85] The language and the methodology of the Court's decision serves Anglo-Australian culture, applying that culture to the Other's cultural perspectives.[86] The High Court chose to use criteria based upon Western ways of identifying a connection with the land. There has been no attempt to take on the ethical vernacular of the Murray Islanders. The High Court requires Aboriginals to share white Australia's reality in order to share in white Australia. This has given Aborigines highly qualified cultural validation.

On one hand, *any* progress for Aboriginal people is welcome. On the other, for the High Court to redraw a new Real (re)confirms the old hierarchy of white Australians over Aboriginal people. It is an existential problem. *Mabo* confers an immediate political advantage for Australian Aboriginal people as a *single* category of oppressed by creating a new, but still simplistic, Real. This new Real ignores the pluralities and differences of those within the category, as surely as the old Real did. It fails to grapple with identity.

Aboriginal Australians continue to be placed in a process dependent upon *differentiation* with white Australians. Indigenous conceptions of land tenure are never present on their *own* terms. The extent of perceived differentiation has been guided solely by the extent of sameness (eg, geographical landmarks that signify the equivalence of Western geographical maps showing land ownership boundaries). There is a nudging commitment to another way of viewing reality, but the judgement as text has reinforced the role of white Australia as the speaker, as the centred subject.

Mabo has emphasised the different narrative form in Aboriginal Australian and Anglo-Australian laws and cultural myths. Their foundational epistemologies are based upon different stories. The *Mabo* decision is a cultural product — it operates as a cultural or social text. *Mabo* purports to stand as a text of decolonisation, but ultimately absorbs elements of difference within an existing system in the interests of stability. It continues the capture and control of a culture by the written, European word. The difficulties of understanding a cultural tradition that is mostly oral have not begun to be addressed.

The 'unutterable shame' of the 'dispossession' admonishes, but ultimately exculpates, Law. Culpability lies with those decisions (absent human construction) that misconstrued the law. Law as *institution* is not implicated in the misconstruction. The ultimate restoration common law's integrity reinscribes the dominant culture in the speaking position. Objectification of the image of the indigenous Australian as Other reinstates the old hierarchy. The possibility of selfhood and subject status of that Other is denied.

Perhaps the most interesting element revealed by this judgment/text structure is the relationship of 'justice' to the act of system maintenance that both majority judgements effect. While Brennan J.'s judgement concluded by emphasising the common law's capacity to include the concept of native title and remain systemically intact (and even further valorised), this is reached through a process of reasoning that cures the cause of injustice by effecting a resolution to the conflict. Gaudron and Deane J.J.'s judgement, on the other hand, foregrounds the capacity of the common law system to cope with the issue of native title. They locate the problem, reject *terra nullius* as a legal principle, and position the rights of native title when the offending principle is abandoned. Justice is obtained. Justice is an argument in and of itself.

There are two important consequences of the 'justice' approach. The approach of conflict resolution suggests a process of negotiation, debate and decision designed to accord with the common law idea of justice. And since the discourse of justice is designed to ultimately ensure the continuing existence of the legal system, the possibilities for radical change are, to an extent, short circuited from the outset. Secondly, while the judgements seemingly operate as legal texts, the stakes are social. This means that *Mabo* as an entity in Australian culture, quite apart from *Mabo v Queensland* or even the *Native Title Act* 1993, has an intertextual life of its own. *Mabo* can be accessed in steadily growing numbers of media and journal articles and in the plain English interpretation of 'What the High Court Said.' '*Mabo*-ness' has pervaded Australian culture to the extent that it is possible to trace the lines of *Mabo* through discussions ranging from equality rights to tourism to political correctness.

The question remains if *Mabo* has altered or simply embedded the Anglo-Australian discourse of land tenure. Constructed through the coastal shores of their islands, the Murray Islander relationship to the land is more obvious than the nomadic practices of mainland Aboriginal peoples. Murray Islander land practises are more like 'civilised' peoples — they are 'settled' and do not rove through a vast region. Anglo-Australian land practices have a centred view of the farmer and a diminished view of the land:

> (For the Aboriginal people) topographic features and creatures were diffused throughout a vast region. They were not all visible at once and human products were always mixed with the non-human.[87]

The High Court's assessment of Murray Islander land tenure was a search for ways in which that system was similar to Anglo-Australian *institutional systems* of identifying land tenure. Because the means of identifying boundaries and perimeters was crucial, the High Court has situated the Anglo-Australian land tenure system as superior, against which the Murray Islanders 'system' (a tree, a rock) is evaluated. Necessarily, the Anglo system is impliedly superior — it is more definite, more complex, more reliable. Impliedly, it is more equitable and just. The legal text of *Mabo* does not provide a strong legal precedent for Aboriginal land claims on mainland Australia. If the High Court had attempted to identify Aboriginal spiritual songlines, for instance, and legitimated those in their judgment through 'hearing' ('seeing') them, the implications of the decision would be wider.

The High Court decision is, of course, of enormous legal importance.[88] But the High Court judgements are only a part of the discourse. The decision is only one type or instance of *Mabo*-ness. The High Court judgements are not important so much for what they say about native title, but what they tell us about the role of the law, and particularly the High Court, in the generation of discourse in our culture. The judgements signify legal authority and consideration of disturbing elements within this system of authority. Aiming to resolve conflict, this legal text is a site and moment of legal and social change.

**Helen Endre-Stacy is Professor of Law at Queensland University of Technology.* *My thanks go to Jan Rohde and Derek Wilding for their assistance in preparation of this article. My thanks also go to participants of the Eighth Round Table of Law and Semiotics, Penn State, 1994, for their valuable comments and insights when this paper was first presented.*

ENDNOTES

1. There are two long written judgements of the majority view; Brennan J. (with whom Mason C.J. and McHugh J. concurred) and a joint judgement of Deanne J.J. and Gaudron Dawson J. and Toohey J. both dissented, both delivering lengthy written judgements.

2. For example, the Australian state that is most likely to attract native title claims is Western Australia. Not surprisingly, pastoralist and miners groups in this state argue that the High Court decision has strayed beyond the boundaries of context that is 'relevant' to Eddie Mabo's claim. The new Native Title Tribunal, formed under the Native Title Act 1993 (Cth), is to have its headquarters in Perth, Western Australia. Most federal public sector agencies are headquartered in the national capital of Canberra, or the two most populous eastern seaboard cities, Sydney and Melbourne.

3. Culler, 1988, *Framing the Sign*, 151.

4. Indigenous Australian people have been called 'Aboriginal and Torres Strait Islanders' from the 1970s, and especially so since the inception of the federal *Aboriginal and Torres Strait Islander Commission Act* in 1989. Amongst local Aboriginal people, southern Queenslanders are knows as 'Murris' and south-easterners are known as 'Kooris.' In Western Australia, indigenous and non-indigenous still use 'black fella.'

5. The *Australian Heritage Commission Act* 1975 (Cth) gave this Commission the responsibility, inter alia, to identify places of cultural significance for a cultural group as part of the National Estate (s4(1A); the *Aboriginal and Torres Strait Islander Heritage Protection Act* 1984 (Cth) was established to preserve and protect areas and objects of particular significance to Aboriginal and Torres Strait Islanders in accordance with their traditions; other Commonwealth (ie, federal) legislation containing specific provisions relating to indigenous peoples are the *National Parks and Wildlife Conservation Act*, 1975; *World Heritage Properties Conservation Act,* 1983; *Protection of Moveable Cultural Heritage Act*, 1986; *Australian Institute of Aboriginal and Torres Strait Islander Studies Act*, 1989. State governments of Australia have passed similar legislation.

6. In the case of Brennan J.'s decision, the structure of the judgement plays an important role he conceives of the issue to be addressed. The judgement can be divided into three sections: acknowledgment of an injustice, pp 2-12; location of the legal problem to which this injustice relates and its place within law, pp 12-47; offering a solution to this problem, pp 47-65. This solution cures the injustice and maintains the integrity of the 'system' as a whole. This contrasts to the approach of Gaudron and Deane J.J., (whose judgement also takes a three-part structure) but is most concerned to locate the potential for the legal system to recognise native title so as to establish the integrity of the system itself, pp 67-92; followed by an identification of the same disruptive element of injustice as the legal problem, pp 92-101; and finally, an explanation of the co-existence of native title and the common law in a state of justice, pp 101-111.

7. See *Dictionary of Semiotics*, eds. Sebeok and Umiker-Sebeok, Mouton de Gruyter.

8. The Australian federal government has used the *Mabo* judgement to introduce the *Native Title Act,* 1993, suggesting that 'The High Court has made its decision and now we have the chance of legislating away the fiction of *terra nullius* (sic) and basing our national social policy with Aboriginal and Islander people on a truth

rather than a lie.' Paul Keating, Prime Minister of Australia, quoted in *The Australian*, October 20, 1993. Of course, the federal government could have done so at any time under the doctrine of parliamentary sovereignty and was given an obvious opportunity to do so with *Milipprum* in 1971.This legislation validates all existing land titles up to December 31, 1993 and sets up a joint federal and State tribunal system to determine where and how native title coexists with mining leases. The federal government is to meet 85% of the cost of compensation for native title that has been extinguished (the State of Victoria is taking this aspect to the High Court, claiming that the federal government should pay 100%). A social justice package and a land acquisition fund is to be established to benefit Aboriginal people who have been dispossessed of native title rights (the larger proportion of Aboriginal people).

9. *Eddie Mabo and Ors v. The State of Queensland* 1992 175 CLR 1.

10. There was no dispute that *terra nullius* was a fiction in fact. That had been stated by the Northern Territory Supreme Court in 1971, although following English precedent in that case persuaded the judge to hold that Australia was practically empty on white occupation as a matter of law. *Milirrpum v. Nabalco and The Commonwealth of Australia* (1971) 17 FLR 141, following a decision of the Privy Council in *Cooper v. Stuart* (1889) 14 App Cas 286.

11. 'Native title' is the term used by the Judges of the High Court throughout the Judgement. The Court further held in the *Mabo* judgement that native title could be extinguished by legislation and also by Crown grants of freehold and leasehold interests in land. The Commonwealth *Racial Discrimination Act* of 1975 applied to any extinguishment of native title by state governments of Australia (which would then invalidate any grant made on a basis of racial discrimination). The High Court held by a majority that no compensatory damages are payable by state or federal government to native title holders upon extinguishment of their title, though this is to be subject to the federal *Racial Discrimination Act* 1975.

12. Eddie Mabo died before the High Court handed down its ruling in June 1992. According to the religious custom of Aboriginal and Torres Strait Islander people, it is disrespectful towards the dead to utter the name of the dead. It is ironic that the discourse of '*Mabo*-ness' that has grown up since the decision was handed down should invoke disrespect under customary law at every utterance.

13. The High Court did not decide this issue in relation to portions of the Islands that had been used for (white) administrative purposes and under the leases to the Trustees of the Australian Board of Missions.

14. Citation from SC case. This finding can be criticised for its entrapment by Western metaphysical dualism. See N. Sharp, 1993, 'No ordinary case: reflections upon *Mabo*,' 15(2) *Sydney Law Review* 143.

15. It seems that the High Court is willing to allow native title to inhere where traditional land rights do not necessarily resemble Australian property rights (Brennan, p 51 and Deanne and Gaudron, p 85). That leaves an opening for a claim

on mainland Australia from nomadic Aboriginals, provided they can demonstrate that traditional lands have been retained through traditional laws and customs, and that native title has not been extinguished by inconsistent government action or that the land has been granted to someone else — a very tall order.

16. Per Toohey J., 181.

17. *Supra*, 267.

18. Moynihan J. from the Supreme Court of Queensland and cited by Brennan J. in the High Court decision, 3.

19. *Mabo*, 67. This initiation into the retelling of Australian history is followed by qualifications to the *extent* of the historical re-write. While the cultural outlook may have changed, the narrative of Australian settlement and the development of Australian law still proceeds in the proscribed style of legal judgement/texts. The legal position of native title is recast within the traditional legal pattern.

20. *Ibid.*

21. *Ibid.*

22. *Ibid.*

23. *Ibid.*

24. *Ibid.*

25. *Ibid.*

26. *Ibid.*

27. For example, when he describes the decision that original inhabitants had no interest in land as 'an unjust and discriminatory doctrine' (p 30), it comes after a lengthy discussion of the nature of Crown ownership, sovereignty and the operation of the common law and the principle of *terra nullius*. First there is a re-examination of the circumstances of 'habitation' that have been applied to the state of the common law and the operation of *terra nullius*. All this is not to say, however, that Brennan J. does not place just as much investment as Gaudron and Deane J.J. in the technique of narrative to embody his retelling of Australian history — just that his Honour probably constructs a better history text than his fellow Justices.

28. *Ibid.* 58.

29. *Ibid.*, 47.

30. Brennan J.'s position throughout the judgement is that Aboriginal and Torres Strait Islander interests of some kind did exist at the time of arrival of Europeans, and although the Crown gained ultimate radical title, the rights of the original inhabitants survived. They needed a clear act of withdrawal or a clearly inconsistent grant to be

extinguished. Thus in some cases those rights can still exist to the present, and the common law itself can quite ably recognise this.

31. Reinforced by surrounding aspects of the text such as the 'argument for counsel,' headnote, title of the case etc.

32. Brennan J.'s vocabulary continually reinforces his concern that the common law ought not be able to snatch land surreptitiously from the Murray Islanders. From the beginning of his judgement he introduces the evocative terms of 'expropriation' and 'centuries past.' Later in the judgement, he uses the terms 'dispossessed' and 'time immemorial.'

33. The movement from the 'facts' of the case to the 'principles' involved (and from the findings of Moynihan J. in the Supreme Court to those of Brennan J. himself in the High Court) relies on the assumption that the law as it stands has evolved case by case from an original principle: to even consider amending this requires careful consideration of what has gone before, an attempt to 'distinguish' the present case.

34. *Ibid.*, 15-16.

35. *Ibid.*, 16.

36. *Ibid.*, 16.

37. Richard Delgado makes the point quite clearly: 'Implying that objective, correct answers can be given to legal questions . . . obscures the moral and political value choices at the heart of any legal inquiry' and 'case and case analysis purport to be objective, impartial, rigorous, rational, quasi-scientific. the proceed to a pre-determined conclusion, leaving the reader little opportunity to reach a different one, or the same one in a different way.' See F. Delgado, 1988, 'Derrick Bell and the Ideology of Racial Reform: Will We Ever Be Saved?,' Vol 97 *Yale L.R.* 923, at 927 and 947.

38. A true narrative style would give the reader a choice of interpretations and outcomes.

39. *Mabo*, 1.

40. *Mabo*, 11.

41. *Mabo*, 100.

42. This retrospective fault-finding seems to ignore the act of construction of the past 204 years that has taken place through reproducing the social world of today and yesterday. This presents a problematic treatment of the temporal aspects of cultural construction.

43. Schlag provides a good description of some of the criteria for 'sound legal thought.' 1. representational accuracy (the theory must not rely on assumptions or advance propositions that do not correspond to its referents); 2. consensual acceptability (the

theory must not rely on assumptions or advance claims that are or entail offensive, absurd, or unbelievable implications for the relevant audience); coherence (the theory must avoid internal contradiction and performative contradiction); elegance (the theory must rely on as few explanatory or justificatory variables as possible); sweep (the theory must be as encompassing as possible and must explain or justify all aspect that are within its legitimate scope); determinacy (the theory must restrict as much as possible the number of relevant and plausible conflicting interpretations it can sustain), and realisability (the theory must be capable of guiding its own realisation in practice). P. Schlag, 1991, 'The Problem of the Subject,' *Texas Law Review*, Vol 69:1627, at 1740.

44. *Ibid.*, 47.

45. Especially with respect to the subsequent dealings with the land by the Queensland Government, 47-65.

46. The two legal propositions explored by the court were whether the territory of New South Wales was in 1788 *terra nullius* in the sense of unoccupied or uninhabited for legal purposes, and whether full and beneficial ownership of all lands of the Colony vested in the Crown, unaffected by any claims of the Aboriginal inhabitants.

47. Brennan J., 29.

48. Deane J.J. and Gaudron, 100.

49. This repeats the findings of fact of Moynihan J in first instance in the Supreme court of Queensland. These findings were the basis of the High Court's decision that the Meriam people had maintained a traditional and customary connection with their land since white settlement. Moynihan J.'s findings were that 'Communal life based on group membership seems to have been the predominant feature of life . . . Daily life . . . was of a ceremonial or ritualistic nature . . . Behaviour was regulated . . . by social pressures . . . The people lived in groups of huts . . . organised in named villages (that is) far from obvious to the uninitiated but is patent to the islander . . . Garden land is identified by reference to a named locality . . . The Islands are not surveyed . . . Gardening was of the most profound importance . . . prior to European contact . . . Marriage and adoption involved the provision of exchange or considerable quantity of produce . . . Considerable ritual was associated with gardening . . . social cohesion (was inculcated) by a constant pattern of example, imitation and repetition and reinforcing behaviour . . . A sense of shame was the outcome of a failure to observe. It could be reinforced by group pressures leading to retribution. Ultimately force might be resorted to by those who had access to the means of exerting it. Sorcery, magic and taboo were obviously important cohesive factors and a source of sanction.' Brennan J. said (p 4) that '(these) findings show that Meriam society was regulated more by custom than by law,' drawing the distinction between law as culture (tagged 'magic') and legal culture as a culture of law.

50. But not their ghosts. The old lie of *terra nullius* is exposed as against the contemporary view of equality between indigenous and non-indigenous people. 'Equality' is problematic, of course.

51. *R v L* (1974) CLR 379. In a speech delivered in Sydney in March this year, Mason C.J. said that judges will increasingly become '. . . a constructive interpreter of legislation . . . spell(ing) out the interstices of the legislative provisions . . . by reference to the policies and purposes which are reflected in the legislation.' ('The Australian Judiciary In The 1990s,' Address to The Sydney Institute by The Honourable Sir Anthony Mason, A.C., K.B.E., Chief Justice of Australia, 15 March 1994) Mason C.J. did not refer to the public furore over *Mabo* in this speech. As an example of High Court decision acting to change outdated principles of substantive law, he pointed to the Courts decision in 1974 to overturn the common law right of a husband to rape his wife (delicately referred to by Mason CJ as the 'common law . . . entitle(ment of) a husband to sexual intercourse with his wife against her will'), but an implied reference to *Mabo* seems to palely loiter: 'It is no longer feasible for courts to decide cases by reference to obsolete or unsound rules which result in injustice and await future reform at the hands of the legislature. There is a growing expectation that courts will apply rules that are just equitable and soundly based except in so far as the courts are constrained by statute to act otherwise. Nothing is more likely to bring about an erosion of public confidence in the administration of justice than the continued adherence by the courts to rules and doctrines which are unsound and lead to unjust outcomes.' To an American audience, this may sound a tame statement. Legal formalism has been the accepted role of the High Court, regardless of the deeper critique that may lie behind a High Court judgment. Mason C.J. recognised this skewed view of the High Court's approach by continuing in this Address to say: 'What I have just said may not be welcome news to those who believe that the courts do no more than apply precedents and look up dictionaries to ascertain what the words used in a statute mean. No doubt to those who believe in fairy tales that is a comforting belief. But it is a belief that is contradicted by the long history of the common law. That history is on judicial law-making which shows no sign of coming unaccountably to an end.'

52. *Ibid.*, 9.

53. This raises the question of the High Court representing a 'best possible' reflection of public opinion, rather than a 'majority view' reflection of public opinion — the potential constituents of the rape in marriage rule (females in Australia/married females in Australia/females of marriageable age in Australia) are a much larger group than the potential constituents to the *terra nullius* doctrine (the 1984 census showed Aboriginal and Torres Strait Islander people to constitute 1.5% of the Australian population). On the other hand, Mason CJ was clear in rejecting any role for the High Court that made it a slave to public opinion. For a judge to 'act . . . as a representative of a section of the community . . . would be completely inconsistent with the judge's paramount responsibility to act impartially.'

54. *Mabo*, 2-11.

55. *Ibid.*, 3.

56. Brennan J.'s framing of Murray Island life within known Western lifestyles is so embracing that it extends to projecting Western gender indices upon Murray Islander society: Prestige depended on gardening prowess . . . and the cultivation of yams to a huge size . . . Boys in particular worked with their fathers and by observations and imitations reinforced by the rituals and other aspects of the social fabric gardening practices were passed on (p. 4).The association of men with work skills, responsibility for ritual, and the prestige of things of size is not new. There is a complete absence of women with respect to the notion of 'work' in this observation of traditional Murray Island society (whether at the hands of Moynihan J., or in Brennan J.'s citation of his Honour). Perhaps a measure of acceptance of another culture is the ready transfer of prejudice from one group in the dominant society to its corresponding group in the marginal society.

57. *Ibid.*

58. *Ibid.*

59. *Ibid.*

60. *Ibid.*

61. *Ibid.*

62. *Ibid.*

63. *Ibid.*

64. *Ibid.*

65. *Ibid.*

66. *Ibid.*

67. *Ibid.*

68. *Ibid.*

69. *Ibid.*

70. *Ibid.*, 95. The structure of their judgement at this point is interesting. The six pages which immediately follow are under the heading '(x) The 'dispossession of the original inhabitants.'

71. They provide an overview of the four offending Australian precedents which maintain the *terra nullius* position, concluding that any support these cases lend to the operation of *terra nullius* and the principle of absolute Crown ownership is 'little more than bare assertion' and ought be confined to *obiter dicta*. The authority of the four cases is 'formidable,' 92-95.

72. *Ibid.* 100. The first line of this segment (x) begins with 'The first days of the Colony . . .' — a mark of narrative introduction and an echo of the initial introduction to the narrative ('The starting point lies . . .' on page 67). This recollection of the early history of the colony is fundamental — it marks the development of the plot. Up to this point, recognition of the facts of the case has been suspended. Even for the first 30 pages of their judgment, Deanne J.J. and Gaudron have barely considered the operation of *terra nullius*. Now they go on to discuss how it could be, were it not for *terra nullius*.

73. *Ibid.*, 95, 101.

74. *Ibid.*, 100.

75. Deanne J.J. and Gaudron state '. . . one is compelled to acknowledge the role played, in the dispossession and oppression of the Aborigines, by the two propositions that the territory of New South Wales was, in 1788, *terra nullius* in the sense of unoccupied or uninhabited for legal purposes and that full legal and beneficial ownership of all the lands of the Colony vested in the Crown, unaffected by any claims of the Aboriginal inhabitants, 100.

76. 28 lines long — the shortest segment in their Judgement.

77. Unlike Brennan J., they consider that compensation ought to be paid where title has been wrongfully extinguished.

78. *Ibid.*

79. *Ibid.*, 111. In segment (xi) Deanne J.J. and Gaudron state that the act of dispossession constituted 'the darkest aspect of the history of this nation' and that '[t]he nation as a whole must remain diminished unless and until there is an acknowledgment of, and retreat from, those past injustices' (p 100). There is a very well established tradition operating here of the modernist narrative — the exposition of the heart of darkness and the fear within the human/national soul. This conception of the history of Australia as a tale of 'settlement' in the rhetoric of 'invasion' is problematic. It is accomplished within the discursive realm of decolonisation and the judgment in *Mabo* brightens the horizon. The nation is no longer 'diminished' because the revolutionary judgement overhauls the system (or purports to).

80. The very act of 'framing' something decides what is, and what is not, context to the field that has been framed. I have adopted this metaphor from J. Culler, *Framing the Sign*, 1988, Oklahoma Press, Norman, because of its metaphorical significance to 'frame up.'

81. That is why it is just as important to understand the positioning of the High Court judges to the legal issues at stake as it is to understand the legal issues as the judges' object of study. Part of the reading of *Mabo* must entail a reading of the judges as objects, not only as subjects. Together, these have helped contribute to a new position on and relationship between the people and issues contained within the

Mabo decision. New standards now govern the functioning of rules. The conditions of possibility have altered.

82. It has been suggested that white suburban property owners are at risk of losing that symbol of the Australian way of life, the backyard, to claims of native title. The criteria used by the High Court in *Mabo* makes this unlikely simply as a result of the decision.

83. P. Butt and R. Eagleson, 1993, *Mabo: what the High Court said*, Federation Press, Sydney. Luce Irigaray's mimicry is at work here — that is, the playful reproduction of a discourse. The 'plain English' book of the High Court decision undermines the privileged position of the original legal discourse. Although it is a repetition, it is also a displacement. L. Irigaray, 1985, *Speculum of the Other Woman*, Cornell University Press, New York.

84. Since its inception at Australian Federation in 1901, the dominant style of the High Court has been legal formalism. Constitutional decisions have depended much upon the presumed intentions or assumed meanings of Australia's 'founding fathers' who drafted the Constitution. To many who criticise the decision, the *Mabo* Justices have joined the ranks of the disloyal and the unfaithful in deciding in a way outside the likely anticipation of the authors of the Constitution that created the High Court, As Jane Gallop has noted in another context, 'Infidelity is not outside the system . . . but hollows it out, ruins it from within.' J. Gallop, 1982, *The Daughters Seduction: Feminism and Psychoanalysis*, Cornell University Press, New York.

85. The challenge to the High Court in writing in a narrative form would be to forego its authoritative claim to the one 'true' discourse. The legal decision relies on coherence, continuity and consistency. In *Mabo*, the essentialising effect of this upon Murray Island identity is all too obvious. The quasi-narrative of history situates a white Australian in the mindscape/landscape of a Murray Islander.

86. In this sense, the High Courts narrative is grounded in a geography that is not the geography of the Murray Islands. If *Mabo II* were to included Aboriginal and Torres Strait spiritual information, the High Court decision would need to be written in mythic language. Sharp has suggested that the High Court has overlooked the 'depth and richness of Meriam cultural life' because it has not considered the spiritual/religious aspect of land ownership, *supra*, 155.

87. P. Shepard, 1982, contrasting Australian Aboriginal people with white farms, in *Nature and Madness*, Sierra Club Books, San Francisco, 23.

88. Australians have been told repeatedly for several years that the decision in *Mabo* will be/is/was of enormous cultural importance.

Editor's Note: Some referential documents appended by the author are not included here. They are available from the author.

Chapter Twenty-Two

The Mentally Retarded Defendant as Interpretant: Semiosis of Admissions

Donna E. West*

I
Introduction

This inquiry constitutes an attempt to offer rationale from the disciplines of Linguistics, Cognitive Developmental Psychology, and Semiotics to suggest means by which mentally retarded defendants' Fifth and Sixth Amendment rights can be adequately safeguarded. It is easily demonstratable that law enforcement agents, legal counsel, and judges alike possess inadequate rationale and inappropriate case law and statutory standards to fairly adjudicate mentally retarded defendants, not to speak of the jury's related fact-finding sufficiency.[1] A two-pronged analysis is posited to suggest first the likelihood of mentally retarded defendants to lack the requisite intent needed to prove the elements of intent crimes bolstered by their illequipped cognitive-moral reasoning level. The second prong of the analysis focuses on why it is that confessions/admissions of mentally retarded defendants are at greater risk to violate the right against compelled self incrimination and the Fifth and Sixth Amendment right to counsel. Linguistic theoretics, as well as empirical data of actual mentally retarded defendants plea colloquies/confessions support the latter contention. Suggestions as to alternative safeguards to differentiate truth-bearing confessions/admissions from non-truth-bearing statements comprise the concluding remarks.

A discussion of the former prong (proof of the element of intent) is paramount to a thorough investigation of substantive and procedural due process for this population. Given that proof of intent beyond a reasonable doubt is necessary to convict, and given that many serious crimes require proof of intent, lack of capacity to form intent should constitute the defense 'innocent because of mental retardation.'[2] A charge of a lesser included offense (one devoid of the element of intent) might follow. 'Intent' in its legal sense should not be confused with 'motive' — the former refers to purpose or desire to commit the offense and to cause the outcome, namely, the injury which materialized; the latter encompasses reason for commission of the offense, an element of any and every crime. Among the crimes of intent are: murder, arson, sexual abuse offenses, prostitution, larceny, and the like. Such offenses range from class A felonies to class B misdemeanors. In the event that capacity to form intent to wrought the outcome is unlikely or is a factual impossibility, charge and trial for intent crimes should likewise constitute a legal impossibility.

Mentally retarded defendants (not merely those whose degree of intellectual impairment is profound/severe) should be eligible to assert the defense: 'innocent because of mental retardation,' to the end that the charge is dropped and the factual and legal impossibility of formulation of intent is recognized. Mentally retarded defendants are particularly at risk in terms of such factual and legal impossibility by virtue of their relative incapacity to connect means to potential ends or to relate cause to its likely effect(s).[3] The very notion of intent (cognitive/conceptual framework) is founded upon a relationship between two if not three events: 1) the 'feeling-event' of desire to injure; 2) the 'empirical-event' of initiating a change in state of the injured party/property; and 3) the 'result-event' of the injury. The relationship among the three events is not merely that of a simple connective aggregate; its very essence determines a cause and effect alliance. The marriage of the requisite events to constitute intent by its nature necessitates an understanding of means-ends or cause-effect connections. Understanding the character of these particular connections presupposes discernment of the sequential nexus between and among events. Hence, it is not merely comprehension of a positive correlation of two or three events which is required; but, somewhat invariant temporal affinity between certain event types must be fathomed.

II
Semiotic Continuum and the Element of Intent

To possess intent as an element of the crime an offender must have the means to form a cognitive kinship between two indexical events — that of feeling the 'brute force'[4] of volatile emotion, and that of channeling that 'brute force' into destructive conduct — an instance of indexicality.[5] Symbolic representation[6] is likewise vital to conceptualize the cause-effect affiliation.[7] At the time of the commission of the crime the offender is presumed to have determined the likelihood of the result-event from his/her own feeling-event and empirical-event. Commission of murder necessarily entails a symbolic construct, namely, that the result-event (death) by deduction is an immanently likely prospect. The sequentially prior indexical events do not merely point toward the result-event, but contribute to a rule-based paradigm that feelings and injurious conduct of a certain gravity perpetuate intentional killing.

It is not the complex nexus among cognitive events which need be considered to appreciate the wrongfulness of the act or to possess intent, but the semiotic classification of such events. A given defendant must perceive that the feeling-event together with the empirical-event are indicators of the resultant injury event if conduct is uncontrolled. Moreover, any dislinkage in discerning the specific indexical message could result in the necessity to draw upon a still more complex mode of representation — symbolic knowledge.[8] Symbolic representation is dependant upon the cognitive ability to generalize from a set of propositions, as to the character and parameters of actualization of a distinctly different event which typically is not within the cognizor's experience.[9] It consists of the means to assert a rule that an event is likely to actualize were a particular context of event structures to materialize. Symbolic processes do not rest upon experience of contextually defined event structures with which the cognizor has direct experience;[10] rather, the context like the perpetuated event is a deduction grounded perhaps on analogous experiences. By the fact that analogy can contribute to formation of a deduction it is founded upon some iconic reasoning.[11] Nonetheless, a deduction based on non-experience or on abstract constructs devoid of empirical involvement approximate the type of symbolic thinking imperative to intentional criminal acts.

The relationship between and among events of a criminal act (including *mens rea, actus reus*, and consequent event for which the charge has been made) is seemingly more easily discernable if the defendant were to have experienced a similar set of criminal act-event sequence (either by observation of another's perpetration, or by his/her own involvement). Such empirical experience creates little need for abstraction in any subsequent analogous criminal event. The cognizing defendant can recall by means of mental imagery both the sequence and character of each link in the series of contributors to the consequent crime, thus abolishing the need for more abstract symbolic mental processes to determine the likely result. Were a defendant to envision him/her- self performing a prior criminal act with the same person or property, the iconic mode of semiotic representation would be called upon. Were it the case that a defendant recalled prior participation in a crime whose event structure was similar, but the objective person(s) or property was different, semiotic representation is of a distinctly higher cognitive order — that of indexical thought and the still higher form of symbolic reflection. Hence, if a defendant engages for the first time in a particular criminal act an element of which is intent to commit such act, dependance upon symbolic representation appears to be essential.

The semiotic analysis proffered herein has particular import to mentally retarded defendants in that their degree of cognitive capability is, by the very nature of the classification, descriptive of a group whose intellectual functioning is slow or below standard.[12] Their intellectual disorder is not merely distinct from the norm, as in the case of learning disabled persons;[13] it identifies a group which cognizes less abstractly and more slowly such that the deliberateness of each fact connection can obscure relationships across connections. Continuity across fact connections is critical not merely to efficient mental processing, but to making the connections at all. To perceive two distinct cause and effect relationships in the chain of the three event components of an intentional criminal act well reasoned symbolic processing is paramount, unless prior experience permits less elevated mental representation — a more iconic means of determining the outcome. Iconic processing draws upon concrete data, as does indexical processing — memory of actual participation in a like experience represents the grounds for assertions as to possible consequences. Conversely, symbolic processing is derived from a more arbitrary nexus across events: When relevant experience is absent, connections are governed by thought similarities and differences, rather than by a motivated resemblance baring image of an experienced event to a subsequent like event. The latter (iconic, indexical mental operations) is alone based on similarity as opposed to contiguity relations the essence of symbolic reasoning.[14]

According to Ellis and Luckasson, conceptualizing a single cause and effect relationship is an unlikely accomplishment for mentally retarded persons,[15] even for those whose condition is mild (IQ between seventy and fifty).[16] Application of a semiotic analysis could yield some interesting rationale regarding the possible developmental course of simple cause-effect relations as they impinge upon social perspective taking skills foundational to ability to form intent, were they perceivable by the more promising of mentally retarded individuals. Such analysis suggests that direct participation in an identical cause-effect scenario (the most iconic in terms of subsequent determination of which effect might follow in the same context) constitutes the initial level in the developmental sequence toward cause-effect acquisition as applied to increased awareness of the consequences of an intent based criminal act.

The second semiotic level might likewise entail a requirement of some prior personal participation in a similar crime experience; but, such experience need not be identical to the subsequent crime experience in which the element of intent is alleged. It is sufficient that the initial crime experience bear some analogous quality to that which is subsequent; if not, any cause-effect affiliation between even two events is at risk of loss/perceptual failure for mentally retarded defendants. Since direct personal involvement is a more iconic mode of representation which mentally retarded persons are more likely to employ, requirement for more symbolic means of mental imagery in discerning consequences constitutes a prospective cognitive misfire in making abstract connections.

The third semiotic stage requires a dependence on Social Learning Theory — reinforcement of means-end learning through observation of the participation of another in an identical or similar context to the character of the alleged crime. The rationale is that the mentally retarded defendant could be taught or could learn to formulate more complex cause-effect concepts as a consequence of less direct involvement — by means of observation of another's participation, as opposed to mentally retarded persons' own direct participation in a like event. Hence, the essence of determining whether intent is present as an element of the crime charged could be more easily, and more accurately assessed. The mentally retarded defendant might be shown a film in which a similar or identical crime was initiated without presenting the consequent event — without displaying death in the context of murder. In the event that the mentally retarded defendant is able to articulate which result-event is likely to materialize from the precedent actions/feeling manifestations depicted in the film, the presence of intent in the alleged crime at bar exists as a possibility.

The fourth and last stage in ascertaining a developed concept of cause-effect is founded upon symbolic means ('thirdness') for determining the likely outcome of an event which has neither been experienced directly nor observed such that experience is indirect. Abstract forms of mental representation are beyond the reach of even mildly mentally retarded persons' capabilities.[17] Since abstract thought is the very essence of symbolic representation, cognitive reach of this most advanced level necessary to form intent is likewise unascertainable. To exhibit cognitive patterns characteristic of this advanced developmental stage envisaging others (not merely imaging the other participant of an event exchange), as well as one's self as initiator within a compound means-end scenario is imperative.[18] The envisagement must remain independent of prior experience, and must take on an objective perspective.[19] An objective perspective constitutes a liberation from a uni-dimensional ego-based perspective. Ego-based perceptual patterns are confined to a static psycho-social dimension[20] in which iconic means of representation is primary, if not exclusive. Mentally imaging one's self as an initiator only within a cause-effect scenario falls short of the realization of person reciprocity vital to the knowledge that intending injury is undesirable, and is a violation of another and/or of the law.

Selman et. al. have proposed a developmental stage scheme tracing the ontogeny of social perspective-taking.[21] Selman claims that until the perspective of another can be taken/assumed such that other is considered not merely to be a distinct physical entity, but an entity with a unique psychological perspective(s), ascertaining the import of conventional rules (laws) is remote at best.[22] Appreciating how conduct affects another and, in turn, how violation to another might wrought consequences to ego, is exemplary of reasonably mature social perspective-taking skills (typically not present until ten years of age).[23] Until a defendant perpetrator is psychologically and socially able to treat his/her own thoughts/feelings/actions objectively, as a non-involved party (third person perspective) empathic consideration is not possible. Without empathy, reflection on extent of injury to another within the context of intent crimes is hardly likely, not to mention the still more complex notion of consequent sanctions to the self. The complexity consists in the plurality of the cause-effect connections, as well as in the relatively advanced psycho-social maturation crucial to separating self from other.

Psychological differentiation of ego from other points of view is foundational to the eventuality of forming the element of intent. Unless harm is purposeful it can scarcely be intended. Purposeful harm, by its very nature, can materialize only with the conscious realization both that from the point of view of the victim physical/economic/psychological harm is imminent, and that from the point of view of societal legal convention injurious conduct is sanctioned. These two latter realizations rest upon the defendant's capacity not merely to stand in a reciprocal relationship to one other person (the victim, as in Selman's stage two),[24] but to objectify his/her contemplated action to the degree that it is wholly distinct and autonomous from the self and from any participant with the self to constitute meritorious influence immediately prior to the crime. This objectification requires symbolic mental agency; whereas simple reciprocity draws upon more iconic and indexical mental operations. The latter is indicative of shifting of two perspectives only, at any one point in time from ego/initiator of action to receiver. Means to place ego in the perspective of any observer, independent of whether the observer has a participant role, is not a characteristic of indexical operations but of symbolic operations. Pure objectivication (symbolic reasoning) requires more than dependence on experience in role taking exchanges; it entails the more abstract skill of perceiving many potential perspectives and many potential outcomes from those perspectives.[25]

By the fact that crimes of intent are founded upon use of two cause-effect symbolic relationships, together with the fact that mentally retarded population is at risk for failing to ascertain these mental operations, judges need to especially safeguard mentally retarded defendants against unfounded presumptions of normalcy. Even the most precocious children do not attain symbolic operations of the objectification of self until ten years of age or beyond.[26] Few mentally retarded defendants are documented as having an IQ of more than sixty-eight or a mental age of more than seven years.[27] It is well documented that mentally retarded individuals exhibit behavior/linguistic responses not toward any truth purpose, but simply to please an observer/instructor.[28] Rationale for such universal practice has received insufficient recognition in terms of procedural safeguards in criminal adjudication contexts.

Perhaps it is such populations very developmental insufficiency of non-objectification — of failing to take the view point of a non-involved observer — which determines their propensity to attempt to assume for each instance the perspective of a reciprocal partner. The frequent attempt to please the partner falls far short of a semiotically symbol-based thought operation. Reciprocal mental operations, which appear to be inherent to mentally retarded persons' thought patterns throughout adulthood,[29] are responsible for perpetual shifts in the character of a defendants' pattern of responses, whether during plea bargain exchanges, admissions on the stand, or confessions taken in custody. The mentally retarded defendant automatically attempts to discern what the listener (questioner) wishes to hear and complies, thus accounting for the frequent shift in his/her perspective. Reciprocal operations fail to go beyond the immediate context of the two role-takers in the adjudicative exchange; neither do they comport with a solidified, comprehensive and consistent perspective type. Hence, operations founded primarily upon reciprocal rationale are destined to remain indexical: — the other party's point of view virtually always indicates the course of response of mentally retarded defendants.

III
Supreme Court Precedent

The Court in *Penry v. Lynaugh*,[30] implicitly addresses the issue of intent with regard to mentally retarded defendants. At trial in the state of Texas, Penry was convicted of murder and was sentenced to death. Penry had an IQ of between fifty-nine and sixty-four, and a mental age of a six and one half-year-old.[31] Appeal to the Fifth Circuit was sought primarily on the issue of constitutionality of the Texas sentencing scheme. The sentencing body (the jury) was required to respond 'yes' to each of three special issues, the first of which is relevant equally to guilt for a crime of intent, as to sentencing. 'Whether defendant committed the act with deliberateness,' presupposes some degree of intentionality to be distinguished from intention. Intentionality is necessary to forming intent, but is not sufficient. 'Deliberateness' assumes a state of intellectual awareness preexisting the alleged criminal act. It likewise presumes that the preexisting mental state constitutes an awareness of complex cause-effect relationships to victim and to the actor, and that the presumed awareness of potential outcomes to the criminal act are durative, such that knowledge of the consequences continues to exist throughout the 'feeling-event,' the 'empirical-event,' and the 'result-event.' It is well documented that even mildly mentally retarded persons/defendants fail to make the most simple of cause-effect connections.[32] Defendant Penry was at the low end of the subcategory mild mental retardation; and he still was determined by the jury to have been capable of intent.[33]

On appeal the jury's decision (conviction) was affirmed. The explicit issue on appeal is whether 'deliberateness' was overly vague to allow the sentencing body to proceed with unreigned discretion. The issue of whether deliberate conduct is possible for mentally retarded offenders did not seem to engender any notice for the courts; and even the Supreme Court fails to set the precedent that the charge of an intent crime is less appropriate for mentally retarded than for 'normal' defendants. In the majority opinion, Justice O'Connor remands on the grounds that the lack of definition of deliberateness could preclude the jury's consideration of Penry's mitigating factor of diminished mental capacity. 'In the absence of jury instructions defining 'deliberately' in a way that would clearly direct the jury to consider fully Penry's mitigating evidence as it bears on his personal culpability, we cannot be sure that the jury was able to give effect to the mitigating evidence of Penry's mental retardation and history of the abuse in answering the first special issue.'[34]

Mentally retarded defendants are twice disadvantaged as to their presumed capacity to form intent (at the guilt and at the sentencing phase). The disadvantage is attached to degree of culpability, and additionally to the existence of deliberateness at the sentencing phase — the mental state of knowledge/reflection that an act is wrong and to do it anyway. The Supreme Court primarily considered the issue of deliberateness with respect to the Eighth Amendment, and not as a Fifth or Sixth Amendment right. Nonetheless, the fact that the Court has accorded greater protections to mentally ill (psychotic) defendants, as well as to minors, indicates an unwillingness to acknowledge any analogy of mentally retarded defendants' disadvantage(s) to those of other special groups.[35]

To illustrate, the Court has ruled execution of insane defendants and defendants under 16 years of age to be violative of the Constitution's precept against cruel and unusual punishment.[36] That same protection is not extended to mentally retarded defendants. The Court's unwillingness not to perceive a need for like protections for mentally retarded defendants in sentencing contexts is likely to represent a far reaching approach, applying to the guilt phase as well, hence to the issue of intent. A Supreme Court precedent fails to exist on the issue of whether proof of intent for a defendant of diminished mental capacity violates Eighth Amendment strictures. Greater protections in the sentencing phase may indicate a willingness for greater caution/scrutiny at the guilt phase to prove intent. Although standards of proof are not lower in the context of intent crimes in the case of insane and minors, a greater burden may implicitly exist for the prosecution to adequately prove such element. The typical presumption is that while any adult is capable of intent, children's capability is more questionable and increases with age. The fact that a mentally retarded defendant's mental age might be consonant with a child defendant's chronological age is not a comparison which the Court accepts.

> . . . the 'mental age' concept, irrespective of its intuitive appeal, is problematical in several respects. As the AAMR acknowledges, 'the equivalence between non-retarded children and retarded adults is, of course, imprecise.' The 'mental age' concept may underestimate the life experiences of retarded adults, while it may overestimate the ability of retarded adults to use logic and foresight to solve problems.[37]

Justice O'Connor apparently presumes experience to be a factor which separates the two groups, and accords special learning significance to increased experience over time. Mentally retarded persons' inability to connect cause-effect[38] events may never be afforded facility of understanding even with the most careful of intervention strategies.

Quantity of experience does not translate into quality of experience; nor does quantity of experience guarantee diversity of experience types, critical to discerning novel connections across events as related to means-end scenarios. Lower expectations of mentally retarded persons, on the part of care-takers, may account for exposure to fewer experience types,[39] despite greater succession of experience. Moreover, decreased opportunity to interact as a participant within any experience/event likewise contributes to a possible diminished qualitative opportunity for mentally retarded individuals.[40] Justice O'Connor's contention that mental age and chronological age fail to contain sufficient semantic similarity, and that experiential advantage on the part of those whose mental age is equivalent to a child's chronological age constitutes the attribute of characterized distinction is unfounded.

The first Texas special issue (deliberateness) is responsible for but a portion of the procedural disadventagian whose consequence is to assign more severe degrees of culpability for more stringent sanctions. The third special issue which the Court upholds is whether the defendant is likely to engage in future conduct which would be dangerous or pose a threat to society.[41] Most jurors unrelentingly are in accord that mentally retarded persons, as a group, have a predisposition toward future dangerous acts.[42] Mentally retarded defendants' reputation to inherently commit criminal acts, however unfounded, coupled with the fact that rehabilitative services are of minimal benefit to their relatively permanent cognitive state,[43] contribute to jurys' perceptions that such defendants are dangerous to society. The upshot is that mental retardation serves not as a mitigator, but as an aggravater; and the issues of deliberateness and dangerousness overshadow diminished intent. Weak evidentiary status to prove the commission of the crime (the element of intent) becomes insignificant in the face of jury presumptions which have no validity, or which may place blame on the offender where it is better placed on deficiencies in the criminal justice system.

IV
Confessions: A Trap for the 'Unwise'

While federal Constitutional standards fail to exist for mentally retarded defendants regarding the admissability of confessions/admissions, some have been formulated with respect to defendants with other, distinct mental conditions: mentally ill/psychotic offenders.[44] In *Colorado v. Connelly*,[45] the United States Supreme Court held the suppression of a confession of a delusionary defendant to be admissible, despite Colorado's highest court's decision to the contrary.[46] Defendant Connelly claims to have heard God's voice lending an ultimatum — 'to confess to the killing or to commit suicide.'[47] Even the psychologist testified that Connelly was experiencing 'command hallucinations.'[48] The majority (Justice Rehnquist writing for the Court) concluded that without police coercion in the context of custody, confession is voluntary, notwithstanding that defendant's delusionary mental state foreclosed potential exercise of free will.

> We think that the supreme court of Colorado erred in importing into this area of Constitutional law, notions of free will that have no place there. . . . The sole concern of the Fifth Amendment on which Miranda was based is governmental coercion. Indeed, the Fifth Amendment privilege is not concerned with 'moral and psychological pressures to confess emanating from sources other than official coercion.'[49]

Justice Rehnquist more than implies that extrinsic factors only specifically law enforcement or coercion from law enforcement agents, and not intrinsic forces from the defendant him/herself, are legitimate to reach the question of voluntariness. Presumably, the Court accepts police coercion to affect the internal psychological volition of a defendant to elicit a confession, while rejecting the validity of internal psychological factors as a primary source for a claim of involuntariness. Can it be that the Court endorses the use of intrinsic psychologically based threats as a secondary source in the context in which coercion rallies psychological subjugation while de-legitimizing their use as a primary source?

Justice Stevens concurred in part and dissented in part. He comments that defendant's incompetence to stand trial at the outset is inconsonant with the Court's decision that defendant was capable of waiving his right against Fifth Amendment self incrimination.[50] Justice Stevens further comments that the Court's decision to admit the confession stands in opposition to precedent, more specifically, the standard expressed in *Moran v. Burbine*.[51]

> The relinquishment of the right must have been voluntary in the sense that it was the product of a free and deliberate choice. . . . We have learned the lesson of history, ancient and modern, that a system of criminal law enforcement which comes to depend on the confession will, in the long run, be less reliable and more subject to abuses than a system which depends on extrinsic evidence independently secured from skillful investigation. [52] . . . Only if the 'totality of the circumstances surrounding the interrogation' reveals both an uncoerced choice and the requisite level of comprehension, may a court properly conclude that the Miranda rights have been waived.[53]

Free will, and not police coercion only, should unquestionably become the federal standard to determine voluntariness for mentally ill, as well as mentally retarded defendants. Even if the Court determines voluntariness to be the appropriate test for non-disordered populations, it is improper to apply such test to defendants of mentally diminished capacity. The use of extrinsic factors (police coercion) as the measure of voluntariness is illogical since such population has little control over how they affect their own conduct, as well as how others influence their conduct. It is unlikely that delusionary defendants have any awareness of coercion directed toward them by law enforcement agents, while they experience an hallucination-like mental state. In most cases the coercion fails to have any effect, and hence should be disregarded even as a less material factor. Does it not extend the stretch of the obvious to make explicit the proposition that coercion fails to unduly affect an organism incapable of recognizing the awareness of the presence or destructiveness of a police agent while coercion is in progress?

In terms of mentally retarded defendants, the standard of voluntariness is likewise in error, but for distinct reasons. Mentally retarded defendants' lack of comprehension of Miranda (resultant from their predisposition against making cause-effect affiliations intrinsic to glean the significance of

Miranda warnings) should invalidate the coercion standard. But, invalidation/suppression on the grounds of involuntariness is less likely to be the case, if New York State courts are at all exemplary of state trends.

Since *People v. Williams*,[54] a Court of Appeals decision in 1984, the state precedent has created a less strict standard to show voluntariness — that defendant understood the 'immediate' meaning of Miranda warnings. Such standard increases the burden on defendant to counter with evidence of involuntariness. At the evidentiary hearing for confession suppression, prosecution need demonstrate by a preponderance standard, only that during administration of Miranda, defendant was read his/her full rights; presumption of capacity to comprehend removes any burden on prosecution to prove any actual understanding on the part of defendant.[55]

> An effective waiver of Miranda rights may be made by an accused of subnormal intelligence so long as it is established that he or she understood the immediate meaning of the warnings. An inability to comprehend the import of the Miranda warnings in the larger context of criminal law generally does not of itself vitiate the validity of the waiver.[56]

Defendants' lack of understanding of long term effects of Miranda no longer suffices to show involuntariness of confession. Prior to *Williams* any significant failure to comprehend implications of Miranda warnings invalidated the confession on grounds of involuntariness.[57] Since it is failure to comprehend the 'immediate' implications of Miranda rights which has become the standard, far fewer confessions indiscriminately provided by mentally retarded defendants are being or will be suppressed.[58] It is a tall order indeed to prove, if only by preponderance, that awareness of 'immediate' Miranda implications was inaccessible simultaneous to the crime event, especially since the *Williams* court never defines 'immediate;' nor is long term ever rescued from its intrinsically vague semantic captivity.

'Immediate' and longterm distinguish poler extremes of a temporal sequencing continuum for which affinity between two or more often times non-contiguous events is a primary requirement. Hence, comprehension even of 'immediate' implications (those more contiguous both temporally and spatially to administration of Miranda warnings) presupposes facility to causally connect an inherently prior event (Mirandization) to one or more contemplations of the consequences of relinquishment of rights. The fact that the implications/consequences are 'immediate' does not change the fact that the events are causally related, a mental operation requiring skills which mentally retarded defendants lack. Despite such lack, courts still uphold a standard which is unsuitable because of the presumption of mental capacity, as apposed to incapacity. Proof of mental incapacity, on the part of the defense, regarding a specific set of past events is a heavy burden to meet.

Even at the state level, coercion constitutes the more desirable criterion to demonstrate involuntariness in the face of mentally retarded defendants because it is still presumed that Mirandization provides safeguards to the 'wise,' as well as to the 'unwise,' as to the consequences of a confession should one be forthcoming. Those who are 'unwise,' for whom Miranda warnings constitute insufficient protection — a consequence of failure either to understand or to appreciate implications of Miranda rights — demonstrates the inappropriateness of police coercion as the measure. Since mentally retarded defendants are unlikely to have been warned of the consequences of confessing, a measure short of police coercion represents a more fair standard on the part of the courts. Inability to connect means-end relations across events (connecting refrain from silence to the recording of the confession, and then to the use of such statement against defendant at trial) should, in the context of mentally retarded defendants, preclude the police coercion standard, and warrant its substitution with a less narrow measure. Less psychologically oppressive contexts may 'coerce' mentally retarded defendants to the same degree as police coercion affects non-mentally retarded defendants.

Furthermore, immature perspective-taking skills which translate into an inability to take an observer's point of view to discern whether silence or verbal explanation is preferable in the context of in custody questioning requires some objectification. Simple means of reciprocal perspective-taking falls short of the skills needed to make a free and deliberate/intelligent choice whether to respond to police questioning. If the law enforcement agent's point of view is alone considered, the very fact that questioning is underway might determine, for mentally retarded defendants, that the reciprocal wish is that the defendant respond, and the response is forthcoming. Hence, anything short of a third person observer perspective exemplary of a semiotically symbol-based mental procedure, decision whether to speak or request counsel constitutes poorly formed contemplation, and should not be determinative on the issue of Miranda waiver.

More intrinsically-based criteria such as whether police questioned defendant at all, might provide a more fair approach. The rationale is that in custody questioning without administration of Miranda, itself is sufficient to suppress a confession. Failure to comprehend the implications of Miranda is tantamount to failure of police to articulate such rights, especially in light of the strength of Miranda not to exist as a prophylactic, mechanistic standard of mere platitude-based procedural compliance. The suggestion is not that a subjective standard be employed specific to the individual retarded defendant, rather, that objective criteria be developed commensurate with the cognitive skills of the population. [59]

V

Plea Bargain: An Escape for the Judiciary

Certain distinctions (linguistic, psycho-social, legal) exist to establish the attractiveness of plea bargaining as a tool to dispose of cases involving mentally retarded defendants.[60] Defendants experience far greater relinquishment of legal rights as pleaders than is the case were their case to be tried. Relinquished Sixth Amendment rights are: right to confront witnesses against them (cross examination);[61] right to assist counsel on their own behalf;[62] not to mention the right to have counsel defend their non-guilt.[63] Additional rights relinquished as a consequence of entering a plea include: right to present one's case before a jury of one's peers; and the Fifth Amendment right against self incrimination[64] (since plea bargaining necessitates an admission of guilt to a lesser included offense). It is evident that many far-reaching unfavorable consequences materialize were a defendant to 'opt' to plead. Pressures to plead are intense for any defendant; how much more confounding to mentally retarded defendants are attempts to convince them to relinquish rights which are less likely to be understood?[65]

Perseveration at the reciprocal level of perspective-taking increases still more the likelihood of compliance with the plea inducer's prodding. Were mentally retarded defendants capable of stepping outside of the experience exchange such that the inducer's perspective is interpreted to be one of several equally legitimate formulations, strength of the inducement would decline to leave the pleader free to make an informed decision. It appears as though high incidence of plea bargaining[66] to resolve cases for mentally retarded defendants can be attributed to an absence of advanced semiotic representation (use of symbolic operations). The cognitive bondage to assume but a single other's point of view cripples any opportunity to voluntarily or intelligently consider the best means of proceeding to result in the best outcome for mentally retarded defendants' reputation. The symbolic mode of semiotic operation affords more than mere reflection of static consequences from defendant's own idiosyncratic isolated rendition; it includes the perspective of many other societal validative perspectives.

The standard for entering a valid plea supersedes that necessary for a valid (admissible) confession, which, at first glance, indicates that a pleading defendant is more protected against due process violation than is a defendant who is tried. In *Henderson v. Morgan*,[67] Justice White concurs in the judgement:

> The Constitutional rule relevant to this case is that the defendant's guilt is not deemed established by entry of a guilty plea unless he either admits that he committed the crime charged, or enters his plea knowing the elements of the crime charged.[68] . . . Out of consideration for those accused of crime, courts are careful that a plea of guilty shall not be accepted unless made voluntarily after proper advice and with full understanding of the consequences.[69]

Nonetheless, the fact that pleas are interpreted judicially to be inviolate/permanent such that pleas are seldom invalidated interferes with the aforementioned advantage of close scrutiny for plea acceptance. In *Henderson*, Justice White expresses the Court's rule regarding appeal to invalidate a plea: 'The Court has repeatedly emphasized that a guilty plea for federal purposes is a judicial admission of guilt conclusively establishing a defendant's factual guilt.'[70]

After a more than cursory analysis of the relative merit of the two dispositional approaches (pleading, submitting to trial) the conclusion is that the latter represents a more fair adjudicative procedure. At very least, a non-pleading defendant is afforded opportunity to confront witnesses against him/her at an evidentiary hearing; the same opportunity is absent to a defendant who pleads. Consequently, protections for pleaders fail to provide greater safeguards called for when risk of deprivation is increased. Undoubtedly, deprivation of primary Constitutional Fifth, Sixth, and Fourteenth Amendment rights is present where mentally retarded pleaders have no means to consider potential consequences,[71] independent of blind acceptance of the prosecutor's influence. Without access to symbolic semiotic mental operations to liberate the pleader from static contemplation (non-objective perspective-taking), pleading constitutes not a knowing abandonment/forfeiture of primary rights, but larceny of such rights by the courts.

For prosecutors, plea bargaining is an attractive alternative to trial when there is any question as to defendant's intellectual categorization. Competency to stand trial,[72] competency to take the stand, as well as difficulties proving the intent element of the crime,[73] are factors which account for the greater proportion of plea bargains with mentally retarded defendants. Like-cases which do go to trial face distinct controversies. More often than not, defense attorneys convince mentally retarded defendants to waive their right to a jury. Apparently, the suspicion is that juries, as apposed to judges, characteristically evaluate the conduct of mentally retarded defendants more harshly. Rationale for this unfortunate practice lies in juries' presumed lack of education and experience with members of the retarded population, and stereotypes of future dangerousness which reek of the unfounded belief that mental diminished capacity is somehow positively correlated with criminal activity.[74]

Judges' lack of knowledge and sensitivity to linguistically-based difficulties particular to mentally retarded defendants compounds any disadvantage for which juries are responsible.[75] The fact that plea bargains more frequently dispose of mentally retarded defendants' cases obscures any realistic account of whether the questions posed to such defendants are less often understood. Written records of plea colloquies are typically accessible only at the local level; and expense copying transcripts is costly. More important, the very nature of the verbal exchange within plea bargain scenarios defines the disadvantage. Plea bargain interactions are predisposed by their very character — powerful to powerless dialogues — to consist of an exceedingly high proportion of binary questions and consequent binary 'yes,' 'no' responses. Several factors contribute to mentally retarded defendants' vulnerability for linguistic misinterpretation or non-interpretation of questions posed by judges: non-symbolic perspective-taking skills; use of overly complex terms whose semantic components exceed the grade level of defendant's mental age; use of syntactic structures which are more advanced than what defendant's mental age allows; an overuse of distinct question types which preclude revelation of incomprehension; defense counsel's inability to explain (linguistically) the elements of the crime; and/or defense counsel's lack of recognition of retardation as an attribute of the defendant.[76]

All of the aforementioned disadvantaging factors, other than the question-type factor, require extensive efforts to remediate. Interdisciplinary teams of experts, consisting of: special educators, clinical and experimental psychologists, applied linguists, and the like, need to set standards to evaluate the linguistic and cognitive skills which can be expected of mentally retarded persons of distinct mental ages. The single disadvantaging factor which is easily changeable is the increased degree of binary questions directed to such defendants typically by judges.[77] To generate a far greater proportion of substantive questions ('wh' questions) constitutes a simple but effective remedy. Asking 'what happened at x time,' or 'why the lesser included offense has been admitted,' represent better means to elicit something other than a 'yes,' 'no' response.

> In *Monroe v. United States*,[78] the Fifth Circuit Court of Appeals[79] recognized the limitations of posing such binary question types, when it vacated and remanded the trial judge's acceptance of the plea. While a trial court need not follow any particular ritual, a routine boiler-plate question to the defendant as to whether he understands the charges is not sufficient; and a single response by the defendant that he understands the charge gives no assurance or basis that he does. . . . The affirmative responses of defendant and his counsel to the court's inquiries, whether defendant understood the charge, are not a substitute for knowledge. . . . Matters of reality and not mere ritual should be controlling.[80]

'Yes/no' responses hardly reveal comprehension of the binary question. They signify only an acknowledgement that some interrogative[81] was directed toward the addressee, and perhaps that such addressee feels compelled to make some response in view of the authority figure of the questioner.

Some data, however sparse, were taken from plea colloquies [82] to illustrate the following two hypotheses:

> I) That a significantly greater proportion of questions addressed to mentally retarded defendants are binary in nature, as compared to questions to non-mentally retarded defendants.
>
> II) That mentally retarded defendants' responses to binary questions more often consist of affirmative 'yes' responses, relative to non-retarded peers.

The sample consists of plea colloquies from four mentally retarded and four non-mentally retarded defendants, all of whom had originally been charged with intent crimes (larceny, murder, rape).[83] Chronological age for all defendants is within an eight year range — between twenty-one and twenty-nine — to ensure that age was not a confounding factor. A coding scheme was developed to chart the type of question posed by the judge and the type of response made by the defendant. Question types include the categories of binary and substantive; response types consist of: affirmative ('yes') answers, negative ('no') answers, and substantive answers. The absolute and relative frequencies represent mean frequencies averaged over each sample. Means were charted to simplify the data; not to force outcomes. Since range of frequencies were not wide, mean scores should not under or over-represent performance.

Findings regarding Hypothesis I reveal an insignificant[84] difference, if any, in type of question (binary, substantive) to mentally retarded as to non-mentally retarded defendants: relative frequency for retarded, .88, and for non-retarded, .85. Absolute frequencies of binary and substantive questions are: 8 + 1 for retarded; 7 + 1 for non-retarded, respectively. Whereas for the mentally retarded Group, frequencies of affirmative answers to binary questions are 7 (absolute) and .84 (relative); for the 'normal' group they are 4 and .69. Such findings manifest some meaningful difference in how the two groups answered binary questions. Frequencies of negative responses to binary questions are found to be less than an absolute frequency of 1 for both groups; but, a difference in relative frequencies is observable, .03 (retarded) and .13 (non-retarded): .09 and .13 represent proportions of substantive answers to binary questions for retarded and non-retarded, respectively (revealing no meaningful difference between the groups). For both groups frequency of substantive responses to substantive questions is 1.

To interpret some of the more notable findings: no meaningful difference exists in the question type directed to the retarded and non-retarded defendants, revealing that Hypothesis I is unsubstantiated. Although some difference exists in the absolute frequencies between the groups, relative frequencies show that the difference is slight. Hypothesis II, however, is substantiated, in that the mentally retarded group answered the binary questions with a notably greater proportion of affirmative responses, as compared to their peers.

VI
Conclusion

The underlying premise is that semiotic analysis of the function (not merely the form) of the linguistic sign can bear fruitful information regarding particular meanings which mentally retarded defendants' assign to their adjudicative-based utterances, to the end that the utterances may fail to constitute the admissions/confessions deemed to be so at superficial glance. The linguistic sign which mentally retarded defendants use as signifier is identical in form to convention; but, the signified may not match that used by convention. Whether with respect to admissions or responses to judges' binary questioning within plea colloquies, or whether regarding issuance of in custody confessions, mentally retarded defendants seem to assign a distinct meaning to their utterances even though utterance form (phonemic, morphemic representation) is by observation the same as that of non-retarded defendants.

If the logic employed in making the utterance is to please the reciprocal partner or the police agent to the exclusion of objectifying, the meaning of the linguistic string may be unreliable. A response of 'yes' to all and any inquiry represents the simplest means to take the perspective of the reciprocal questioner; and any such response on the part of mentally retarded defendants should be suspect in terms of its conventional interpretation of truth value. 'Yes' might evoke a distinct meaning for the mentally retarded interpretant-defendant than for the judge-interpretant or for a non-retarded defendant-interpretant.[85] For the former a 'yes' response may serve as an index — a precedent cause whose purpose is merely to draw attention away from their inability to process the respective question, and hence affects the consequence of satisfaction whereby judge proceeds to another matter. The judge-interpretant typically construes the 'yes' response conventionally, as attaching to the truth or falsity of his/her own assertion/question. Presence of more than a single interpretation, together with the fact that each interpretant lacks awareness of the other interpretant's presumption, account for linguistic misinterpretations on the part of the criminal justice system, resulting in far reaching deprivation for mentally retarded defendants.

Judges and prosecutors should refrain altogether from use of binary questions, and should take special notice of distinct meanings which mentally retarded defendants attach to linguistic forms, especially if the form is as devoid of specific semantic content as is the 'yes' response. 'Yes' only derives its specific meaning from an individual use. Apart from such use 'yes,' in its invariant sense, is assigned little semantic content. Nevertheless, in its use from context to context meaning changes as referents shift. For example, a response of 'yes' to one interrogative might convey willingness or affirmation of the truth value of the preceding assertion; whereas, in another context 'yes' could falsify the prior assertion. An affirmative answer to: 'you did commit murder, didn't you?' is likely to verify the truth value of the question; but the same response form to a different tag is indicative of non-affirmation. A 'yes' response to: 'you didn't commit the crime charged, did you?' if interpreted conventionally, rejects the proposition rather than affirming it.

The point is that many interpretations can be attached to the affirmative response due to its dependance on context for specific meaning; therefore, conventional interpretation should not automatically be assumed, especially when cognitive deficits can contribute to unconventional linguistic use obscured by isomorphism of form. Judges participating in plea colloquies, as well as police recording confession data need to posit substantive questions, or to request a paraphrase of Miranda in defendant's own words.

An additional procedural safeguard, effective in contexts of police custody and in the court room, is the requirement that a legal guardian be assigned when there exists any question that defendant is mentally retarded. Such guardian should be familiar with consonant legal proceedings, that defendant might be apprised while in police custody or before the judge of how to best understand incoming information, and how best to respond. Police agents should be foreclosed from taking any statement from a suspect/defendant who is even borderline mentally retarded; and a reliable system should be in place to make such determinations. Similarly, judges should consider admissability of the truth value of confessions as a matter of law to protect against gross miscarriages of justice from misperceptions founded upon stereotypes, all too frequently presumed on the part of the fact-finder.

Perhaps such suggestions appear to be simplistic/overly intuitive; they nonetheless represent practical, easily implementable modifications, given economic and educational restrictions prevalent within the criminal justice system. The aforementioned protections are vital to the provision of due process under the Fourteenth Amendment, since without them a significant portion of defendants[86] will remain stripped of basic fairness, as in the opportunity to make an informed decision whether to proceed to trial, and means to weigh the consequences of providing a confession. Mentally retarded defendants have not the cognitive hardware and software to

DECIDE these most essential issues; let us not condone 'decision' by default.

**Donna E. West is conducting advanced research at Cortland, New York.*

ENDNOTES

1. 'Ninety percent of the police officers, lawyers, and judges in New York State had no training regarding mental retardation,' according to a 1979 survey conducted by Jeffrey Schilit. Jeffrey Schilit, 'The Mentally Retarded Offender and Criminal Justice Personnel,' *Exceptional Children*, September 1979, 16. See also, James McAfee & Michele Gural, 'Individuals with Mental Retardation and the Criminal Justice System: The View From States' Attorneys General,' 26 *Mental Retardation*, February 1988, 5.

2. Mental retardation may provide a defense only if it precludes the finding of the requisite *mens rea*, but standing alone will not constitute an excuse (affirmative defense) even though it may be accorded mitigating weight at sentencing. Accordingly, in most jurisdictions, it appears that mental retardation is a far less effective basis for a defense than is mental illness. Hermann, Singer, & Roberts, 1988, 'The Mentally Retarded in the Criminal Justice System Symposium: Sentencing of the Mentally Retarded Criminal Defendant,' 41 *Ark. L. Rev.* 765.

3. James Ellis & Ruth Luckasson, 1985, 'Mentally Retarded Criminal Defendants,' 53 *Geo. Wash. L. Rev.*, 414, 439.

4. Charles Sanders Peirce, referred to as the father of American semiotics, used 'brute force' somewhat differently. His construct as applied to indexical signs or 'secondness,' materializes only in the context of simultaneous experience as part of an event. Such 'secondness' is so because it is existential, and hence derivable from another entity. David Pharies, 1985, *Charles S. Peirce and the Linguistic Sign II*, John Benjamins Pub. Co. Peirce's 'brute force' applies to facts only, not to emotion which is an exemplar of 'firstness.' 'Firstness' comes into existence out of nothing. *Id.*, at 10. An entity which is existant from nothing, or which is so independent of other stimuli, appears to me to constitute a more appropriate exemplar of 'brute force' than does the indexical, existential sign. I determine that emotion/'feeling-event' is aptly characterized as 'brute force' because it springs from a sense of surprise or from vulnerability of lack of control.

5. This destructive-like behavior is, by Peirce's scheme, characteristic of indexical representation by virtue of its dependence on empirical access or direct experience to the perceiver, which characterizes indexical signs as propositions of 'secondness.' 'The mode of being of secondness is thus actuality: brute facts are not mere possibilities, they *Exist*,' *Id.*, at 11.

6. This form of representation is founded upon well formed logic considered by Peirce to constitute 'thirdness.' Peirce asserts that 'thirdness' is the highest mode of representation, since it is characterized by general laws or rule based axioms. *Id.*, at 12. 'Thirdness' is distinct from 'secondness' in that experience is not its defining attribute. 'Thirdness' and its distinct manifestation of symbolic representation are likewise indivisible from 'firstness;' while the very essence of 'firstness' is its unpredictable nature, 'thirdness' could not be characterized as 'thirdness' apart from its predictable law governed abstract quality, Id.

7. In fact, without symbolic representation most cause-effect relationships are undiscernible. 'Its (thirdness) being consist in active power to establish connections between different objects,' *Id.*

8. Mentally retarded defendants mental operations do not consist of the high form of representation necessary to think symbolically. Since the mental operations necessary to perceive cause-effect relationships are lacking to mentally retarded defendants (according to Ellis & Luckasson, *supra* note 3, at 439), and since ability to make such cause-effect connections is foundational to symbolic representation (Peirce's 'thirdness,' *supra* note 4, at 12), it remains more than a likelihood that mentally retarded defendants are incapable of higher symbolic processes.

9. David Pharies, *supra* note 4, at 17.

10. *Id.*, at 11.

11. Iconic representation is so by the fact that it draws upon likeness to be characterized such. Since analogy, by its essence, is constructed upon some similarity or likeness between entities, it necessarily lends itself to iconic modes of representation, although not exclusively. Symbolic modes of representation can equally give rise to analogy: Their quality as rule based mental generalizations fail unless classification, a categorization founded upon like characteristics among distinct entities, is operational. *Id.*, at 12.

12. '. . . Retarded and non-retarded individuals differ in the speed with which they can carry out the different mental operations,' Penelope Brooks & Charley McCauley, 1984, 'Cognitive Research in Mental Retardation,' 88 *American Journal of Mental Deficiency*, at 480.

13. Learning disabled persons do not process information more slowly than do non-learning disabled individuals, but, portions of the data may not be processed at all, or may be mis-processed. It is not the case that this population characteristically experiences disfunctions connecting events in which they have not participated. Processing difficulties of a significant proportion of learning disabled students entail cognitive attention or linguistically-based deficits, not a general delay in processing.

14. 'Every mind which reasons must have ideas which not only follow after others but are caused by them; and every mind which is capable of logical criticism (not ascertainable without symbolic 'thirdness' reasoning operations) of its inferences

must be aware of this influence of one idea upon another,' *Writings of Charles S. Peirce: A Chronological Addition Volume III*, 102, Indiana University Press, 1986.

15. James Ellis & Ruth Luckasson, *supra* note 3, at 430.

16. *Id.*, at 423.

17. *Id.*, at 441.

18. '. . . To become conscious of one's own view point involves distinguishing it from other view points, and by the same token, co-ordinating it (ego's view point) with them (other view points),' Jean Piaget & Barbel Inhelder, 1967, *The Child's Conception of Space 209*, W. W. Norton & Co.

19. 'The third-person perspective permits more than the taking of another's perspective on the self; the truly third-person perspective on relations which is characteristic of level three (between ten and fifteen years of age) *simultaneously* includes and coordinates the perspectives of self and other(s), and thus the system or situation and all the parties are seen from the third person or generalized other perspective,' Robert Selman, 1980, *The Growth of Interpersonal Understanding* 39, Academic Press.

20. '. . . The child's outlook is at first completely egocentric and tends to change appearances which are in fact purely relative to his own perception and activity, into false or spurious absolutes,' Jean Piaget & Barbel Inhelder, *supra* note 18, at 210. See also, Robert Selman & William Damon, 1975, 'The Necessity (But Insufficiency) of Social Perspective Taking for Conceptions of Justice at Three Early Levels,' *Moral Development: Current Theory and Research* 64, John Wiley & Sons.

21. Robert Selman, *supra* note 19. Selman's theoretical perspective is derived from the long-standing work of psychologists Jean Piaget and Lawrence Kohlberg. Each of the two theorists has proposed a developmental sequence of stages (the former, cognitive; and the latter, moral) upon which current experts legitimately rely. Both Piaget and Kohlberg take a modified experimental, but naturalistic approach of data collection to test and support hypotheses. Although Selman initially collaborated with Kohlberg, he later refined his theory as a result of independent investigations. Selman offers rationale distinct from that of Piaget and Kohlberg, in that focus is to characterize the course of social development as an outgrowth of moral reasoning during childhood and adolescence, as opposed to a simplistic characterization of moral development which presumes no connection to social reasoning.

22. *Id.*, at 40.

23. Robert Selman & William Damon, 1975, 'The Necessity (But Insufficiency) of Social Perspective Taking for Conceptions of Justice at Three Early Levels,' *Moral Development: Current Theory and Research* 70-71, John Wiley & Sons.

24. A child is approximately ten years of age at this juncture, *Id.*, at 70.

25. '. . . Thought is rational only in so far as it recommends itself to a possible future thought. Or in other words, the rationality of thought lies in its reference to a possible future,' *Writings of Charles S. Peirce*, *supra* note 14, at 108.

26. Robert Selman & William Damon, *supra* note 23, at 71.

27. 'Approximately three percent of Americans have IQs below seventy and accordingly are deemed retarded, but eighty-nine percent of all mentally retarded persons are within the mild category (IQ between fifty-two and sixty-nine),' Zigler, Balla, & Hodapp, 1984, 'On the Definition and Classification of Mental Retardation,' 89 *Am. J. Mental Deficiency* 215, 227.

28. James Ellis & Ruth Luckasson, *supra* note 3, at 446.

29. Persons whose mental operations stagnate at reciprocal points of view 'are still tied to real or concrete experiences in the ability to reason logically,' John Dougherty & James Moran, 1983, 'The Relationship of Piagetian Stages to Mental Retardation,' 18 *Education and Training of the Mentally Retarded*, 260, 262.

30. *Penry v. Lynaugh,* 492 U.S. 302 (1989).

31. *Id.*, at 303.

32. According to Ellis and Luckasson, *supra* note 3, at 429, 439, mentally retarded persons experience deficits controlling impulses. Such deficit accounts for limitations in cause-effect concept formation in that: 'The ability to control impulsive behavior is related to the ability to understand both the nature of behavior and the social circumstances that make an action appropriate or inappropriate to a particular occasion. . . . The mentally retarded person might accompany perpetrators or actually commit a crime on impulse without weighing the consequences of the act.'

33. *Penry,* 492 U.S. at 308.

34. *Id.*, at 323.

35. *Ford v. Wainwright,* 477 U.S. 399, 1986 and *Thompson v. Oklahoma,* 487 U.S. 815, 1988.

36. *Ford v. Wainright*, 477 U.S. 399, 1986 and *Thompson v. Oklahoma*, 487 U.S. 815, 1988, respectively.

37. *Penry*, 492 U.S. at 339.

38. James Ellis & Ruth Luckasson, *supra* note 3, at 439.

39. 'The very nature of the cognitive deficits inherent in the classification of a person as mentally retarded means that most individuals with mental retardation will know less than most people without mental retardation. This knowledge deficit is often aggravated by the special education curriculum for the mentally retarded children,

which is less informative than the regular curriculum. Special education students will often be excluded from certain classes and activities that teach general knowledge about the world, in order to focus more time and attention on learning basic skills or participating in vocational training. For example, while other students are learning the concepts and vocabulary of civics and social studies, students with mental retardation may instead receive extended instruction in reading or engine assembly. Although special curricula are necessary for most mentally retarded students, their exclusion form certain courses is not without cost,' James Ellis & Ruth Luckasson, *supra* note 3, at 431.

40. This same exclusion from participation in exchanges is not particular to mentally retarded persons; but, is generalizable to other disabled populations. Diminished opportunity for participant role-taking can present disadvantaging consequences in language development, concept formation, and social perspective-taking, Elizabeth Bates, 1976, *Language and Context The Acquisition of Pragmatics*, 342, Academic Press. Non-disabled children and disabled children and adults are frequently not addressed even when they are present during the inquiry and when they constitute the topic/focus of such inquiry. Cathy Urwin, 1979, 'Preverbal Communication and Early Language Development in Blind Children,' *17 Papers and Reports on Child Language Development*, 119, 125. Mentally retarded individuals, as a particular disability subgroup, are at greatest risk regarding prolonged exclusion from participant exchanges: lack of maturation readiness (cognitively, linguisticly, and socially) makes it less likely that others might draw them into conversational or behavioral interaction.

41. *Penry*, 492 U.S. at 310.

42. James Ellis & Ruth Luckasson, *supra* note 3, at 417.

43. 'Mental retardation is not a disease, but a permanent deficiency state which is not properly classified as mental illness and not responsive to psychotherapy or other psychiatric therapies including drug interventions,' Hermann, Singer, & Roberts, *supra* note 2, at 765.

44. Although an explicit standard regarding voluntariness of mentally retarded defendants' confessions has not been proffered, it is likely that the courts will apply to such group the standard set forth in Connelly infra note, at . Courts have often employed the identical legal test for responsibility and disposition to the entire broad category of mentally deficient defendants, including those who are mentally retarded, as well as those who are mentally ill (insane). Judicial economy, and the precepts of equal protection are reasons for applying the same standard to both the mentally ill and mentally retarded defendants, *Id.*, at 765.

45. *Colorado v. Connelly*, 479 U.S. 157, 1986.

46. *Id.*, at 158.

47. *Id.*

48. *Id.*

49. *Id.*, at 170.

50. *Id.*, at 172.

51. *Moran v. Burbine*, 475 U.S. 412, 421, 1986.

52. The introduction of a confession makes the other aspects of the trial superfluous, and the real trial, for all practical purposes, occurs when the confession is obtained. E. Cleary, 1972, *McCormick on Evidence*, 316, 2nd ed.

53. *Moran*, 475 U.S. at 421.

54. *People v. Williams*, 476 N.Y.S.2D 788, (Ct. App. 1984).

55. The fact of past arrests is a primary determinant for the New York trial courts that defendant understood the 'immediate' warnings of Miranda, *People v. Matthews,* 148 A.D.2d 272, 275, 544 N.Y.S.2d 398 (Sup. Ct. N.Y., 1989); *People v. Lippert,* 525 N.Y.S.2d 390; *People v. Munoz,* 521 N.Y.S.2d 299; *People v. Gates,* 475 N.Y.S.2d 158.

56. *Id.*

57. *People v. Bruce,* 403 N.Y.S.2d 587 (Sup. Ct., N.Y. 1978); *People v. Randolph,* 294 N.Y.S.2d 933 (Genesse Cty. Ct., 1968); *People v. Lux,* 289 N.Y.S.2d 66 (Suffolk Cty. Ct., 1967).

58. *People v. Sanchez,* 486 N.Y.S.2d 76 (Sup. Ct. N.Y., 1985); *People v. Avilez,* 503 N.Y.S.2d 102 (Sup. Ct. N.Y., 1986); *People v. Matthews,* 544 N.Y.S.2d 398 (Sup. Ct. N.Y., 1989); and *People v. Mitchell,* No. 86-713-1 (Onondaga Cty., 1987). In the three former cases confessions were held to be voluntary; whereas, in the latter only, confession was suppressed.

59. This approach to treat such disabled population differently is founded upon due process rationale; whereas, 'equal' treatment for disabled and non-disabled alike is an outgrowth of an equal protection argument.

60. The approach is typically the reverse with regard to victims who are mentally retarded -- if they are marginally competent to take the stand prosecutors are likely to prefer them to testify. Their very presence on the stand, together with their distinct, subnormal linguistic and paralinguistic patterns while testifying, creates an ambiance which evokes an almost involuntary sense of emotional alliance, on the part of the fact-finder, with victim's condition, and against the perpetrator who caused victim's injury.

61. *McCarthy v. United States,* 394 U.S. 459, 1969.

62. *Drope v. Missouri,* 420 U.S. 162, 1975.

63. *Escobedo v. Illinois*, 378 U.S. 478, 1964.

64. *Miranda v. Arizona,* 384 U.S. 436, 1966.

65. 'It is fundamental to an adversary system of justice that an individual whose mental condition is such that he lacks the capacity to understand the nature and object of the proceedings against him, to consult with counsel, and to assist in preparing his defense may not be subjected to a trial,' *United States v. Masthers,* 539 F.2D 721, 724, 1976.

66. James Ellis & Ruth Luckasson, *supra* note 3, at 460.

67. *Henderson v. Morgan,* 426 U.S. 637, 641, 1976. This defendant's IQ is documented to be between sixty-eight and seventy-two, which falls approximately two standard deviations from the norm of one hundred. Given that courts, psychologists, and special educators have determined an IQ below seventy to constitute the upper limit of mental retardation, this defendant's categorization is questionable because of the overlapping age range. Defendant Henderson pled guilty to a charge of second degree murder; it was accepted, and defendant appealed. Permission to appeal was denied by New York's Court of Appeals, and certiorari was granted. The United States Supreme Court invalidated the plea.

68. *Id.*, at 650.

69. *Id.*, at 653.

70. *Id.*, at 647.

71. *Henderson v. Morgan,* 426 U.S. 637, 1976; *Johnson v. Zerbst,* 304 U.S. 458; *United States v. Masthers*, 539 F.2D 721, 724, 1976.

72. James Ellis & Ruth Luckasson, *supra* note 3, at 452.

73. Hermann, Singer, & Roberts, *supra* note 2, at 776.

74. The latter is likely to occur as a direct consequence of the former.

75. Salvador Uy, 1990, 'From the ashes of *Penry v. Lynaugh* The Diminished Intent Approach to the Trial and Sentencing of the Mentally Retarded Offender,' 21 *Colum. Hum. Rts. L. Rev.* 565, 592.

76. All too frequently defense counsel confounds mental retardation with unenriched language patterns of economically and socially disadvantaged youth. Further lack of discernment of retardation results from the presence of race related sub-cultural linguistic differences, in which distinct labels (signifiers) are used to refer to the object in question (signified). It requires a well informed psycholinguist to determine which speech patterns are suspect, and afterward, which are attributed to which unconventional environmental influence.

77. 'Judge Bazelon, writing for the court (in *Masthers,* 539 F.2D 721), noted that the defendant's answers in the colloquy almost never went beyond a simple affirmation ('yes' responses),' James Ellis and Ruth Luckasson, *supra* note 3, at 462.

78. *Monroe v. United States,* 463 F.2d 1032, 1972. Defendant Monroe's IQ is documented to be seventy-six, and his mental age was twelve years. Monroe's intellectual level is beyond that of most adjudicated mentally retarded persons, according to Ellis and Luckasson. In fact, defendant is likely to be considered borderline mentally retarded, as apposed to mildly mentally retarded, and hence his language patterns may not be representative of those of mentally retarded defendants — they may overstate the 'true' linguistic disadvantage. Monroe originally pleaded not guilty to second degree murder; but, when a jury was impanelled he withdrew the not guilty and substituted a guilty plea. Since the court concluded that evidence of intent existed (defendant dug up his knife from its burial place, and previous animosity between defendant and victim) the plea was accepted.

79. The issue of whether binary questions can ever suffice to demonstrate that any defendant understands the crime charged has not yet reached the Supreme Court. Since understanding of the charge is required to show plea validity, the tool to measure the understanding should be valid.

80. *Monroe*, 463 F.2D at 1034.

81. This term is used in its linguistic sense to refer to question-based sentences, as apposed to declaratory sentences. The legal sense (type of discovery technique) is not intended.

82. Transcripts which comprise data from the mentally retarded sample are taken from the following cases: *Henderson v. Morgan,* 426 U.S. 637, 1976; *Monroe v. United States,* 463 F2d 1032, 1972; *People v. Zampi,* No. I-92-380-1 (Onondaga Cty. Ct., N.Y. 1993); *People v. Kelley,* (Onodaga Cty. Ct., N.Y. 1991). Transcripts from which data were taken to represent the control group were derived form the following cases: *North Carolina v. Alford,* 91 S.CT. 160, 1970; *Nash v. LaFollette,* 707 F.2D 298, 1983; *Alessi v. United States* , 593 F.2D 476, 1979; *R.C. Marshall v. Lonberger,* 103 S.Ct. 843, 1983.

83. Caution must be taken not to generalize findings to either of the populations. Small sample size, together with relatively few questions contained within each colloquy, can be misleading — numerical representations (especially absolute frequencies) can make the appearance of the occurrence of an event which must be considered relative to other event types.

84. 'Significance' is not used in its statistical sense since total frequencies are low.

85. An interpretant is a sign which makes 'explicit reference to the person whom the sign is addressing, i.e., the interpreter of the sign. The sign addresses somebody, that is, creates in the mind of that person an equivalent sign,' David Pharies, *supra* note 4, at 18.

86. Whereas three percent of the general population is documented as being mentally retarded, approximately ten percent of the prison population is characterized such, Hermann, Singer, & Roberts, *supra* note 2, at 766.

Chapter Twenty-Three

Seeing Rhetoric as Law as Literature

Willem J. Witteveen*

I
Confrontation

A man named K. — his case is no doubt familiar to you — is one day arrested without being informed of the crime he has supposedly committed. Throughout the story he tries to justify himself against these unknown charges and in doing so encounters a number of people that may or may not be involved in the proceedings against him. He is never subjected to real trial proceedings and confronts the words and deeds of unofficial and official representatives of the law in a futile struggle that takes place in an atmosphere of absurdity and strangeness. The legal proceedings are never completed, K. is not judged in a public trial and in a recognisably legal manner; and yet he ends being executed. This is, of course, a summary of Kafka's *The Trial*, designed to bring out that for K. there is only the law in action and that the law in the books, which could provide meaning to all that transpires, is closed to him. K. remains outside of the law in the sense of the system of ideals and norms and instead is perpetually 'before the law' (*Vor dem Gesetz*).[1]

For a lawyer reading this novel, one of these confrontations with the law in action is especially significant. K. finds a lawyer to represent him in court. But the man who is supposed to help him confront the law, who is himself an insider to the world of law, in fact only confirms and deepens the powerlessness and injustice that K. experiences. The lawyer does not offer effective legal assistance, but useless rhetorical advice and ironical reflections on the very limited possibilities available to all participants in the legal process, including the prosecuters, the advocates and the judges. 'Now and then he gave K. a few vacuous admonitions, such as children are given. These speeches were as boring as they were useless, and K. had no intention of paying a penny for them when the time came to reckon up their accounts.'

One such supposedly boring and useless speech follows. It is a threatening rhapsody of motives that is vaguely reminiscent of a rhetorical treatise on advocacy, turned upside down, mixing analyses of the workings of the court and considerations on the influence lawyers can have on the courts officials with intimations of an unfathomable complexity of the legal world and of a fundamental uncertainty and unpredictability of outcome that baffles not even experienced lawyers but even the highest judges on the court. This long speech makes many contradictory turnings and has the rhetorical effect of placing the lawyer in the camp of the court officials instead of on the side of K. The whole point of the speech is apparently to offer justifications for delaying the presentation of a plea for the defence. It begins thus:

> Naturally, he said, he had set to work on the case immediately, and the first plea was almost ready for presentation. This plea was very important, because the initial impression made by the defence often decided the whole course of the proceedings. Unfortunately, he had to warn K., it sometimes happened though, that the first pleas were never read at all by the Court officials, who simply placed them with the documents and added the rider that, for the time being, interrogation and observation of the accused were more important than any written plea. If the petitioner pressed the point, it was stated that, before the final decision, as soon as all the material connected with the case had been assembled, all the documents, including the first plea, would be examined. But unfortunately this was often not true, the first plea was usually mislaid or went completely astray, and even if it was preserved until the very end, it would scarcely ever be read — judging by what the lawyer had heard, though of course this was only a rumour. That was all very regrettable, but not entirely without justification.

The quality of the whole speech, which is considerably longer, comes out well in this one paragraph. It contains a fundamental contradiction: promising rhetorical advantage with a strong first plea; and then destroying any influence a first plea can have when it is read at the end of the proceedings or not read at all. It mixes the confident tone of the professional rhetorician explaining some of the tricks of the trade with the admission that nothing is certain, that rumours are all the lawyer can go by. It begins with the points of view of the lawyer and K. but imperceptibly slides into the internal logic of the court system. It offers no emotional or ethical reassurance by splitting regret of standing practices with the admission that they are in some measure justified. Small wonder that at the end of the lawyers speech, the situation is thus:

> The lawyer had an inexhaustible supply of speeches like this. They were rehearsed at every visit. It always turned out that progress had been made, but it was never possible to say exactly what this progress was. More work was always being done on the first plea, but it was never finished, and at the next visit this was usually shown to have been a great advantage, since, for reasons which could not have been foreseen, the last few days would have been a very unfavourable time for submitting the plea.

Notice, again, the pattern of contradictions. Speech for the lawyer (as a professional rhetorician) never wears out but is never productively used to further the cause of his client. The plea which might or might not be an effective means of obtaining justice for K. simply is never brought to the courts' attention. And when K. protests and wants to know why nothing is happening on his behalf, all rhetorical ingenuity is put to the task of explaining why nothing can be done at this moment. The lawyer is a master of anti-rhetoric. His is an art concerning the 'impossibilities of persuasion,' in which formula Aristotle's famous words in the *Art of Rhetoric* are inverted.[2] The lawyer representing K. is not a helper but an opponent.

The problems K. encounters in his efforts to find justice can be variously interpreted. *The Trial* can fruitfully be read as a book about bureaucracy, about the absurdity of modern life; it can be read in a theological, a psychoanalytical or a deconstructive mode, to mention just a few possibilities. But for a legal reading these problems have significance as indications of very real problems encountered in the practical operation of legal systems everywhere. K. is in the position of any person experiencing powerlessness and injustice in the face of the law. The lawyer's movements in circumventing a defence of K. are similarly meaningful: the lawyer's craft shows the dangers of legal rhetoric when this art is not operating within the theatre of legal communication, not working towards judgments in accordance with the ideals of the rule of law, but instead is subservient to power and at the same time ineffective, like a running engine disconnected from a machine. These twin problems of the powerlessness of people caught up in the machinery of the legal process and lawyers unable or unwilling to act as mediators are both important and neglected in traditional jurisprudence, especially in the positivistic schools. This is a natural result from placing rules and rule-following at the centre of attention. Questions that do not fit the frame of rule-following acquire marginal importance at best. The categories of legal thinking cannot be brought to bear upon the problems of those who, as in K.'s case, are before the law and are unable to enter legal discourse. And when it comes to addressing the dangers of failing mediation by lawyers through their rhetoric, a rule-centered approach easily supplies moralistic advice but does not lead to penetrating insights in the strategic choices of legal rhetoricians. In order to grasp these problems that are so eloquently raised in Kafka's writings, we propose to turn to rhetoric and to literature.

II
Semiotic Possibilities of Rhetorical Systems

Systems of legal rhetoric have a long history. Since the fifth century B.C. manuals of the art of persuasion in public discourse have been written, first in Greece in the Athenian polis, later in the Roman Republic. Rhetoric was incorporated in the classical writings that have been part of humanist curricula since the renaissance. The influence of this rhetorical tradition on forensic theory and practices has been vast, though difficult to reconstruct. Rhetorical systems show tremendous variety. But all of them have the empowerment of the speaker or writer as a central concern. Even simple treatises are systematic in discussing a range of connected subjects: the three genres of rhetoric (judicial, political and epideictic), the relations between speakers and hearers, the stages of composition, the parts of a speech, the stylistic devices. Insight in these topics serves to increase the speaker's abilities. But a rhetorical system is a body of knowledge that can be put to different uses. The terminology being employed, the examples of effective speech being given, can serve different functions. It can be asked what possibilities for the generating of meaning, for starting and sustaining semiotic processes, are contained in them.

In looking at rhetorical works, written in different periods, the same types of meaningful use keep emerging, notwithstanding the different concerns of their authors. All in all, there appear to be four basic and three complementary semiotic processes at work when rhetorical manuals are used in order to reflect on persuasion. First, and foremost, there is the option of *empowerment*. A rhetorical system is a body of knowledge that generates power. Readers of rhetorical works are always looking for ways of improving their performance, in the sense of being able to influence their audiences more effectively. Secondly, and in line with the first option, is the possibility that knowledge of rhetoric leads one to be better able at *unmasking and interpretation* of the moves of other participants in processes of public argumentation. Not only is rhetorical power in part the power to unmask other speakers (for instance by showing their 'real motives' behind an honourable argument), the conscious striving for more effective persuasive techniques calls forth the reaction that these sophisticated moves are seen through. Interpretation is the suave face of unmasking activities, where there is less anatagonism between the 'author' and the 'reader.' Without training in interpretation and a vocabulary to observe what goes on in interpreting the arguments of speakers and writers, critical reflection on rhetoric is impossible and improvement of one's own rhetorical skills unlikely. Thirdly, rhetorical knowledge is used to make discourse beautiful, in the sense of esthetically appropriate (decorum). This option of *beauty* is originally tied in with efforts at increasing rhetorical power and being able to unmask or interpret. It soon becomes an independent purpose of rhetorical reflection. To many people, rhetoric is even preponderantly associated with esthetics, in a wide variety of fields. And fourthly, a rhetorical system serves the semiotic need of providing *cognitive organisation*. This basic semiotic possibility is least controversial (while Plato denounces the rhetorical arts generally, he develops in his dialectical method of interrogation a powerful tool of cognitive organisation). In the arts of memorisation, of stylistic figuration and of narration, the purposes of cognitive organisation are most clearly present.

The three complementary possibilities concern *cultural expression, regulation and truth*. Rhetorical systems can, especially with the passage of time, be read as texts about the culture within which they were written. They provide evidence of cultural expressions, of values and practices of a community. The agonistic nature of Greek public debate can, for instance, be inferred from the body of writings of the sophists. A rhetorical system can, on the other hand, also be studied for its regulatory effects upon the practicies in which it is embedded. Sometimes there are even explicit sets of rules for speech and writing to be both effective and normatively acceptable. Strategically valuable ploys become conventionalized; the strategies become not so much cunning moves as ordinary speech acts facilitating communication. The original idea behind the five parts of the oration (exordium, narration, proof, counterproof, peroratio) may well have been to provide a structure that makes it possible to be maximally influential with the audience, but as everybody starts to speak in this order, its communicative value increases: speeches following the five-part order make it easy for the audience to follow the deliberations of both parties to the debate. The semiotic possibility of truth, finally, is a rare bird in rhetorical manuals, being the obverse of the alluring promise of empowerment. Yet, during the heydays of rhetorical culture the publicly known rhetorical system did provide a method and a way of life conducive to the expression of truth, relative to the time and the place. In our own time, legal procedures that are antagonistically structured are an example of rhetoric organised to be of service to ideals of truth and justice. The rhetorical situation — in which two debating parties confront an independent and impartial judge — allows for freedom in the selective presentation of the case and yet provides the judge with the materials needed to form a judgment that discounts the selective presentations and approximates truth and justice. Of course, the truth thus achieved depends on probable knowledge, not on certainty, and it is expressive of the dominant normative convictions of the community the judge belongs to (the Aristotelian *doxa*).[3]

Within the assumptions of the classical rhetorical tradition, notably in the Aristotelian heritage, it is supposed that these uses, these semiotic possibilities, reinforce and presuppose each other; the picture is one of harmony. In modern rhetoric, after Nietzsche and the poststructuralists, it is easier to see the semiotic possibilities as being in conflict with one another; the picture is one of clashing functions, of instabilities and disharmonies.

III
Harmony

The harmonious picture shows the seven semiotic possibilities as corollaries of coordinated action in a well-organised community. Strategies of influence are mirrored in strategies of unmasking and interpretation, both employing esthetic means in order to achieve their effect. Cognitive organisation automatically results from the full use of the available instruments. The repertoire of the system as a whole is understood as expressive of the communities' concerns and its knowledge and aspirations, so that it also responds to the socially accepted rules that make the rhetorical art into a working and useful practice. Truth may well emerge from its operation. In the classical rhetorical writings this is the optimistic picture that emerges. Responding to Plato's indictments of the dangers inherent in rhetoric, Aristotle sees within rhetoric mechanisms at work that constrain its use.

While Plato sees rhetoric as a collection of tricks, designed to make the weaker argument appear the stronger, Aristotle believes that speakers who want to persuade their audience will invoke the shared understandings of the community and so will rely on arguments that are at least culturally strong. For Aristotle the rhetorical syllogism or enthymeme is structured in such a way as to make this happy coincidence of striving for influence and achieving socially supported results possible. The person who argues employing enthymemes forces the listener to complete the reasonings for himself and thus exercises some control over the deliberative process, but on the other hand this strategy can only work when the omitted arguments can be easily supplied by the listener; for practical reasons this means they have to belong to the stock of common knowledge. The hope that technically effective language can be ethical simultaneously, is even clearer in the use of the gnomè or maxim. This is introduced by Aristotle because of its expediency; maxims give the argumentation an appearance of generality. 'To express in general terms what is not general is especially suitable in complaint or exaggeration, and then either at the beginning or at the end of the demonstration.' As an example of a maxim Aristotle discusses 'The chances of war are the same for both,' used strategically to persuade an army to fight, even though it is numerically in the minority. And Aristotle explains this strategy in these strategic terms: 'One should even make use of common and frequently quoted maxims, if they are useful; for because they are common, they seem to be true, since all as it were acknowledge them as such.'[4] A classical case of making the weaker argument appear the stronger? Not quite. Aristotle mentions another, and greater advantage of maxims. 'Maxims make speeches ethical. Speeches have this character, in which the moral purpose is clear. And this is the effect of all maxims, because he who employs them in a general manner declares his moral preferences; if then the maxims are good, they show the speaker also to be a man of good character.' Maxims are conducive to building up an image of moral trustworthiness which far exceeds the importance of the maxims themselves. The general speaking to his men about the equal chances in war shows them by taking this socially accepted line of thinking that he is himself a good person, asking them to be equally good. Rhetorical tricks performed with dignity and at the right moment (decorum) are expressive of a collective rationality because they lead to decisions that correspond to the norms of the group.

This picture may well be too optimistic. Aristotle's harmonious picture of the ethical effect of strategic ploys is situated in the context of the Athenian polis of free and equal men, performing their tasks as citizens in practices of public argumentation. Once these and similar republican assumptions are absent, rhetoric may be an instrument of power that is inadequately checked; it may be speech operating as a command or as verbal manipulation.[5] As a social practice rhetoric may reflect positions of power and exclusion in a society, it may require bureaucratic competence that is confined to a small group, it may even actively create divergent codes that distinguish an upper class from a lower class.

These social aspects of rhetoric can be inferred from the technical manuscripts themselves. When rhetorical advice is preoccupied with stylistic matters, for instance, listing a large number of acceptable figures of speech, this is instrumental to a cleavage between those who are competent speakers and those who are not; it signals a practice of exclusion. When rhetorical writings in a Ciceronian vein extol the virtues of speech according to rules of taste (decorum), there is also a distinction that divides citizens that do from those that do not count. These rhetorics tend to equate decorous with ethical speech, blurring the ethical dilemmas that arise when rhetoric is at the service of power. All these variants fail in the most crucial Aristotelian demand on a rhetorical system: they codify forms but do not invite reflection on the further possibilities of persuasion and of its limits and limitations.

These are the troubling questions put to a rhetoric of harmonious uses, and they can already be found in Plato. How can it be prevented that rhetorical systems are put into the service of domination, of exclusion, of bureaucratic performance? How can it help the stronger argument to assert itself against weaker arguments that are uttered by those in positions of power? How can rhetoric be ethical in conditions of inequality in debate? How can it actually help to further conditions of democratic citizenship? Big questions indeed. They raise the troubling problem of rhetorics relation to outsiders, to those not trained in its precepts. There are many situations in which the insiders speak to the outsiders or about the outsiders, using language that excludes them, or turns them into manipulable objects, or hides the strategic choices underlying it. K.'s lawyer symbolizes the empowered rhetorician talking over the head of the uninitiated person whose interests depend in part on the rhetoricians speech.

IV
Clash

The modern picture of rhetoric stresses strife. Rhetoric aiming at influence over the mind of the listener or reader would rather be perceived as spontaneous argumentation, but is being unmasked as an act of strategic power-wielding. Similarly, evolved standards for good rhetorical speech tend to prevent the creativity that rhetoric as beauty strives for. The truth that resides in cultural expression is always bound to a certain community and its history and so cannot be a general, encompassing truth (*et cetera*). These are clashes of a pragmatic nature that manifest themselves in the uses to which rhetorical insights are put. Some of them fit in well with the aim of making law sensitive to rhetoric, the prime example being the conflicting uses made of rhetorical techniques for exerting influence and for unmasking influence. This basic conflict at the heart of reflection on persuasion in fact helps persons equipped with approximately equal rhetorical knowledge to participate in rhetorical situations in which the collective goal of well considered judgments must be practiced, such as the courtroom. Absent such an equal division of knowledge among all concerned, the clash of semiotic possibilities may be a one-sided affair. When there is too little unmasking, weak arguments may well be decisive in debate. When there is too little empowerment in the face of a sceptical attitude on the side of the audience, the debate may well be brought to a premature end. These difficulties in the social practices of rhetoric are compounded when the clash between semiotic possiblities does not in itself reinforce the humanist tendencies in the rhetorical tradition. Overregulated speech that limits creativity, threatens the quality of discourse subjected to it. The prevalence of culturally expressed truths over universal truths may have serious consequences for the protection of human rights.

Rhetorical interactions actually do not exclusively take place in the context of the public argumentation of free and equal members of a homogeneous community. In fact, rhetoric has long left the traditional arenas and it has spread out through large and heterogeneous societies, where not everyone with an interest in its functioning is a competent speaker according to the prevailing rhetorical mode. Two historians of rhetoric note that our age is one of *rhetoricality*, 'of a generalized rhetoric that penetrates to the deepest levels of human experience.' According to them:

> The classical rhetorical tradition rarified speech and fixed it within a gridwork of limitations: it was a rule-governed domain whose procedures themselves were delimited by the institutions that organized interaction and domination in traditional European society. Rhetoricality, by contrast, is bound to no specific set of institutions. It manifests the groundless, infinitely ramifying character of discourse in the modern world. (. . .) Rhetoric is no longer the title of a doctrine and a practice, nor a form of cultural memory; it becomes instead something like the condition of our existence.[6]

K. lives in exactly such a world of rhetoricality, where the rhetorical practice of law has spread out throughout the normative universe he inhabits. When rhetoricality is not confined to well-defined areas of life but instead becomes the 'condition of existence,' the cultural presuppositions of the classical rhetorical tradition evaporate.

This brings us to the questions raised in relation to Aristotelian rhetoric. Much of the insights of classical rhetoric are still relevant in assessments and interpretations of contemporary practices in which legal rhetoric takes place. Studies of contemporary courtroom interaction are, when they are stripped from the jargon of sociology, exercises in the classical tradition of the possiblities and obstacles to the art of lawyers pleadings.[7] The basic mechanisms of law talk about facts of the case and about rules that have to be interpreted have not changed dramatically; any research into existing court practices can usefully start with these, with the possibilities for persuasion in the Aristotelian and Ciceronian sense. But we can also see that there is no need to be complacent about this continuing relevance of classical insights. When rhetorical ideals are embedded in legal practices, they also reflect the biases of the culture of public argumentation. The arts of rhetoric were never developed as value-neutral instruments in the service of everyone, but were often dedicated to people with power and written for people aspiring to be in power. Rhetoric as a tradition had an aristocratic air and it has flourished not only in democratic conditions but in oligarchic circumstances as well. Machiavelli's *The Prince*, dedicated to the idea of the absolute power of worldly monarchs, is the ultimate rhetorical manual, as Kenneth Burke for one has shown.[8] Rhetoric, which in principle has a liberating and democratizing effect, too often has been put to uses of domination. Like rhetoric, legal science has been of great interest to social elites. Legal science promises its own particular version of empowerment: a science for social control, offering neutral methods that can be used to attain politically or economically determined ends. In many legal systems the complaint can be heard that the instrumentality of law has overgrown the ideals of the rule of law. Formalism, proceduralism, neutralism, positivism: the monster has many heads. It is seen as a monster only when law has been made into the technical language of politics and business rather than into a widely accepted system of social justice.

When the law has in recent times become one of a number of autopoietic systems, these social 'uses' of the law have become ingrained into its very language and discourse.[9] Rhetorical analyses from a vantage point outside these cognitively closed systems may bring a new relevance to legal rhetoric, in showing exactly how language is made to serve which interests. But precisely because rhetoric is forced in this situation to take the perspective of the unmasking critic, under the pretty banners of postmodernism, poststructuralism, critical legal studies or feminism, it can easily be marginalized by those who are identifying with the systems and allow only constructive interpretations of the Law. Rhetoric as a new brand of critical reflection on legal practice, in alliance with some critical work in legal theory, may not by itself be strong enough to provide such a broad fostering of a selfcritical attitude among lawyers and non-lawyers. At this point the importance of literature for both rhetoric and law can be argued for. In literature, the autopoietic closure of the law can be brought to consiousness. In literature, the social consequences of a dominant rhetoric can be shown.

V
Seeing Rhetoric as Law as Literature

The theme of powerlessness in the face of rhetoric appears in many literary works in a special way, which is not provided by rhetorical studies. Literary works often capture the perspectives of those who are subjected to legal rhetoric, remaining silent about the promise of empowerment rhetorical treatises hold out to the aspiring rhetorician. Rhetoric is, in these literary works, not an instrument offered in order to engage in law-talk; rhetoric is mirrored in the activities of those already competently speaking the language of the law; rhetoric parades as law. The law in action, perceived as strings of legal arguments presented in dialogue, refers to a symbol system beyond talk, to the realm of legal rules that are being 'applied' or 'interpreted.' The outsider does not understand such law-talk, even when the reference to the legal rules is accepted as constitutive of the conversation.

A moving story by Pirandello makes it plain that even telling the truth as one sees it, need not count as a strong argument in discourse that takes valid legal rules as its core. The Sicilian farmer Tarara has murdered his wife by splitting her head with a hatchett upon finding out that she has been unfaithful to him. Returning home on saturday night after a weeks work on the land, he finds the whole neighbourhood astir over a horrible scandal which has broken out in his home. His wife has been discovered in his bedroom with the young Count Fiorica, the wealthy landowner. Fiorica's wife has informed the police and has caused them to be arrested. It was impossible to hide these events from Tarara, for his wife was still detained at the police station when he returned. When his wife had indeed come home, Tarara killed her. Standing trial Tarara has to tell the true story, even though everyone knows what happened. Tarara has already admitted to having killed his wife. The only legal issue remaining concerns motive. If the killing has been committed at the crash of the moment, in order to defend honor, the valid rules of Sicilian law result in a light punishment. If there has been premeditation, this leads to a heavy sentence. All Tarara has to do is, tell the truth. Tarara does not follow the long story the clerk reads to him. 'Your Honor and you, too, gentlemen, you are learned people who understood all that is written in those papers, but I live in the country. If the writing in those papers says that I have killed my wife, then it is true and let us talk no more about it.' This statement leads to general laughter in the courtroom. Tarara explains that he means to say that he did it. 'I did it because I couldn't help it.' This turns out to have been a dangerous remark. What does Tarara mean by saying he couldn't help it? Whose fault was it then? Answering the judge, Tarara blames Count Fiorica's wife for causing the scandal. Does this mean that Tarara knew his wife was unfaithful to him? The judge asks him now whether Tarara is actually confessing that he was aware of his wife's relations with Count Fiorica. While everybody in the courtroom realizes the consequences of such a confession, Tarara is not aware of the legal rule and does not seem to realize that his rhetoric has to take a preestablished course. Instead, he relates a more complicated truth.

> And the truth is this: I knew it and yet it was as if I didn't know it. The thing, Your Honor, was on the quiet and nobody could have dared to face me and tell me that I knew it. I am a peasant, gentlemen, and what can a peasant know when he toils like a beast in the fields from monday morning till saturday night? What does a peasant know of his troubles at home? Of course, if somebody had

> come to me and told me: 'Tarara, your wife and Count Fiorica are too friendly,' I would have rushed home and split my wife's head with my hatchet. But nobody had ever come to tell me, your Honor, and in order not to raise trouble I even sent someone to give warning when I had to return home earlier than the end of the week. Men are what they are and women too. Of course men should know that women have it in their blood to be untrue even if their husband is never away, but women too should know that men cannot so slightly stand the scorn of their friends.

So Tarara both didn't know (because nobody had ever told him) and he did know, for adultery is in a woman's blood. In the binary terms of the legal code this subtle answer was interpreted as an admission of foreknowledge. 'As truth — even so candidly confessed — is not always easy to be accepted, the jury found Tarara guilty of murder with only mild provocation and a sentence of thirteen years' imprisonment followed,' concludes Pirandello. Commenting on this story, 't Hart asks the right rhetorical question: 'Would criminal law's ways of establishing the facts and endowing them with meaning correspond closely to what 'really happened'?'[10] The answer is of course negative. In fact, the criminal procedure leads to an official version of events that is alienated from direct experience. For Pirandello, this is the nature of law. Tarara, waiting for the beginning of his interrogation, reflects upon the law in the following metaphorical terms.

> All this staging of Justice appeared to him as something inevitable, as Fate. Justice was for him like a bad year on land, nothing more. And justice, with all its solemn setting of high benches, bells, robes and uniforms was for Tarara something as mysterious as the great new steam mill of his village which had been opened with great pomp the previous year. One could bring his own grist to that mill, but who could guarantee that the flour one received back was from the same grist? It was a question of accepting with blind eyes and with resignation the flour which it pleased the miller to give . . . Tarara could not help thinking that his case was like the grist brought to the mill: one had to accept the result which would come out of the trial as one had to accept the flour which came out of the mill.

This metaphor of law as a great steam mill captures both the powerlessness in the face of the legal system and hints at some reasons the lawyer should have for being concerned about the question of justice that is structurally constrained by the official rhetoric and the valid rules. The legal truth should coincide with the experiential truth, even if it never can. That demand brings out the desire for equal treatment and for sensitivity to the individual circumstances of the case. The metaphor is not chosen from an internal perspective on the law, however. Seeing the machine of justice is a way of watching from an outside observation post. Those inside the machine need not worry over much, secure in their conviction that the rules are valid and the ideals upholding the rules true principles of justice. The cognitive reorganisation the metaphor achieves, yet turns on values that are important for law's insiders. When the legal system evokes or invites comparisons with machines this relates to the fact that in the argumentative practices of the law legal concepts and predetermined rules are employed (three cheers for the rule of law) in order to decide in equal manner on the great variety of cases in real life (three cheers for equal treatment). The lesson for lawyers is not that all legal systems, all machines are necessarily bad as instruments for the repression of knowledge. It is that the danger is always there that the ideals of justice that legitimate an operating legal practice are perverted in the process of doing justice. Such an insight leads to considerations on the desirability of adequate mediation between lawyers and lay persons. The lawyer who only takes an internal point of view need not worry about the kind of grist put into the mill: the quality of the flour is an average. But for the legal subject, in the sense of the person recognised by and subjected to law, his story can never be averaged down to the size of accepted stereotypes.

Literary texts such as this one by Pirandello offer a privileged place in which to see rhetoric as law and law as rhetoric. Any lawyer taking such a story seriously cannot fail to contemplate the discursive possiblities on the side of the representatives of the Law in relation to the vocabulary available to the simple speaker of truth. Tarara does not know the language of the law but does have notions of justice that are at least equally valid as the official legal ideas. The tensions generated by this insight lead one to be aware of what Martha Nussbaum calls 'the fragility of goodness.'[11] Also, one may discover what Isaiah Berlin finds in Vico, a finite plurality of values: 'equally genuine, equally ultimate, above all equally objective; incapable, therefore, of being ordered in a timeless hierarchy, or judged in terms of some one absolute standard.'[12] Literature in this vein can sensitize readers to the difficulties that arise when rhetoric is like law and law like rhetoric, and when both are used to decide on the lawful application of violence against people.[13] Literature is an immensely powerful way of stimulating the imagination of readers that of themselves would not be in the habit of taking the point of view of those subjected to the law with sufficient seriousness. In his sketch of a program for a literary jurisprudence, Richard Weisberg rightly concludes that some stories can teach the empowered practitioner of law through law's only medium (language) that:

> 1. The law cannot *do* justice without fathoming the inner worlds, aspirations and values of those who are different from itself;
> 2. The law cannot *speak* justice unless its practitioners continuously scrutinize their *own* values to strive for what is most fair and least hostile in them;
> 3. The striving for justice can finally be accomplished only through an act of communication with an audience whose own prejudices and values must be engaged, without sacrificing or even compromising the speaker's informed sense of fairness.[14]

A literary jurisprudence along these lines is in my view especially promising when the interrelationships of law and language are at stake. Literary experiences may reflect the legal appearance of rhetoric or the rhetorical dimension of the law. When literature forces such reflections on the reader, in or outside class rooms and seminars, the same processes are at work that accompanied the reflective use of rhetorical systems since antiquity. Thus Pirandello's story becomes a meeting ground for various semiotic possiblities that we have noticed in rhetorical reflection. It shows strategies of discursive power and it unmasks these. Doing that, it points lawyers to an interpreteve effort in order to make sense of the assumed ideals inherent in the legal system (justice, equality et cetera). Simultaneously, the story shows something of the moral structure of the community in which it is unfolding. One cannot help wondering whether the rules of courtroom interaction allow for adequate judgment. The whole point of the story, expressed in the Italian title, is to discuss the social construction of The Truth. The web of semiosis that is spun in rhetorical reflection generally, is already present in the compact format of this Pirandello story about rhetoric and law.

Willem J. Witteveen is Professor of Law at Tilburg University.

ENDNOTES

1. Derrida has analysed Kafka's parable, 1992, incorporated in *The Trial*, ed. Derek Attridge, in his masterful address 'Before the Law,' republished in *Acts of Literature*, New York, 181-220.

2. Aristotle defines the art of rhetoric as 'the faculty of discovering the possible means of persuasion in reference to any subject whatever.' Aristotle, 1975, trans. J.H. Freese, *'Art' of Rhetoric*, Loeb Classical Library, London, 1355b.

3. For an extended discussion of these seven semiotic possibilities inherent in a rhetorical system, see W.J. Witteveen, 1989, *'De mogelijkheden van de retorica,' Recht en Kritiek*, 240-262.

4. Aristotle, 1395b, *'Art' of Rhetoric*, II. xxi. 15, 16.

5. And remember that within the Aristotelian harmony women and strangers were excluded from taking part in public deliberations.

6. John Bender and David E. Wellbery, 1990, 'Rhetoricality: On the Modernist Return of Rhetoric,' in *The Ends of Rhetoric*, Stanford, 25.

7. William Twining, 1990, 'Lawyers' Stories,' in *Rethinking Evidence*, Oxford, 219-261.

8. Kenneth Burke, 1962 (1950), *A Rhetoric of Motives*, Berkeley, 158-166. See also Q. Skinner, 1978, 'The foundations of modern political thought,' Vol. I, *The Renaissance*, Cambridge, 93, 138.

9. Gunther Teubner, 1989, *Recht als autopoietisches System*, Frankfurt am Main.

10. A.C. 't Hart, 1991, *Recht als schild van Perseus*, Arnhem, 27.

11. Martha C. Nussbaum, 1986, *The Fragility of Goodness. Luck and Ethics in Greek Tragedy and Philosophy*, Cambridge.

12. Isaiah Berlin, 1990, *The Crooked Timber of Humanity. Chapters in the History of Ideas*, London, 79.

13. Rovert Cover, 1992, eds. Martha Minow, Michael Ryan and Austin Sarat, *Narrative, Violence and the Law. The Essays of Robert Cover*, Ann Arbor, 1992.

14. Richard Weisberg, 1992, *Poethics and other Strategies of Law and Literature*, New York, 46.

Subject Index